Harbans Singh was born in Samba, in the Jammu region of Jammu and Kashmir. He began his career as a college professor before moving on to journalism and occasional writing. Over the years, he has worked as a reporter for the *Observer of Business and Politics*; been a book critic and reviewer for *The Tribune*, Chandigarh for over twenty years; and was a regular columnist for *Dainik Bhaskar*.

As a bilingual, Singh has authored books in both Hindi and English. His primary area of interest is Jammu and Kashmir. He is the author of *Sufi Satta aur Samaj*, written in Hindi, which examines the impact of Sufism on Jammu and Kashmir and the overall Indian society. His books in English include a trilogy on the history of Jammu and Kashmir that spans from 1925 to contemporary times.

A MODERN HISTORY OF JAMMU AND KASHMIR

VOLUME THREE

The Times of Turbulence
(1975-2021)

HARBANS SINGH

SPEAKING TIGER

SPEAKING TIGER BOOKS LLP
125A, Ground Floor, Shahpur Jat, near Asiad Village,
New Delhi 110049

First published in paperback by Speaking Tiger Books in 2024

ISBN: 978-93-5447-728-7
eISBN: 978-93-5447-729-4

10 9 8 7 6 5 4 3 2 1

Typeset in Minion Pro by SŪRYA, New Delhi
Printed at Chaman Enterprises, New Delhi

Contents

Foreword

Harbans Singh has emerged as a significant re-interpreter of Dogra history, specifically dealing with the period that begins with the reign of Maharaja Hari Singh. This volume is the second part of a trilogy—*A Modern History of Jammu and Kashmir*—about the contemporary political history of Jammu and Kashmir.

The first volume of the trilogy deals with the events during my father's reign. The author holds that it is unfortunate that Maharaja Hari Singh is remembered only for the accession of the State, which had come under very severe pressure due to the tribal invasion from Pakistan. He points out that from when my father ascended the Gaddi (throne) in 1925, all the way to 1946, he undertook a series of far-reaching and progressive measures, including throwing all temples doors open to the Harijans (Dalits); abolishing the obnoxious Forced Labour System of begar; paying attention to girl's education, which was far ahead of the situation in most of the rest of India; setting up first-class hospitals and colleges both in Srinagar and Jammu; beautifying the Dal Lake by constructing a boulevard; and so on. His first statement, after assuming the high office in 1925, was 'justice is my religion'. In a memorable speech at the Round Table Conference on Indian Constitutional Reforms held in London in 1930-1931, he had stated, 'As Indians and loyal to the land of our birth, we stand as solidly as the rest of our countrymen for our enjoyment of a position of honour and equality in the British Commonwealth.' All these seem to have been forgotten and his rule has been overshadowed by the accession imbroglio, which is grossly unfair. Sheikh Abdullah, who was bitterly anti-Dogra, had launched a protracted movement against the Maharaja way back in 1931, which fructified in the crisis of 1947. Abdullah had seized the opportunity during Partition and had come to oust Maharaja Hari Singh and assumed power himself with the blessings of Pandit Nehru. All of this led to my father virtually going into exile in Bombay (Mumbai) in 1949. It was only his ashes that I brought back to Jammu after he passed away in April 1961.

From the vantage point of hindsight, it may be easy to say that the Maharaja could have handled the entire crisis better but, in my Autobiography, I have recounted in some detail the events that took place during those tumultuous times, the difficulties my father faced during the political crises of Partition and also my ideological divergence from his views. Regretfully, he has received a lot of negative press and, therefore, I am glad that this first volume not only puts the Maharaja in the right focus but also highlights the valiant role of the Jammu and Kashmir State Forces that historians have generally ignored. Readers will, no doubt, judge my father more fairly than contemporary historians have done.

The next volume in this series covers the events of the eighteen years that I was the Head of State under three different appellations—first as Regent, then as Sadar-i-Riyasat and finally as the Governor. This period also saw the ten-year rule of Bakshi Ghulam Mohammad and also the advent of G.M. Sadiq, who drastically moved towards further integrating the State into the Indian Union. The Presidential Order was welcomed in 1964 and the nomenclature of the Sardar-i-Riyasat and Prime Minister was changed to Governor and Chief Minister respectively, in line with the other States of the Union. Harbans Singh brings out the fact that right from the beginning, in my correspondence with Pandit Jawaharlal Nehru, I constantly put forward the importance of Jammu and Ladakh, which were generally neglected due to the Delhi Kashmiri-centrism. This period also covers the arrest and prolonged exile of Sheikh Abdullah for over ten years, until he finally returned as Chief Minister in 1965 after an accord with Indira Gandhi. The second volume takes the story up to March 1967 when I resigned as Governor and joined Indira Gandhi's Cabinet as Minister for Tourism and Civil Aviation.

The third and final volume in this trilogy—*The Times of Turbulence (1975-2021)*—traverses the period of the history of the

State from 1975 to contemporary times. This covers the beginning of aggressive militancy in 1988, which resulted, among other disasters, in the mass exodus of the highly talented Kashmiri-Pandit community from the Valley. The volume also studies the drastic and dramatic events of 5th August 2019 whereby the State was bifurcated for the second time, with Ladakh and Jammu and Kashmir becoming Union Territories. Harbans Singh has evidently studied this whole period closely and his trilogy will surely become essential for all those interested in the history of Jammu and Kashmir. The series is a welcome opportunity to understand the Dogra point of view and set right the blatant anti-Dogra distortions by some historians.

I commend Harbans Singh for performing such a valuable service and congratulate him for his detailed research, which, I am sure, will be widely read and appreciated.

KARAN SINGH

March 2023

Preface

This book is final part of the trilogy about contemporary political history of Jammu and Kashmir. The first, *A Modern History of Jammu and Kashmir, Volume One: The Troubled Years of Maharaja Hari Singh* dealt with the events that took place during Maharaja Hari Singh's time and alluded to the past only in as much as it had a bearing on the events as they unfolded. During the course of the events, he found himself confronted by the rising powers represented by Pandit Jawaharlal Nehru, Sheikh Abdullah and Mohammad Ali Jinnah. It also informs the readers of the various social, political, economic and revolutionary agrarian reforms that took place in the thirties of the twentieth century. For the record, his agrarian reforms were far ahead of the times and preceded the acclaimed reforms initiated by Sir Chhotu Ram in British Punjab. It also brought forth the political events of the era and the communal nature of, first, the Muslim Conference and later, in its new birth, National Conference. Importantly, it also focused on the systematic policy of Sheikh Abdullah to not only weaken the Dogras but also crush their pride as symbolized in the form of their last Ruler. In this he found Prime Minister Jawaharlal Nehru and other central leaders allied to him. By convincing them of his indispensability in winning the plebiscite in favor of India Abdullah, more often than not, was responsible for the unfair treatment Maharaja Hari Singh often faced. The 'coup de grace' moment for the Maharaja came when Sardar Patel, in whom he had reposed great faith, not only told him to go into virtual exile after appointing the eighteen-year-old Yuvraj as his regent but also refused to accept his request of honorably giving him a position of respect in the national affairs.

That book also focused on the indomitable Jammu and Kashmir State Forces. Barely 6,000 in number, they were called upon to defend a border that stretched from the northern feudatory States, bordering Afghanistan and China, to the southern tip of the State at Lakhanpur, which became the entry point to the State after Partition. The fact that nearly one fourth of the State Army gallantly laid down their lives in that effort, is unheard of in the annals of modern warfare. In comparison, the Indian Army suffered only a few hundred while losing vast tracts of the territory, particularly, the geo-strategically important region of Gilgit-Baltistan. This also brought to the fore Sheikh Abdullah's attempts to have these Forces under his control, failing which he went out to destroy its reputation with false accusations and vicious propaganda about its participation in the killings of the Muslims. The fact that the Government of India asked Maharaja Hari Singh to leave the State is testimony to his success. In the process, the State has had to pay a heavy price since it alienated the Dogras from the Kashmiris and left deep and festering wounds. It must also be added that the alienation between the two major communities now is mutual.

Karan Singh: Jammu and Kashmir (1949-1967), which has now been revised as *A Modern History of Jammu and Kashmir, Volume Two: The Karan Singh Years (1949-1967)* follows the events subsequent to the departure of Maharaja Hari Singh and the appointment of Yuvraj Karan Singh as the Regent, and therefore, the head of the State. Instead of making a new start and effort to reach out to Dogras, this success only whetted the appetite of Sheikh Abdullah for wreaking further revenge upon them. He began to relentlessly target not only the Dogras but also those who had a word of caution for him. In the process he also charted a course independent of India. He spared no effort to keep the State out of the Indian Constitution till he was satisfied with the provisions of Article 370. Ironically, all these years he had continued to rule under the provisions of the Constitution of 1939 of the State, which vested ultimate authority and power in the Ruler and, by extension, his Regent but which was actually to be exercised by the Prime Minister appointed under the Maharaja's 5th March 1948 Proclamation. Finally, this brought him in conflict with the Regent and the

Government of India when he wanted to initiate land reforms that were prejudicial to the Dogras and would have affected the other States of the country too. Hence began the process of framing a Constitution for the State as sanctioned by the process of Accession. It, however, began on a wrong foot.First, the electoral process was manipulated by either intimidating the opponents into dropping out or arbitrarily rejecting their nomination papers. This was followed by the Praja Parishad boycotting the polls. The situation was further aggravated when the Assembly had been convened, and Sheikh Abdullah resolved to selectively follow the process of finalizing the Constitution. Thus, it was decided that before other Articles were discussed and finalized, the dynastic rule be abolished and land reforms undertaken immediately. Obviously, the Dogra dynasty and the people were targeted by this decision thereby setting the stage for another round of confrontation between the Dogras and the Kashmiri leadership. In the end, it also earned Sheikh Abdullah and his family antagonism and hostility of generations of Dogras.

The pusillanimous nature of Delhi leadership in the face of an aggressive Sheikh Abdullah is also illustrated by the exchange of letters between Jawaharlal Nehru and Yuvraj Karan Singh, who was pressurized by Delhi to accept the office of Sadar-i-Riyasat. Effectively he was asked to preside over the annihilation of the dynasty he belonged to, and which had created the State as it existed on the eve of India's Independence and had ruled it for a century. Sheikh Abdullah was in too much of a hurry to wait for the process of the drafting of the complete Constitution of the State and its ratification. At the same time, the Yuvraj was understandably reluctant to accept the office of Sadar-i-Riyasat without knowing the rest of the provisions of the proposed Constitution. It was widely believed that there would be a provision to try the Sadar-i-Riyasat for treason, if so felt by the Assembly. It was also widely believed that the provision was being added to give Sheikh Abdullah leverage against Yuvraj Karan Singh! Pandit Nehru conceded that he agreed with the Yuvraj in principle and wrote to him that he too was not comfortable with the piecemeal manner in which the Constitution was being drafted. However, he fell back on the argument about the indispensability of Sheikh Abdullah and the need to have the reliable eyes and ears of the Yuvraj for the Centre in the State. It is clear from the exchange of letters that by then Nehru had realized that his trusted friend Sheikh Abdullah had drifted away from him, and that he was capable of going to any extent to realize his ambition of a completely autonomous Kashmir within the safety net of India. Simultaneously, without saying that in words, he was bent upon reducing the Dogras to an abject state of second-class citizenship. This confrontation was to come to an end only with the dismissal and arrest of Sheikh Abdullah under the signature of Yuvraj Karan Singh.

Thereafter, began an era of reconstruction under Bakshi Ghulam Mohammad. He has been a much-reviled politician from Kashmir because of the misdeeds of his brothers and unorthodox manner of running his administration, and soon became the target of the propaganda machinery in the Valley and Pakistan. But some of the blame must also be attributed to the intellectual class of the State that mocked his deficiencies in elitist education. He was a pragmatic politician, more rooted in the streets of Srinagar than the debate clubs of universities, who had realized that the fate of the State and the Kashmiris was closely linked to India, and that the interests of the Kashmiri people were safer with India than Pakistan. Hence, he followed the middle path of integrating the State with the Indian Constitution without fully losing its autonomy. He also enjoyed the confidence of Sadar-i-Riyasat Karan Singh and the two gently made it possible for a great number of Indian laws and provisions of the Constitution to be extended to the State.

There is no reason to believe that the people of the Valley did not accept the process of integration. Though there were a few discordant voices from the diminishing followers of Sheikh Abdullah, the positivity among the people was so pervasive that there came a time when Bakshi Ghulam Mohammad, encouraged by Prime Minister Nehru, became confident enough to first free Abdullah's chief lieutenant Mirza Afzal Beg and then him. What followed is mostly forgotten. Twice the followers of Bakshi and Abdullah confronted each other and on both occasions the latter had to abjectly eat the proverbial humble pie. One of the occasions was to celebrate the Republic Day and the manner in which the nationalist Kashmiris outnumbered the separatists remains a glorious chapter in the history of integration. Bakshi had conclusively proved that the priorities of the people were different from what the Plebiscite Front activists demanded and that people, in conjunction with sensitive and participatory administration can far outweigh the emotional appeal of narrow sub-nationalism. Sheikh Abdullah, indeed, had been effectively neutralized by him.

It is unfortunate that this period also coincided with the rise of Bakshi's brothers that led to charges of nepotism and corruption against him. During this period, the Congress party too had run into rough waters because of rising aspirations of the people and the increasing failure of the leaders to rise to the occasion. Finding the ground slipping, the Congress hit upon the novel strategy of asking the well-entrenched Chief Ministers of some states to resign and go back to organizational work. It might not appear so incongruous today but at a time when Congress had no foothold in the State and the executive head of the State was known as Prime Minister and belonged to a separate entity—the National Conference—Bakshi hitched his fate along with Congress and resigned to devote himself to organizational work. It is still not clear why his services were not utilized by the Congress at the national level. Had that been done, he would have been the first Kashmiri leader to play a role in the national affairs and surely it would have been a very significant development for the sub-continent. On the contrary, he was subjected to wild accusations, harassed and hounded by his opponents and former friends, thereby alienating him.

However, the good work begun by Bakshi was carried forward by Ghulam Mohammad Sadiq, who, like Bakshi had been a close associate of Abdullah. If Bakshi provided the strength and energy of the streets to National Conference, Sadiq lent ideology and intellectual fervour. The Sadar-i-Riyasat too was very comfortable in his relationship with him and both combined to bring the State closer to the Constitution of India. The landmark change of nomenclature in the executive and constitutional heads of the State took place during that momentous period. But this period was also marked by the assertion of democratic rights and rising aspirations among the people. It was also marked by the changing nature of discontent among the Dogras. It was no longer just the demand for the abolition of Article 370 and complete integration of the State but the more mundane, yet important issues of equitable development and facilities in health, education and infrastructure. Discontent of the Jammu people still boiled over on to the streets but now the issues were different and were similar to the ones that were being voiced in various other states of the country. But even during these agitations, the forces demanding the abrogation of Article 370 marked their presence by adding the slogans demanding its repeal since the Article was considered by vast numbers in Jammu to be the reason for the politico-economic inequity among the various regions of the State. The country, however, could live with such protests.

The inference obviously is that wise leadership that is responsive and understanding has the ability to reshape the discontent and change the destiny. Historian Alastair Lamb, although not very sympathetic from India's point of view, contends that if the plebiscite had been held soon after the accession or during the early years of Sheikh Abdullah's administration, the result would have been overwhelmingly in favour of India. That was the time when the memory of the atrocities of the invaders was fresh. But it was also because Sheikh Abdullah had unreservedly hitched the fate of the State with that of India. He found shared values with India. But no sooner had he begun to have second thoughts about the Accession that a section of the Kashmiri population began to nurse the ambition of independence. Subsequent leaders, in their own way, tried to wean this section away, but once Pakistan decided to meddle in the affairs of the State, using the vulnerability of people to religious appeals as a crutch, India had its hands full combating the challenge. Among all these developments, what is certain is that as long as Bakshi Ghulam Mohammad and Ghulam Mohammad Sadiq were in the saddle all efforts of the secessionists were futile and it is in this context that the decision of Prime Minister Indira Gandhi to reopen the chapter and conduct negotiations with Sheikh Mohammad Abdullah appears baffling. G. Parthasarathy and Mirza Afzal Beg had held protracted negotiations before reaching an accord that paved the way for the return of Sheikh Abdullah to the mainstream politics.

This final volume deals with the return of Sheikh Abdullah in 1975 to head a Congress-supported government and the events that followed. Since this period culminated in the State and the country getting engulfed in terrorism, an attempt has been made to understand the origin of terrorism in this region and the factors that support and fan it. An effort has also been made to understand Pakistan and its army, as both play a very significant role in keeping the specter of separatism and terrorism alive.

The accord reiterated that the State of Jammu and Kashmir which is a constituent unit of the Union of India, would continue to be governed by Article 370 of the Constitution of India. As for the residuary powers of legislation, they were to remain with the State but Parliament will continue to have power to make laws relating to the prevention of activities directed towards disclaiming, questioning or disrupting the sovereignty and territorial integrity of India or bringing about cession of a part of the territory of India or secession of a part of the territory of India from the Union or causing insult to the Indian National Flag, the Indian National Anthem and the Constitution.

It was also agreed that where any provision of the Constitution of India had been applied to the State of Jammu and Kashmir with adaptation and modification, such adaptations and modifications can be altered or repealed by an order of the President under Article 370, each individual proposal in this behalf being considered on its merits. However, provisions of the Constitution of India which had been already applied to the State of Jammu and Kashmir without adaptation or modification were to be unalterable.

These points of convergence were something on which most of the political parties agreed but then the understanding on assurance of freedom to the State of Jammu and Kashmir to have its own legislation on matters like welfare measures, cultural matters, social security, personal law and procedural laws, in a manner suited to the special conditions in the State, had seeds of mischief. Even then, it was agreed that the State Government can review the laws made by Parliament or extended to the State after 1953 on any matter relatable to the Concurrent List and may decide which of them, in its opinion, needed amendment or repeal. If that was to be so then appropriate steps may be taken under Article 254 of the Constitution of India and the grant of President's assent to such legislation would be sympathetically considered. The same approach was to be adopted in regard to laws made by Parliament in future under the Proviso to clause 2 of Article 254. The Government of India agreed that the State Government shall be consulted regarding the application of any such law to the State and also conceded that the views of the State Government shall receive the fullest consideration.

After yielding considerable ground, the Government of India extracted minor concession in the form of an 'arrangement reciprocity to what has been provided under Article 368 and a suitable modification of that Article as applied to State should be made by Presidential order to the effect that no law made by the Legislature of the State of Jammu and Kashmir, seeking to make any change in or in the effect of any provision of Constitution of the State of Jammu and Kashmir relating to any of the under mentioned matters, shall take effect unless the Bill, having been reserved for the consideration of the President, receives his assent; the matters were (a) the appointment, powers, functions, duties, privileges and immunities of the Governor, and (b) the following matters relating to Elections namely, the superintendence, direction and control of Elections by the Election Commission of India, eligibility for inclusion in the electoral rolls without discrimination, adult suffrage and composition of the Legislative Council, being matters specified in sections 138, 139, 140 and 50 of the Constitution of the State of Jammu and Kashmir.'

The Agreement, to the chagrin of many, also reopened the question of nomenclature of the Governor and the Chief Minister and the matter was, therefore, remitted to the principals. It was believed by many that the single act of changing Prime Minister to Chief Minister and Sadar-i-Riyasat to Governor had broken a huge psychological barrier between the State and the rest of the country and also assuaged the feelings of the Dogras who felt a proximity to the safety net of India. But the truth was that the ghosts that had been laid to rest had been awakened by the Accord.

If the first tenure of Sheikh Abdullah was not known for efficient administration, then in his second coming, Sheikh Abdullah had packed the power centers with his relatives and cronies. It took some time but the people did get disillusioned, and it needed only a moment of illumination for the Abdullah magic to vanish. Simultaneously, there were other developments in the State and Delhi that were to have long term influences and that continue to reinvent themselves when they appear to be waning.

Experts and Kashmiri politicians tell us that the key lies with our relationship with Pakistan and that unless there is some kind of understanding with our neighbor, there cannot be a lasting peace. On a number of occasions normalcy seemed to have prevailed only for the nightmare to return because of some ordinary looking incident. Sometimes, a deliberate act of a politician has plunged the State back to the abyss, giving credence to conspiracy theories. There is some grain of truth in the belief that militancy has become an industry with multiple stakeholders enjoying the fallout on both sides of the border. What, however, is not articulated is that Kashmir, a predominantly Muslim region and Jammu, a Hindu-majority region are living in an embrace of death. The distrust and dislike for each other feeds upon their mutual fears of insecurity. The State of Jammu and Kashmir, it needs to be remembered, was the result of the ambitions of the Jammu rulers and the politics of the nineteenth century. In fact, none of the constituents of the State are its natural organs. Even a cursory look at the diversity and dissimilarities between Jammu, Ladakh, Gilgit-Baltistan and Kashmir prove this and among them all, Kashmir has always boasted of, an uninterrupted, rich, cultural and political history. Similarly, Jammu has always had a distinct identity, the meagre natural resources notwithstanding, and, at certain times in history, Ladakh has been closer to Tibet than the subcontinent. But because of the demographic composition of the State and the fact that for long centuries it had been ruled by outsiders, it was easier for the Dogras to rule Kashmir without any ripples till the arrival of a new generation equipped with the modern education. However, history is replete with examples where minorities have successfully ruled the majority by the judicious use of the tool of accommodation and sharing of power. There are also examples where brute majorities have failed to keep the countries together because of arrogance and refusal to yield ground to minorities. Thus, much depends on the ability to govern wisely and judiciously.

During the past four decades, the persistent and active role played by Pakistan with renewed vigor, has morphed the non-violent separatist streak into an almost permanent state of violence, making it a potent force. Pakistan, more specifically, its army has always been an integral part of the narrative of the State since 1947. From its sponsoring and finally coming out openly to aid and abet the invaders in 1947 to the present, it has been there in one form or another. Such has been its magnitude of involvement in recent years that it can no longer be wished away as was India's wont in the 1960s. In addition, since 1998 both the countries have become nuclear, which in Pakistan's opinion, gives it an insurance against full scale war by India. Thus, convinced that it will be difficult for India to inflict deterrent punishment, Pakistan has been emboldened to launch a low intensity war against India in the Valley and occasionally in the Jammu too. In fact, it has been audacious enough to even launch a terrorist attack in Dinanagar in 2015 and on an Indian Air Force base in Pathankot in 2016 respectively, both in Punjab, and the ghastly killing of 42 Central Reserve Police Force (CRPF) personnel in Pulwama in Kashmir in 2019. Therefore, it is imperative to look inwards, and to focus on the internal developments in the State and New Delhi, but it is also necessary to delve into the role of Pakistan and related perspectives.

Over the years, the role of Pakistan has bordered on brinkmanship. It has been fueled by the trends and events that have influenced the policies and thinking of not only the governments all over the world but also societies too. Post World War II, what began as a movement to carve a homeland for the Jews so that no future Hitler could harm them, turned out to be a campaign to oust the Palestinians, mostly Muslims, from their homeland. The consequences of the alienation have taken many forms, the most dangerous being the emergence of hijackers, jihadists, armed freedom fighters or terrorists (depending upon which side one is sitting), and finally the coming together of violent Islamic forces. Jammu and Kashmir too did not remain out of the range of influences of these global patterns. In another development, the erstwhile USSR had marched into Afghanistan that immediately invited a strong response from the USA-led western world. This turned out to be a windfall gain for Pakistan that had lost all relevance for the western world because of another failure in democracy and imposition of martial law after another military coup that was followed by sham elections.

Thus, with the blessings of USA, Pakistan became host to *jihadis* from all over the world. After the defeat, withdrawal and disintegration of USSR, these Islamic warriors became, in the hands of Pakistan, a handy tool to use against Kashmir, which was projected as a legitimate target. It has now unfolded with all its tragic consequences, hurling the State towards an increasingly uncertain future.

1

The Year After

In the contentious history of Indo-Pak ties, the year 1999, after India and Pakistan's nuclear tests, was eventful. Hope, despair, anger, frustration and the familiar resignation—there was never a dull moment that year.

It began with the Indian Prime Minister Atal Bihari Vajpayee visiting Lahore, and notwithstanding the reluctance shown by the hosts, visited Minar-e-Pakistan. This sent a strong message that India recognized and accepted Pakistan's separate identity in the subcontinent.[1] Vajpayee had taken a bus ride from the border post of Wagah, on the Indian side of Punjab, to Lahore to a tumultuous welcome from cheering Pakistanis on both the sides of the road. Apparently, the visit promised a paradigm shift in the Indo-Pak relations. It also contrasted the desire of the people with the publicly expressed antagonism and posturing of the governments.

The visit was significant since Vajpayee belonged to the Bharatiya Janata Party (BJP), a right-wing political party that made no bones about its hostility and rigid stance on issues concerning Pakistan. If anyone could re-write a new chapter at that time in Indo-Pak relations then it was he, for he had the right stature as a parliamentarian and leader of BJP as well as the masses. Prior to his visit, no Indian Prime Ministers had dared display friendliness towards Pakistan after the 1965 Indo-Pak war. This was particularly after Prime Minister Lal Bahadur Shastri had signed the Tashkent Agreement in 1966[2] and had returned areas captured by India after the war. Similarly, Indira Gandhi had repatriated 90,000 Pakistanis, taken as prisoners during the 1971 war, after the 1972 Simla Agreement. However, Pakistan had still not accepted the Line of Control (LoC) in Jammu and Kashmir as the international border. On both occasions, Pakistan had disappointed India. The failed attempts of the past to establish peace notwithstanding, Vajpayee had been backed by media and the people, and the pervading optimism preceding the visit enhanced the cheerfulness of the approaching spring.

Those who were surprised by the decision of Vajpayee to visit Pakistan forgot that even if he belonged to a political party that was seen to have not reconciled to the existence of Pakistan yet, he was not an ideological fundamentalist, and that he, as Foreign Minister, had broken ice in Indo-Pak relations in 1979 by becoming the first leader of eminence from the RSS/Jana Sangh/ BJP[3] school to visit Pakistan and express the desire of normal relations. Vajpayee's 1999 visit was therefore the first visit of an Indian Prime Minister to Pakistan after Rajiv Gandhi's in 1989.

In 1979, as foreign minister in Morarji Desai's Janata Party government, he had also become the first Indian minister to visit China after the Sino-India war of 1962. Vajpayee was a realist and unlike others from the RSS/BJP was not overly burdened by the baggage of history and irredentism, nor was he a prisoner of any political shibboleth.

Apparently, his visit had come suddenly. But by the time it happened both, India and Pakistan, had already conducted nuclear tests the year before, while an alarmed world had been putting considerable pressure on them. In comparison to Vajpayee, who was erudite and seasoned, Nawaz Sharif was, 'no great visionary, only a businessman committed to Pakistan's development (and) was convinced that without replacing enmity with cooperation Pakistan's development was not possible.'[4] The two countries had tried to forge cooperation in recent times, first when Deve Gowda was the Prime Minister and then during Inder Kumar Gujral's tenure. However, Deve Gowda was there only for a short time and Gujral's time was not only short but he was politically too weak to steer the country in uncharted direction. In contrast to both, Vajpayee had the greater will and stature to take the peace process to its logical conclusion.

On the other hand, one of the main poll planks of Sharif's landslide victory was negotiating a peace deal with India. According to then foreign minister Jaswant Singh, the bus ride to Lahore was a brilliant idea that emerged, as Vajpayee and Nawaz Sharif (Mian Sahib, as everyone called him) met for lunch on the sideline at the United Nations General Assembly in New York, in September 1998.[5] Earlier that year, on 11 and 13 May, India had conducted nuclear tests for the first time after 1974. The then Deputy Prime Minister, L.K. Advani had warned that now that India had a bomb, Pakistan should be careful while meddling in Kashmir! However, given the history of the two countries, it was a foregone conclusion that 'no inducements or penalties the United States and other capitals could identify were powerful enough to prevent Pakistan from following suit.'[6] Pakistan had responded with its own tests on 28 May, and both the countries were back to square one—putting to rest the hope that a bomb could give strategic advantage to either of the two. It is another matter that both the countries were yet to use their nuclear weapons.

During the lunch in New York, Sharif had casually mentioned that in 1982 he had driven his own car from Lahore to New Delhi to witness the Asian Games. This little bit of light conversation crystallized into starting a bus service between Delhi and Lahore and as the date for the first bus service neared, Sharif invited Vajpayee to come ride on it to Lahore. Vajpayee seized upon the idea and drew a list of 20 eminent Punjabis, including actor, late Dev Anand, who was an alumnus of famed Government College Lahore, Sardar Parkash Singh Badal, alumni of Ferguson College, Lahore, cricket star Kapil Dev, journalist Kuldip Nayar etc. Vajpayee boarded the bus from Wagah from where Sharif too joined him. They were given a rousing reception by the people. The evening banquet was held in Lahore Fort's Diwan-e-Khas and the next day, Vajpayee expressed his wish to visit Minar-e-Pakistan, though the hosts were reluctant, not sure what a right wing Indian Prime Minister might say that may cause protests. As it is, the parties aligned with the fundamentalists were already on the streets protesting against the visit. It was known that BJP had never accepted the Partition, therefore, this apprehension was understandable.

That visit to the Minar-i-Pakistan became the highlight. At the monument Vajpayee signed the visitor's book and wrote: 'A stable, secure and prosperous Pakistan is in India's interest. Let no one in Pakistan be in doubt. India sincerely wishes Pakistan well.' During the civic reception hosted by Lahore mayor, Vajpayee disclosed that initially he had intended to come only up to the border, greet Mian Sahib and then return home but Mian Sahib convinced him to come to Lahore by saying, 'Dar taka aye ho, ghar nahin aaoge?'[7] (You have come to the door, won't you come inside?) A new dawn, it was felt, was about to break.

It, however, turned out to be a deceptive spring and no sooner had the snow melted with the approaching summer that the Indian Army discovered that the posts that it had vacated in winter on the strategic heights of Kargil[8] in the then State of Jammu and Kashmir had been occupied by the Pakistani soldiers. These posts were located in the Batalik and Dras sector of Kargil and dominated the entire of the Kargil sector and the Srinagar-Leh highway. The Pakistani Army had taken India by surprise and threatened to cut not only Leh but also the Siachen[9] region. It also left borders with China, defenseless and vulnerable.

Pakistan initially denied it had anything to do with what had happened and, instead, suggested that the posts were occupied by the Kashmiri secessionist insurgents who had been waging a war against India! Eminent experts like, retired Brig. Shaukat Qadir and American political scientist Christine Fair, however, are unambiguous in their opinion that Kargil was an operation conceived and executed by General Pervez Musharraf and a handful of other generals. Christine Fair concluded that 'the army was seeking to redeem itself (and also) to punish India for the 1971 defeat, India's occupation of the Siachen glacier, and India's periodic shelling of the Neelum Valley road...'[10]

According to A.S. Dulat, Pakistan had three goals, 'To internationalize Kashmir as a nuclear flashpoint, requiring urgent third party intervention; to alter the LoC and change its sanctity by capturing unheld areas in Kargil; to achieve a better bargaining position for a possible trade-off against positions held by India in Siachen.'[11] In fact, it is said that as early as 1996, when General

Musharraf was Director General of Military Operations before being appointed the chief, he had approached Prime Minister Benazir Bhutto with the Kargil plan. Khaled Ahmed, a political commentator wrote that General Musharraf said: 'The time window for the resolution of the Kashmir dispute is short because with the passage of time, the India Pakistan equation, military as well as economic, is going against us.'[12] However, Benazir had refused to take the bait. Major General Javed Hassan, then heading Pakistan's Force Command Northern Areas (FCNA) agreed with General Musharraf and also opined that India had by that time run out of options in Kashmir but the timidity of Pakistan's political government had weakened the cause of Pakistan!

However, Nasim Zehra, a Pakistani commentator on military and strategic affairs, who has done extensive research of the subject for eighteen years, has exposed not only Musharraf's complicity but a web of deceit and deception that was woven by him and his loyalist Generals. She finds that even as Sharif and Vajpayee were exploring some way of establishing peace 'a clique of senior Pakistani Generals had interpreted the post-May (after the nuclear tests) global concern for the settlement as an opportunity to reinvigorate the smoldering Kashmiri movement…and to force Delhi's hand on Kashmir, or at least on Siachen. They had moves and they had ideas for untying this Gordian knot.'[13]

For the Indian side, there was no doubt that even as Vajpayee had gone to Pakistan with good will for its people and State, Pakistan must have been planning such an operation though Prime Minister Nawaz Sharif suggested that it was a rogue operation by the Pakistani Army without the knowledge of the elected government. Many years later, the then Pakistan President and Army Chief, General Pervez Musharraf, who, in fact, had master-minded the whole operation, was categorical in claiming that Prime Minister Sharif was kept in the loop. In recent years, during some of the talks of the retired Pakistani Generals at literary festivals, it has been suggested that General Musharraf had indeed taken his Prime Minister in confidence but only casually, resulting in the matter slipping out of the mind of Nawaz Sharif! But now, with the publication of Nasim Zehra's book, more light is being thrown on the Kargil misadventure of Pakistan.

Since Zehrais a defence and strategic studies journalist and has access to commentators and people in the defence forces, she has based her book not only on interviews with the people involved but also documents. There is, therefore, no reason to dispute her version of events. Before her book was published in 2018, the subject of Kargil 1999 and the debacle of the Pakistani Army had remained a taboo with no enquiry or official or informal discussion taking place. In contrast, a committee headed by a civilian, had been instituted to ensure that the country is not caught in such a situation again. But with the publication of *From Kargil to The Coup: Events that Shook Pakistan*, the facts are now out in the public domain and the debate of whether the Pakistani Prime Minister knew about the operation too has been settled.

There is little doubt now that the Kargil operation, code named by the Pakistani Army as 'Koh Paima', was conceived as a local operation planned in such a manner that even the troops movement did not require approval from the army headquarters. It was planned and executed by the Rawalpindi-based 10 Corps which was responsible for all Pakistani Army actions in the Kashmir area. Thus, a cabal of Generals whose views converged on the intent of seeking revenge for the 1971 dismemberment and humiliation, the occupation of Siachen by India, and Pakistan's inability to grab Kashmir, got together to execute Operation Koh Paima. A careful reading of Zehra's book will also suggest that contrary to her suggestion that the plan was conceived by a few Generals and then presented to General Musharraf for approval sounds hollow since the Chief of the Pakistani Army had handpicked all those Generals to post them in such strategic positions where no General outside of them needed to know what was going on in that sector. Moreover, after the military coup that dislodged Sharif government, General Musharraf promoted all of them.

The operation was so shrouded in secrecy that even the all-knowing ISI had no clue to it. The Pakistan Air Force and Navy too were kept out of the loop and informed only when the forward areas under India had been occupied. This, according to the FCNA (Force Command Northern Areas) commander Major General Javed Hassan, had taken place in October 1998, before the peace strategy between the two countries was to unfold.

In November 1998, addressing the Defence Committee of the Cabinet, Prime Minister Sharif unveiled his plans for peace and instructed the foreign minister and chief of the ISI to implement the new policy with their mandate being to discontinue armed support for the Kashmiris and 'broadening and deepening of APHC (All Parties Hurriyat Conference) and to highlight the violations of human rights and political rights by the Indians.'[14] Unknown to Sharif, about five weeks before Prime Minister Vajpayee was to visit Lahore, the clique of Generals informed their Chief of the whole operation, and after securing General Musharraf's consent went into a full offensive, even though by then they had already occupied the Indian Territory overlooking Srinagar-Leh highway.

As the battles turned into war, the authorities and people of India became aware of the magnitude of the threat. In Pakistan too, the Navy and Air Force were brought in the loop but it was more in the nature of fait accompli. Finally, on 17 May 1999, Prime Minister Sharif too was informed. Pakistan's Director General Military Operations, Lieut. General Tauqir Zia claimed that Pakistan's army would soon infiltrate freedom fighters into Leh and Ladakh to start an insurgency, thus cutting off any help from the mainland and then, as a next step, a large number of 'freedom fighters' will be rushed in Kashmir, thereby locking in much of the Indian Army in Kashmir and Ladakh. This, he said, would bring the Indians 'on their knees begging for talks and Pakistan would dictate its own terms.'

The presentation of the DGMO was followed by the Chief of the General Staff, Lieut. General Aziz Khan's flattering words to Nawaz Sharif: 'Sir, Pakistan was created with the efforts of Quaid and Muslim League and they will always be remembered for creating Pakistan and now Allah has given you the opportunity and the chance to get Indian held Kashmir and your name will be written in golden letters...after Quaid it is unique opportunity to be remembered as the Fatah-i-Kashmir (Conqueror of Kashmir)'[15] As it turned out, the temptation was too great to resist and Nawaz Sharif wasted no time in taking the bait.

India paid a heavy price for having lowered her guard. However, after suffering 473 casualties and 1,060 wounded it not only recovered all the strategic heights in the Dras and Batalik sectors but also Point 13620 in Kargil that was an important military town in Kargil and overlooked the Kargil-Leh highway. Ever since the 1965 war, Point 13620 had been captured a number of times by the Indian Army at heavy cost and every time it had surrendered it at the negotiating table. That phase was consigned to history with the Kargil war of 1999.

It was only the middle of the year, and there was to be more drama before the year came to an end. Instead of 'facing the punishment for his failings, its planner-executioner (Musharraf)... staged a coup against the democratically elected government of Nawaz Sharif in October 1999, grabbing the reins of power for nearly a decade. An already crippled economy, struggling under the weight of the sanctions imposed by the US after the previous year's nuclear tests, Pakistan had to cough up $2 billion for the botched war. The damage to Pakistan's international standing was no less significant: In the eyes of the world, Pakistan was perceived as a dangerously unstable state led by military officials with little to no accountability.'[16] In Pakistan, on 12 October 1999, General Pervez Musharraf followed the footsteps of General Zia-ul-Haq and deposed the person who had appointed him as the General of Pakistan Army, put him under arrest and promulgated martial law.

In India, another drama of far-reaching consequences was to take place before the year ended. As the year was ending, Indian Airlines flight IC-814 was flying from Kathmandu to Delhi on the eve of Christmas with 178 passengers on board, including eight cabin and three flight crew. It was a happy flight back home for most people on board after enjoying the holidays in Kathmandu, the favorite holiday spot for the emerging middle class, when suddenly armed men took over the Air bus. The ATC was informed of the hijacking at 4.52 p.m. The Captain was asked to take the flight towards 'west' and when he tried to make excuses, such as insufficient fuel, one of hijackers made it known that not only could he read the fuel gauges but was also conversant with flying jargon. In western direction lay Lahore, the preferred direction of hijackers while hijacking planes from Indian soil. Finally, by using the ruse of low fuel, the Captain managed to land at the Amritsar airport in the hope that Indian authorities would be able to do the needful. The standing instructions to Indian commercial pilots was to follow what the hijackers said and leave the job of dealing with them to the people on ground. Later, former Punjab police chief, K.P.S. Gill reconstructed the whole ordeal and published it as a book, which was edited by him and Ajay Sahni.[17]

According to the paper, the ATC Delhi had received the warning of the hijack at 4.52 p.m. and the information had been duly passed on to the Government's Crisis Management Group (CMG). But nothing was done since the Prime Minister was traveling and his plane was in the air. As a result there was no coherent response as no one was in-charge and there was no blue book for such exigencies. The CMG could meet only at about 6 p.m. and the National Security Guard (NSG), an elite group, based on the outskirts of New Delhi and specially trained to deal with such situations was informed at 6.10 p.m. It was ready to fly in less than an hour but no one had made the necessary arrangements to send them to Amritsar. It is appalling that though senior ministers, including the National Security Adviser, Brajesh Mishra, were told of what had happened, none had the presence of mind to alert the NSG. Meanwhile, at 7.01 p.m. the flight landed at Amritsar but during that crucial one hour no preparation had been made to hold it there and senior members kept passing the responsibility. After the fiasco and the vain bid of the Captain to stall take off, the flight took off for Lahore without fueling since the hijackers had got fidgety by the delaying tactics of the Captain. It now flew in the destination of two earlier incidents of hijacking, one from Srinagar and the other from Chandigarh.[18] The flight carrying the NSG arrived at 8.15 p.m. three hours and twenty three minutes after the first information had been received and twenty six minutes after IC-814 had taken off. The fact that India was no stranger to hijacking had apparently taught nothing and even in 2008 when Mumbai was attacked by a group of ten terrorists, no effort had been made to have at least zonal centers for stationing the NSG and equip them with their own planes and helicopters so that it can reach anywhere in the country at a short notice.

Sarabjit Singh, DGP, Punjab had his own version that he narrated to A. S. Dulat, who was a master spy before he ended his career as the point-man for Vajpayee in Kashmir. According to Singh, 'the state police had commandos at Amritsar and Virdi (Inspector General Border posted at Amritsar) had two companies sent immediately to the airport. The deputy inspector general (border), Jasminder Singh, had the presence of mind to reach the air traffic control (ATC) tower even before IC-814 landed. Jasminder kept reporting to Sarabjit on the development as they unfolded... Sarabjit decided to monitor the situation from Chandigarh and await instructions from CMG in Delhi, because he felt he was not in a position to act on his own...(He) did consider that he had at his disposal in Punjab commandos who were trained in anti-terrorism, and that they could storm the aircraft, but there would be casualties. He told Delhi, which responded that the government's top priority was that there be no casualties.'[19]

Adding to the woes of Sarabjit Singh was the response of the chief minister of Punjab, Parkash Singh Badal. 'Be careful,' he cautioned his DGP. Thus, Delhi did not want any casualties and the state chief minister in whose jurisdiction the hijacked plane was parked had washed his hands off by instructing his DGP to be careful. Almost a decade after that fateful day, Sarabjit Singh told Dulat that no one in Delhi told him that the plane should not be allowed to takeoff from Amritsar even though Deputy Prime Minister Advani had taken charge of the CMG. All that they were prepared to say was that there should not be any casualties. The bottom line was that there was a crisis of leadership in Delhi and Punjab. In Delhi no one wanted to take the responsibility of an action gone wrong; in Punjab, the chief minister did not want any part in it and the DGP was too timid to assume leadership and initiative. As he put it to Dulat, he was no K.P.S. Gill, the legendary Director General of Police in Punjab who had faced a similar situation in 1993 in Amritsar when a hijacked Indian Airlines flight from Delhi to Srinagar had landed there. Gill had taken charge and the hijacking was over in twelve seconds with the NSG commandos storming the plane, immobilizing the four hijackers and killing their leader. But 1999 was different. The result was that India lost the chance to act. After that there was no choice but to yield to the demands of the hijackers.

When the flight approached Lahore, Pakistan did not want to be seen having any connection with the hijackers and the incident. The Pakistani authorities pretended to disown hijacked victims, refusing to give the aircraft permission to land and switching off the lights of the airport.

Throughout the 1990s, Pakistan had been playing an active role in the terrorism in Kashmir and the Americans had been pressurizing it to end the support. The Americans had also come to see the folly of having funded and armed Pakistan without controls and checks during the fight against Russians in Afghanistan. As a consequence, it had come close to being declared an international pariah. International community had also come close to viewing Pakistan as a failed state since once again a democratically elected government had been ousted by a military coup led by General Pervez Musharraf, the third in the history of Pakistan in sharp contrast to India where successive elections had been conducted and governments elected, reelected and ousted through the ballot. This coup had taken place soon after the Kargil misadventure of Pakistan by the General who was primarily responsible for the Kargil conflict. In response to the American pressure, the Inter-Services Intelligence (ISI) had only covered up its tracks and carried on with its activities. Now pretending to wash its hands off the whole affair, Lahore ATC refused landing. However, with the danger of a crash due to low fuel, the Captain scared the Pakistani authorities into allowing him to land after threatening to land the plane on a highway! Pakistan authorities, in fact, made no effort to deal with the situation but fueled the plane to send it back in the air.

The destination of the hijackers was Kabul but the Captain was able to convince them that the plane could not land there as the runway was ravaged by the war and there was no facility for landing at night. Most of the countries in the region were Islamic and as a rule either stood by Pakistan or stayed out of the Indo-Pak conflict, and in this instance, the Pakistan distancing notwithstanding, this part of the world was convinced of its involvement and, therefore, were not willing to get involved by letting the plane land and then have the responsibility of neutralizing the hijackers. India tried through the US to pressurize UAE into allowing Indian commandos to storm the plane while it was in Dubai, but the request declined. Finally, UAE allowed the aircraft to land and tried to convince the hijackers to release some of the passengers in lieu of fuel. It turned out to be a short delay and IC-814 was back in air to finally land at Kandahar airport, close to the border of Baluchistan in Pakistan. Kandahar was a hotbed of Mujahideens and also had a heavy presence of ISI and Afghanistan's Taliban.

The plane remained parked in Kandahar till the New Year's Eve when the hostages were released after a deal was struck between the Government of India and the hijackers and their handlers. A team of negotiators, including Ajit Doval, who would later become Prime Minister Narendra Modi's National Security Adviser in 2014, also arrived in Kandahar and were struck by the close coordination between the hijackers and the Taliban. It was also very clear that at almost every stage, they had been consulting a third party which could have been none other than the ISI.

It was very clear that the ISI had not been deterred by the American warnings. Even the missile attack that President Clinton had ordered in Afghanistan over the Pakistani space targeting Osama bin Laden had not dislodged them from their course. Finally, when the deal was finalized, it was agreed that notorious terrorists, Maulana Masood Azhar[20] and Omar Shaikh[21] of Pakistani descent and a Kashmiri militant Mushtaq Ahmed Zargar[22] were to be released in exchange for the passengers. Senior cabinet minister, Jaswant Singh accompanied the terrorists for the exchange. Dulat, who was present all through the CMG meeting narrates that when some of the passengers were released in Dubai, Sharad Yadav, a senior cabinet minister, was the first to raise his hand and fly out to bring back the rescued passengers, and when the flight back home was to take off, he had triumphantly waved to the media. But now when no minister was willing to go to Kandahar, where the terrorists were in control, to bring back the hostages, it was left to Jaswant Singh who had to go and face the wrath and frustration of the rescued hostages.

India, indeed, had paid a heavy price. Not only were three terrorists released but the lack of will and low confidence of the government coupled with institutional failure to act in stopping the flight at Amritsar brought about the description of the country as a soft state. Conversely, the confidence of Pakistan also rose since ISI had made the release of Azhar a matter of prestige and, in fact, the arrest of Omar Shaikh in Delhi by Indian authorities was because of its persistent attempts to secure his release.

Azhar had played a prominent role in the battle against Soviets in Afghanistan and had been instrumental in getting the two Islamic jihadist groups, Harkat-ul-Mujahideen (HuM) and Harkat ul-Jihad-i-Islami (HuJI), to merge in 1993 as Harkat-ul-Ansar. Both had played a prominent role in Afghanistan under the leadership of Maulana Fazlur Rehaman Khalil while being in close contact with the ISI.

Masood was a native of Bahawalpur (South Punjab, Pakistan) and belonged to a family connected with the Ahrar[23] movement but had got associated with the Binori[24] school of Islam, the breeding ground of Jihadists. Like other Jihadists, after the Soviet withdrawal, Masood went to Kashmir to wage Jihad against India, but was captured in 1994 by the Indian Army. How valuable he was to the Pakistani plans can be judged by the fact that Harkat-ul-Ansar and ISI went to great lengths to get their man freed, the favored technique being taking foreign tourists hostage to use as bargaining chips. For the mission to liberate Masood Azhar they sent Pakistan-born British Ahmed Omar Saeed Shaikh, better known as Omar Shaikh, to Delhi where he took western hostages but ultimately the operation got botched and Omar Shaikh was arrested. More cases of abduction took place in the Valley in 1995 with the same goal and in one of them, four of the hostages were executed while one escaped.

However, nothing explains the relationship of the Pakistani Army with the terrorists in Kashmir better than the activities of Ilyas Kashmiri who hailed from Pakistan-occupied-Kashmir (PoK). He was from the Pakistani Army's elite corps, Special Service Group (SSG) and was deputed in the mid-80s to train Afghan Mujahideens. 'As a Harkat-ul-Mujahideen cadre, he worked first as an instructor in a training camp near Miramshah (North Waziristan). After being "asked by Pakistani establishment to work with Kashmiri militants", he joined the Kashmir chapter of Harkat-Ul-Jihad-e-Islam in 1991 but eventually created his own movement, the 313

Brigade. He multiplied guerrilla operations across the LoC in the 1990s. The Indian army arrested him but he escaped from jail after two years and immediately became a legend in Pakistan. Musharraf himself, as COAS, gave him a cash award of rupees one lakh for one of his operations. Ilyas Kashmiri built a training camp in Kotli (PoK).'[25] Masood's career is a testimony to the relations which existed between the Pakistani Army and Jihadis—who sometimes came directly from its ranks, as in this case.

Much of the decade of 1990s had passed in this struggle between the Indian security forces and the multiple incarnations of the jihadi militants to gain control of Kashmir. The Pakistani Army developed a different strategy for Kashmir since its goals were different from what they were in Afghanistan. Now it was not interested in conquering the Indian Territory since it knew that India had the wherewithal to defend it. Instead, it chose to 'bleed India through a thousand cuts' without being in the frontline. It launched an 'outsourced' war that was low in intensity yet it tied the Indian forces in the Valley. One General involved in this strategy to 'bleed India' by infiltrating jihadists into its despised neighbor explained to Ahmed Rashid the predominant rationale in the 1990s in very simple terms: 'It kept 7,00,000 Indian troops and paramilitary forces in Kashmir at very low cost to Pakistan; at the same time, it ensured that Indian Army could not threaten Pakistan, created enormous expenditures for India, and kept it bogged down in military and political terms.'[26]

ISI was the mastermind of this strategy and having been so successful in defeating a super power had gained in confidence and decision-making space in Pakistan. 'Cultivating the art of "plausible denials"...(the) Pakistan Army will always deny remote-controlling jihadists operations in...Kashmir. Yet, the ISI has never ceased training, funding and arming paramilitary troops...Until the early 2000s, with ISI support (LeT) maintained three camps in Pakistani Kashmir. The largest of them near Muzaffarabad, trained 300 mujahideens per month. In all, the movement had at its disposal between 1,00,000 to 3,00,000 youths who had undergone military training.'[27]

A historian might well be intrigued by the doggedness of

Pakistan to pursue Kashmir and might wonder as to why when the international community too has stopped questioning the accession of the State to India, Pakistan continues with its efforts, even at the cost of jeopardizing the well-being of its people. While this question will be addressed in the following chapters any student of contemporary developments will know that from 1999 onwards, Pakistan had grown in confidence due to the developments of 1998. That was the year when both India and Pakistan had declared themselves as nuclear powers after Pakistan detonated five blasts in the Chagai hills. It had followed India which too had conducted its tests in Pokhran, Rajasthan, two weeks prior to Pakistan's detonations. Myra Macdonald, a journalist specializing in South Asia studies, has depicted a dramatic contrast in the manner in which both the countries announced their nuclear status in her book, *Defeat is an Orphan.*[28] She says that after summoning a press conference at short notice, Prime Minister Vajpayee casually sauntered in and made a short crisp announcement in English that India had conducted nuclear tests, and then gave a few technical details and left. Obviously, a Hindi-speaking Prime Minister had deliberately chosen English as the language of communication in the country with a purpose—the communication had been addressed to the international community as much as to the domestic audience.

In sharp contrast, Pakistani Prime Minister Sharif chose the national television to make the announcement in Urdu. Obviously, his targeted audience was domestic, and he wanted to reassure his countrymen that by becoming a nuclear power, Pakistan had not only bought insurance but also established parity with India. But the contrast was not lost on observers: Vajpayee casually dressed in his everyday dress and Sharif in the more formal sherwani; one choosing English to announce to the world that India was occupying its rightful place in the nuclear club, and the other, formally wanting to be accepted as a nuclear country. These tests, Pakistan believed, gave it a guarantee against any Indian invasion since it was convinced that it was a deterrent. Right from its inception, barring democracy and its institutions, Pakistan viewed itself in relation to India and where it stood in terms of India's war capabilities. Founded on the Two Nations theory, Pakistan's core philosophy had been knocked out by India when it facilitated its break-up and creation of another Muslim State, Bangladesh, in 1971, a mere twenty-four years after coming into existence. Its Prime Minister Zulfikar Ali Bhutto had then vowed to fight a 'thousand-year war' against India.[29] In 1974, India had conducted its first nuclear test and in response Bhutto had again vowed that Pakistanis will eat grass but will also have their nuclear bomb. In fact, Pakistan had put itself at the forefront of Islamic countries and had promised an 'Islamic' bomb on behalf of all Muslim countries. However, when it finally possessed that bomb, it failed to see it as deterrence to both the sides and blissfully believed that only the 'Hindu' India would be scared of using it and inviting international opprobrium. This explains the earlier bold bid to wrest control of Ladakh by initiating the Kargil conflict and now by a bolder action of hijacking an Indian airlines plane to secure its most strategic assets in the, sometime overt but mostly covert fight, to wrest Kashmir from India. In the following two chapters, an attempt has been made to understand the State of Pakistan, its driving force, the impulses and ambitions.

2

Understanding Pakistan

'So we march on, following our leaders, toward an "Armageddon" of our own making.'

—Noam Chomsky, *Failed States: The Abuse of Power and the Assault on Democracy*

The fundamentals of Pakistan were as much a product of the British parliamentary system as of India. Yet, within its first few years, Pakistan had slid into being identified and defined only by its religion and army. Not surprisingly, some critics characterize it as a State whose birth has been riddled with insecurity and indecision, comparing it to a child whose parents were unsure if they wanted the child or not. Till the very end, the leaders of the Muslim League had remained muddled in their thinking and ambivalent to the idea of Pakistan. This was in stark contrast to the leaders of the Congress who were clear headed in their approach to their goal of independence and the kind of India they wanted to build. As early as 1928, a Congress committee headed by Motilal Nehru, that included the next generation of leaders in Jawaharlal Nehru and Subhash Chandra Bose, had made recommendations for the framework that Congress wanted for India.

Ever since the Indian National Congress was established in 1885, it had grown at a fast pace and attracted large sections of the population in its struggle to achieve independence. Though led by educated and largely rich members of the society, its ranks soon swelled in numbers of ordinary and poor people from all walks of life. By 1906, the Muslims, feeling insecure at the possibility of losing considerable space and prestige to the vast multitudes of Hindus once the British left, organized themselves into the All-India Muslim League or simply Muslim League to safeguard the Muslim interests, as they understood them. As independence drew near, the Muslims began to fear their fate in South Asia and demanded separate Muslim constituencies, and later, a separate homeland. Their fears were best illustrated by an Urdu couplet by the century's most eminent poet and orator, Muhammad Iqbal, who was commonly known as Allama Iqbal[30]:

> *Jamhūriyat ik tarz-e-hukūmat hai ki jis meiñ*
> *bandoñ ko ginā karte haiñ taulā nahīñ karte.*
>
> (Democracy is one form of government in which
> Men are counted not weighed.)

In a democracy only the numbers matter and not the quality! Nothing has illustrated the fear of the majoritarianism more than this couplet.

Although Pakistan was led by the charismatic Mohammad Ali Jinnah[31], it was given ideological fervor by Allama Iqbal. Jinnah might be acknowledged as the founder of Pakistan and is reverentially addressed as 'Quaid-e-Azam'—the Great Leader—but it is Iqbal who is credited with being the spiritual father of Pakistan. However, ironically, Iqbal had only demanded a Muslim State within India rather than separate homeland in the subcontinent, though the debate about what exactly he meant by 'State' continues to be part of 'roshan-khyali'—liberalism—debates among many Pakistanis.

Ironically, till 1946 Jinnah continued to work for preserving Muslim interests within United India. Both, Christophe Jafferlot[32] and Ayesha Siddiqa[33] are of the opinion that Jinnah used Islam as the 'cultural basis for an ideology of ethnic nationalism that was intended to mobilize the Muslim community in order to defend the 'minoritarian Muslims' Iqbal's thinking was equally complicated. He is said to have written a letter to the editor of The Times, London, protesting its 'out of context' reporting of his famous 1930 Allahabad address to the Muslims, which seemed to hint at the fact that he had demanded a Muslim homeland! His protestation notwithstanding, that selective quote from his address, came to be known as 'Iqbal's call', and the foundational myth, for the making of Pakistan. However, Iqbal had, rather than making a call for a separate Muslim homeland, in fact, said:

> The Muslim demand for the creation of a Muslim India within India is, therefore, perfectly justified. The resolution of the All-Parties Muslim Conference at Delhi is, to my mind, wholly inspired by this noble ideal of a harmonious whole which, instead of stifling the respective individualities of its component wholes, affords them chances of fully working out the possibilities that may be latent in them. And I have no doubt that this House will emphatically endorse the Muslim demands embodied in this resolution.
>
> Personally, I would go farther than the demands embodied in it. I would like to see the Punjab, North-West Frontier Province, Sind and Baluchistan amalgamated into a single State. Self-government within the British Empire, or without the British Empire, the formation of a consolidated North-West Indian Muslim State appears to me to be the final destiny of the Muslims, at least of North-West India.[34]

While on the one hand, Iqbal's speech was used as an argument for the creation of Pakistan, the Muslim Bengalis also used it to claim a separate State for themselves in the east! Significantly, in the same address, he had also said; 'The unity of an Indian nation, therefore, must be sought not in the negation, but in the mutual harmony and cooperation, of the many. True statesmanship cannot ignore facts, however unpleasant they may be. The only practical course is not to assume the existence of a state of things which does not exist, but to recognize facts as they are, and to exploit them to our greatest advantage. And it is on the discovery of Indian unity in this direction that the fate of India as well as of Asia really depends. India is Asia in miniature.'

But Ayub Khan, late President of Pakistan, records in his autobiography, *Friends Not Masters*, that Iqbal 'spelt out the broad outlines of a plan under which the Muslims of India were led to aspire to an independent state in which they would be free to follow their own way of life.' The problem, however, was that Iqbal's political philosophy was as complicated as that of Jinnah. Both shared concern for the future of Muslims in a democracy driven free India and offered a solution in making territorial arrangement to consolidate Muslim-majority states. But neither he nor Jinnah had a vision for Muslims, spread all over the subcontinent, to remain limited to the north western region of India comprising Punjab, North-West Frontier Province, Sindh and Balochistan. Later the north-eastern region of Bengal and Assam too was added to this consolidation plan. But this practical understanding of a Muslim community that realized the importance of geography was at odds with his idea of universal Muslim community—ummah.[35]

Territorial Islam was not something that Iqbal could reconcile to and considered a territorial Islamic state a blow to communal harmony. Often this philosophy was at odds with his dream of the dominance of Islam in this world, as repeatedly expressed in his poetry. The difference between him and Jinnah was that though the latter used the word 'Sharia' as a foundation of the new State, it is doubtful if he really understood it, and the former understood it so well that he rejected the Quranic Hadood laws, which were later introduced by General Zia-ul-Haq.[36] Ultimately, the doubts and reservations of Iqbal notwithstanding, the Pakistani Army and other Pakistani institutions appropriated him and have insisted that it was his philosophy that gave the historical thrust to the making of Pakistan. It has been noted by scholars that it also explains why almost all Pakistani defence publications frequently quote his verses in justifying the prevalent notions, from faith to jihad. It is interesting to note that though the Muslim League was born in 1906, it was not till 1933 that the word 'Pakistan', meaning 'Land of the Pure', was first articulated and it was only during the historical Lahore session of 1940 that the philosophy behind a separate homeland for Muslims was articulated.

It was during Muslim League's 1940 Lahore session that Jinnah propounded the theory that Hindus and Muslims should comprise separate nations. This theory came to be known as the Two-Nation Theory. There is much debate and controversy about the words used in that Resolution and the meaning thereof but it came to be generally believed as a call for the partition of India.

> Islam and Hinduism are not religions in strict sense of the word, but are; in fact, different and distinct social orders…The Hindus and the Muslims belong to different religious philosophies, social customs, and literatures…To yoke together two such nations under a single State, one as a numerical minority and the other as a majority, must lead to growing discontent and the final destruction of any fabric that may be so built up for the government of such a state.[37]

This theorizing notwithstanding, nowhere did the main resolution of the session use the word Pakistan or the Partition of India. It only wanted subsequent constitutional dispensations to be reconsidered in light of the claim that Indian Muslims constitute a nation. It was argued in vague terms by the League that Muslim majority areas of the northwest and northeast and east should be 'grouped to constitute Independent States in which constituent units…(would) be autonomous and sovereign.'[38] Ironically, it was these words that were used by the Bangladesh separatists to demand a separate state for themselves, arguing that it had been resolved that there would be independent 'states' and not just a single 'state'.

The idea of a separate state did not resonate in the Muslim-dominated Punjab and northwest and northeast provinces; it was only in the United Provinces (present day Uttar Pradesh) that the Muslims feared most, the domination of the majority community, and hence were the most vocal. What followed is beyond the scope of this book but suffice it to say that till the very end the tall Muslim leaders of the Muslim League, including the tallest, Jinnah, remained ambivalent towards the idea of a separate state. No wonder when the reality of Pakistan dawned, Jinnah termed it as 'moth eaten'.

Adding further confusion to defining Pakistan was Jinnah's speech on the eve of its creation, when the British hurried to leave their former colony and in the process created an ill-defined state that equally hurriedly tried to define and justify itself. After having unleashed the monster of communal hatred and violence, Jinnah found himself saddled with the responsibility of running a state in an orderly manner. In a bid to stop the violence that was raging, he delivered a speech to the Pakistan Constituent Assembly on 11 August 1947 wherein he declared:

> You are free, free to go to your temples; free to go to your mosques or any other places of worship in the state of Pakistan. You may belong to any religion or caste or creed that has nothing to do with the business of the state...[You] will find that in course of time Hindus will cease to be Hindus and Muslims would cease to be Muslims, not in the religious sense, because that is the personal faith of each individual, but in the political sense as citizens of Pakistan.[39]

This speech is used by some secular Pakistanis as evidence to prove that Jinnah wanted a Pakistan that was inclusive rather than exclusive. Unfortunately, Jinnah died within a year of this speech without having the time to give shape to his idea of Pakistan and leaving his followers confused and unable to define his dream. In his lifetime, he had said different things at various times, leaving his followers confused and squabbling and 'divided...about whether to take their cue from his independence eve call to keep religion out of politics or to build on the religious sentiment generated during the political bargaining for Pakistan.'[40]

Ironically, it is now known that, Jawaharlal Nehru and Jinnah both regretted their decision about Pakistan. Both had seen the consequences and were horrified at what they saw. Even Lord Mountbatten was not really keen about it but he was clear that the responsibility for Partition should be with the leaders of the subcontinent. Stanley Wolpert, American historian and Indologist wrote that Mountbatten said: 'The most we can hope to do, as I have said before, is to put the responsibility for any of these mad decisions fairly and squarely on the Indian (pre-partition India) shoulders in the eyes of the world, for one day they will bitterly regret the decision they are about to make.'[41]

Within a year of Partition Pandit Nehru was in a contemplative and revisionary mode, and said: 'Perhaps we acted wrongly...The consequences of that partition have been so terrible that one is inclined to think that anything else would have been preferable... Ultimately, I have no doubt that India and Pakistan will come together...some kind of federal link...There is no other way to peace. The alternative is...war.'[42]

Surprisingly, Jinnah was equally mortified at what he saw and his doctor reported that on his deathbed when he saw Liaquat Ali Khan, he told him: 'Pakistan was the biggest blunder of my life.' Jinnah also added in a slurred whisper, 'If now I get an opportunity I will go to Delhi and tell Jawaharlal to forget about the follies of the past and become friends again.'[43] In another account it is said that during a flight to survey the extent of refugee crisis in the Punjab, Jinnah had held his head in his hands and remarked, 'Oh, my God, what have I done?'[44] And, finally, within months of Partition, Jinnah had asked Sri Prakasa, the first Indian High Commissioner to Pakistan to convey a personal message from him to Pandit Nehru—'Tell Jawaharlal not to break my heart...you do not know how much I love Bombay. I still look forward to going back there.' The man who had demanded a 'homeland' for the Muslims and in the process had been the cause of more than a million deaths and many more displaced, now wanted to abandon his 'homeland' for the city he loved and the home he had built.[45]

Another shock that Jinnah had got was the outcome of his obsession with the word 'Pakistan' as the name for the new country. He was certain that with independence, India will call itself 'Hindustan' or would revert to the myth,* invoking the name of 'Bharat'. However, when it chose to call itself 'India that is Bharat' he was outraged. With a single word, 'India', Nehru and India had appropriated culture and the civilization that had flourished on the banks of Indus and its tributaries as also claiming the title of that property![46]

In popular perception, General Zia-ul-Haq is held responsible for the Islamization of Pakistan but the reality was that this process had already begun before Pakistan's creation with acceleration being provided by the labors of political and military leadership. It became the principal tool of strengthening the new born state and when the discussions for the Constitution were going on there were demands for an Islamic Constitution. Thus, the Islamic clerics and scholars

---

*According to the Mahabharata (Adi Parva), Bharat was the son of King Dushyant and Shakuntala. Bharat conquered the world, ruled for twenty-seven thousand years. The kingdom that he inherited and expanded—the Indian subcontinent—came to be known as Bhārat, named after him.

gained a bigger space in the Constituent Assembly than Jinnah would have allowed them, but that is how the chief lieutenant of Jinnah, Liaquat Ali Khan put before the assembly in the Objectives Resolution on 7 March 1949 and adopted on 12 March 1949:

> Sovereignty over the entire universe belongs to Allah Almighty alone and the authority which He has delegated to the state of Pakistan, through its people for being exercised within the limits prescribed by Him is a sacred trust…The state shall exercise its powers and authority through the chosen representatives of the people. The principles of democracy, freedom, equality, tolerance and social justice, as enunciated by Islam, shall be fully observed. The Muslims shall be enabled to order their lives in the individual and collective spheres in accordance with the teachings and requirements of Islam as set out in the Holy Quran and Sunnah.

Pakistan was clearly struggling after Jinnah—to manifest its communal underpinnings or to recognize the needs of consolidating and securing a multiethnic and multi-religious polity. Finally, they ended up formulating a state ideology that was based on Islam. Khaled Ahmed, a columnist and political commentator, draws our attention to the fact that when in 1949 the Constituent Assembly of Pakistan was adopting its Objectives Resolution, 'it used the less-threatening terms "Quran" and "Sunnah" rather than Sharia, which later came to be embedded in Article 203(C) of the Constitution… The politicians who signed the resolution knew nothing about what the "guiding code" zimmis (non-Muslim subjects of a state governed according to the shariat) who would have to pay a special tax.'[47] The civilian and military leaders alike agreed on this principle though it was not possible to be unanimous on defining what that ideology meant.

Thus, the Islamic ideology of Pakistan had clearly defined the new state, more so since leaders like Liaquat Ali Khan belonged to the secular elite of Pakistan and if they were supporting the idea to employ Islam as a tool to unify the state in the face of multiple identities then it meant that they had conceded that nothing but Islam could keep the state together. This idea was strengthened by the loss of Bangladesh in 1971, after which Prime

Minister Zulfikar Ali Bhutto made conscious effort to promote Islam as a unifying factor among the remaining ethnic groups. The government and the Islamists were unanimous in their opinion that only Islamic ideals of governance could maintain cohesion. Ever since, Arabic has occupied greater space in school education, Ahmediyas declared non-Muslims, drinking and gambling outlawed and Islamic socialism promoted. In addition, the Constitution of 1973 recognized for the first time Pakistan as an Islamic state. After Bhutto was replaced by another spell of martial law and General Zia-ul-Haq became the Chief Martial Law Administrator and then President, Sunni Islam was given greater space in the state and Pakistani polity. He reconstituted the Council of Islamic ideology, established shariat federal courts[48] and also gave role to conservative and orthodox ulemas[49] to ensure that the government was functioning within the goals of Islamization. In 1979, Zia went a step further and introduced Hudood Ordinances[50] that prescribed punishment for crimes in accordance with the laws that were applicable during the times of Prophet Mohammad. In this line, Zakat[51] too was introduced by the state but it only outraged the Shias for whom it was a personal affair and not to be interfered by the state. Since this period was closely followed by the Iranian revolution and the war between Shia Iran and Sunni Iraq, the tremors were also felt in Pakistan with sectarian violence taking a bloody turn. In this potboiler was added the Soviet invasion of Afghanistan and the consequent involvement of Pakistan as a frontline state for the Jihadis.

The Pakistani Army which had come to identify itself with the ideology of Pakistan in the 1960s became another pillar of the idea of Pakistan. Overtime, only two undercurrents of Pakistan's ideology remained—Islam and perpetual hostility to India—and the Pakistani Army was quick to appropriate to itself the role of the defender of this ideology. However, writers like Husain Haqqani are of the opinion that this process had begun no sooner than Pakistan was created since this ideology was present in the garb of 'resistance to Hindu India'. Some analysts find it hard to accept that though the Indian and Pakistani Army came from the same stock of British Army that inculcated similar ethics and approach to life, yet the Pakistani Army was quick to morph into a religion-driven force. But considering the fact that the British Indian Army had long used religion as tool, with the concept of martial races being its pivot, it was easy for Pakistani soldiers to completely identify with Islam. After all, the British raised regiments based on ethnicity and religion. The Sikh regiments were separate as were the Baloch and Frontier, almost all Muslims. Even the Punjab regiment was organized as Hindu/Sikh battalion and Muslim battalion. So, the transition of the Pakistani Army to becoming the defenders of the ideology of Pakistan was not difficult.

The role the British Indian Army played in inculcating the spirit of religious identity is brought out by Brig. Mirza Hamid Hussain who was a cadet at the Royal Indian Military College in Dehradun between 1926 and 1932:

> We lined up according to our religious beliefs and marched to our respective places of worship. There were three main religions, that of the Sikhs, Hindus and Muslims and we fell in line in accordance with the number of people in each religious group. This meant that if Sikhs were more in number then they took the front position, the Hindus and Muslims, depending on which group was greater in numbers, occupied the second position…It always struck me as strange that the British who ran the school and were so very anxious to keep religion as far as possible from the boys during the day, would in the evening, without fail, undertake this duty of separating us into various religious groups. This, I presume, was to impress upon us that we were really different people following different religions.[52]

But this religiosity soon made the Pakistani Army believe that among its duties was to also defend the ideological frontiers of Pakistan. A reading of President Ayub Khan's *Friends not Masters* would show that he had a healthy contempt for orthodox religious leaders and wanted to guide Pakistan towards a modern Islamic State. His ambition was to build a strong central government that would be reinforced by Islam.

For guiding Pakistan towards modern Islam, President Ayub Khan's first task was to contain and use the powers of the numerous Sufi shrines and the Pirs who wielded enormous powers but mostly for their own advantage. He created a Department of Auqaf to oversee these shrines and used their enormous resources in building hospitals, schools and other facilities. The occasion of Urs of these Pirs was used to host agricultural and industrial exhibitions. In other words, he sought to appropriate the space created by them for state activities and thereby give the message that the ideology of Islam is best defined and defended by the state in general and the army in particular.

Paradoxically, while on one hand, President Ayub Khan never failed to flaunt his secular credentials, on the other, he also never felt shy of using Islam in the name of the nation. The confusion about Pakistani identity is best analyzed by him in an article written in *Foreign Affairs* magazine in 1960:

> ...none of us was in fact a Pakistani, for the simple reason that there was no territorial entity bearing that name...Prior to 1947, our nationalism was based more on an idea than any territorial definition. Till then, ideologically we were Muslims, territorially we happened to be Indians; and parochially we were a conglomeration of at least eleven smaller, provincial loyalties. But when suddenly Pakistan emerged as a reality, we who had got together from every nook and corner of the vast subcontinent of India were faced with the task of transforming all our traditional, territorial and parochial loyalties into one great loyalty for the new state of Pakistan.[53]

It is clear that for President Ayub Khan, as many others, the idea of Pakistan was driven not only by pan-Islamism but also the fear of Hindu domination. His Hindu complex and fear of Hindu hegemonic impulses finds greater articulation in his autobiography *Friends not Masters*:

> India was not content with her present sphere of influence and she knew that Pakistan had the will and the capacity to frustrate her expansionist designs. She wanted to browbeat us into subservience. All we wanted was to live as equal and honorable neighbors, but to that India would not agree. It was Brahmin chauvinism and arrogance that had forced us to seek a homeland of our own where we could order our life according

> to our thinking and faith…There was [a] fundamental opposition between the ideologies of India and Pakistan.[54]

Evidently Ayub Khan feared that if the ideology of Pakistan failed, the state of Pakistan too would fail. Hence the need to secure the legitimacy of this ideology within the state was necessary—using every tool that was available, from school education to media, radio and television. With the restriction on the debate about Pakistan's ideology and state, the process of creation of myths about both, began in right earnest. The central myth made the army the key institution of the state. He also laid down a new education system in which Pakistan's roots with the subcontinent were severed and replaced by Arabic roots to strengthen this ideology. This has continued to serve Pakistan till now.

With the aim of developing national consciousness, President Khan instituted the Sharif Commission,[55] which completed its task in 1959. This Commission had two main objectives: one, achieving national integration, and two, homogenization of modern economy of society. It invoked religion for national integration. It was natural too since it was the only common factor between diverse regions and interests. However, the new education not only gave Pakistan deeply problematic histories of Islam and xenophobic characterization of India and Hindus but also emphasized Sunni Islam to the exclusion of other Muslims and non-Muslims. Thus, it was Ayub Khan and not Zia-ul-Haq who began the use of Islam in promoting the idea of Pakistan and its ideology and in the process made all other state tools subservient to this goal.

Islam was invoked time and again to keep reminding the people about Pakistan. In fact, beginning with Ayub Khan, Pakistan has had a total of four separate periods of military take over and rule. Of the four, Ayub Khan, General Zia-ul-Haq and General Pervez Musharraf have used the same ruse to impose military rule: 'All justified their rule in terms of saving Pakistan from chaos—and from politicians.'[56] It also must be added that of the four, General Ayub Khan and General Yahya Khan were invited by the civilian government to take charge of the administration to ensure that the idea of Pakistan does not collapse. In comparison, General Zia-ul-

Haq and General Pervez Mushharaf were the ones who executed a genuine coup d'état to exercise power on their own.

To General Zia-ul-Haq, goes the dubious distinction of assigning a role to the Pakistani Army in defending the ideology of Pakistan along with its frontiers. He contended that the 'preservation of ideology and the Islamic character of the country was…as important as the security of the country's geographic boundaries.'[57] What Zia intended to do was made clear by the wording of the referendum on his rule put before the electorate, which is more revealing and unambiguous. Voters were asked to: 'endorse the process initiated by General Mohammad Ziaul Haq, [sic] the President of Pakistan, for bringing the laws of Pakistan in conformity with the injunctions of Islam as laid down in the Holy Quran and Sunnah of Holy Prophet (Peace be upon Him) and for the preservation of the ideology of Pakistan, for the continuation and consolidation of that process and for the smooth and orderly transfer of power to the elected representatives of the people, and in case of answer "Yes", General Mohammad Ziaul Haq [sic] shall be deemed to have been duly elected President of Pakistan for a term of five years from the day of the first meeting of the House of Parliament in joint sitting.'[58]

Zia-ul-Haq also deviated from Ayub Khan in his approach to the Sufi shrines, Pirs and the ulema. Whereas the former used the shrines and circumscribed the powers of the Pirs, the latter did not feel the necessity of associating with Sufi Islam and attempted to reinstate the original Islamic order as it existed during the time of Prophet Mohammad.

The next military dictator to follow Zia-ul-Haq was President General Pervez Musharraf. Although a curious mix of ostensible personal secularism, he too did not resist the temptation of using Islam to further his cause as President of Pakistan. Musharraf encouraged the bloc of Islamist parties—Muttahida Majlis-e-Amal (MMA)—who constituted the opposition of his choice. His core philosophy is best illustrated by the speech he gave to the citizens of Pakistan on 19 September 2001, in the wake of the choice given to Pakistan by USA, 'with us or against us', after the 9/11 attack on USA. He said:

> Our forces are on full alert and ready for do or die mission. In this situation if we make the wrong decision, it can be very bad for us. Our critical concerns are our sovereignty, second our economy, third our strategic assets (nuclear and missile), and fourth our Kashmir cause. All four will be harmed if we make the wrong decision. When we make these decisions they must be according to Islam...[59]

After saying this he went on to narrate the incident when for the survival of nascent and not yet strong Islam, Prophet Mohammad had decided to migrate from Mecca to Medina. The Prophet also had to sign an unequal treaty with the Meccan when faced with threat from the Jews but had soon succeeded in turning the tables by isolating the Jews from Meccan support, defeating them and then soon after having Mecca too acknowledge his supremacy.

Musharraf had used the life of Prophet Mohammad to justify the actions that he was determined to take to safeguard, what he considered, were the core challenges before Pakistan. Thus, Islam was once again declared integral to the existence of Pakistan. Moreover, making Kashmir an integral issue of Pakistan and Islam's interests, he had propounded the theory that by securing the interests of Pakistan he was advancing the interests of Islam! Apparently, there were great deal of similarities between the approach of President Ayub Khan, Zia-ul-Haq and President General Pervez Musharraf though each put his view in his own distinctive style.

The 'yes/no' referendum was also resorted to by Musharraf and he asked the voters: 'do you want to elect President Musharraf as President of Pakistan for the next five years for: survival of local government system; restoration of democracy; continuity and stability of reforms; eradication of extremism and sectarianism, and the accomplishment of the Quaid-i-Azam's concept.'[60] On the face of it, this question lacks the cynicism of the referendum held by Zia-ul-Haq. But by equating his rule with that of the dream of Jinnah, Musharraf was invoking the two-nation theory and the protection of Islam as Pakistan's ideology.

General Ashfaq Pervez Kayani, who succeeded Musharraf as the Chief of the Army Staff too followed in the footsteps of his predecessors in repeatedly referring to the ideology of Pakistan and the need to protect it. Addressing an audience on the occasion of Day of the Martyrs[61] he said, '...We would be successful when we have a strong belief in the ideology of Pakistan. Any doubt about this ideology would weaken the country.'[62]

On 14 August 2011, addressing the annual Azadi Parade, he further declared, '...We must stay committed to the ideals of Pakistan and remain ever ready to protect our motherland...The basis of our existence is the "Ideology of Pakistan". Therefore, each one of us must endeavor to pass it on to the next generations. We have the firm belief that by following the golden principles of Islam, we shall progress and win a respectable place in the comity of nations. We should never forget that Islam is the religion of peace. This great religion is the bond that binds us together and should not in any way divide us.'

The need to repeatedly refer to the bonds of Islam had begun to be felt once the ideology of Pakistan had been defined in reference to Islam. The Islamist forces, dormant earlier, had now begun to rear their head because of the international environment and the confrontation between the army and these forces. Making the situation even more problematic was the inability of the rulers and army of Pakistan to cut the umbilical cord that had raised Jihadis to fight in Afghanistan. Now Pakistan began to desperately make a distinction between the good Jihadi and bad Jihadi. The good ones, it goes without saying, were those who did not unleash terror on fellow Pakistanis, for they reserved their energies for attacking the Indian forces in Jammu and Kashmir and the forces in Afghanistan in order to further the interests of Pakistan in the 'so-called Great Game'. But unfortunately, the genie of Jihad was not one to remain in control of those who had opened the bottle and hence it would strike at those of their own countrymen who the Jihadis thought had been betraying the ideology of Pakistan, and by extension, Islam.

Religion has always been there in the British Indian Army, and later, in the Indian and the Pakistani armies. But in the Pakistani Army, special emphasis is laid on inculcating Islamic principles. What Zia-ul-Haq had done was expand the canvas to promote Islamic values all across the social life of Pakistan. He went to the extent of changing the motto that Jinnah gave, 'Faith, Unity,

Discipline' into 'Faith, Piety, holy war (struggle) in the name of God'. When he brought about this change not much resistance was offered and that which was, was easily brushed aside. However, the down side of this was that there were many Islamic thoughts that prevailed in society, some of them mutually antagonistic and hostile.

Zia-ul-Haq had also encouraged Jamaat-e-Islami, the Islamic religious party founded by Maulana Abul A'la Maududi, and allowed its literature to be distributed among officers, enlisted men and officers, and employees of other services. Even other Islamic groups, like Tablighi Jamaat, too were encouraged to influence these forces. The dismay this caused to Zulfikar Ali Bhutto is best expressed in the underlying exasperation of his statement before the Supreme Court during his trial that 'I appointed a Chief of Staff belonging to the Jamaat-e-Islami and the result is before all of us.'

The ideology of Islam had been distorted and the need to keep the control over the levers of power had begun to force those wielding it to embrace all kinds of non-state actors in defining the ideology of Pakistan and its association with Islam. The process of working closely with the Sunni kingdoms of Arab that began in 1967 when Pakistan signed an agreement with South Arabia to formally come in defense of the kingdom, reached its zenith during Zia-ul-Haq's times when unspecified number of Pakistan's soldiers were deputed to that kingdom. The result was intense exposure of the army to orthodox Islam and Wahhabism. This gained acceptability in the society and soon scholars like Stephen Cohen discovered that 'expressions like "ideology of Pakistan" and the "glory of Islam", normally outside a fighter's lexicon, were becoming stock phrases… The Service Chiefs sounded more like high priests than soldiers.' One retired officer wrote that the cumulative effect of Zia's policies was the 'rise to religious orthodoxy among a cross-section of the armed forces. For this small group, ideology can be stretched to radicalism and can take precedence over professionalism. Their attitude needs to be countervailed otherwise it will erode the very foundation of a cohesive, professionally competent, and technologically adept armed-force.'

What began as a tool for nation building became a master of those who were supposed to wield it. It began as an exercise of the 'rulers…[attempting] to "manage" militant Islamism, trying to calibrate it so that it serves its nation-building function without destabilizing internal politics or relations with western countries. General Ziaul Haq [*sic*] went further than others in "Islamizing" Pakistan's legal and educational system but his policy of Islamization was the extension of a consistent state ideology, not an aberration.'[63]

In the post Zia-ul-Haq era, some generals like General Asif Nawaz Janjua (August 1991-January 1993), have tried to push back the efforts to politicize Islam within the force and restore the earlier value of making Islam a component of professionalism. Unfortunately, the debate about the ideology of Pakistan and the role of Islam will continue since it has been the backbone of Pakistan. As a consequence, the Kashmir question will remain integral to Pakistan because its removal from the agenda will be an acknowledgement of the fallacy of the two-nation theory. To fight for Kashmir then becomes integral to the defence of the idea of Pakistan and hence the Pakistan Army keeps finding ways of instrumentalizing Islam, so as to motivate the Pakistanis to fight. There is a threefold strategy to achieve this: 'First, the army employs Islam as a means of unifying the country via an identity that can supersede ethnic affiliations and the fissiparous tendencies stemming from Pakistan's ethnic diversity. Second, the army uses Islam to rally the citizenry in times of war and to prepare them to accept adversity as well as the army's continued domination of national affairs. Third, the army has used Islam to motivate soldiers by focusing on the purported supernatural advantages conferred by Islamic faith. Numerous authors writing in Pakistan's military journals suggest that a pious Muslim can defeat his adversary even if outnumbered. These writings also essentialize the enemy, reducing him to the category of Hindu despite the fact that India's armed forces include Sikhs, Muslims, Christians and Parsees as well as Hindus.'[64]

Thus, among the multiple uncertainties that have plagued Pakistan since its birth, the one certainty about which there is no debate is that because of its ideology and the need to emphasize its identity, Kashmir has been made integral to preserve said ideology and identity. It has used every mean to get hold of it, first by force and then by influencing the internal politics in the hope that whenever the Plebiscite was held, the Kashmiris would willingly become part of their ideological identity. After all, the history of Kashmir is replete with periodic bouts of feverish Islamization of the society resulting in mass proselytizing. Such a society, they have believed, would always be susceptible to the sustained pressure of propaganda. In this regard, it needs to be remembered that more people have embraced Islam under the benign influence of indigenous Kashmiri Sufism and hence the use of persuasion by example has played such an important role. This strategy underwent a radical change when Pakistan realized the power of Jihadis after the Soviet intervention in Afghanistan. Ever since then, India has been battling a rejuvenated, aggressive Islam, and targeted violence unleashed by Pakistan to bleed India by a 'thousand-cuts'.

The error of judgment made by Pakistan in dealing with East Pakistan was born of the same prejudice that it had against the 'Hindu' India. It ignored the fact that unlike West Pakistan where Punjabis, Pathans, Balochs and Sindhis vied for space, the East was dominated by the single ethnic group of Bengalis. In 1947, 12 million Hindu Bengalis lived with 32 million Muslim Bengalis and their total was greater than that of the West Pakistani inhabitants. Both spoke the same language and shared same culture and values in spite of the differences of faith. If genuine democracy had been put in place in Pakistan, with the principle of one person one vote, the East Pakistanis would have dominated the politics of Pakistan during its earlier phase. This, the dominant Punjabis and Mohajirs in West Pakistan were determined to prevent. Apart from this, the political and military elite of West Pakistan looked down upon the Bengalis because they were not categorized as martial races and were therefore nearly excluded from military service. Another sin of equal magnitude was that as Bengalis they objected to the imposition of Urdu as the national language and of treatment as second-class citizens. West Pakistan, on the other hand, objected to an oral and written language that used a script that was derived from Sanskrit and was used by Hindus and Muslims as part of their culture. West Pakistan tried to convince Muslim Bengalis in vain to replace the Sanskrit-based script and vocabulary with that of the Perso-Arabic. Rather than giving up on their mother tongue, the East Pakistanis mobilized to canvass for the national status of Bengali. West Pakistanis also believed that their eastern counterparts were less Muslim because of their cultural, historical, linguistic and social proximity to Bengali Hindus. These differences between the two had begun to hurt with the realization that the only common bond between the two was Islam. Even here, the West Pakistani Muslims were convinced that the Islam of Bengalis was contaminated because of long exposure to Hindu culture and practices.

These differences were aggravated by divergent views on sharing political power and were rooted in the Objectives Resolution of 1949.* This came to a head in early 1971 when for the first-time elections to the National and Provincial Assemblies on the principle of universal suffrage were held. The results and the subsequent inability of the leaders from West Pakistan and the Military Generals to hand over power to the Awami League and its leader Mujibur Rahman exploded the myth of a unified Pakistan. The idea of Pakistan based on Islam too stood exposed. However, living in a state of denial, leaders of what remained of Pakistan not only clung to the idea of an Islam-driven Pakistan but also the need to subvert the idea of India. Consequently, the goals remained the same though the strategies had to be changed.

In the struggle to rationalize the existence of Pakistan, developments in India in recent decades have been a boon for the ideologues of Pakistan. The rise of Hindutva forces in India and the coming to power of BJP under Narendra Modi and the unrelenting attack on the secular forces in India, has finally validated this ideology. In an insightful analysis, Ayesha Siddiqa wrote:

> ...perhaps, a Modi-led right-wing government is a wish come true for the ideological right-wing in Pakistan. For the first time since 1947, people do not have to convince each other of how right Muhammad Ali Jinnah was in creating Pakistan: Not that Pakistan

---

*The Objectives Resolution of Pakistan, as adopted by the Constituent Assembly of Pakistan in 1949, proclaimed that Pakistan would be modeled on the ideology and democratic faith of Islam rather than European counties.

> was ever designed for all Muslims of the Indian subcontinent, but it now sees its formula for ideological nationalism justified in the face of rising religious-ideological nationalism next door in India. I have lived through the times when Pakistan's intelligentsia was confused in the face of Indian secularism and democracy. Despite having [their] own country, there would be an internal conversation about the Indian experiment being better. The last four to five years has brought about a change in that thinking... New Delhi no longer represents a secular ideal. For Islamabad, a non-secular India is easier to contest.[65]

The reaction of Pakistanis to the rise of Hindu right wing in India is best summed up in Fahmida Riaz's poem written in the wake of the demolition of the Babri Mosque and the communal riots that followed:

> *tum bilkul hum jaise nikale...*
>
> (So finally you have turned out exactly like us)

With that, curtains ought to have been drawn on the self doubts within Pakistan.

These are hopes of a Pakistani but the existential challenge to Pakistan has dimensions that cannot be defined by the failure or success of India's secular and liberal tradition as built by Jawaharlal Nehru. Pakistan's real problem lies within the nature of Islam that has grown and developed over the centuries in south Asia and its relations with the Islam that dominates the Gulf countries. The ideological debates developing in Saudi Arabia and Iran, and the schism that they cause in the subcontinent are the real challenges for Pakistan to deal with. It is in the context of this challenge that Pakistan finds India as a tool for its validity since it is visible, in the neighborhood and, therefore, easier to understand and simplify for its masses.

3

The Sentinels

'The eyes, like sentinels, hold the highest place in the body.'
—Marcus Tullius Cicero

Pakistan, as we have seen, is also a child of insecurity, born out of doubts about its own legitimacy. A number of historians are of the opinion that the demand for Pakistan was to be used as a tool for bargaining more constitutional concessions for the Muslims of the subcontinent and was never meant to actually create a State that could not accommodate all the Muslims and was divided in two parts, set apart by thousands of kilometers. The insecurity of Pakistan, because of its doubts about its own legitimacy, has been made even more excruciating by its inability to grab Jammu and Kashmir even though it was a Muslim-majority State and is also geographically and economically contiguous. Its annexation could have validated Pakistan's existence and its failure to get Jammu and Kashmir motivates it to make repeated attempts to wrest its control. Thus, Pakistan's strategists have placed Jammu and Kashmir at the Centre of its existence.

In 1947, in its greed, Pakistan displayed impatience even after having signed a Standstill Agreement with Maharaja Hari Singh, by sending raiders from its territory in an obvious bid to intimidate the Maharaja into signing the accession in its favor. Its argument, that the raiders were non-state actors trying to help out co-religionists, is the same as the one that it advances today while sending and supporting terrorists in Kashmir. Down the years, it has scripted a long history of trying to use force to annex Jammu and Kashmir.

The fact that no sooner had the idea of Pakistan been realized than it was assailed by the thoughts of insecurity is supported by developments within the Pakistan Army. This is borne out by the detailed defence strategy drawn by the English General of the Pakistani Army, General Douglas Gracey.[66] According to the said strategy, it was perceived that the new-born nation faced threat not only from India but also Afghanistan and the tribes of its Frontier area. This raised the phantom of India and Afghanistan joining hands to dismember Pakistan. In this, as a first step, Gracey opined that it was essential to push the India border as far away as possible from the key cities and strategic locations. Thus, when it became abundantly clear that the Muslim majority of the population notwithstanding, the ruler of Jammu and Kashmir was not inclined to accede to Pakistan, it involved the military to forcibly occupy Kashmir. But Jammu and Kashmir alone does not explain Pakistan's posturing towards India and the resolution of the Jammu and Kashmir issue alone is never going to guarantee an end to Pakistan's conflict with India. Other aspects too have to be considered and addressed.

The 'so-called Great Game' of the nineteenth century had the western frontiers of the north-western Indian subcontinent as one of the core themes. British India spared no effort to thwart the movement of Russia towards this direction and the British employed various strategies to achieve their goal.[67] By the late nineteenth century, Afghanistan had become the active theatre and continued to be so till the Afghans accepted the Durand Line,[68] demarcating the border between Afghanistan and the British Frontier area, in 1893. However, when Pakistan came into being, Afghanistan thought that it was an opportunity to reopen the Durand Line by reclaiming the tribal areas which were under Pakistani control by virtue of the said line.

The demand for the creation of Pakhtunistan only strengthened the fears of Pakistan; and when the 1946 elections in that area rejected the idea of Pakistan by voting to power the Abdul Ghaffar Khan-led Congress Party, these fears were doubly aroused. They were further strengthened when Abdul Ghaffar Khan, betrayed by the Congress' acceptance of the Partition Plan, demanded a Referendum with the option of creation of a separate Pashtun Province. The Referendum was held though not with the option of independence but with accession to either India or Pakistan. From thence began the fear of the possibility of India and Afghanistan colluding to destabilize the western borders of Pakistan. Ever since, Pakistan has sought to limit India's influence in Afghanistan by trying to manipulate the policies of its western neighbor. This policy of Pakistan continues even today.

As it is, this part of the Pakistan conundrum is not easy to solve, but what's perplexing is its persistent refusal to accept the status quo in Kashmir and allowing the state's people to live in peace. In the recent past, in its bid to change this status quo it has raised and supported a number of jihadi groups who, quite often, turn on their patron and indulge in sectarian violence. Pakistan also wants to be treated as an equal of India by the international community, even though it is apparent that it is fragile with anemic state institutions, and is struggling to contain insurgency in Baluchistan and Khyber Pakhtunkhwa. Furthermore, it is not equipped to contain 'non-State' players from using its territory to launch terrorist activities at home and abroad. It can also not match India's natural and human resources.

Even in other parts of Pakistan, ethnic and sectarian violence is a recurring threat, both in the rural and the urban areas. In fact, one of the earliest secessionist movements, along with that of Pakhtunistan, was of Sindh that was led by the champion of Sindhi language and culture, G. M. Syed, and called for 'Jeay Sindh' demanding a separate Sindhudesh.

Terrorists, active under the banner of Tehreek-e-Taliban-Pakistan (TTP), in short Pakistan Taliban, have not only been targeting politicians and certain groups of people, police and bureaucratic institutions but also intelligence and military wings.[69] Pakistani terrorists operating under the banner of Pakistan Taliban have killed thousands of their own citizens, as estimated by the Pakistan Institute for Peace Studies and the University of Maryland's Global Terrorism Database. In other words, Pakistan is, and has been, at war with itself. Economically, it has long lost the edge that it had over India in the 1960s and today has abysmal human development indicators and also suffers from chronic shortages of power, potable water and gas. A cursory glance at their comedy shows reveals the pervasive presence of these challenges in the consciousness of Pakistan's citizenry.

In contrast, India has been enjoying sustained economic growth, even during the period of global recession. As a result of this, it has undertaken steady modernization of defence structure while still keeping the spending under 3 percent of its gross domestic product. India has also cultivated strategic partnerships with United States, the European Union, Israel, Iran, Saudi Arabia, Qatar, and in recent years, with Japan and Australia. Simultaneously it has also retained its historically robust ties with Russia. Ignoring these parameters, Pakistan continues to believe to be an equal of India in all respects and expects the world to treat it as such. In fact, former Pakistan president and army chief, General Pervez Musharraf had boldly demanded of India to accept Pakistan as an equal as a precondition for peace.[70] But all the parameters of socio-economic and political development indicate to the significant disparity between the two countries in favor of India. By acknowledging this reality, Pakistan should have come to some kind of accommodation with India which would have made it easy to develop neighborly relations with Afghanistan instead of channeling all its energies to cultivating a client state on its north-western border. '...the longer Pakistan defers this ultimate concession the more costly its eventual concessions will be.'[71] Ashley Tellis, a prominent South Asia analyst had the following opinion to offer to the United States: 'Pakistan has to recognize that it simply cannot match India through whichever stratagem it chooses—it is bound to fail. The sensible thing, then, is for Pakistan to reach the best possible accommodation with India now, while it can, and shift gears towards grand strategy centered on economic integration of South Asia—one that would help Pakistan climb out of its morass and allow the army to maintain some modicum of privileges, at least for a while. The alternative is to preside over an increasingly hollow state.'[72]

In this light some analysts argue that since Kashmir is central to Pakistan's behavior, the best option to bring peace to the region—

India, Pakistan and also Afghanistan—is to resolve the issue and prevent Pakistan from adventurism and reliance on Islamist militants, by accommodating Pakistan's preferences. While this could have been possible sometime in past, it is no longer relevant since Pakistan is already on an irreversible journey of undermining territorial status quo not only in Kashmir and the region but also beyond. Status quo in these respects will never be acceptable to the Pakistani Army since that will be construed as genuine and total defeat since adversarial role in relation to India is more ideological than based on secularism or the lack of it. Many scholars and analysts (including Charles Glaser, a scholar of international relations theory) have tried to look at Pakistan from this point of view and concluded that by encouraging its anti-status quo policies, the world powers will do greater disservice to the region since it is feared that Pakistan falls in the category of 'greedy states'. Glaser has defined greedy states as 'fundamentally dissatisfied with status quo, desiring additional territory even when it is not required for security.' Such states have multiple goals that are targeted simultaneously, like increasing their prestige, propagation of their ideology and spread of their religion. Appeasement of such states is counterproductive and dangerous since they thrive on competition, which also becomes their only strategy. Some scholars like Alastair Johnston, Zionts and Christine Fair opine that understanding the strategic culture of the Pakistani Army is the key to understanding the strategic culture of Pakistan since both are interchangeable, with the Army continuing to dictate foreign and domestic policies.

It is instructive to recall that in the mid-fifties of the nineteenth century, after having declared itself an Islamic Republic, the civilian government had fallen victim to internal dissensions and chaos whereby the army was invited to help it out. But having once realized that the job of governing can be done in a much efficient and better way by it, the next step by the army was an easy one. It was in 1958 that Major General Iskander Mirza took over as the Martial Law Administrator and appointed his close associate General Ayub Khan as the army chief who, in turn, wasted little time in displacing Iskander Mirza and declaring himself as the Martial Law Administrator. Ever since, the Pakistani Army has come to believe itself as the defender and savior of not only Pakistan's borders but also the very reason of its existence.

The strategic culture of the Pakistan Army developed as a collective of its core beliefs, values and norms, as well as the collection of its historical experiences. Unlike other armies, the Pakistan Army does not limit itself to defending the country's borders. It actively involves itself in the management of domestic affairs too, thereby creating a linkage between the two. In doing this, the Pakistan military, like those of Turkey and Indonesia, have developed a parent-guardian relationship. 'These armed forces are known for institutionalizing their political power through constitutional and legal provisions. Such changes are brought about through the help of civilian partners that are dependent on the military for their survival.'[73] From its early days the army has appropriated to itself the dual role of defending the territorial as well as ideological frontiers. This ideology has been enunciated by successive army chiefs as Islam, which is the founding logic of the State, and is used to drill some cohesiveness in a multiethnic State, while at the same time to whip up support against the 'Hindu' India.

Over the years the interpretation of Islam might have undergone changes but the army has embraced it to protect the ideology and has made it a core function for itself. In the end, this Islamist ideology becomes a tool to resist India's rise, restrict its presence and ability to harm Pakistan, and overturn territorial status quo. Ironically, in this quest, if the Pakistani Army is seen to be just resisting India, it is interpreted as victory. Conversely, concessions such as trade, travel and peace talks, granted to India are equivalent of total defeat not only of the army but also of the ideology of Pakistan and the erosion of its legitimacy. This explains why Pakistan has managed to redefine victory in the face of repeated setbacks and defeats in wars against India. Meena Menon a journalist from *The Hindu* records in her book, *Reporting Pakistan* that she found it very confusing and amusing that though Pakistan had never won any war against India, the state still celebrated many 'Victory Day' parades very seriously. But that is the narrative that the Pakistani state and the army have constructed and believed in. Even more ludicrous is the manner in which Pakistan lives in denial about the events of the 1999 Kargil

War. While Nasim Zehra, in her monumental work, *From Kargil to the Coup,* has brought out all the facts about the attempt of a group of Pakistani Generals to wrest Siachen if not Kashmir, she too believes, like the official myth of the Pakistani Army, that the Pakistani soldiers were firmly entrenched and were winning the war but the political leadership surrendered on the intervention of US President Bill Clinton!

In more than seventy-five years of its existence, Pakistan has initiated several conflicts with India because it has suffered from false optimism. During each of these conflicts, it has misread not only the military strength of India but also its political will. This has been so because of the feeling of inherent superiority that the Pakistani Army have because of its 'Muslim' and 'Islamic' character. This syndrome has roots in its faulty reading of history. It is true that almost all the invaders, including Muslim, arrived in India with a numerically weak army yet they had prevailed over the bigger 'Hindu' armies. This is factually correct since one after another the Indian (read 'Hindu') princes fell before the more ferocious foreign adversaries. But an objective analysis of those defeats will reveal that though Muslim forces, notwithstanding the fact that they were small, were tactically and strategically superior and did not follow the conventional methods of warfare of the times, the indifference of the large masses of India to victories or defeat of the kings and princes, played a critical part in the eventual outcome. But more importantly, many Muslim and European historians misread the abject acceptance of defeats by the Indian masses. India of that period was not only politically divided (which it had usually been in the past) but also fragmented in mind and spirit, and socially too. The bulk of the masses had no stakes in the fortunes of the state and a change of rulers hardly affected their daily life. Because of the absence of any allegiance in a cohesive manner, these fragmented sections rejoiced in the defeat of fellow countrymen or were plainly indifferent. That was a time when India had created and perfected the caste system—the gargantuan machine for oppressing fellow human beings with the class above obsessed with the passion to keep the one below in a state of abject submission and humiliation. In addition, the meaning of dharma as understood then was quite different from what is conveyed by ancient texts and understood by others. Thus, even offering water to a thirsty soldier was part of dharma, even if he happened to belong to the enemy force. This was practiced as late as the period of Aurangzeb, where the example of a Sikh, Bhai Kanhaiya, offering water in the battlefield to both the injured Sikh as well as Mughal soldiers shines brilliantly. Same went for giving shelter even if the enemy soldier was being pursued by the Hindu forces. Thus, the arrival of Muslim invaders was a clash of civilizations; one effete and decaying and the other possessed of raw energy and fired by ambition; one professing multiple, but mutually antagonistic faiths and goals and the other united in aggressively, asserting its monotheism and the finality that it had come to believe and was determined to impose upon the non-believers.

The political conquest of India by Islam has been interpreted in Pakistan as a victory over the people of India. However, they forget that although, before arriving in India, the Islamic juggernaut had not only defeated armies but had converted all those lands that they had conquered to Islam, that same cultural and civilizational victory of the Islamic conquerors was thwarted in India, in spite of the barbaric acts unleashed upon the Hindu population. It was here that the irresistible force of Islam failed to move the mountain of faith of the Indians. Thus, it was only a partial victory that Islam enjoyed over the Hindus. The limited conversion that had finally taken place in India had been more because of the influence of the benign philosophy of Sufis and the rewards given to those among the aristocracy who embraced Islam. To a great extent, it was due to the fragmentation of the Hindu society which was at war with itself as Brahminical dominance had kept the vast multitudes beyond the periphery of the society. Thus, most of the conversions came from the lower classes. It should also be noted that in many regions of Europe where Islam had imposed itself, people had reconverted to Christianity soon after the Christian forces had reasserted themselves. On the other hand, in India, there was no going back to Hinduism since the Brahmins disallowed it. Pakistani historians also forget that India has always been the land where Hindus have not hesitated in debating and accepting new ideas and faiths, which also explains why there are overlapping philosophies and why multiple religions have co-existed here. Instead, those historians need to question as to why Islam failed to replicate its success by converting the entire multitude in the subcontinent. This, is what should have been considered as defeat.

Centuries later, after the British gained complete control, the Muslims in India were given more preference. Thus they had to had to reconcile to the loss of power. This happened after 'the mutiny of (East India Company's) Bengal Army in 1857'. After the British thwarted the Revolt, they restructured the armed forces, preferring the Punjabi Muslims and Pathans over upper-caste Hindus from the Ganges Valley. This created the myth of the 'martial race', particularly with reference to Punjabis, who, ironically, had been ousted by the British as rulers from Punjab. Unlike India, in Pakistan, 'the myth of Punjabis and Pathans from the NWFP as the "martial races" was propagated even after…[I]ndependence in 1947; and served the purpose of retaining the ethnic composition and inherently elitist fabric of the armed forces. Moreover, the British bias against recruitment of Bengalis, Sindhis and Baluch was maintained. The continuation of the recruitment pattern also fed into the tension between the Centre and the smaller provinces, particularly Baluchistan. As a result, Baluch leaders view the armed forces "not as a national military, but a Punjabi force with a mercenary and exploitative character".'[74]

Out of the British policy, later perpetuated by Pakistan, the theory of the martial race proved to be a boon to the Muslims who had also been the backbone of the Mughals. It also helped in their rehabilitation after defeat since they were the ruling and hence warrior class. Thus, the British Indian Army was composed of people who had supported the British in fairly large numbers in 1857, particularly Punjabis, Pathans, Rajputs and Dogras, who were then labeled as 'martial'. This was ironic since it was the army of Tipu Sultan, from the south (derisively called Madrasis in Pakistan and also in India for a few more years after Independence), that came closest to evicting the British from India. Even in the Indian Army there are components made up of the now defunct concept of martial races that included, Sikhs, Rajputs, Marathas, Dogras etc. But while India has given up this practice and is in the process of raising more and more mixed battalions, retaining only a few of the pure race-based units, Pakistan continues to revel in the martial race syndrome, thereby excluding large sections of its own population from combat forces and also perpetuating the myth of the superiority of the Pakistan forces since they are composed of martial races and are driven by the Islamist spirit.

A unique characteristic of the Pakistani Army, because of the inbuilt anomalies, is that it is afflicted by 'persistent and even expanding revisionist goals.'[75] In this it is supported both by the military regimes and civilian governments. These revisionist goals target Jammu and Kashmir, which acceded to India and has accepted and is governed by the provisions of the Indian constitution. This insistence is despite the fact that no international forum claims that the State had not acceded to India in the legal sense and none considers it as a justifiably disputed territory. But Pakistan has claimed that it is disputed because it has made Jammu and Kashmir's acquisition integral to its national identity. Thus, even after its plans were defeated in 1947 it remained committed to acquiring the territory one way or another. In this context, the following observation is worth noting:

> A common definition of tragedy is that of a noble figure betrayed and destroyed by some inner flaw. The Pakistani military is in some ways an admirable institution, but it suffers from one tragic feature which has been with it from the beginning, which has defined its whole character and world view, which has done terrible damage to Pakistan and which could in some circumstances destroy Pakistan and its armed forces altogether… This is the military obsession with India in general, and Kashmir in particular.[76]

It was because of this obsession that soon after the failure of 1947, Pakistan continued to wage a low-level proxy war in the State, hoping to make its possession by India too costly, and therefore forcing it to abandon. In the 1950s, newspaper articles being published in Pakistan were already advocating the idea of launching a guerrilla war in Kashmir. Though the Government of India chose to withdraw the 'Kashmir Conspiracy case'[77] against Sheikh Abdullah, Mirza Afzal Beg, and others, the fact was that there was enough evidence that suggested that preparations were on for rebellion and armed insurrection, aided and abetted by Pakistan.

After 1947, as the two countries settled to face the challenge of feeding millions of refugees, Pakistan wasted no time in aligning with the western powers to take advantage of their training systems and weapons. In fact, 'even before Partition, Jinnah had indicated that Pakistan's foreign policy would be oriented towards the Muslim world but there would be an expectation of US support.'[78] He had further said that Muslim countries would stand together against any possible Russian aggression but would look to the US for assistance. Apparently, Jinnah was still viewing central Asia and Afghanistan from the prism of the 19th century's obsession with the 'Great Game'.

After the creation of Pakistan, Jinnah emphasized on an alliance with the US and also believed that because of the geostrategic location of Pakistan it could extract a good bargain from it. The famous photo-journalist, Margaret Bourke-White, of *Life* magazine reported that Jinnah told her in an interview that 'America needs Pakistan more than Pakistan needs America...Pakistan is the pivot of the world, as we are placed...[on] the frontier on which the future position of the world revolves.'[79] Jinnah was so obsessed with this importance of Pakistan for the US that his thesis percolated down to the government officials. Bourke-White remarked 'This hope of tapping the US treasury was voiced so persistently that one wondered whether the purpose was to bolster the world against Bolshevism or to bolster Pakistan's own uncertain position as a new political entity.'[80]

After initial disinterest in Pakistan, USA did turn to it as it assumed greater role in the world affairs. Pakistan became a member state of the Baghdad Pact, later the Central Treaty Organization (CENTO), and it received about a billion dollars' worth of aid from the USA with which it bought modern military weapons. This Treaty was specifically designed to contain the communist Soviet Union. However, ultimately it led Pakistan into an embarrassing situation when the US Air Force spy plane U-2 made a sortie from an airbase near Peshawar over Soviet Union but was shot down by a Russian MiG in 1960.

The USA and UK also trained the officers of the Pakistani Army to bring them at par with the western countries. Ironically, Pakistan was also a member of South East Asia Treaty Organization (SEATO) that was designed against Communist China and was still a member of this Treaty when it began opening up to China as it saw its rift with India widening.[81] The fact that both, Pakistan and China had claims to the territories that were part of the Jammu and Kashmir State in Ladakh were brushed aside by Pakistan to cultivate this new found friendship, and it ceded large tracts of land, which were under its control, in order to cultivate an ally that was in direct confrontation with India. As a consequence of this new found confidence, Pakistan made a second major military attempt to wrest control of Kashmir and change status quo in 1965 under the code name 'Operation Gibraltar'. Following an audacious plan, it sent regular and irregular troops disguised as local fighters in the hope of igniting an insurgency thereby forcing the international community to pay attention to it.

The timing and the background of that attempt was of Pakistan's choosing, when India was most vulnerable because of sluggish economy, the looming drought and internal unrest in some states after the death of Pandit Jawaharlal Nehru. In contrast, the economy of Pakistan was at its strongest, industrial growth superior to India's and it had won the complete support of the western world after having entered into alliances with them against the communist bloc. In addition, Kashmir was still recovering from the jolt it had received after the theft of the holy relic from Hazratbal in Srinagar and consequent political upheaval. However, the factor that weighed most in favor of war was the ingrained prejudice against the 'Hindus'. Pakistan was convinced that 'Hindu' India was by nature weak and no match for the supposed martial Islamic force of Pakistan.

President Ayub Khan believed that the weakness of the Indian Army had been explored during the Raan of Kutch confrontation earlier in 1965 in Gujarat. This was notwithstanding the Pakistani Army having failed in its objective, with India holding the greater part of the Raan, and the International Tribunal making a favorable judgment for India. It is believed that more than that, what helped

President Ayub Khan make up his mind was a meeting between him and Prime Minister Lal Bahadur Shastri during the Commonwealth Heads of the States conference in London in 1965. Looking down at the small size of the *dhoti*-clad Indian Prime Minister, the burly Pathan was convinced of the vulnerability of India!

The plan misfired, as the insurgency that Pakistan hoped for in the Valley never materialized. The adventure soon slid into the second Indo-Pakistan war when India opened a second front across the international border to endanger two major cities of Pakistani Punjab—Lahore and Sialkot. Scholarly accounts say that this war ended in a stalemate with Pakistan failing to grab Kashmir yet again, and India failing to capture either Lahore or Sialkot. However, scholars believe that India could have continued to fight a few days longer than Pakistan to deliver a decisive defeat if India had not accepted UN ceasefire.

Ironically, when India opened the front on the international border, President Ayub Khan tried to give it a spin during his address to his countrymen. He claimed that '...Indian aggression in Kashmir was only a preparation for an attack on Pakistan. Today [the Indians] have given final proof of this and of the evil intentions, which India has always harbored against Pakistan since its inception. The Indian rulers were never reconciled to the establishment of an independent Pakistan where the Muslims could build a homeland of their own...Then (India) exploited the Chinese bogey to secure massive arms assistance from some of our friends in the West who never understood the mind of the Indian rulers and permitted themselves to be taken in by India's profession that once they were fully armed they will fight the Chinese. We always knew these arms will be raised against us.'[82] Notwithstanding President Khan's claims, the fact remained that as a member of CENTO and SEATO, it was Pakistan who had got the latest Sabre and Starfighters for its air force and Patton tanks for its armored divisions to fight Soviet Union and China. In comparison, India fought the war with Second World War's Gnat fighters and Hercules and Vampire bombers, long retired by other countries.

Parallel to the war, Pakistan's state-controlled media generated a frenzy of Jihad wherein the virtues of the 'soldiers of Islam' were extolled. Many years after the war an officer of Pakistan wrote, 'There was a spurt of gallantry stories, of divine help, of superhuman resistance and of unrivalled professional excellence in the face of overwhelming odds…The story of the suicide squad—a band of dedicated soldiers who acted as live mines to blow up the advancing Indian tanks in the Sialkot sector—became one of the most popular legends. There was no end of stories about divine help. People, both soldiers and civilians, had actually 'seen with their eyes green robed angels deflecting bombs from their targets—bridges, culverts, mosques—with a wave of their hand. Soldiers were reported shooting enemy aircraft with their .303 [rifles].'[83]

Post ceasefire, USA suspended aid to both countries which hurt Pakistan more than India because Pakistan was more dependent on the US military aid. Consequently, India was soon to outstrip its neighbor in growth. After the war had ended, the world saw that Lahore and Sialkot were on the verge of being severely damaged if not captured and the strategic bulge of Uri-Poonch, the Haji Pir Pass fell into Indian hands. Pakistan's General Headquarters' approved account of the 1965 war written by Lieut. General Mahmud Ahmed of Pakistan Army describes it as, 'watershed in the military history of the subcontinent. It marked the turning point in the balance of power in South Asia. After 1965, the Indian military power grew by leaps and bounds while Pakistan's strength declined appreciably.' The events that followed the aftermath of the 1965 war exposed Pakistan since not only had the US stopped military supplies, but also ended economic aid. This hatred for the US gradually firmed up within the Pakistan Army. Thus it was present many years later when Osama bin Laden master-minded the attack on American soil in 2001. In this context, political commentator Khaled Ahmed noted: 'His hatred for US was shared by many senior military officers. Secular officers hated the US for its post-1965 tilt in favor of India and the subsequent non-recognition of Pakistan as long-term nuclearized ally.'[84]

In addition, there were political consequences amidst the frustration of Pakistan. During the war, a Canadian diplomat asked President Ayub Khan what Pakistan wanted, and he replied, 'We want Kashmir but we know that we can't win it by military action.

If only you people would show some guts, we would have it.'[85] Clearly, Pakistan wanted something which it knew it did not have the strength to have but was still trying to grab it by force in the hope that the western powers would intervene on its behalf. Its problems compounded after the Tashkent Agreement because of the propaganda unleashed by the state-controlled media had fed the Pakistani people with the narrative of victory. Therefore, the people did not understand the rationale behind the imposition of an 'unfavorable' settlement on Pakistan. 'The Tashkent agreement made no mention of Pakistan's demand for a plebiscite in Kashmir either, which made the people wonder why Pakistan's "military victory" did not bring it any gain in territory or at least the promise of future favorable settlement.'[86]

The unrest that followed exposed the imposed unity among the various ethnicities and regions, notably East Pakistan that had virtually refused to use the Urdu language. It was also questioning the skewed economic disparity between the two wings. The fact was that East Pakistani people, all Bengalis 'suffered from economic exploitation. The revenues reaped from their exports were used to finance the industrialization of West Pakistan. Between 1947 and 1962, East Pakistan exported 13.08 billion rupees worth of goods (particularly jute) and West Pakistan only 9.9 billion worth. Imports into East Pakistan amounted to only 7.9 billion compared to 18.7 billion for West Pakistan, which was clearly able to purchase equipment abroad with the trade surplus produced by East Pakistan. The Bengalis complained all the more bitterly of this practice as their per capita income in the early 1960s was about 25 percent below that of West Pakistan and the growth rate of their province amounted to half that of West Pakistan. Per capita income only rose by 17 percent in East Pakistan from 1959-60 to 1969-70 whereas it grew by 42 percent during the same period in West Pakistan'[87] Clearly, East Pakistan was dissatisfied and aggravating this was the political imbalance and the abysmally low representation in the services and other related opportunities. Soon Pakistan realized that it had been failed by Ayub Khan's military and political leadership, and with the general unrest, fanned by his erstwhile lieutenant Zulfikar Ali Bhutto, President Ayub Khan handed over power to

General Yayha Khan and the army to bring order to the rising chaos. Thus, the country was put under another spell of military rule. For the second time in its short history, the government of Pakistan had asked the military to take over administration and save it from chaos and disintegration.

Most accounts do not consider General Yahya Khan as a person interested in politics. He was a career soldier who had simply obeyed the command of Field Marshal Ayub Khan in imposing martial law and taking charge of the office of the President. The inability of democratic institutions to take roots forced the army to resort to the tactic of using its ideological indoctrination to keep the country together. During the nearly three years of his rule, General Yahya Khan took steps that were a precursor of what was to happen at the end of the next decade. The ideological commitment of the military took firm roots and senior officers sounded like high priests. This was to come gradually but, immediately on takeover, General Yahya Khan began on a very positive note by announcing that general elections will be held on the basis of universal suffrage and the new Assembly will be tasked with drawing up a new constitution within a period of 120 days. He did everything right till the elections had been conducted but no sooner were the results announced, and Mujibur Rahman's Awami League won a majority, that it was realized that the power centre was about to slip away from the grasp of the Punjabis and Pathans and the western wing. As soon as this happened, the Pakistan People's Party (PPP) and Zulfikar Ali Bhutto refused to accept the rules of democracy and wanted equal partnership in government even though compared to the Awami Party, the PPP was a distant second. Moreover, the PPP had not contested even a single seat in East Pakistan. General Yahya Khan brokered negotiations in Dacca though neither Bhutto was prepared to travel to Dacca and nor was Mujibur Rahman prepared to come down to West Pakistan. Finally, when negotiations failed to yield any compromise, 'Yahya appeared to blame Mujib more and committed the Himalayan blunder that propelled Pakistan to civil war, war with India, and the secession of East Pakistan to form the independent country of Bangladesh: he had attempted to find a military solution to a political problem. This fatal error would undo all his achievements at home and abroad in his brief period in office and seal his fate as one of the most reviled rulers in both Bangladesh and Pakistan as well as around the world.'[88]General Yahya has been referred to as the 'Grave digger of Military Regime and national unity'[89] but it must be said that he was not alone in digging that grave. His fatal error was that when negotiations between Bhutto and Mujib failed and East Pakistan was virtually taken over by the Awami League, with the party flag being hoisted on 23 March 1971, he and his corps commander decided to launch 'Operation Searchlight', leading to the April massacre of students and teachers in the Dacca University. That massacre has been a wound in Bangladesh's psyche that refuses to heal since it was a diabolical plan to eliminate a whole generation of educated and the thinking class in Bangladesh. Yahya Khan had failed to 'realize that no matter what the problems with politics and politicians, there can be no military solution to a political problem.'[90]

It was in this context that the next war between India and Pakistan took place in 1971.Unlike the earlier two occasions, it was not because of Kashmir. This had roots in the shabby treatment of East Pakistan where the numerically superior Bengalis were treated like inferiors by the arrogant Punjabis. What began as a protest against the declaration of Urdu as the national language and its imposition over the numerically larger Bengali-speaking East Pakistan, soon snowballed into an uprising and became a full-fledged civil war. East Pakistan had come to conclude that, though numerically less but more active, West Pakistanis will not allow them to enjoy full citizenship within Pakistan and hence this debate and confrontation became a secessionist movement. It also drew moral strength from the Lahore Resolution of the Muslim League that envisaged 'states' for the Muslims and not just 'state'. But after Operation Searchlight and the university massacres in Dacca and Khulna, India was inundated with refugees pouring in from the east, and its plea to the world community to intervene largely fell on deaf ears. India was left with no choice but to intervene. When the war was over, Pakistan had lost East Pakistan with more than half of its population emerging as Bangladesh, an independent country; the Pakistan Army was disgraced by the humiliating defeat and the fact that over 90,000 soldiers had been taken prisoners of war after surrender made it look even more ignominious.

On the face of it, the years following the '71 Indo-Pak war were by and large peaceful, but as subsequent events developed, it was evident that Pakistan was smarting under the burden of the humiliation of defeat and had not given up its agenda. It was soon to find appropriate conditions to implement a new strategy to wrest Kashmir. It took advantage of the currents that were dominating the Islamic world and began forging ties with Islamists of the extreme kind. It was now reiterated with greater emphasis that Islam was at the core of Pakistan's ideology and the army was its sole guardian and protector. With it, a campaign was introduced, first, to indoctrinate the society of Pakistan by Zulfikar Ali Bhutto and then the army and the society by General Zia-ul-Haq. As a consequence, the civil-military dispensation that has dominated the Pakistani narrative has left the civil society stunted and handicapped. The emphasis laid on Islam has allowed the *Deeni Madarsas* (religious schools) to have its shadow cast on every aspect of life. Their influence has been so pervasive that any attempt by the state to curb their activities or influence is met with stiff resistance. 'In FATA (the semi-autonomous Federally Administered Tribal Areas, now merged in Khyber Pakhtunkhwa) this conflict has led to an outright insurgency. In Islamabad, the Red Mosque[91] episode demonstrated the striking power that a "fighting mullah" could mobilize.'[92] The *Deeni Madarsas* had owed their rise and spread to the army patronage and to fundamentalist Islam that gradually tightened its grip not only on the army but also the society. By the time the Pakistani Army came under sustained pressure from the USA to act against these forces, the *Madarsas* had become too entrenched and powerful, as witnessed in the Red Mosque episode.

By now, there were three parallel forces that dominated Pakistan and were not controlled by the civil government. On the one hand was the military which was convinced of its role in safeguarding the territorial and ideological identity of Pakistan, and in the process had developed fears about politicians politicizing the army. An officer of the army told British author and journalist, Anatol Lieven: 'We have a great fear of the politicians interfering in military promotions and appointments. This could split the army and if you split the army you destroy the country. Look at what happened under Nawaz Sharif's last government…' The officer went on to rationalize the military takeovers by adding, 'Whenever civilian government starts trying to interfere in this sector, we have to act in self defence.'[93] Needless to say, this philosophy was detrimental to the growth of democracy and democratic institutions. The second was the ISI which has come to believe that it owned the victory over the Soviet Union in Afghanistan.[94] Emboldened by that success, it is no longer under the control of either the civilian government or the full control of the military though its Director General is still drawn from the military. It has its own financial resources to fund and run its operations in Afghanistan and India. The third force is the Islamists who have their presence in every sphere of life, particularly the ISI, the military and politics. Ironically, Pakistan faces greater threat from this third dimension than from India because it can lead that country to auto-destruction by its complete takeover as it had conspired to do in 1995 when Benazir Bhutto was the Prime Minister.

Loud warning signals for the Pakistani establishment had been sounded in the 1990s when a conspiracy involving Islamists army officers to assassinate PM Benazir Bhutto in 1995 came to light. 'The plan was radical, it included the murder of PM Benazir Bhutto, Army Chief Waheed Kakar and some generals, with the goal of establishment of Pakistan-Afghanistan Caliphate.'[95] The career of the leading conspirator, Major General Zaheer ul-Islam Abbasi is representative of the mindset that had developed within the army establishment. Abbasi had been posted to New Delhi where he was an active ISI station leader and had been removed in circumstances that were never disclosed. Later, commanding a division in the Northern Areas, he had authorized an unsanctioned attack on Indian military posts in the Siachen area in which his unit suffered huge losses. He was disciplined by the Chief of the Army Staff but had soon become the master mind of the conspiracy against PM Benazir Bhutto. 'After the revolutionary plan was uncovered, Abbassi [*sic*] and his co-conspirators were sentenced by a military court to harsh detention for several years. They were prematurely released after the coup by Musharraf in 1999.'[96]

Interestingly, though it was a conspiracy hatched by the army officers, there was also an Islamist, Qari Safiullah Akhtar, a key figure of the Pakistani Jihadi nebula. If Abbasi spent four years in prison, Qari remained there for only five months and because of his close links with the ISI, was released. However, he remained steadfast to his goal of murdering Benazir Bhutto and once she was killed, President Musharraf had no option but to detain him again. This time he spent only three months in detention. By now the nexus between politicians, Islamists, military and terrorists had become so intertwined that it had become difficult to distinguish one from the other. The Government of Benazir Bhutto had been hobnobbing with the Afghan Taliban since 1994 'the dubious honour of being their midwife and godfather goes to PM Benazir Bhutto, her husband Asif Zardari and her Minister of Interior Naseerullah Babar.'[97] In fact, civilians, ex-officers and Islamists have often formed an explicit alliance. The Defence of Pakistan Council is a case in point since the organization founded in 2001 was re-launched ten years later in November 2011 in reaction to the killing of twenty-four Pakistani soldiers by a NATO aircraft in Salala near the Durand Line. This Council chaired by Maulana Samiul-Haq, the JUI(S) leader, includes former ISI officials (such as Hamid Gul[98] now deceased) and politicians (such as Sheikh Rasheed[99]), leaders of Islamic parties such as the JI and the JUI, as well as jihadists (including leaders of the Jama'at-ud Dawa, the new name for LeT).[100]

The relationship of the Islamists and jihadis with the army officers had become so deep that the army was in danger of being taken over by them at some future date since most of the young officers were influenced by their philosophy. In 1999, Malik Rehman[101] stated on television that 'officers of the rank of major in intelligence agencies with links with the Taliban and Al-Qaeda had been arrested because they wanted to target army generals.' With threat knocking at their doors the army generals were shaken and soon afterwards, the 'army stepped up operations in the Pashtun areas, 211 of them took place from 2007 to 2010, involving 150,000 of its 550,000 soldiers. Losses were heavy, estimated at around 2,000, including three generals, five brigadiers and seventy-three intelligence agents.'[102]

The Frankenstein that the Pakistani Army's ISI raised in the jihadis has now begun to turn on Pakistan. In 2018, Washington lobbied and succeeded in convincing the global watchdog, Financial Action Task Force (FATF), to put Pakistan in the 'grey list'. 'The move is part of a broader US strategy to pressure Pakistan to cut alleged links to Islamist militants waging chaos in neighbouring Afghanistan.'[103] India and USA tried to put pressure since all evidence suggested that terror in Afghanistan and Kashmir was being funded from the Pakistani soil. 'According to the FATF summary report released, Pakistan needs to continue to work on eight specific areas, including demonstrating it is "identifying and investigating" all terror financing activity in the country, freezing the funds of all designated terrorists and that its prosecutions result in "effective, proportionate and dissuasive sanctions" against all terror entities in Pakistan.'[104]

Prior to USA recognizing that, for too long it had been supping with the forces in Pakistan in the belief that its geostrategic goal will be achieved in the region. Indian protestations had largely fallen on the deaf ears in USA and the west. It was only when the flames of terrorism began to scorch the western world, and the USA and NATO continued to lose soldiers in Afghanistan, that they realized that the Frankenstein that they had helped Pakistan to create to fight their war in Afghanistan had spun out of their hands and had in fact turned on them. On the other hand, India had been suffering from terror, funded and exported from Pakistan, since the 1990s. They had begun to face a more belligerent Pakistan since 1999 when an opportunity was surreptitiously created by General Pervez Musharraf, a year after both the countries had become nuclear in 1998 and had begun a new and meaningful process of peace with Indian Prime Minister Atal Behari Vajpayee's 'Bus' journey[105] to Lahore. It was not only a momentous gesture on the part of the Indian Prime Minister considering the political party he belonged to, but a bold one too since it could boomerang with devastating political consequences for him and his party.[106]

All along the Wagah-Lahore route, he was given a rousing welcome by the people of Pakistan, lending hope of normalization of relations. Giving a further boost to the peace process and reiterating the message that contrary to misgivings in Pakistan, India acknowledged Pakistan as an independent sovereign country, Vajpayee visited Minar-e-Pakistan and wished Pakistan well. However, these peace overtures were not appreciated by the Pakistani Army and soon in the spring of that year, Pakistan made another attempt to redraw the map of Jammu and Kashmir by military force.

Known as the Kargil conflict, Pakistan used paramilitary soldiers belonging to the Northern Light Infantry along with regular Army soldiers to take control of Kargil–Dras sectors in the Ladakh region of Jammu and Kashmir. India paid dearly for dropping guard in the winter months when normally both the sides abandon their position in the higher reaches of the region, but after an intense war and high cost in personnel and the use of air power, it succeeded in vanquishing the Pakistani intruders. Pakistan not only failed in its attempt but also emerged as a conflict-prone and reckless nuclear power. It was also suggested (wrongly as it turned out) that General Pervez Musharraf, Chief of the Army, had not fully informed Prime Minister Nawaz Sharif of the operation and its implication. Because of this rogue act, the Pakistani Army cut a sorry figure in public perception. India, on the other hand, though bruised by the short war, emerged not only as the victor but also received accolades for its forbearance and restrained response particularly when the temptation to open another front to ease pressure on Kargil was great.[107]

The Kargil war turned out to be a watershed moment in the subcontinent's geo-strategic relations with USA, with India occupying greater space in them, and the space for Pakistan considerably shrunk. The belief that finally the USA had seen through Pakistan's irresponsible behavior, was, however short lived. The rise of Al-Qaeda and the ghastly 9/11 terror attack on the World Trade Centre, Pentagon and the American Airlines in 2001 forced USA to once again align with Pakistan because of the need to have an ally in the neighborhood of Afghanistan from where the Al-Qaeda leadership and its Amir, Osama bin Laden was operating.

By now, General Musharraf had replaced the civilian government of Nawaz Sharif, imposed martial law and arrogated to himself wide and sweeping powers. He had decided to be on the side of the Americans, albeit reluctantly, after President George Bush had given the ultimatum of 'if not with us then against us' and the Assistant Defence Secretary had warned that Pakistan would be bombed to stone age.

Thus, Pakistan has periodically indulged in overt and covert military operations against India to change the map and wrest control of Jammu and Kashmir. These have not just been confined to Jammu and Kashmir. In the north-east in the mid-'50s, Naga rebels were supported not only by China but also Pakistan. In the 1960s Pakistan fanned the Mizo rebellion. But Pakistan lost an important launching pad for these rebels. With the breakup of Pakistan in December 1971, these movements became increasingly weak. With the passage of time, they also became India-friendly as the environment changed. However, never the one to give up, Pakistan's propensity to fan trouble in India found another opportunity in the late 1970s in Punjab. 'Beginning in the late 1970s and through the early 1990s, Pakistan supported the Sikh insurgency in India's northern state of Punjab.'[108] The big opportunity had arrived in the 1980s when it was recovering after its dismemberment in 1971and was growing confident because of the progress it was making in its nuclear program. Confident that its nuclear program will buy insurance against a fully fledged war by India, it once again picked up the thread of games that it had been playing in the Valley since the fifties. Emboldened by the American reliance on it for conducting the war against Soviet occupation of Afghanistan, as the operations of Mujahideens was coming to an end there, it successfully turned them towards India in the Valley of Kashmir. Ironically, Pakistan was aided in no small measure by India that made political miscalculations at home out of myopic vision and short-term political goals of the ruling party.

This began with the return of Sheikh Abdullah in 1975 as chief minister of Jammu and Kashmir, and was soon followed by a period of intense struggle for power between Prime Minister Indira Gandhi on the one hand and Sheikh Abdullah and his successor Farooq Abdullah on the other. All the three, obsessively pursued power with the consequence that when the State began to go through a period of uncertainty it ended up sliding into a hitherto unknown field of terrorism among the Kashmiris. The most tragic consequence of this was the disruption of the Kashmiri society with killings of Pandits and their eventual migration. The fallout of this still echoes across the country and has considerably altered the tone and tenor of political discourse.

Experts like Ashley Tellis, Christine Fair and Jamison Jo Medby in their work *Limited Conflict Under the Nuclear Umbrella: Indian and Pakistan Lessons from Kargil Conflict* contend that '...As Pakistan continued to expand its nuclear program, and thus its confidence that India would be deterred from taking punitive action, it also increased its reliance on militant proxies in India'.[109] Thus, as it became an overt nuclear power, it became aggressive in its design to intensify low-intensity conflict through the Islamist militant proxies. In doing so, it no longer confined its operations to the State of Jammu and Kashmir and has boldly targeted high value recipients like the Indian intelligence operations center located near Red Fort, Delhi in December 2000, strike on the Indian Parliament, a year later in December 2001, housing for the families of army personnel in Kaluchak, Jammu, coordinated bomb attack on Mumbai's commuter rail system in 2006 and the most audacious and deadly siege of Mumbai in 2008 that also dragged in Israel. After that there have been periodic attacks such as on a police station in Dinanagar in Gurdaspur district of Punjab, an important Air Force Station in Pathankot, again in Punjab and the Uri Brigade headquarters in the Valley. Most of these terrorist attacks were carried out by the Lashkar-e-Taiba while the attack on the Parliament was executed by Jaish-e-Mohammad which was also responsible for the Pulwama suicide bomb attack in February 2019. Pakistan had also created Indian cells which carried out the bomb blasts in the Mumbai commuter rail system, though with the support of Lashkar-e-Taiba.

In between these major acts of terror, Pakistan has kept up the pressure by terrorist attacks of smaller dimension. But it would be naïve to explain Pakistan's rivalry with India over possession of Kashmir if not the whole of Jammu and Kashmir. This antagonism has seeds in its stubborn refusal to admit that India is a bigger country, with better resources and also a superior ideology acceptable to the rest of the world without reservations. This naturally makes India a preeminent State in the region. Pakistan, afraid of Indian hegemony resists this, thus putting its army in the front to ensure that it is internationally accorded the same status as that of India. For achieving this goal, it believes that the ideology of Pakistan, the foundation of that state and one that sets it apart from India, has to be defended. The Army of Pakistan has taken upon itself the responsibility of not only defending the borders but this ideology too. So, the goals set by Pakistan for preserving itself are to resist India's regional dominance and its steady global rise. Both of them are viewed from the prism of ideology and in terms of conflict of civilizations.

4

The Threat of Jihad

'This is an enemy for life, as well as an enemy of life.'
—Christopher Hitchens

Apart from the ideology and army of Pakistan, the third element affecting the Kashmir conundrum that India has to contend with is the evolution of the transnational nature of Jihad. Islamic scholars may debate about the true meaning of Jihad but the layman knows only its impact and has seen how lives have been devastated and the social fabric shredded. Three events, spread over twelve months, determined the course that human history took during the next few decades. All three sucked the rest of the world into a vortex of turbulence, violence, divisions and upheavals that history witnessed rarely during its course. Combined together, they have proved too hard to deal with, and the more the countries try, the more it mutates in many more devastating forms.

The first cataclysmic event was the exit of the Shah of Iran, Reza Shah Pehlavi, from his country in the middle of January of 1979, after a long-drawn struggle against his rule. There is little doubt that under the influence of the western countries, the Shah had led his country to new heights of economic development and modernity. But, at the same time, his rule was also marred by allegations of corruption against him and other members of the royal family, as well as the muzzling of all political protests and dissidence by the kingdom's notorious secret service. Importantly, there was the question of legitimacy about a monarchy created after a legitimately elected government had been overthrown by a western-funded revolution. The Shias, the main component of Iranian society, too had been displeased by the Shah's modernity, westernization and, what they perceived, licentious behavior of the society. In addition, he had changed the Iranian calendar from Islamic *Hijri* to marking it from the date of Cyrus, the pre-Islamic king-emperor of the empire known as Achaemenid.

From 1977 onwards, opposition to the Shah had become stronger though it was met with brutality by the authorities. In October of that year, a 10-night poetry festival organized by the Iranian writers' association at the Goethe Institute in Tehran attracted thousands of participants for lectures criticizing the government. On 23 October, Mostafa Khomeini, the eldest son of the exiled cleric, Ayatollah Sayyid Ruhollah Musavi Khomeini, died of unknown causes at age 47 in Najaf, Iraq. The elder Khomeini, also simply known as Ayatollah Khomeini, had been living in exile since 1963, when he was arrested for leading protests against the Shah's modernization program. Thereafter, protests became rampant and hundreds of clerics were arrested. Things boiled over to a point till 16 January, when Shah and his family left Iran for Egypt, and on 1 February 1979, Ayatollah Khomeini returned to Iran to be greeted by millions of people in the streets of Tehran.

Westernization of the Islamic world had extracted its first victim. But, a greater upheaval of long-term consequences was about to burst upon the world a few months later in Kaaba, the holiest shrine of the Muslims. Hundreds of Jihadist Salafists[110], known as Juhayman's Ikhwan[111], rebelled against the House of Saud[112] and occupied Kaaba. Their leader was 43 year old Juhayman al-Otaybi. He declared that according to the Islamic scriptures, the Mahdi[113] who was to appear just before the Day of Judgment at the Kaaba and conquer the world for Islam had appeared. It was very obvious to everyone that dislodging the occupants required greater force but the place being the holiest shrine of Islam, the Saudi king and the government hesitated. Finally, it was decided that it was ideal to seek the support of the Islamic clerics to issue a fatwa unbinding the State from the injunction of not using force in the holiest shrine and sanctioning the use of force to have it vacated.

The ulema 'agreed to issue the fatwa in exchange for some promises. The regime…had to put an end to women on television, ban licentious films and prohibit alcohol. Most importantly, the regime had to put petrodollars to spread the Wahhabi[114] version of Islam, not only to reform Muslims, but also convert infidels.'[115] The clerics had, in fact, not just extracted their pound of flesh but had asked the Saudi royals to adopt the agenda of Juhayman. In *The Siege of Mecca*, Yaroslav Trofimov, a journalist of *The Wall Street Journal*, wrote, 'As is often in the case in the kingdom, this quid pro quo was implied, and not necessarily enshrined in clear, unambiguous words. But nobody questioned the meeting's outcome and the royal household accepted the bargain.'[116] The consequences were to be felt worldwide, including India.

Armed with the fatwa, the Saudi forces tried to storm the Kaaba. Unsuccessful in their attempt, help had to be sought from the French. Finally the holy shrine was cleared but not before the forces had killed 117 rebels. The Saudi military is said to have lost 127 soldiers. On 9 January 1980, 63 rebels, including the self-styled Mahdi, were beheaded in public executions. In the following weeks, more rebels were killed—among those arrested were 23 women and children. With this incident, modern-day Jihad had arrived.

Islamic scholars make a fine distinction between the struggle that is waged within to overcome evil and the external manifestation that means killing of the infidels. In fact, Markaz ad-Dawat wal-Irshad (MDI) and Jamaat-ud-Dawat (JuD) use either *qital* (killing, as in *qatal*) or *jihad-o-qital* that is jihad and killing. Killing and being killed is part of Islam and scholars tell us that in the 'Qur'an and Hadeeth, Allah and his last Prophet tell the believers that if they kill a non-believer or got killed by a non-believer, they will get paradise without being questioned on the Day of Judgment.'[117]

The Islamist scholars had begun the revivalism of fundamentalist Islam with renewed vigor when oil was first discovered by Americans in Saudi Arabia in 1938 and USA had entered into an agreement with it. The newfound riches were immediately used for the modernization of the state on the western pattern and it soon invited a backlash, triggering a process that insisted on the literal interpretation of the Qur'an and Hadeeth and also the revivalism of the period of Prophet Mohammad. The resistance to modernity and change also led to the periodic crackdown by the government, leading to the exodus of the Islamic scholars to other countries. Thus, by 1979, when the siege of Mecca took place, and the consequent crackdown on the fundamentalists and proponents of extreme Islamism began, there was a large-scale migration or exile of such scholars to other Muslim countries. The seeds of Wahhabism/Salafism had been spread wide across the world wherever Muslims lived. The events of 1979 in Mecca and Medina had been treated as a rebellion by the Saudis and, therefore, treated as a law-and-order problem. However, what at that time had not been realized was that it was rather a rise of an ideology, and should have been to be treated as such. The Saudis had failed to comprehend the consequences of not dealing with it accordingly and letting the believers of that philosophy get out of the country and spread it all over the world. In 2004, Prince Khalid al Faisal, the Governor of the province to which the supposed Mahdi belonged, said, 'We have eliminated the individuals who committed the Juhayman crime, but we have overlooked the ideology that was behind the crime. We have let it spread in the country, ignoring it as if it did not exist.'

In this Islamic upheaval, December of 1979 had arrived but had not yet ended when on the night of 24 December 1979, Soviet Union's tanks and armored vehicles rolled into Afghanistan in support of the government headed by Babrak Karmal. In other words, communism had not only taken over Afghanistan but had also come to the borders of Pakistan, and this was, to the western world, a threat as it was not too far away from the 'warm waters' of Persian Gulf and the shores of resource-rich Middle East and Africa. As a consequence, all forces, belonging to different schools of thought, and with different motives, joined hands to resist the communist regime and its patron—the Soviet Union. Meanwhile, the periodic purging that had taken place in Saudi Arabia, meant that the survivors of the Juhayman's thoughts had also spread all over the world. They were to announce their presence in 1981 when Egyptian President Anwar Sadat was assassinated for having accepted the American-brokered peace treaty with Israel. Such forces not only existed but also began to close rank over the Soviet invasion of Afghanistan and by mid 1980s a new force and organization, Al-Qaeda, was born with the goal of defeating the super power.

Jihadi volunteers from all over the world arrived in Pakistan to go into Afghanistan and fight the Soviets. It was a God-send opportunity for Pakistan, since the military coup against the elected government of Zulfikar Ali Bhutto had made it a pariah state. The fact that the military dictator, General Zia-ul-Haq, had gone back on his word of holding elections and handing over power to the civilian government on multiple occasions, had not gone down well with the western world. But at this juncture of history in the 1980s, the geostrategic location of Pakistan came to its rescue. This was the same scenario that Jinnah had visualized before Partition. He had indicated that Pakistan's foreign policy would be oriented towards the Muslim world but there would be an expectation of US support.[118] He firmly believed that the Muslim countries would stand together against possible Russian aggression and would, therefore, expect US assistance. *Life* magazine's celebrated reporter-photographer Margaret Bourke-White, reported after an interview with Jinnah that he said, 'America needs Pakistan more than Pakistan needs America...' She also wrote in her book the underlying assumptions of Pakistan's relations with the United States for the next five decades. "Russia," confided Mr. Jinnah, "is not very far away."...In Jinnah's mind, this brave new nation had no other claim on American friendship than this—that across the wild rumble of roadless mountain ranges lay the land of the Bolsheviks.'[119] Pakistan, in that early stage had read the USA right for soon thereafter it had become a part of the Baghdad Pact, later CENTO and SEATO, against Soviet Union and communist China, and received not only modern military weapons, equipment and training but also financial aid to build the economic infrastructure of that fund-starved new State.

With the Soviets sitting in Afghanistan, USA needed Pakistan more than ever before. Funds came pouring from all over the world in support of the jihadists as they gathered in the area that Jinnah had described as the 'pivot'. The Saudis pitched in with funds and the USA with the weapons and other logistics support. General Zia-ul-Haq grabbed at the opportunity with both hands and with Pakistan becoming the centre of interest for the entire Muslim world, he initiated the process of the Islamization of Pakistani society. Since the fervor of jihad was all pervasive, few objected to what he was doing and those that dared were quickly made to hold their peace. It was during this period that ISI assumed larger than life role in the affairs of Pakistan. During this period, the CIA-ISI relations also grew stronger though the two had been cooperating since the 1960, when Pakistan first became an ally of the USA against the Soviets, and then when some disgruntled Indian Sikhs launched a movement for Homeland in London in 1970 under the banner of the Khalistan movement. But now Pakistan thought its opportunity to extract revenge plus Kashmir for the break-up of Pakistan in 1971 had arrived. This alliance remained for the next fifteen years till Prime Minister Indira Gandhi was assassinated by her Sikh bodyguards.[120]

The longer the process of jihad went on, the stronger grew the hold of Zia-ul-Haq on Pakistan and that of the clerics on its society. Consequently, it 'gained strength throughout the 1980s...and also involved in forming the alliance of opposition parties, the Islami Jamhoori Ittehad (IJI), and Mohajir Qaumi Movement (MQM) to counter Bhutto's PPP.'[121] However, in 1988 the Soviets declared that they were pulling out of Afghanistan. Soon thereafter, General Zia-ul-Haq died in a mysterious air crash and with his death, political activity picked up in Pakistan and among the Islamists, Jamiat Ahle Hadith (JAH), became active and assertive in its involvement with elections. JAH was one of those organizations that had opposed Zia-ul-Haq's martial law and had participated in strikes and sit-ins. For this reason, the ISI had not involved it in the Afghanistan jihad. However, it had raised funds for the Jihad and a trickle had begun to be active in the war in Afghanistan. But by and large, it was the foreigners who constituted the Jihadis in Afghanistan.

The Afghan war brought the JAH and the Juhayman Ikhwan closer and its influence grew. With the death of Zia-ul-Haq in 1988 and the return of the process of electoral politics, Ahle Hadith, which had a history of participation in the elections, once again got involved. The rise of Benazir Bhutto, her victory, and the beginnings of rumbling in the Kashmir Valley injected a new strategy where Benazir did not fit in and consequently in a soft military coup she was removed. This was followed by the ISI bringing different Islamist factions together, in which the different factions of Ahle Hadith united to form Muttahida Jamiat Ahle Hadith (MJAH), which in turn merged with the Nawaz Sharif-headed and ISI-sponsored, Islami Jamhoori Ittehad (IJI), to contest elections. However, divisions, splits and mergers continued to haunt the clerics and the jihadists till 1996 when a combination of circumstances following a debate over-international Jihad and Kashmir-Jihad left Hafiz Saeed as the leader of Markaz ad-Dawatwal-Irshad (MDI). This has not stopped the proponents of international Jihad from pursuing their agenda, though the ideologists, clerics and foot-soldiers kept uniting and splitting all too frequently. This was to test the patience and mettle of India in the following years.

The coincidence of the closure of the Jihad in Afghanistan in 1988 and the disillusionment of many Kashmiri sections and youth with the establishment and the electoral process of the 1987 elections to the Jammu and Kashmir Assembly proved fortuitous for the ISI and Pakistan. While many Jihadists moved to Europe, where the collapse of the Soviet Union and the breakup of Yugoslavia were to cause havoc and trigger a civil war among the Christian and Muslim populations of the region, it also created an opportunity for them. Many of the regions that formed parts of Yugoslavia had at one time in history been part of the Ottoman Empire where the Christians had failed to dislodge the Islamic rule. In a way, therefore, jihad in that part of Europe was a continuation of an old struggle for supremacy and it attracted most of the foreign jihadists of Afghanistan. But Pakistan was not interested in that since its focus was on gaining control of Kashmir. It is in this context that the MDI from Pakistan was more than eager to enter into the fray. Simultaneously, the Kashmir front too had opened up an opportunity for them though the ISI knew that the 'young boys from Kashmir were more street fighters than guerrilla fighters, and hence needed military training. The ISI did not have sufficient training facilities for the incoming Kashmiri boys at that time. Therefore, the ISI connected the young Kashmiri fighters with Pakistani Jihadist groups, such as the MDI.'[122] The ISI also knew that in the developing circumstances, unlike the failed attempt to rouse the people to rebellion in 1965, this was their best chance since they could now depend upon the logistic support of the local population. Their assessment had proved correct when almost the entire Valley, the towns, villages and hamlets in unison unleashed the psychological terror against the Pandit community on 19 January 1990. These developments convinced Pakistan that it could successfully launch a low-cost war against India without getting directly involved and that soon Kashmir will fall into its lap. This was a dream that had sustained Pakistan and now it grew in confidence and was certain that its ideology would be soon validated.

Soon thereafter, on 25 January 1990, MDI participated in the first militant activity when its 'mujahidin gunned down one squadron leader and three pilots of the Indian Air Force.'[123] This attack and the deaths, demonstrated the diabolical nature of Pakistan as a State since apparently they were in retaliation of the Indian Air Force which had made many sorties during the last week of October and early November 1947 to ferry Indian soldiers to the Valley to thwart the Pakistan-supported tribal invaders from capturing the Valley. The Pakistan plan had been in works for quite some time and MDI had, in fact, started setting up its jihadist infrastructure in Pakistan-occupied-Kashmir (PoK) since early 1989. The first lot of Kashmiri youth that came for training belonged to Yasin Malik-led Jammu and Kashmir Liberation Front (JKLF). But it did not take long for the ISI and MDI to realize that JKLF would not be furthering the cause of Pakistan or international Jihad and hence very early in the militancy, they started raising Hizbul Mujahideen(HM) and Lashkar-e-Taiba (LeT) mujahidin, and subsequently the first lot of LeT entered Kashmir independently in August 1992 to attack a military convoy in Kupwara. Between 1989 and 1992, various other factions had started supporting the Jihad in Kashmir. The MJAH, the political face of MDI, held a Jihad-e-Kashmir conference in Lahore on 16 March 1991. A former vice-chancellor of Medina University assured the conference of cooperation of the Saudi people, ulema and government. Finally, the conference declared support for the ISI-sponsored Jihad and encouraged Muslims to join it under the banner of MDI.

After winning support from various factions, the ISI moved quickly to establish control and direction of the militant activities by demanding and getting all the militants registered with it. In order to be eligible to receive money and paramilitary training, this registration was made mandatory. It also decided on the number of militants who could be sent into India at any given time. 'The ISI decides how many mujahidin a certain group can send across the LoC, and the groups are then required to periodically update the ISI about their members and operations to stay eligible to receive money. The ISI pays the entire amount of operational funding for Jihad in Kashmir to each group operating there…as they are not supposed to be working in Pakistan. The Pakistani members of Kashmiri groups, including the Hizbul Mujahideen, are required to pay for their living while in Pakistan.'[124]

In those early years, competing groups vied for control of the campaign launched in the Valley. On the one hand were the ulema who were more interested in the missionary work of proselytizing as opposed to those who did not want to deviate from the path of Jihad. The latter was led by Hafiz Saeed. Thus, in the early years of terrorism, there were three distinct groups pursuing their agenda. On the one hand was the JKLF, which wanted to pursue its political agenda of uniting the whole of Jammu and Kashmir State and attaining independence through the armed struggle but on the other end of the spectrum were the Hizbul Mujahideen and the Lashkar-e-Taiba, who were both proxies for Pakistan. The most brutal atrocities were committed by HM in the early days on the tiny Pandit population of the Valley. As a result of targeted killings and massacres, within the first two years of terrorism, the Valley was nearly purged of all Hindu population. In addition, 'The ISI had asked the Hizbul Mujahidin and other Kashmiri militant groups to attack Hindu temples and properties along with the Hindus themselves.' When the LeT entered the fray, it also joined in on the destruction of temples. The state government admitted that the 'Muslim militants had damaged and vandalized 208 of the 438

Hindu temples in the Valley during the 20-year-old Jihad...(but) the Kashmiri Pandit Sangharsh Samiti...disputed the figures. They put the number of total vandalized temples at 550, and 50,000 *kanals* [1 *kanal* = 1/8 acre] of land that had been encroached.' In addition, the LeT had been tasked by ISI to target areas in the Jammu region so that the ambit of Jihad spreads in the whole of the State and in the process triggers communal riots. It was not only the State of Jammu and Kashmir that was on the target of ISI and its puppets but the whole of India because the persecution, killings and desecrations of holy places was also intended to arouse the majority community in the rest of the country and trigger communal riots.

The ISI calculated that since Jammu had witnessed communal violence in 1947, by reigniting those flames, it could be used as a template for the rest of India. Praveen Swami, one of the most informed analysts, opined 'Terrorist activity here intervenes in all-India discourses, legitimizing itself as a defence of the vulnerable Muslim communities. For Hindu communal politicians, similarly, terrorism is a platform through which their all-India concerns can be amplified and broadcast. Protecting the people from terrorism in Jammu is for politicians of the Hindu right, an exercise in defending a besieged Hindu minority.'[125] As far as the Islamic and Kashmir-centric terror groups' operations in the State were concerned, they were under such a tight control of the ISI that only Hizbul and LeT were allowed to enter it.

The first major attack in Jammu took place in the Kishtwar district in August 1993. Terrorists killed 18 Hindu bus passengers triggering communal riots, as Hindus attacked Muslim businesses and homes. Largely, the authorities succeeded in keeping the rioting under control. The next target was the neighboring district of Doda, which had a very heavy population of Muslims. Between 1993 and 2001, the militants killed 310 Hindus. In all, there were 39 major massacres in the State between 1996 and 2006. As in the Valley, the LeT tried to do the same in the Jammu region by attacking the temples. But unlike Hizbul, LeT was no longer limited to damaging and vandalizing the temples and tried to expand its area of activity by targeting not only temples in the Jammu region but also the rest of the country. Thus, they targeted not only the Raghunath Temple of Jammu but also the Akshardham Temple of Gujarat. This had led to the vice-president of the Vishwa Hindu Parishad to warn the terrorists to 'understand that they had many shrines related to their religion in the rest of the country which can also be made targets.'[126] The ISI had very nearly attained its goal!

The attacks of the LeT had a definite plan since each time initiative for peace talks was taken, the LeT carried out brutal massacres. On 19 February 1999, as Indian Prime Minister Atal Behari Vajpayee prepared for his bus journey from Wagah border to Lahore, militants attacked a marriage party at Bal Jaralan in Rajouri, killing two[127]. The toll would have been much higher but for the presence of two brothers, one from the Central Reserve Police Force (CRPF) and the other from Jammu and Kashmir (JAK) Rifles, who were on leave to attend the marriage. In another remote village of Rajouri, the LeT massacred another family of four and in a separate incident that night, a family of nine in a remote village of Udhampur was brutally massacred. Indian Army intelligence intercepted signals on frequencies used by terrorists, saying 'give Nawaz Sharif a present…by turning the snow red.'[128] It is a different matter that the peace process was not allowed to be disrupted by these incidents till Kargil happened.

Emboldened by the successes, three LeT terrorists carried out an attack on the family quarters of the Indian Army on 14 May 2002, at Kalu Chak cantonment near Jammu. They killed 31 people including eight women and 21 children.[129] It was a morning attack when the mothers had accompanied their children to the bus stop to see them off for school. The *fidayee*[130] attackers had carried 30 grenades, 2,000 rounds of ammunition, AK-47s and Chinese pistols and it took three hours to neutralize them. The macabre planning and its ruthless execution demonstrated that this attack achieved multiple goals: worldwide media attention, low cost 'war' on India, infliction of psychological pain on the people and possible fear and insecurity in the minds of families of soldiers. From *The New York Times* to London's *Guardian,* all took notice of the killings.

The Jihadist attacks on the noncombatants in the Valley were equally sinister in design. In right earnest they began to propagate the principles of Juhaymans, and any perceived obscenity and un-

Islamic behavior was severely punished. In 2000, a LeT operative in a Sopore village killed two residents for engaging in the un-Islamic behavior of gambling. In June of 2005, Pakistan-based LeT operatives came down to a hamlet in north Kashmir, addressed the village gathering in the mosque, and warned the young boys and girls there against the use of mobiles. The three girls in the village who were found to be possessing mobiles were severely reprimanded in public. These deeds were a natural progression from the early days of terrorism when the LeT had shocked the Kashmiri society by targeting Sufi shrines in 1989. The historic Baba Reshi[131] shrine in Tangmarg was targeted in 1994. Pilgrims were fired at and the shrine burned.[132] Even more outrageous was the attack in 1995, when the holiest of holy Sufi shrine of Kashmir, the Charar-i-Sharif, was occupied and finally destroyed by burning. In 2005an attempt to murder Abdul Ahad, a well-known custodian of Sufi's Islamic traditions in the Valley, was made in Sopore. In the same year the shrine of Zainuddin Wali at Aishmuqam in Anantnag district was attacked and destroyed. It was obvious that those perpetrating these acts were not just Pakistani agents trying to wrest Jammu and Kashmir from India but were adherents of fundamentalist Islam who had taken upon themselves the responsibility of purging the world of impurities, as they understood them, and establish the *Nizam-e-Mustafa*[133]. In their scheme of things Kashmir had either deviated from the true path of Islam or had never learnt it, and, therefore, the people in the Valley needed to be reconverted to it!

In a multipronged strategy, the terrorists from Pakistan were also carrying out *fidayee* attacks on military targets. *Fidayee* attacks are different from suicide bombers though both are conscious of the impending and certain death. Suicide bombers commit suicide to kill others whereas a *fidayee* is someone who exerts to avoid death although death is certain in the end. But as long as he is not dead, and his weapons are working, his aim is to inflict maximum casualties on his targets. In fact, the attackers did succeed in some of the most spectacular attacks on army establishments, like the high security zone of the Badami Bagh Cantonment in Srinagar where the soldiers were held off for more than 12 hours and eight soldiers lost their lives. A few years down the line, the Red Fort in New

Delhi was targeted and 12 soldiers laid down their lives to meet the attack. Equally deadly and full of symbolism and importance was the attack on the camp of the Electrical and Mechanical Engineers near Akhnoor in the Jammu region where even after one of the *fidayee* was killed at the gate, the other killed six soldiers before he was killed. The third, who had hidden himself, threw a grenade at Lieutenant General Prasad who came out on hearing of the attack and though he escaped with his life, a Brigadier, who was in-charge of the Corps headquarters was killed. Lt General Prasad was the highest rank officer of the army to have sustained injury during the militancy.

In these, and other *fidayee* attacks, the casualties by the army were much greater than the LeT attackers killed. Such acts had begun to influence public opinion in the Valley though a majority of the Muslims of the Valley were adherents of *Sufi Islam*, and its clerics had repeatedly issued *fatwas* excommunicating the LeT terrorists. The ominous signs appeared when *fatwas* appeared useless after a LeT operative was killed in an attack on the Srinagar airport on 16 January 2001. About 6,000 local residents protested against the killing, marking a new phase in the Valley. By now, many in the Valley had begun to recognize and accept the *mujahideen* as *mehman* (guests) *Mujahideens* 'who were fighting for their cause and dying on their behalf'. Soon, public funerals, at the expense of the local people began to be held and shrines built for the slain terrorists.

Ever since 1990, the focus of the world has been on the militant and terrorist activities in Jammu and Kashmir, and this has drawn the attention away from the bigger picture of Islamic Jihad against the world of the infidels at large. The scholars and the media have remained obsessed with the so-called 'Kashmir' issue because of its being an integral part of the Indo-Pak narrative. However, for forces unleashed since 1979, as has been seen earlier in this chapter, the Islamic struggle for Jihad has global dimensions in which local issues are mere catalysts. Terrorism in Jammu and Kashmir has to be seen from this prism too.

In India, the communal problem has been endemic, notwithstanding the fact that the country has enjoyed enlightened leadership and a constitution that guarantees equality and secularism and is committed to achieving these goals. However, the prejudices and suspicion based on the legacy of an acrimonious past and the partition of the country has been periodically exploited by some for their immediate goals. As a consequence, communal riots have been the bane of free India. Serious rioting and killings were witnessed in the decades of 1970s and 1980s, particularly in Bihar and Maharashtra. Of the two states, Maharashtra was the worst affected as the textile town of Bhiwandi would periodically explode into rioting and then there would be reports of police complicity with the rioters of one section of the society. It was in these circumstances that Ahle Hadith became the vector for the Juhayman Ikhwan's philosophy in India, though there is no evidence that there were direct links between the two. But, as one of the Saudi Prince's had warned, Juhayman Ikhwan was less of a law-and-order problem and more of an idea that needed a superior philosophy to deal with. Within a few years of its being banished from Saudi Arabia, it had spread and by 1985 its tentacles had reached India where the insecurity and communal tensions had created a fertile ground. The Indian LeT too was to be born in the wake of the Bhiwandi riots. The Salafists and the Wahhabis too had discovered a place which had a sizeable population of Muslims that could provide volunteers for the proposed worldwide Jihad that, they thought, was inevitable and necessary.

The demolition of the Babri Masjid in 1992 and the subsequent riots, communal killings and bomb blasts in Mumbai and elsewhere, accelerated the rallying of Islamic extremist forces and by the mid-1990s, LeT had established links and cells in Mumbai, Bhiwandi, Delhi, Hyderabad, Coimbatore and in Bangladesh and Nepal. The Indian Muslim Mohammadi Mujahideen (IMMM) and Students' Islamic Movement of India (SIMI) too was formed during this period. By the time LeT was organized in India, the Pakistan based MDI had started preparing to take its jihad into the heart of India. It saw the bigger picture of jihad in Kashmir 'as only the first stage of the global jihad against the forces of unbelief worldwide.'[134] The MDI/JuD discourse on the jihad in Kashmir was presented as a conflict between Islam and *kufr* (non-believers of Islam) and in

October 1993, Hafiz Saeed said that MDI was preparing to turn Kashmir into an entry point to India where the real jihad will be fought. By 1999, Hafiz Saeed, on behalf of MDI, declared that it had entered India. During one of the Friday sermons on the last day of the annual congregation in Muridke (Pakistan) he warned the Prime Minister of India that if the Indian forces were not withdrawn from Kashmir, then the Prime Minister's office will be invaded! In the same breath, he also warned the Pakistani opponents of jihad: 'Those who are not honest with jihad don't have a place in Pakistan…The Jihad is not about Kashmir only. It encompasses all of India…' He went on to add, 'About 15 years ago people might have found it ridiculous if someone told them about [the] disintegration of USSR. Today, I announce the breakup of India, *Insha-Allah.* We will not rest until the whole of India is dissolved into Pakistan.'[135]

There is little doubt about the ambition of MDI and Hafiz Saeed and in their own way they tried their best, and obviously they were blinded to the reality of the present times. Without saying it in words, India was making up for the lost centuries of its disunity and divisiveness. The institutions, including the army and other security forces, were no longer the preserve of any one class or caste and hence the unity was impregnable. On the other hand, organizations like MDI and JuD and their agents like Hafiz Saeed continued to reminiscence of times when the gale of Islam had swept aside the fragmented and passionless Indian society. On the other hand, Pakistan and the forces dominating the discourse of that country were actually struggling to keep that country together since they had to find rational reason for its existence. This obvious difference visible to India and the west, was beyond the comprehension of Hafiz Saeed and hence their quixotic efforts to break India. This explains the attacks that were launched in various parts of the country, particularly in New Delhi.

After the attack on the Red Fort, an even more audacious attack was launched on the Parliament when five LeT and Jaish-e-Mohammed (JeM) terrorists attacked the Parliament of India on 31 December 2001, resulting in a 45-minute gun battle in which nine policemen and parliament staffer were killed. The terrorists wearing commando dress had entered the Parliament in cars carrying Ministry sticker through the VIP gate of the building.[136] Ironically, the attack achieved the opposite of what the LeT wanted. Instead of demoralizing the country or creating dissensions it brought not only the country together but also forced the political parties to close ranks and express solidarity with the security forces, reaffirming the resolve to defeat and destroy the menace of terrorism. The High Commissioner to Pakistan was recalled, troops massed at the borders and war appeared imminent, alarming the world. India also handed over a list of 20 dreaded terrorists living in Pakistan, demanding their surrender.

Internationally, the attack drew widespread condemnation and President George Bush, speaking on the hundredth day to mark the 9/11 attacks on USA, designated the LeT and Ummah Tameer-e-Nau (UTN) as terrorist organizations and their assets were to be frozen. This was the time when Pakistan had reluctantly decided to be on the side of USA in its war on terror. Therefore, President Bush also said, 'I also look forward to working with the governments of both India and Pakistan in a common effort to shut it [LeT] down and to bring the killers to justice...Lashkar is an extremist group based in Kashmir. LeT is a stateless sponsor of terrorism and it hopes to destroy relations between Pakistan and India and to undermine Pakistan's President Musharraf.'[137] This speech of President once again demonstrated the ability of Pakistan to exploit the needs of USA since, as in the 1950s when USA needed an ally against the Soviet Union or 1979 when the US once again needed an ally to be a frontline state against the Soviet occupation of Afghanistan, now too, USA needed Pakistan to fight the Al-Qaeda based in Afghanistan. Thus, President Bush absolved Islamabad of all complicity in terrorism in Kashmir and other parts of the country. All that it resulted in was that the State Bank of Pakistan asked all banks to freeze accounts of the MDI/LeT and the UTN. However, it is speculated that before that the ISI had already asked all of them to withdraw funds and leave only token money. Additionally, Hafiz Saeed announced that the name of the MDI had been changed to Jamaat-ud-Dawa (JuD). He also said that the LeT would be separated from the MDI, would work independent of the JuD, and would be restricted to Jammu and Kashmir. Zakiur Rehman Lakhvi became LeT's operational commander. Obviously, everything was happening with the blessings of the ISI, the Pakistan Army and the government. Pakistan also arrested Hafiz Saeed and Maulana Masood Azhar to demonstrate its will to act against terrorists but soon enough all those arrested were released one by one.

In connection with the relationship of the ISI and the Pakistani Army with the terrorists and fundamentalist, it is interesting to recall what Condoleezza Rice records in her book, *No Higher Honor*, about the remarks of Vladimir Putin while talking to President Bush in 2001 during the G-8 meeting: 'He [Putin] excoriated the Musharraf regime for its support of extremists and the connections of the Pakistani army and intelligence services to the Taliban and Al Qaeda…' Putin had gone on to prophetically warn that it was only a matter of time before it resulted in a major catastrophe. His remarks had been dismissed by Bush and Rice—who was then the National Security Adviser—as exaggerated fears. When it was too late, the American strategists grudgingly acknowledged that greater threat to the US was posed not by Afghanistan but by Pakistan which had a stockpile of nuclear weapons and was plagued with instability. Rajiv Dogra, a career diplomat, in his insightful book *Where Borders Bleed* cites that Mike McConnell, the Director of National Intelligence in the Bush administration, had focused on this threat in his first briefing of President-Elect Barack Obama. He had said bluntly: 'Pakistan is a dishonest partner of USA in Afghan war…in exchange for $2 billion a year from US, Pakistan's powerful military and its spy agency (ISI) helped USA, while giving clandestinely weapons and money to the Afghan Taliban.'[138]

The MDI also forged ties with other groups of India who for their own reasons were at war with the country. One of the earliest allies of LeT were the Sikh separatists. Soon enough the ISI put them in contact with the Kashmiri separatists. Arif Jamal writes, 'Sikh separatists from India and their supporters outside India very often openly take part in MDI/JuD activities in Pakistan. Occasionally, they also get mentioned in the MDI/JuD publications. In March, 2000, *Mujallah A-Dawa* reported that a group of Babbar Khalsa also participated in the Kashmir Day rally on February, 5, 2000, in Lahore. They raised slogans against India.'[139] He further informs that a Sikh charity called Khalsa Aid U.K. sent its volunteers to provide relief to the victims during the October 2005 earthquake in Pakistan-occupied-Kashmir. Since this was known to the Indian authorities, when a list of the most-wanted terrorists was handed over to Pakistan in the wake of the international outrage after the attack on the Parliament, five were of the separatist Khalistan movement. They continue to enjoy the hospitality of Pakistan and also the collaboration with the Kashmiri separatists. ISI and JeIP are known to have conducted camps for training the Sikh youth when that movement had appeared to be gaining momentum in Indian Punjab.

In addition, LeT is also believed to have established contacts with Maoists and Naxalites as well as separatist groups in north-east India. The Maoists help LeT agents cross the Indo-Nepal and Indo-Bangladesh border and also find hideouts. In return, LeT pays them huge amounts and sophisticated weapons. Mohammad Umar Madani, a trusted lieutenant of Hafiz Saeed, upon his arrest in South Delhi on 5 June 2005, allegedly confessed that the LeT was working in tandem with the Naxalites. Madani confessed that the LeT had approached the Naxals with the proposal that if they triggered blasts in the country, the LeT would provide them with sophisticated weapons. In addition, the LeT had offered them logistical support in penetrating the cities for their activities since it had created cells almost everywhere.

Thus, *jihad* has transnational dimensions and is a global threat and India is its special area of interest for multiple reasons. For the Pakistani establishment and army, it is the Kashmir factor, and what they consider is the unfinished business of Partition. However, for the ideologists, the unfinished agenda dates back to the centuries when Muslim rulers reigned supreme in India and yet failed to secure the kind of complete victory that Islam had marked wherever its *jihadi* armies had marched. The defeated Hindus had shown remarkable resilience in holding their own against the might of Islam. They did not fight. They accepted the Muslim rule and suffered ignominy under many fanatic rulers. Yet, only a small percentage of Hindus could be proselytized by incentives of the rulers and the persuasion of Sufi saints. Even a lesser number converted out of fear. India really marked the defeat of Islam for it had failed to replicate its template here. Thus, for the Islamic philosophy, which arose out of the Juhayman's Ikhwan, India was a legitimate target for spreading Islam as they understood. That is why so much focus and energy has been invested in India.

In Jammu and Kashmir, there has been a fortuitous combination of thwarted ambitions of a section of Kashmiri youth, and the rise of fundamentalism for the separatists and the agents of Pakistan. The politics became the façade for them to work freely without being accused of any sinister design. In fact, the political events have often found a catalyst in religion with the result that the fallout of the developments taking place in the State had spread out to the mainland with the ordinary man not distinguishing one from the other. Unfortunately, this has suited a section of the polity that had been struggling to right the perceived and genuine wrongs of history. Not visualizing the long-term consequences, this section has grown rigid in its stance. This has suited the Islamic fundamentalists since they thrive on confrontation and suffering. Having tried to understand Pakistan as a State in search of reasons and ideology to validate its existence; the army, to suffer from the compulsion of arrogating to itself the role of the sentinel of the Pakistani ideology; and, revivalism of Islam across the globe, the following chapters will try to understand the politics of the Union and the State governments and the consequences of all these elements for the state of Jammu and Kashmir when they combined.

5

Disillusioned Followers

'I knew nothing but shadows and I thought them to be real.'

—Oscar Wilde

In sharp contrast to Pakistan, India had developed sound democratic institutions which earned it the respect of the western democracies in spite of the fact that it had not only developed friendly ties with the communist bloc but also followed its economic development model. At a time when the entire world was becoming part of one military alliance or another, India, a democracy had, to the chagrin of western democracies, chosen to be non-aligned. 'Emerging into a world of established powers and the Cold War, independent India subtly elevated freedom of maneuver from a bargaining tactic into an ethical principle…The essence of this strategy was that it allowed India to draw support from both Cold War camps—securing the military aid and diplomatic cooperation from the Soviet bloc, even while courting American development assistance and moral support of the US intellectual establishment,' noted the eminent diplomat and strategic thinker, Henry Kissinger.[140]

Jammu and Kashmir, understandably, was an issue on which the world remained divided on the lines and the equations of the cold war bloc affiliations. In the wake of the events of 1947 both India and Pakistan had continued to focus on dealing with the challenges posed by the State to them—for Pakistan it was winning the battle for Kashmir in the Security Council with the support of friendly nations in the west, while India faced the challenge of how best to integrate the State and make it accept its Constitution.

During the early 1950s, when the world was literally dominated by the west, the Islamic nations of the world were too powerless and disinterested in the affairs of other countries. The power of oil had not yet been fully discovered to give them a voice in world affairs. Hence, the world opinion was largely formed by the still influential voice of Great Britain. But, it had to work hard to convince USA that because of the geo-strategic location of Pakistan, it needed to be supported by the western world in order to use it as a pivot and strategic partner against possible threat from the Soviet Union and China in the region.[141] By virtue of the occupation of the strategically located large tracts of the State of Jammu and Kashmir (Gilgit and Baltistan), Pakistan emerged as the pivot of the power structure in that region. India, by reason of not comprehending the strategic value of Gilgit and Baltistan, had made no effort to regain these areas from Pakistan during the 1947-48 war, thereby ruling itself out from playing a significant and direct role in the affairs of the region. Pakistan, as we saw in the earlier chapter, seized the opportunity and exploited it to the maximum extent. Readers will recall the conversation between Jinnah and Margaret Bourke-White, the celebrated photographer-journalist of the *Life* magazine, when the former was literally pleading to be an alliance partner of USA with the pivotal position of Pakistan being the sole qualification. But in those early days, lines were still being drawn between the Cold War camps. It was only when the contours of the post-World War II order began to take recognizable shape and after the Korean War of 1950-1953, which underlined the possible threat from China, that USA decided to play a significant role in world affairs by containing the perceived threat from the Soviet Union and communist China in this part of the world and in turn prevent the recurrence of yet another world war. Pakistan, which had been pleading to be included in the western alliance suddenly became its vital strategic partner. Once again, the phantom Great Game had come alive. But in those early days USA was still not convinced that accession of Jammu and Kashmir to Pakistan would be a just solution and was more inclined towards encouraging the State to become independent with the security guarantee from the western countries.

The Pakistani approach to grabbing Jammu and Kashmir changed when Sadar-i-Riyasat Karan Singh decided to dismiss Sheikh Abdullah from the office of Prime Minister in 1953 and put him behind bars. Till then it had been depending upon the Security Council Resolution for plebiscite and covertly extending monetary and material support to those members of the National Conference who had been expelled from the party. Among them, Ghulam Mohiuddin Karra[142] was a leading figure, though not as influential as Sheikh Abdullah, but who appeared to be challenging Abdullah's primacy in the party. The intelligence agencies of Pakistan had decided to extend support to him and his group in the hope of destabilizing the State. He had been put under arrest by Sheikh Abdullah, but upon Sheikh's dismissal Prime Minister Bakshi had released him from detention hoping that he might be won over by him. But Karra was too far gone into his association with Pakistan to take the olive branch. At about the same time, Mirza Afzal Beg too had been released and with his release, the equations changed. In 1955, Beg had established the Plebiscite Front[143], and with pockets of support in south Kashmir, Pakistan found that 'Karra was no longer a winning horse…' Even though they maintained 'contact with him and…[assisted] him financially', it's greater support was given to Beg and his Front.[144] Thereafter, it became easier for Pakistan since the combination of Abdullah and Mirza Afzal Beg was much more formidable than any alliance Karra could have forged. Thus, the Plebiscite Front, became the perfect façade for the Pakistani agents, particularly in Anantnag and the rest of south Kashmir.

Meanwhile, Sheikh Abdullah languished in detention though, in deference to Kashmiri ethos, the successor of Sheikh Abdullah, Prime Minister Bakshi Ghulam Mohammad, remained considerate and pragmatic towards Sheikh Abdullah's wife[145], who was allowed to often stay with her husband in the rest house where he was detained. In fact, she was not subjected to any checks that visitors to the prisoners have to undergo. This had resulted in not only messages passing unhindered to the detainee but also a free run for the family members.[146] Later, taking advantage of this decency and liberty, the Kashmir Conspiracy[147] was born which the Indian agencies succeeded in exposing before material difference could be made and were in an advanced stage of proving it in a court of law when the Government decided to withdraw the case.[148] In the meantime, when Prime Minister Bakshi had decided to free Sheikh Abdullah and confront the consequences, he succeeded in demonstrating the waning influence of Sheikh Abdullah among the people by two successive street confrontations in short duration; the second one being the historic celebration of the Republic Day in 1958.[149] It is unfortunate that though Bakshi proved his superiority in swaying the masses over his mentor, in the end a combination of circumstances, and his acts of omission and commission, marginalized him.[150] This, as subsequent decades proved, allowed not only Sheikh Abdullah to make a comeback but also created an atmosphere conducive for the separatists and the pro-Pakistani elements. In this, not a little help was rendered by human failings in which, first Jawaharlal Nehru and later Indira Gandhi played significant role.[151]

Looking back at the sequence of events, it is apparent that after having enjoyed power and then losing it to be incarcerated for a number of years, Sheikh Abdullah had probably acknowledged the futility of continuing the conflict with the Indian State to create an autonomous Jammu and Kashmir, with guarantees from the Western powers, and which also enjoyed equidistance between India and Pakistan. It is also significant that the 1971 Indo-Pak war had not only humiliated Pakistan but had also, in a way, demonstrated the hollowness of the Two Nations theory. The Sheikh too had read the signals and he acknowledged as such[152] and responded by sending signals of his reconciled position to the Government of India.

Wajahat Habibullah, in his book, *My Kashmir* claims that Kashmiris were shocked by the humiliating defeat and surrender of the Pakistan Army that followed the 1971 war. An Army and a country that could not hold its integrity against India was likely not capable of winning freedom for the Kashmiris! It is also possible that earlier, before Nehru's death, the widely reported emotional reunion of Sheikh Abdullah with Jawaharlal Nehru, his travelling to Pakistan and Pakistan-occupied-Kashmir to see and contrast the difference between the lives of the people on both sides of the Line of Control, and then getting the news of the sudden demise of Nehru had brought about a change of heart and, therefore, Abdullah was amenable to a new arrangement with Government of India. It can also be conceded that Indira Gandhi, once she had established herself as the tallest leader in the subcontinent, embarked upon the mission to complete her father's unfinished Kashmir business. Whatever the reasons, the fact was that Sheikh Abdullah returned to head the State government but, unfortunately, rule it like a family business. The only person within the government and Congress to express reservations to the accord was Dr Karan Singh, who suggested that as a measure of checks and balance, at least, the Congress party, which was making way for the return of the unelected government, be made an equal partner in power sharing so that those who opposed secessionist elements and championed the cause of India did not feel abandoned.[153]

The fact of long years in power, combined with the reality of the post-1953 generation having little reason to hero worship Sheikh Abdullah, was to open a new chapter in the State. When he was politically rehabilitated in the mainstream, Abdullah inherited the same legacy of electoral politics that he had bequeathed while holding the elections for the Constituent Assembly that had doubly ensured that his opponents were kept out of it. Unfortunately, the general elections for the State Assembly in 1967 and 1972 had not enhanced the credibility of the Congress party either and once again the opponents were kept out by means fair or foul. To his credit, however, the Sheikh succeeded in restoring the credibility of electoral process when elections were held in 1977.

Earlier, the accord had been struck after prolonged discussions between G. Parthasarathy and Mirza Afzal Beg. The reason for delay had been mainly because Sheikh Abdullah had been adamant on returning to the pre-1953 constitutional statuses, when he was the Prime Minister of the State, with a Head of the State being elected by the members of the State Assembly. It took a lot of convincing to make him acknowledge that much water had flown under the bridges of rivers Jhelum and Yamuna and that the country would not accept any roll back of the erosion of the State's integration through the Article 370. With the deal sealed, the Congress Chief Minister, Syed Mir Qasim resigned and the party extended support to the accord by supporting Sheikh Abdullah as the new Chief Minister. At that point in time, he had neither any support in the Assembly nor was he or any member of his cabinet, members of the Assembly. He had to govern with the outside support of Congress. It was this incongruous situation that brought his supporters and relatives to the corridors of power. He, however, broke free of the shackles of Congress in 1977 when the house was dissolved under a cloud of controversy and elections were held. By then, Indira Gandhi had been ousted from power by the electorate in 1977 and Sheikh Abdullah, realizing the possibility of rule by anti-Congress forces a reality, had built his bridges with the Janata Party, the new party in power in Delhi. Reacting to the development, Congress had withdrawn support to his ministry and staked its claims. The Governor, however, decided to follow the advice of the Chief Minister and dissolved the House, calling for fresh elections. By then Abdullah had opened his cards and the National Conference re-emerged to win the polls. For the next five years, he once again ruled like he had before. His supporters hero-worshipped him once again for being the *baba-e-qaum* (father of the nation). However, this image and its celebration did not last long.

The realization of an uncomfortable truth often comes without warning, and when least expected. But few could have imagined that an English film made in Hollywood and financed by the Libyan Government of late Colonel Mummar Qaddafi[154], would lift the veil of heroism and trigger an unrest that would degenerate into armed unrest in the Valley of Kashmir. The unrest is more than three decades old now, with no signs of its coming to an end even if it appears to have been abated. This is a cause for concern since the average life of uprisings in India is no more than fourteen years. It was in 1985, after Sheikh Abdullah's son Farooq Abdullah had taken a firm control of the government as chief minister that the movie, *Lion of the Desert,* was screened in Regal cinema hall in Srinagar. Among those watching it intently were young men from various quarters of the city. The strong man from Libya, Colonel Qaddafi, had for long been a thorn for the mighty power of USA and CIA.

It was believed that the CIA had made numerous failed attempts to assassinate him and yet he had continued to grow stronger. In popular Muslim perception, and among many from the developing countries, he, along with the Palestinian liberation leader Yasser Arafat, was perceived as a hero. In the late seventies, he had decided to have a world-class movie made on the life of another Libyan hero, Omar Mukhtar, who had led a rebellion against the Italian occupation of the lands of Libya in the first half of the twentieth century. A popular and genial teacher and preacher, Omar Mukhtar had gradually evolved as a champion of his people who wanted their lands vacated by the foreign occupants. His struggle began in 1911 and continued till 1931 when he was tried by the Italians for treason and hanged in the presence of his people in a camp. Prior to it, Mukhtar had been made offers of compromise and collaboration by the Italians in return for power. He had chosen martyrdom instead. The movie, released in 1981, was a commercial failure for obvious reasons though it was very well made and the legendary actor Anthony Quinn played the memorable role of Omar Mukhtar.

But that day of 1985, three years after Sheikh Abdullah's demise, this innocuous looking film in Srinagar had an electrifying effect as it touched the raw nerve of the youth that had begun to feel disenchanted. The most affected consisted of the young audience and their reaction soon snowballed into a movement. At first, slogans of '*Sheikh Abdullah, murdabad*' were isolated but they soon spread, first, within the cinema hall and then outside, where they caught others, and soon, all billboards having posters of Sheikh Abdullah, were pulled down, torn and burnt. Among the young men, the first to raise his voice was Yasin Malik[155]. The screening of the movie was hastily withdrawn but it had already caught the imagination. Comparison between Sheikh Abdullah and Omar Mukhtar was inevitable—both were teachers who evolved as leaders of their people, articulating their aspirations, giving hope and igniting self-belief. But the comparison ended there. While the Libyan leader had refused to compromise and rejected the offer of power, Sheikh Abdullah had finally succumbed to the temptation of power. According to the judgment of this new generation, by entering into an agreement with the then Indian Prime Minister

Indira Gandhi he had not only betrayed his ideals but the Kashmiri people as well. The new generation of Kashmiris, born after 1947, instantly accused and judged him guilty of betraying their cause. With increasing unease, the youth saw the stark contrast between one who had courted martyrdom and the other who not only sold his soul for state power but, in due course of time, had also promoted his sons and son-in-law, thereby betraying and compromising the objectives of the struggle for Naya Kashmir that he had authored and championed![156]

A few weeks after the screening of the movie, Yasin Malik is said to have procured a video cassette of the movie and screened it for a friend of his. Their instincts of sub-nationalism realized that it put into contrast the two freedom fighters and also, in their opinion, outlined the magnitude of the great betrayal of the Kashmiri cause. That friend was among the first to pick up arms against the State and was to transform from being Syed Mohammad Yusuf Shah to Syed Salahuddin,[157] the head of Hizb-ul-Mujahideen, as well as the chairman of an alliance consisting of anti-India militants by the name of United Jihad Council. Before the spark of rebellion was ignited, he had already been influenced by orthodox Islam and had been radicalized to the extent that he would often be seen advocating *hijab* for the women in the university. This rise of orthodoxy in the Valley was not sudden but a part of a historical process in which the modern transnational jihad played the catalyst. Kashmir had begun to feel the heat that was generated by the deal that had been struck between the Royal House of Saudi Arabia and the Mullahs in return for the fatwa to use violence at the Kaaba to free it of the Juhayman followers in 1979.

Scholars may wax eloquent about the composite culture of Kashmir that gave space to others, but orthodoxy has always lurked behind the liberal eloquence, waiting for an opportunity to assert itself and contribute to the making of the *dar al-Islam* or the land where the law of Islam prevails. The history of Kashmir, since its Muslim rulers, has been replete with short periods of liberal administration and bonhomie among the Hindus and the Muslims, only to be followed by longer periods of persecution of the Hindus leading to another era of either their conversion or exodus. After each such period, those remaining in the homeland have clung to the hope that the shared and composite culture will prevail and help them tide over the difficult times. The periodic sunshine in between the clouds only strengthened this belief. Moreover, who would want to leave the homeland or surrender his faith unless all the other doors are found closed? In modern times, the only period that gave the Kashmiri Hindus respite in the Valley was the rule of the Sikhs and the Dogras. This period is not known for persecution of the Muslims either, though it must be said that even in Lahore during Maharaja Ranjit Singh's rule, an attempt was made by the Sikh Governor to stop the early morning azaan of the Muslims on the pretext that it disturbed the non-Muslims, but it was tactfully and quickly snubbed when brought to the notice of the ruler. But it must also be added that particularly during the Sikh Rule, the Kashmiri Muslim was treated harshly which was more due to the contempt in which they were held by successive rulers, including the Afghans. It is in this light that Khalid Bashir's claim in his book *Kashmir: Exposing the Myth Behind the Narrative*, that beginning with the Sikh rule to the third Dogra ruler Maharaja Pratap Singh in 1891 the number of Muslims to have migrated from Kashmir was 1,12,000, appears vastly exaggerated and motivated. How Bashir arrived at this figure is debatable. However, it must be added that because of the famine of 1876-1878[158]—caused by a combination of inclement weather and corrupt and inefficient revenue officials—a large number of Kashmiris were lost to migration as well as famine-related deaths leading to the dwindled numbers of Muslims in particular.

The fault lines, so dominant in the narrative of Kashmir, have been the feature of all countries and societies that have undergone conversion by the influence of coercive or persuasive powers of the new religion under the patronage of the state. Islam has been criticized for professing to be the religion of peace when it was so only selectively, and certainly, wherever and whenever it has been in a minority, it raised its stock by preaching and practicing it as such, but as soon as it becomes a majority and harbors political ambition, it morphs into the power that, it believes, has been chosen by God to purge the lands of the infidels. It is then that the cycle of a brief period of liberalism is followed by a longer period of forceful assertion of its principles of certitude, primacy and finality. It is a remarkable coincidence that countries following Islamic law are the only societies in the modern world that have remained unaffected by the ideals of the French Revolution and insist upon having their societies ruled by the religion-dictated laws that were enunciated in the seventh century CE. It is this insistence from which the orthodox draw their strength. It was this that infused a new dynamism among the Muslims of the Indian subcontinent after the First World War—the fall of the Ottoman Empire to be precise. In the Valley of Kashmir, the past few centuries, and particularly the nineteenth century, had seen the subjugation of the Muslims. Under the Afghans, numerous indignities were heaped upon them with common religion failing to give them protection and security from atrocities and contempt of the Afghan victors. Yet Kashmiri historians do not blame the Afghans for the migrations that occurred then, but when the Valley was brought under the rule of the Sikhs and Dogras, they found it oppressive, cruel and vindictive. In hindsight, the truth, it is suspected, is that they found it galling to be under the yoke of 'infidels' and hence their memory played truant and transferred the atrocities of the Afghans on to the non-Muslim rulers. It was late in the first quarter of the twentieth century that their gradual awakening began and was soon fanned by the British for pursuing their own geo-strategic interests. This awakening owes much to the last two Dogra rulers of the State since they offered liberal stipends, scholarships and various incentives to acquire modern education.[159] It is not without significance that the awakening in the Valley was led by a person who was very well versed in modern education and yet was a good scholar of the Quran and an excellent orator, capable of appropriately quoting from the Muslim Holy Book for each occasion and situation. It was a shrewd combination of these two gifts that made Sheikh Abdullah the leader that he became.

After establishing his credentials and following among the ordinary Muslims of the Valley as a Quranic scholar and a Muslim leader, Sheikh Abdullah had responded to the secular call of the leaders of the freedom struggle and gained their confidence and support when he rechristened the Muslim Conference as the National Conference.[160] Thus, he enjoyed the privilege of having the best of both the worlds. His influence with the national leaders is best illustrated by the special constitutional position that he secured for the State of Jammu and Kashmir, much against the wishes of not only many stalwarts of the Congress but also Pandit Jawaharlal Nehru who alone bears the albatross of special status for the State around his neck.[161] Article 370 was designed for allaying the fears of the people of Kashmir—who constituted 95 percent of the Muslim population—that at some future date India might turn into a majoritarian State. Sheikh Abdullah made no bones about this as he repeatedly demanded a constitutional guarantee for them in a Hindu dominated India.[162] It is unfortunate that the more guarantees he extracted from the Government of India the more ambitious he became in securing a completely independent status for himself and the State. It was the crossing of this red line that finally forced Prime Minister Nehru's hand. After his dismissal, all the forces functioning in the State not only realigned but also came out in the open. The Plebiscite Front of Mirza Afzal Beg became a force with the support of Sheikh Abdullah. It also provided Pakistan's covert operations a perfect cover and a platform. A little later, how Sheikh Abdullah, Beg and the Plebiscite Front were emasculated by Sheikh Abdullah's successor Bakshi Ghulam Mohammad is history. However, the fact that it only required a combination of moral courage and public support to achieve what he did, proved what a responsive and determined government could achieve and how the demands of Sheikh Abdullah were a ruse to perpetuate his hold over Kashmir. The gains thus secured were consolidated by Ghulam Mohammad Sadiq and the jury is still out if his successor Syed Mir Qasim frittered away those gains, when the Parthasarathy-Beg Accord came into existence, to pave the way for the return of Sheikh Abdullah.

When Sheikh Abdullah returned to power in 1975, much had changed in the Valley. It was 'indeed very different from that to which he had returned from Aligarh some four and a half decades ago. In 1931 when Sheikh Abdullah's Muslim Conference first saw the light of the day, the State possessed a handful of university graduates whose potential prestige was, accordingly, very great indeed. Men like Sheikh Abdullah, G. M. Sadiq, Chaudhari Ghulam Abbas and Mirza Afzal Beg were members of a very small elite group. Leadership came naturally to these men. By 1975 university graduates in Jammu and Kashmir had long ceased to be a rare phenomenon. What was becoming relatively scarce however, were the suitably and adequately remunerated graduates. Advances in education, as has happened in many other developing countries, had not been accompanied by a corresponding expansion of opportunity.'[163] During the interregnum, much economic progress had been made because of Indian exertions but, again, like many other developing countries, the rich had become richer, the poor poorer and the not so rich had become more disgruntled. It is not known if Chief Minister Syed Mir Qasim had realized the undercurrent of resentment and frustration of the youth in the Valley as well as the Jammu region, but it can safely be said that he must have recognized the inherent contradiction between the aspiration of the Kashmir region on the one side and Jammu and Ladakh on the other. In these circumstances, it was a totally unrelated incident that once again brought into focus the unpredictability and volatility of the Kashmiri temperament.

A few days before 17 May 1973, someone discovered the *Book of Knowledge: Children's Encyclopedia* written by Arthur Mee, in the library of Government College, Anantnag. The book, in fact, was a 1911 publication brought to the Valley by a mission school and had somehow found its way to the college library. There it had rested all these years. Alastair Lamb opines, 'It was a work of monumental blandness, which did, however, contain a drawing of Prophet Mohammad to whom Archangel Gabriel was dictating portions of the Holy Koran. Somehow this came to the notice of the Islamic establishment who were not slow to point out that such representations constituted blasphemy.'[164]

Students of Anantnag set the ball rolling when they started demonstrating on 17 May in protest, blaming the Government for permitting that obnoxious publication to see the light of the day! The irony was that the students were demanding that the author of the book that had been brought to the Valley in 1911, be hanged!

They blamed the Indian government for permitting the import of such a book and the British, who, in the first place were responsible for the publication. The protests and violent demonstrations soon spread to the rest of the Valley and in Srinagar, the police had to open fire in which four lives were lost. All this happened despite the Indian authorities promptly banning the book.

Any perceptive person could have seen that the book was the trigger and not the cause of the trouble. It also produced preposterous reaction from across the border and Prime Minister Zulfikar Ali Bhutto, despite the Simla Agreement of 1972[165], waded into troubled waters by criticizing India for not holding the plebiscite in Kashmir. Simultaneously, in an apparently unrelated event, at the beginning of the winter in November, the students once again took to the streets for renaming the women's college in Kashmir University after Jawaharlal Nehru.

The protests continued for about two weeks when Sheikh Abdullah too entered the fray after Mirwaiz Mohammad Farooq had lent public support to the Pakistani Prime Minister's demand about plebiscite. Sheikh Abdullah categorically condemned the Pakistani Prime Minister and reminded him of the dangers of meddling into the affairs of Jammu and Kashmir. Thus, on the one hand, Syed Mir Qasim found out the magnitude, unpredictability and the volatility of a plethora of problems that could rear their head without a warning, and on the other, Abdullah's intervention sent a signal to Delhi that perhaps it was time to mend fences.[166] It was ignored that Abdullah was the author of the process that had rendered formal plebiscite redundant and hence his statements were meant for the protection of his own legacy. It would be recalled that when the Constituent Assembly of the State was convened, only the subjects of abolition of monarchy, land reforms and accession to India were discussed as long as Sheikh Abdullah had remained the Prime Minister. It was because of his initiative that the issue of accession to India was endorsed thereby rendering the plebiscite superfluous. Soon after the Anantnag incident and Sheikh Abdullah's statement, began the talks between Parthasarathy and Beg at one level and Indira Gandhi and Abdullah at another.

The irony cannot be lost that when Sheikh Abdullah was first handed over the reins of the State, he had no constitutional mandate to become the Prime Minister; now too when power was handed over to him, he was without any constitutional mandate. After the resignation of Syed Mir Qasim, it was with the support of the Congress party that he became the Chief Minister. The others to be sworn in with him—Mirza Afzal Beg, Thakur Devi Das and Sonam Norbu—too were neither associated with the Congress nor were members of either the State Assembly or the Legislative Council. The news was viewed with skepticism within the country and in Pakistan it caused hysterical and vitriolic reaction and was unanimously termed a 'sell-out'. Prime Minister Zulfikar Ali Bhutto observed '…this man who set himself up as the champion of democracy was now about to become a Head of a Government dominated by a party Congress, to which he did not belong, in an Assembly of which he was not even a member.'[167] Bhutto also claimed that the Accord had violated the terms of Simla agreement and the UN requirements for plebiscite.[168] Soon China too had joined in the Pakistani chorus but it remained empty words and gestures at best.

Opposition to the accord was not just from Pakistan. Within the State, Mirwaiz Moulvi Farooq[169] in the Valley, representing the traditional opposition to Sheikh Abdullah, was particularly distressed and vocal. He was convinced that it was to preclude forever the possibility of plebiscite. The terms of the Accord 'disappointed many in Kashmir, particularly its youth, for it offered far less autonomy to the State than it enjoyed in 1953…However, the majority accepted the Accord as the only pragmatic course left open to them following the post 1971 changes in balance of power in the subcontinent.'[170] The State unit of the Congress too was unhappy. Midway through the Assembly life, the members of the Congress party had been asked to give up power and adjust to life without it. No one knew what kind of relationship would be developed with Sheikh Abdullah. In Jammu, the reaction of the Jana Sangh against it was violent in its demonstration. In Delhi too the party was extremely vocal and again called for the abrogation of Article 370. In other words, the gains of the past two decades seemed to have dissipated with the return of Sheikh Abdullah.

The new innings of Sheikh Abdullah did little to inspire the Jammu region since the Cabinet also included Mirza Afzal Beg, an unapologetic champion of plebiscite, founder of the Plebiscite Front and responsible for changing the demography of the Udhampur district, and political lightweights like Thakur Devi Das and Norbu who could not be expected to stand up to the two wily stalwarts who had, at some point, vehemently championed the cause of autonomy bordering on independence, and plebiscite at another. But worryingly, in a major deviation from his earlier tenure, this time Sheikh Abdullah opened himself up to charges of nepotism when he put his sons and son-in-law in government positions. Indeed, age had mellowed him and he was now susceptible to the influence of his family and also desired to secure a political future for it. Congress too had depended upon his growing years but for entirely different reasons.

Delhi had believed that because of his old age, Sheikh Abdullah would now become pliant and amenable to its influence. But it soon discovered the bitter reality of his intransigent nature. Indira Gandhi had believed that with long years in the wilderness Sheikh Abdullah would have realized and accepted the futility to battle against India and that by now the Indian state had demonstrated enough mettle and resolve with the comprehensive victory over Pakistan and the creation of Bangladesh out of East Pakistan. This apparent invincibility had convinced her into believing that Abdullah would join the Congress and help dissolve the remains of hostility in the Valley towards India. But Indira Gandhi and the Congress were in for a shock when he suggested that instead of him joining the Congress, the Congress unit of the State should dissolve itself to merge with the Plebiscite Front and then merge with the National Conference.[171] In other words, he was determined to liquidate the achievements and legacy of Bakshi Ghulam Mohammad and Ghulam Mohammad Sadiq and begin again from where he had left in August 1953.

Emboldened, by April 1975, he also began to talk about the merger with Pakistan-occupied-Kashmir in none too subtle suggestions about the separate identity of the State even though the Accord was only to readjust the political balance within the State.

Friction between Delhi and the State began to grow over the issue of reviewing the central laws made applicable after Sheikh Abdullah's dismissal in 1953. No sane person can argue that this arrangement would encompass only reviewing each and every law because this would have meant that the Centre admitted that Sheikh Abdullah was dismissed on the wrong pretext and that it was unjust, unlawful and unconstitutional, and that extension of central laws to the State was a mistake. Moreover, Delhi could not have agreed to review each and every law concerning the relationship of the State with the Centre. The degree of constitutional integration that had been achieved was the outcome of years of patience, diligence and wise application by the Government of India of the provisions provided by Article 370. Sheikh Abdullah wanted to undo all that with the same tactics that he had so effectively used against Pandit Jawaharlal Nehru when negotiating Article 370 and the Delhi Agreement.* What he had not countenanced for was that now he was dealing with Indira Gandhi who had grown so strong after the Indo-Pak War of 1971 that the opposition stalwart and bitter critic of the Congress, the Jana Sangh leader, Atal Behari Vajpayee,[172] had literally called her an incarnation of Goddess Durga.[173] Not surprisingly, the euphoria of the Accord soon evaporated.

The situation was further complicated by the fact that his own party was absent to support him in the Assembly. He had, therefore, fallen back on his own family members, consisting of his wife Begum Abdullah, sons Farooq and Tariq, and son-in-law Ghulam Mohammad Shah. This had raised the questions about nepotism and corruption in the same manner as Bakshi Ghulam Mohammad had faced. The administration was far from being

---

*In 1952, Prime Minister Jawaharlal Nehru and Sheikh Abdullah, Prime Minister of J&K State entered into an agreement that became the basis of the State's relationship with the Union of India. It clearly demarcated the boundaries between the powers of the State and the Union. It was agreed that the residuary powers of the Union, unlike other States, were to be vested in Jammu and Kashmir. The State was also empowered to determine the nature of privileges that it could extend to its citizens. The powers of the President of India were to be extended to the State but the State was allowed to have its own flag which would not be a rival to the national flag etc.

efficient and law based. Not surprisingly, in an ironic turn of events, it was called 'democracy through intimidation and terror'.[174] Clearly the trust and confidence between the State and the Union had not been strengthened; on the contrary, the recalibration had adversely affected it. The Accord had actually failed the moment Sheikh Abdullah assumed power. To the chagrin of Indira Gandhi, the stripes of the tiger had refused to fade. But unlike the impatience and arrogance demonstrated by him in his earlier tenure, this time he was patient and bided his time though he continued to run down the post-1953 period as a 'dark patch of 23 years'. He also described the growth and development of that period as 'an artificial and exhibitionist show of false progress...The people of the State refused to yield before the temptation and the terror that followed August 1953.'[175]

In the meantime, an internally besieged Indira Gandhi had imposed Emergency and as a consequence, she lost the General election of 1977. But this interregnum of two years had been used by Sheikh Abdullah to consolidate his hold on the administration and reviving his agenda of extracting full autonomy in subjects other than the three surrendered by the Instrument of Accession. When Morarji Desai became the Prime Minister, one of the motivating factors for his government was to demonstrate that it was different from Indira Gandhi's. In another significant development, just after the exit of the Congress from the national scene, the party withdrew its outside support to Sheikh Abdullah and asked the Governor to administer the oath of office of Chief Minister to Mufti Mohammad Sayeed. But the Governor L.K. Jha, on the advice of the Chief Minister, promptly dissolved the Assembly. Thus, the attempt of the Congress to oust Sheikh Abdullah from power was thwarted by the Governor who accepted the recommendation and imposition of President's rule, even as he was in a microscopic minority in the Assembly. The decision of the Governor can be debated but what cannot be contested is that it heralded an era that does not seem to end.

The truth was that much had changed since Sheikh Abdullah had begun to articulate the discontent and aspirations of the Kashmiris against the Dogra rule. He had given a dream to his people when he was an outsider to power and had launched a movement against the Dogra rule, first with the tacit understanding of the British and then the open support of the Indian National Congress. He had enjoyed unprecedented success in giving shape to the dream that people shared with him as Prime Minister of the State. But then carried away by his own success and convinced of his own invincibility, and unmindful of what the people of Jammu and Ladakh wanted, he had gone a little too far in creating a separate identity for the State. When ousted from power and put in detention, he was still in a position to rally his supporters; in fact, with the façade of his loyalty to India gone he was even more aggressive in his demands and, therefore, blurred the lines between autonomy and separatism. Thus, when he once again assumed power, the expectations of his loyal supporters had been unrealistically aroused.

In contrast, Delhi was hopeful that long years in wilderness would have taught him not to be unrealistic in expectations and that he would carry on from where Qasim had left and use his influence to integrate the Valley with the rest of the country, emotionally and constitutionally. Unfortunately, this did not happen. He believed that the Accord was an acknowledgement that Delhi had erred in dismissing and arresting him in 1953 and aggravated that error by legitimizing the rule of Bakshi Ghulam Mohammad. Parallel to this development were the facts that fed on the theme of separate and independent identity. The new generation was not satisfied by the hide and seek game played by Delhi and Srinagar and wanted more and immediate, tangible results. By now, the Palestinian leader Yasser Arafat had emerged as an acknowledged hero of resistance in the Muslim world. The Kashmiri Muslim youth had seen how the Palestinian youth was embracing death at the hands of Israel in its struggle to free Palestine, knowing well that Israel was backed by the might of the United States of America. This martyrdom had begun to look attractive to them. It was a new phenomenon that the world neither fully understood nor knew how to deal with. In the early years it was something to be admired from a distance since the culture of this extreme sacrifice was never a part of the Kashmiris. In fact, the struggle for freedom by the Palestinians had divided the world into two: for the west, it was a terrorist movement where the youth were indulging in futile killings and rejoicing in a diabolical death wish; but in the developing world, Yasser Arafat was feted as a hero who had taken on the might of the USA-backed Israel. This situation was further complicated by the fact that India was lending all the moral support to him and his Fatah organization. It was the beginning of a new era in which the narrative of 'one community's terrorist became another community's freedom fighter'.

To add to the frustration of the Kashmiri youth, Sheikh Abdullah's government was under the dark shadow of corruption and nepotism. The youth was in a state of aimless drift and feeling restless when *Lion of the Desert* was released in Srinagar. Thus, their protest was unorganized, leaderless and with no specific purpose except to announce the total disillusionment with Sheikh Abdullah. It was the beginning of a chain of events where Delhi's concept of a strong India was at loggerheads with the State's need to enjoy considerable freedom in the conduct of their affairs, and the people's desire to have a corruption-free government and fair participatory democracy.

6

The Flawed Federalism

'My general plan would be to make the states one as to everything connected with foreign nations, and several as to everything purely domestic.'

—Thomas Jefferson

The decade of the 1970s had marked the highs and lows of Indian democracy. Before its advent, in 1969, Prime Minister Indira Gandhi had clearly drawn lines between her brand of politics and the one that was being practiced by the old guard of the Congress. She had neither the patience nor the persuasive skills of her father, and hence, was impatient of any obstruction in her path. When she became the Prime Minister, much of India was still under the cloud of prolonged drought and famine-like conditions. Shortages were rampant, economy sluggish, the media unsparing in criticism and the stalwarts of her party stalling her every move to shake the system and bring in change. This clash between the old and the new hampered progress but she was determined to shake off the old guard to achieve success. In 1969, she got the opportunity and was successful in achieving her goals but in the process, she had concluded that if the regional leaders were allowed to grow too strong, they would develop the ability of obstructing the policies of the union government. During the last years of his life, even Jawaharlal Nehru had become the victim of this phenomenon. Indira Gandhi was determined not to allow regional leaders becoming too big for the central government's comfort. This, however, is a challenge peculiar to democracies like India where there is no cap over the tenure of the leader or tradition whereby the leader's failure extracts instant retirement. Not so in India and many other developing countries.[176] This explains why they repeatedly fail to encourage new leadership and ideas and also why the same mistakes are repeated over and over again and democracies degenerate into dictatorships.

Post-Nehru, apart from the economic challenges, Indira Gandhi faced a number of political challenges, not the least being the yearning of the States to break free of the control exercised by the Centre. She had also observed the resolve of the centrifugal forces to weaken the Centre[177] so that their relevance became more significant. These forces had also sought to make her a captive of their supposed strength without taking into account her greater determination to keep them at bay and to be her own captain. The abolition of privy purses of the erstwhile princes and the nationalization of the banks, along with the breakup of the Congress[178], were steps in that direction. By having V.V. Giri elected as the President of India, in opposition to her own party's candidate in 1969[179], she had demonstrated that her critics, and those in the party who tried to hem her, were out of touch with the people. Abolition of privy purses established her credentials as someone who would stand up against the established privileges, and the nationalization of banks made her an instant favorite of the middle, poor and the underprivileged classes. Buoyed, in March 1971, she called for general elections and secured a landslide victory, decimating her opponents, particularly the right-wing politicians and sympathizers who had united and offered a free market solution to the economic sluggishness of the country.[180]

Having conquered the domestic challengers, she now prepared herself to face the external enemy and forces that propped it. In Pakistan the ruling establishment, consisting of Punjabis and Pathans, treated the population and leaders of Bengali-speaking East Pakistan with contempt and scant respect, dismissing them because of their dark complexion, shorter height and marginal role in the armed forces in comparison to the Punjabis and Pathans. The arrogance of Pakistan's establishment had not only created rebellion in East Pakistan but had directly affected India with millions of refugees taking shelter here. In fact, the exodus from East Pakistan that was witnessed was described as 'Biblical' by correspondent Sydney Schanberg of *The New York Times*! Moreover, Pakistan had also been using East Pakistan's proximity to the north-eastern states of India to foment armed rebellion by providing arms and financial aid. Thus, opportunity came for India out of the events that took place in the then East Pakistan. They were the outcome of the myopic policies of the rulers of Pakistan and no outside agency had any role to play, though India took full advantage of Pakistan's internal strife without losing any moral ground.

Running parallel to this narrative was the anti-Hindu sentiment among the Islamic fundamentalists against the East Pakistani Hindus who had chosen to stay in their homeland and this resulted in periodic anti-Hindu riots.[181] Adding to the woes of the East Pakistani Hindus was the determination of Pakistan to impose Urdu as the only official language, ignoring the majority of the Bangla-speaking East Pakistan.[182] After both Liaquat Ali Khan and Nawab Nazimuddin[183] had opposed Bangla by February 1948, Mohammad Ali Jinnah himself had flown into Dhaka, and told a public gathering, 'Let me tell you in clearest language that there is no truth that your normal life is going to be touched or disturbed as far as your Bengali language is concerned…but let me make it clear to you that the State language of Pakistan is going to be Urdu and no other language. Anyone who tries to mislead you is really the enemy of Pakistan. Without one State language, no nation can remain tied up solidly together and function.'[184]

As a result of this confrontation of differing opinions, many Hindu heroes of East Pakistan became victims. A notable victim was Dhirendranath Datta. 'A deputy leader of the Congress parliamentary party in Bengal Legislative Assembly, Datta had joined the Constituent Assembly in 1946 and opted for Pakistan in 1947.'[185] He is said to have been offered the post of first Chief Minister of West Bengal in the divided state of Bengal in India but he declined because he did not wish to leave the land of his ancestors and chose to stay in East Bengal that became East Pakistan. When the Pakistani Army cracked down on the university students and intellectuals, Datta was one of the first martyrs to the cause of Bengali and Bangladesh. Apart from being Hindu, his main fault was that he had opposed Jinnah's diktat about the national language and is considered to be the harbinger of the Bengali language movement and a precursor of Bangla nationalism.[186]In order to suppress Bengali in any way they could, the Pakistani leaders went to the extent of banning the entire works of Rabindranath Tagore![187] The fact was that while a sizeable Hindu population had crossed over to West Bengal in 1947, millions had remained there in the hope of the madness passing over. After all, for centuries, the Bangla Hindus had lived peacefully under the Muslim Nawabs and rulers. Soon, however, it was found that it was a false hope. It is estimated that between 1946 and 1958 about 4.1 million Hindus had arrived in India and 1.2 million more arrived between 1959 and 1971. According to Abul Barkat, author of the book *Political Economy of Reforming Agriculture-Land-Water Bodies in Bangladesh*, between 1964 and 2013, 'around 11.3 million Hindus left Bangladesh due to religious persecution and discrimination'.[188] One of the biggest influxes of Hindu refugees was in 1969 which added to the burden on already beleaguered Indian Prime Minister Indira Gandhi and the fragile economy of the country.

A new dimension was added to this influx when Pakistan held the first General Election on the basis of adult suffrage on 7 December 1970. Held in the background of strong linguistic chauvinism in East Pakistan and led by Sheikh Mujibur Rahman's Awami League, the people of East Bengal refused to accept Urdu as the official language. The language riots that followed had indeed taken many lives.[189] Thus when the elections were held the results sent shockwaves through West Pakistan as Awami League won 160 of the 300 National Assembly seats, all of them from East Pakistan. However, General Yahya Khan, the military dictator, refused to allow Mujibur Rahman, the leader of the Awami League, to become the Prime Minister and imposed martial law in East Pakistan.[190]

On the night of 25 March 1971, the Pakistani Army carried out large scale executions of professors, teachers and students in Dhaka and Khulna, in its bid to exterminate the intellectual class of East Pakistan. A majority of them were Hindus. The resultant wave of refugees this time was too big for India to handle, with millions crossing the border to enter India. According to Indira Gandhi's close confidante P.N. Dhar, by the middle of June there were 5,330,000 Hindus as opposed to 4,43,000 Muslims and 150,000 from other groups in the country.[191] Thus the pressure on India was intense. It was in the wake of this humanitarian crisis of unimaginable proportion that Indira Gandhi evolved and emerged not only as a great leader but a fearless stateswoman who refused to be cowed down by the bullying tactics of President Richard Nixon. She undertook a whirlwind tour of world capitals, enlisting support and appraising the world leaders of the humanitarian misery that had crossed her borders and tried to arouse the world conscience.[192]The Pakistani Army was systematically driving out Hindus from East Pakistan so that the Bengalis lose majority in any future elections. It was a tool to 'destroy [the] Awami League as a political force by getting rid of 'the wily Hindu' who was supposed to have misled simple Bengali Muslims into demanding autonomy.'[193] Sensing the marshalling of anti-India forces, Indira, in the process, not only explained the predicament India was in, but also signed a Friendship Treaty with the USSR to checkmate any attempt by western powers to militarily come in support of Pakistan. Thus, she not only appropriated the moral high ground but also, in the eventuality of war with Pakistan, ensured that even staunch allies of Pakistan like the USA and China could do little more than make noise.[194]

Ultimately the policies of Pakistan in its eastern wing were to be the cause of its humiliating defeat, disintegration and creation of Bangladesh from the erstwhile East Pakistan, and also, the trauma, of more than 90,000 Pakistani soldiers having been taken prisoners. With this, Indira Gandhi had reached her zenith, both in her contribution and popularity.

For four years she had proved that she had a perfect sense of timing and had her hand on the pulse of the people. It was in the summer of 1972 that she first betrayed signs of losing control and failing to outsmart her adversaries. The jury is still out if the Simla Agreement, signed between her and Pakistani Prime Minister Zulfikar Ali Bhutto addressed Indian interests, despite the fact that

India had the upper hand because of the 90,000 odd Pakistani prisoners. But as subsequent decades have proved, the Agreement did little to resolve the dispute over Jammu and Kashmir though for some years Pakistan remained quiet. In her defence it can be said that few treaties ensure any permanent solutions and the fact that the Simla Agreement resulted in peace for nearly three decades is a measure of some success. But what is missed by Indira Gandhi's detractors is that the Treaty firmly shut its door to any third-party intervention, including the Security Council. Pakistan had to concede that the dispute between it and India over Kashmir is a bi-lateral issue and would be dealt as such. What, however, is not debatable is that never again could Indira Gandhi achieve the kind of success that had become a habit with her since 1969. The wheels of her policies began to come off from 1973 onwards with the economy becoming even more sluggish than it ever was, with attendant unemployment and its consequence, widespread discontent. Bank nationalization had yielded limited dividends. With the closed fists loosening, the banks were soon swamped by widespread charges of corruption in sanctioning of loans. In a parallel development, the green revolution had raised the expectations of the farmers but the fact was that with the farming class constituting of small land-holders, a majority of the farmers still needed a job to feel secure in life. The agricultural production and productivity had increased, giving the country much required food security but, in contrast to the new breed emerging in the urban areas, it did relatively less for the farmers by way of satisfying their aspirations for a meaningful life. The trade unions too had become restive with the salaries not matching the rising cost of living and the working conditions nowhere near the international standards. Thus, every section of the society was getting restive with even those who had benefited from the social welfare schemes of Indira Gandhi not being happy. The '*garibi hatao*' (remove poverty) and '*roti, kapada aur makan*' (food, clothing and housing) slogans had lost their sheen.[195]

Things came to a head in 1974 when the railways unions went on a 20 days strike. With 17 lakh workers participating in the strike, it was the largest in the world. Indira Gandhi believed that there was a bigger conspiracy behind the strike and saw political motives in it, and, therefore, decided to strike back with an iron hand. Thousands of strikers were put behind the bars, dismissed and their families thrown out of the railways quarters they lived in. The cause of concern for Indira Gandhi was not just the strike of the railway employees. Everyone knew that the working conditions, long working hours against internationally accepted norms, needed urgent reforms but with George Fernandes, a political maverick, leading the unions, she smelt a bigger conspiracy. The electoral rout of the opposition at her hands still rankled among the opposition leaders and they were convinced that it was the invisible ink on the ballots rather than the greater credibility of Indira Gandhi among the voters that defeated them. Thus, they seemed to be resorting to any means to strike back at her. Strangely, Indira Gandhi too had begun to feel insecure and had begun to depend more and more on a core group of advisers.

The year 1974 passed with the opposition becoming more and more desperate and belligerent, and Indira Gandhi becoming suspicious even of the shadows within the Congress. This gave rise to dictatorial tendencies which, in turn, allowed the coterie around her to wield undeserved and unbridled powers. This explains the extra-constitutional rise of Sanjay Gandhi and the hijacking of the government.[196] In the midst of this tug of war came the Allahabad High Court verdict on 12 June 1975, for the State of Uttar Pradesh versus Raj Narian. Prime Minister Indira Gandhi was unseated for violating the provisions of the Representations of People Act, 1951. It was held that her election agent Yashpal Kapoor was a government servant. Most political commentators believe that it was this verdict that led to the imposition of the Emergency later that month on 25 June. However, the judgment had acted as a catalyst for the dictatorial tendencies that had been emerging since 1973 when the tepid economic growth began to expose the hollowness of the socialistic and populist slogans of the Prime Minister. She was convinced that the country would be destabilized if she were to be removed from the scene, and hence, she was indispensable for the security of the country. The preceding period was also marked by innuendos and vicious attacks on her character. No small role was played by Jayprakash Narayan, popularly known as JP, who in the wake of the successful agitations of the students in Gujarat and Bihar had come out of his retreat from active politics and had launched an agitation that bore the romantic name of 'Sampooran Kranti'[197] i.e. total revolution.[198] To this agitation flocked not only the idealists but also opportunists and all those who had failed to make any headway against Indira Gandhi. It is believed that the maximum number of volunteers came from the students' wing of the Bharatiya Jana Sangh, the Akhil Bharatiya Vidyarthi Parishad (ABVP).

In another significant development, in 1973, Akali Dal of Punjab had passed a political resolution during its session at Anandpur Sahib. Subsequently it came to be known as the Anandpur Sahib resolution.[199]It caused much misunderstanding, genuine and contrived, and many believed that the resolution had set stage for an ugly confrontation between the Government of India and the Sikhs represented by the Shiromani Akali Dal. The movement of the Akalis had always straddled the twilight zone where secessionism, autonomy and communal polarization met. Significantly, it also demanded a greater role for the states in the affairs of the country but primarily, the resolution was about the Sikh affairs and ideally, the State should not have played any role in it. Because of the politics of Punjab and the inability of the central government to declare the Akali demands as beyond the scope of the government, they being a matter of the Sikh community, and the dependence of the Akalis upon religion for their thriving, it assumed different connotations. For those who opposed the Akalis, their demand to give greater powers to the states with the view of creating a genuinely federal state was to sow suspicion in the minds of much of the country even though on a number of occasions, the Akalis clarified their position but to little avail owing to lack of trust caused by their own inability to keep religion and politics separate. Subsequently, political development lost direction with Indira Gandhi imposing Emergency[200] and the Akalis got embroiled in the hard-line posturing. The defeat of the former in 1977 did halt the dangerous tendencies that had begun to grow but the failure of the Janata Party to give a stable government increased the frustration of those who desired to get rid of the Congress and Indira Gandhi.

The return of the latter by thumping majority in 1980 added to the desperation of the opposition and, in return, made her more determined than ever to cling to power in the belief that without her the country was in danger of becoming a failed state.

Indira was also convinced that some foreign power was bent upon destabilizing India and suspected that the Akalis had become a tool in the hands of that power. She would often accuse her opponents of being the agents of CIA. The fact that by then the world knew of the periodic attempts of the CIA of America to destabilize and overthrow those regimes in the world that refused to tow its line, helped in making her credible in the eyes of her followers. India, as everyone knew, had not only followed its non-aligned course but had dared to defy the great super power in 1971. It was also a common knowledge that Pakistan, that had sustained insurgency in the north-eastern states of India, had probably recognized an opportunity in the unrest in Punjab. It was suspected that Pakistan's ISI was fomenting trouble and that the hijacking of a plane to Lahore in 1981[201], was its handiwork. A section of the Sikhs was said to have become tools of the enemy state. Thus, she became suspicious even of longtime party loyalists. The political environment in Delhi had indeed turned toxic as there were rumors, that a senior cabinet member was informing CIA every decision being made by the government, particularly during the crucial December 1971 Indo-Pak war.[202] But more worryingly, it was rumored that Indira Gandhi had become susceptible to superstition and the belief that her opponents were using *tantric* powers to harm her, particularly after the death of her younger son Sanjay Gandhi.[203] In reality, her opponents had found more substantial tools and causes to whittle her strength and wisdom by creating situations that forced her into committing errors. With the Janata Party experiment having failed, the opposition focused on the regional leaders and issues rather than trying to replace the Congress at the centre. This proved more successful and apart from Kerala, West Bengal, Tamil Nadu and Jammu and Kashmir, most states including Andhra Pradesh and Karnataka were lost by Congress after elections. In addition, Punjab had become restive as its grievances grew and the hotheads justified their religious history and background to adopt extra-constitutional methods.

As has been said earlier, the Beg-Parthasarathy Accord had not yielded the results that Indira Gandhi had hoped. Sheikh Abdullah had not merged his Plebiscite Front with Congress. His plan was instead to have the Plebiscite Front dissolved, revive the National Conference with the members from the Plebiscite Front and then have the State Congress merge with it! However, this difference of opinion between the State and Centre was not an isolated case. It was not even peculiar to the modern times since this was an age-old challenge in India that often-yielded surprising results. Since times immemorial, the Centre and States have struggled to maintain a balance and the best periods have been when local governments and institutions have been allowed to flourish while the Centre has remained strong. 'When united…India generated currents of vast cultural influence. When divided—as it often was—into competing kingdoms, India was a lure for invaders, traders, and spiritual seekers…whose depredations it endured and whose cultures it eventually absorbed and mixed with its own,' wrote Henry Kissinger in his book *World Order.*[204] However, there have been periods like that of Aurangzeb and the East India Company when the Centre with its imposing and overbearing manner has tried to interfere in local affairs and private beliefs with disastrous consequences. This was a lesson that was well learnt by the British after 1857 and that explains the longevity of their nearly 100 years rule in India after that.

The State of Jammu and Kashmir had extracted considerable autonomy with Article 370 but this had not deterred the Centre from finding constitutional ways of paring it down even as a section of the Kashmiri leadership vehemently opposed such changes, notwithstanding the fact that they were being carried out by an elected Government and Assembly of the State by the exercise of constitutional tools. The rest of the states had apparently been content with the relationship being determined by the Centre till things began to change when non-Congress governments came into existence in some of the states. Most fretted under the yoke of Centre and the Planning Commission till they ran out of patience in the early years of the 1980s. The opposition began to organize itself and in 1983 it held its first Conclave in Vijayawada.

> Fourteen non-Congress parties gathered to criticize the Centre for encroaching upon the powers of the States and the Centre was held responsible for economic problems of the country. In 1984, Delhi conclave was held. It was opined that the Union was only a mother organization to coordinate the activities of various States, helping them to develop. It could not act as an institution that thwarts regional aspirations because then they will find destructive modes of self-expression. The message was clear: do not treat the State governments as its branch offices. If this continued then the States would soon become just puppets dancing to the Centre's tune and unable to exist as viable territorial units. In the Srinagar Opposition Conclave, 10 non-Congress parties gathered and for obvious reasons the first subject on the agenda was the office of Governor. It was through this constitutional office that the centre tried to manipulate State politics after losing at the polls. It was suggested that Governors must be appointed by the President on the basis of a panel forwarded by the State Governments concerned and articles 200 and 201 should either be suitably amended or else deleted.[205]

At about the same time other factors had begun to influence politics. A scholar has noted, 'Arising out of India's diversity, the "fissiparous tendencies" of regionalism, ethnicity and communalism have long been sources of social unrest. In 1983, they converged in eruptions of violence that left 4000 dead in Assam and a cauldron of discontent in the Punjab.'[206] While the tensions were born out of regional and ethnic conflict, soon they began to assume communal contours that led to bloodshed in various parts of the country, including Hyderabad and Uttar Pradesh apart from Assam. Also, '...a more significant development was the attempted religious simplification of India's multidimensional self. A religious construct of Indian identity was vigorously promoted in politics and an effort was made to subsume all other identities, which Indians traditionally had, under an all-consuming religious framing of politics. With this massive simplification arose terror as a mode of quotidian politics. Concurrently, solid conditions for the rise of Hindu nationalism were also created,' commented another scholar in the magazine, *India Today*.[207]

The politics of Indira Gandhi were characteristically different from the liberal politics of her father and 'scholars and long-time observers of Indian politics have noted how unprecedented Mrs. Gandhi's political moves in Punjab were. Nehru, for example, never used religion in politics, keeping thereby the temperature of Indian public sphere in control. In the 1960s, Nehru had refused to allow the formation of a new Punjab state on religious grounds, despite Master Tara Singh's fast unto death. Punjab and Haryana were eventually reorganized into linguistically, not religiously, distinct States.'[208] She, on the other hand, tried to play fire with fire and thought that the forces of communalism could be destroyed by a force of even greater ferocity. The results were disastrous in Punjab.

Her son, Rajiv Gandhi, who succeeded her committed a greater folly when he used his three-fourth strength in Parliament to overturn the Shah Bano verdict of the Supreme Court.[209]

> The other quite awkward and controversial religious moment in politics in the 1980s arrived when the Supreme Court, pronouncing its judgment in the Shah Bano case, questioned both the validity of the *sharia* for Muslims as well as the competence of Muslim jurists and religious leaders to interpret the *sharia*. A secular court, having no expertise in centuries-long traditions of Islamic jurisprudence, showed incredible modernist hubris in condescendingly looking down upon believers. Caught in a Muslim furore and understanding it little, Rajiv Gandhi used his three-fourth majority in the Lok Sabha to overturn the court's judgment.
>
> Thereupon, all hell broke loose. Viewing it as Muslim appeasement and smelling an opportunity for anti-Congress and anti-Muslim mobilisation, Hindu nationalists began to rouse large numbers of urban Hindus. In an attempt to pacify those so mobilised, the Government then allowed the re-opening of the Ram Janmabhoomi temple, a contested Hindu-Muslim site that had remained padlocked since 1948. Riots broke out and the Hindu nationalists launched a movement to 'liberate' Ram Janmabhoomi and purge it of Muslim symbols, including the mosque at the heart of the site.[210]

The success of the Hindutva politics ushered in a new era as it genuinely created an alternative to Congress at the Centre.

In Jammu and Kashmir though, the political narrative was both of a natural progression and then of sudden twists and turns. There was peace in the 1970 and the early 1980s, 'in spite of the State's history of disputed status and the mix of different languages and religious groups. Developments and popular sentiments in the area during this period show that democracy was at least possible and valued. Democracy in Jammu and Kashmir seems to have aided integration and the nation building process in India. Forces disloyal to the nation-state project may always be present in a functioning democracy, but the available evidence suggests that they attracted little support and that the level of violence can remain low as long as political freedoms remain intact and institutions are fairly stable.'[211] In contrast to Punjab and Assam, religious identities were not per se responsible for the conflict that escalated in the 1980s though this theme had been present in the Kashmir politics since 1931 when for the first time in recent history violence broke out against the Kashmiri Hindus in Srinagar. Events in the State during the beginning of the 1980s were not the result of religious polarization though when the events unfolded, religious identity had become a handy tool for the political parties.

The undesirable direction that the State took is entirely due to the stubborn insistence of Sheikh Abdullah to wish away the two decades long process of the integration of the State to the Union. He, therefore, needs to bear much of the blame for what happened in the State. The irony about him is that though in public life he was a champion of human rights, 'this commitment was not always reflected in the internal structure of [the] National Conference.'[212] This was also true of inter-regional affairs and the rights of the three regions of the State. The period of the 1970s and 1980s had also witnessed rapid economic development but it had also increased the debt burden of the State since much of the development investment was the result of the Centre providing the funds. But the development had also brought accusations of inefficiency and corruption in its wake, with corruption charges focusing on the Abdullah family. It was said that the family had used the situation to its advantage and amassed wealth. In addition, there was a heightened level of expectations of the people. Thus, when Farooq Abdullah inherited the party and became the Chief Minister after the death of Sheikh Abdullah in 1982, he found that he had taken over 'a State apparatus that can be characterized as quite large but unfortunately thoroughly soft. The administration saw its function as serving patron-client relationship rather than carrying out development projects'.[213] Thus, Farooq Abdullah inherited a popular but internally a fractured party. The process of fragmentation had begun in 1978 when Sheikh Abdullah's longtime associate Mirza Afzal Beg was expelled from the party. He had begun to oppose Sheikh Abdullah's attempt to promote his dynasty instead of building a political apparatus that was democratic and firmly rooted in local organization. By then Sheikh Abdullah was already seen to be looking for a successor within the family.

The search was focused on Farooq Abdullah but Sheikh Abdullah was not sure since he was considered too young and inexperienced though he had already come into the limelight during the *Moe-i-Muqqaddas* crisis. He had also been sent to Pak-occupied-Kashmir when parleys were on between Beg and Parthasarathy to gauge the Kashmiri sentiments on the other side of the LoC. The other choice was Ghulam Mohammad Shah, popularly called 'Gul' Shah, his son-in-law, but he was considered too arrogant and eager to assume leadership. Thus, the divide was already there within the family when Sheikh Abdullah chose Farooq Abdullah as his successor who promptly removed Ghulam Mohiuuddin Shah from the post of party General Secretary. He was the nephew of Gul Shah and therefore carried weight bigger than he would otherwise do and his removal was considered as a direct challenge to Gul Shah. With the party in divide, the outsiders were waiting exactly for such a moment to strike after the death of Sheikh Abdullah.

In 1977, when Sheikh Abdullah was running the government with the support of Congress, the latter had tried to pull the rug from under his feet by withdrawing the support and demanding of the Governor, L.K. Jha, to swear-in Mufti Mohammad Sayeed as the Chief Minister since Congress still enjoyed the majority in the House. In response to the Congress move, Sheikh Abdullah recommended dissolution of the House and holding of fresh elections. To the disappointment of Congress, the Governor chose to accept the advice of his Chief Minister. This decision of the Governor decisively changed the history of the State. It is a matter of conjecture as to what course the State might have taken if the Governor had not dissolved the Assembly and accepted the contention of the Congress. Not many would have faulted him since the Government existed because of the Congress support and that was the norm accepted of the Governors. Moreover, the National Conference, revived by Sheikh Abdullah after becoming the Chief Minister, did not actually exist in the Assembly when he became the Chief Minister. Subsequent elections of 1977 brought the National Conference back with a resounding victory. The loss of power because of Indira Gandhi's misplaced faith in Sheikh Abdullah and subsequent defeat in the polls still rankled the Congress.

Some observers have said that they believed that Farooq Abdullah was receptive to the idea of cooperating with the Congress but the truth is that like his father he too professed one thing and practiced something else. To this day, he has enjoyed multiple identities at different times, depending upon the time and place as well as the situation. His partisans, like A.S. Dulat, the former RAW head and in-charge of Kashmir affairs for Prime Minister Atal Behari Vajpayee, continue to claim that Farooq is essentially a nationalist. Moreover, he had established his nationalist credentials when he was part of the delegation sent to UN when Pakistan had pushed hard for putting sanctions on India for human rights violations. His role was deeply appreciated not only by the Narasimha Rao government but his opponents too. It is, therefore, difficult to explain why he persisted with the Resettlement Bill[214] knowing well that it would alienate Jammu, particularly Hindus. No doubt, the Bill had been introduced by Sheikh Abdullah but Farooq had the choice of putting it in the cold store, which he did not. The Bill gave those, who had migrated from Jammu and Kashmir to Pakistan but were subjects of the State before May 1954, the right to return and reclaim their lands and property. The rift between the two parties grew because of this Bill and a parting of the ways soon happened when they could not arrive at an understanding about an electoral alliance for the Assembly elections in 1983. The result of the polls set the agenda for the coming decades and was the symptom of the problem that had been afflicting the State. Politically, nothing had really changed since the time when Sheikh Abdullah was made the Prime Minister of the State under the Proclamation of 5 March 1948. What had changed, though, was that the Kashmiri sentiment had become more belligerent and Jammu, after the early shock, had found its voice and was no more willing to be pushed. Thus began a tug of war between the two regions, in the process, one of the first victims was the electoral process which was completely subverted and subjugated to the goal of victory. In this search for victory, religious polarization came to play an increasingly bigger role. All this while, Pakistan patiently waited in the wings and prepared to reap a rich harvest.

7

Dangerous Moves

'The world is dangerous...not because of the people who are evil, but because of the people who don't do anything about it.'

—Albert Einstein

The Assembly elections in Jammu and Kashmir were held in 1983 in an atmosphere of increasing regional and communal polarization that ended up in giving a fateful turn to the politics of the State. Congress had little option but to take a firm stand against the Resettlement Bill since its main support came from the Hindu Jammu which feared that it was an attempt to influence the demographic map in favor of the Muslims. But the election was not as simple an issue as it appeared. By the time elections arrived there had been resurgence among the followers of the Jamaat-i-Islami and the forces were also realigned when support was also forthcoming from the Chief Minister who thought he could use them against the Congress in Kashmir and the Muslim-dominated constituencies in Jammu. It meant that much before the elections, violent clashes had begun to occur among the followers of both the major parties and soon they were to become endemic. It is in this context that the judgment of Chief Minister Farooq Abdullah to push through the Bill needs to be questioned, for the timing and the rising toxicity in political life was inappropriate and fraught with danger. He ignored the fact that he was the Chief Minister of the entire state and should have known the nature of the forces he was about to unleash in his State.

On 19 May, the offices of Congress were attacked in Srinagar and set on fire. The Congress obviously blamed the National Conference which predictably denied it, but in the process one thing was made abundantly clear—there were powerful enemies of the Congress in the Valley, and that the Government of India had lost much ground since the time in 1958 when the followers of Prime Minister Bakshi had worsted the followers of Sheikh Abdullah twice within a short span. One of the occasions then was the Republic Day which was celebrated with great fanfare by the masses.

But now things had changed with the Congress and Farooq Abdullah battling for survival. During the election campaign Farooq Abdullah was careful not to challenge explicitly the finality of the accession of the State but still making it clear that over the years Article 370 and the autonomy of the State had been greatly eroded, and that it needed to be restored. Indira Gandhi, on the other hand, publicly refrained from challenging the significance of Article 370 and yet could not help from championing the cause arising out of regional imbalances and emerging as the protector of the largely Hindu population of Jammu against the oppressive policies of the Valley leaders. 'Thus in 1983 Indira Gandhi, who at the beginning had set out to conciliate Dr Farooq Abdullah and bring about an effective National Conference-Congress (I) collaboration…now found that the whole issue had been so polarized that she and Dr. Farooq Abdullah stood facing each other like boxers in the ring after the first round of what promised to be a long and bloody contest.'[215]

It must be acknowledged that, apart from the political compulsions, as a matter of principle, Congress could not have been supporting a Bill that paved the way for the return of those State Subjects who had opted for Pakistani citizenship during these long decades while there were thousands of Hindu State Subjects who had been displaced from that part of the State which was forcibly occupied by Pakistan and were still without allotted lands. The insistence of the National Conference to pave the way for the former Muslim State Subjects without addressing the Hindu grievances gave a new twist to the relationship between the National Conference and the Congress and the National Conference and the Hindus. In addition to this, there was the suspicion in the minds of people of Jammu that it was a ploy to alter the demographic balance in Jammu region in favor of Muslims. The number of people who had migrated from Kashmir to the Pakistan occupied region was negligible and in contrast the number of those who had chosen to migrate from Jammu to Pakistan was substantial as was the number of those who had been forced to migrate from the Pakistan-occupied-Jammu region to the State. If all those, after so many years, chose to return then the demography and the consequent political equations too would change, thereby leaving the Hindus of Jammu at the mercy of Muslim communalists. Thus, overt communal polarization got injected in politics though, careful analysis will prove that it was always present because of the National Conference's inability to take an unequivocal view of the subject. Many commentators tend to lay all the blame for communalism at the door of the Hindus of Jammu but the politics of vendetta unleashed by Sheikh Abdullah had pushed the humiliated Hindus into the lap of the only party that was willing to stand up for their rights.

To reverse this trend, tolerant, just and wise leadership was the need of the hour which, unfortunately, was not forthcoming from the National Conference. In such conditions prevarication on the part of the National Conference was to soon degenerate into a no holds barred fight. The Congress, on the other hand, was willy-nilly sucked into a situation that forced it to espouse a cause which, in the hands of a cunning adversary was easily painted as communal.

The poll results were startling as well as paradoxical. The two political parties—BJP and Jamaat-i-Islami—that identified itself as Hindu and Muslim parties respectively, were completely wiped out. The Hindus of Jammu and the Muslims of the Valley had rejected both. While the National Conference had won 46 seats (most of them from the Valley) out of the 75 Assembly seats, the Congress had bagged 26 seats, all of them from Jammu. In reality, it reflected the outcome of the proposed but aborted the plebiscite proposal of the Dixon Plan.[216] Only three seats had been won by the Independents. While both the National Conference and the Congress professed their secular credentials, the struggle for power had transformed both to the extent that they came to represent the two faces of communal as well as regional polarization. Ironically, even in the face of this blatant communal picture, both insisted that they were secular at heart.

Another dimension, of equal concern, was the trend of increased violence and fraud. Violence, in fact had become widespread. Beginning with attacks on Congress workers and their deaths in police firing while demonstrating, violence had soon degenerated into selective and targeted killings. The symptoms had begun to emerge during the run up to the Assembly elections and boiled over in October 1983 during the one-day cricket match between India and West Indies in Srinagar. The Indian players were subjected to abuse and pelted with rubbish. The match was interrupted by protesters and rain before the visitors won after curtailment. Historian Alastair Lamb opines that the anti-Indian acts of the crowd represented powerful Muslim feelings feeding upon Muslim fundamentalism and, in his words, this clash of parties on a cricket pitch 'can only be described as the first phase of a general Islamic rebellion against the Hindu domination of New Delhi.'[217]

This conclusion, however, is challenged by another western historian, Sten Widmalm. He has pointed out that threats of violence and disruption of the North Zone Ranji Trophy cricket matches in Kashmir was present even 1978, but the situation then was different. Farooq Abdullah recalls in his book *My Dismissal* that, 'I was the Chairman of [the] J&K Cricket Association at the time [1978], and with the backing of the State Government, we had to seek the intervention of the President of India, Shri Sanjiva Reddy, and the match was played without any incident.'[218] The reasons therefore have to be found in the circumstances that must have changed between 1978 and 1983. Probably the Cricket Board and the Government of India were too optimistic and believed that the love of cricket would make the Kashmiris forget politics. They therefore added Srinagar in the itinerary of the touring side. The fact though was that the State should have been warned of this, since the Centre must have gauged beforehand that bringing international cricket to Jammu and Kashmir would be a provocation to the Jamaat-e-Islami, which was critical of the accession of the State to India and had not accepted it in 1978, as well as in 1983. But before drawing a Lamb-like conclusion of India's inadequacies, one must remember that in 1978 Sheikh Abdullah was at peace with New Delhi; Farooq Abdullah in 1983 was not, Had he been at peace, the troublemakers would not have created a hostile environment for the Indian team.

This cricket incident had international ramification and was not to be ignored by Indira Gandhi, who expressed her concern at Farooq Abdullah not taking stern action against the 'insurgents'.[219] Any serious student of political situations will know that the kind of developments that took place could not be attributed just to electoral fraud and that there was a greater import, deep rooted issues and a greater design of the perpetrators. Electoral fraud had always been integral to the State elections with the worst having taken place in 1952[220] when members were to be elected for the Legislative and the Constituent Assembly. Four subsequent elections too were seen as tainted but by the end of the 1970s, no political party had the kind of monolithic presence as the National Conference or the Congress had in the earlier decades. The situation of 1980s was, as an author put it, 'Democratic credibility had, however, begun to be undermined by electoral malpractice and institutional decline. The events in the following years would only accelerate the process.'[221]

By 1984, Indira Gandhi warned that she will not accept any antinational activity in Jammu and Kashmir. There was talk of an invasion of the State by Pakistan. A member of the Congress party went to the extent of accusing Farooq Abdullah of being a member of the Jammu and Kashmir Liberation Front which was vehemently denied by Farooq; the party member also clarified the circumstances that had led to that speculation.[222] This accusation was rather farfetched but there is no doubt in the minds of observers that the Chief Minister was guilty of political incompetence with alleged corruption charges flying around.[223] By now the State was getting unhinged as violent killings became the order of the day.

Former Governor Jagmohan has mentioned quite a few such incidents in his book *My Frozen Turbulence in Kashmir*. What began with an obscene demonstration by a few men in Iqbal Park in front of Indira Gandhi soon deteriorated into killings.

> On January 15, 1984 four supporters of the Congress Party were killed in police firing in Anantnag. Bomb blasts occurred with alarming frequency in the Valley. There were explosions at the

> time of [the] Independence Day Parade, in Srinagar's Indian Coffee House, in the house of Justice A.S. Anand, Justice of the High Court, in Palladium Cinema, in the Lal Chowk, in the University Library Block and in house of the Sessions Judge (Retired), N.K. Ganju.
>
> In those days, processions were also being taken out with telling frequency. People shouted such slogans as "Pakistan Zindabad", "Khalistan Zindabad", "Noor-e-Chashm, Noor-e-Haq, Zia-ul-Haq Zia-ul-Haq". A new slogan, "Muslim-Sikh Bhai Bhai, Hindu Quam Kahan se Ayee", had particularly sinister implications.[224]

It was the last slogan that had Indira Gandhi worried since a combination of the Kashmiri separatists and Khalistani forces, aided and abetted by Pakistan, would have made that a formidable threat for India. 'Punjab had already been engulfed by the fire of fanaticism and fundamentalism. Flames of terrorism were leaping and threatening to reach Jammu and Kashmir. The Valley was littered with dry, combustible faggots which could catch fire even by a stray spark. The entire border from Siachen downwards was in danger of getting destabilized.[225]

Campaigning had been violent not only because of the polarization of communities but because of the intense desire of the elite to win and capture power at any cost. There were widespread allegations against the National Conference of planning the rigging of elections a month before they actually took place. In May, the Congress office was attacked and set on fire in Srinagar and re-poll was ordered in two of the polling stations. In Doda, there was an investigation regarding malpractices and in all, Congress demanded that re-poll be held in eighteen constituencies. These protests notwithstanding, the political opposition and the media conceded that Farooq Abdullah and his party had emerged victorious. In other words, it was accepted that while the ruling party had emerged victorious, it had unnecessarily gone for overkill by indulging in violent booth capturing and corrupt practices. This trend was to continue in the future, but its long-term impact proved disastrous since many individuals and political groups came to believe that they were denied a legitimate chance of victory.

One of the lessons from the great epic Mahabharata is that when victory becomes the sole objective, ethics, principles and rules are the first casualty. Abhimanyu was killed in an unfair battle, when unarmed, surrounded by a group of Kaurava stalwarts. This set a chain reaction when the battle was carried well beyond the sunset, contrary to the rules of the war, by the Pandavas so as to use the power of Ghatotkach, which grew stronger with darkness; Arjuna, on the instigation of Krishna, severed the arm of Bhurishrava when he was about to slay Satayaki, Arjuna's bosom friend; the killing of Dronacharya, Bhishma and Duryodhana were similarly in contravention of the rules of war. In fact, history is replete with such examples. Similarly, if the National Conference was too strong for the Congress in the battle of rigging and booth capturing, then the Congress had to use a different stratagem. It had powerful resources at its command to act against the adversary by (mis)using the Constitutional institutions. In the process, the already fragile democratic process in the state was further dealt a blow from which recovery has only been brittle.

The critical moment in the history of the State came when Farooq Abdullah was removed from office in an operation that could well be called a coup, carried out by none else than the Governor Jagmohan. Years later, historian Sten Widmalm wrote, 'The blow that put a definite halt to consolidation of democracy and the integration of Jammu and Kashmir came on July 2, 1984 when Farooq was told by the new Governor, Jagmohan, that his party had lost its majority in the state Assembly through the defection of thirteen Members of the Legislative Assembly (MLAs), twelve belonging to the National Conference and one independent.'[226]

It is true that Farooq Abdullah's government was plagued by corruption and governance issues but then these afflictions were not peculiar to the State and Farooq Abdullah. The earlier governments too had been similarly flawed, as were many others in the country, but they at least wore the cloak of democracy. But now, for the first time, the central government had blatantly distorted the constitutional provisions to dismiss a democratically elected government of Farooq Abdullah in 1984. For this, Prime Minister Indira Gandhi earned universal opprobrium and was roundly condemned by critics at home and abroad. If Farooq was removed because of the sloth, inefficiency and corruption of his government and administration then many other governments of other states were equally guilty; and, if the removal was necessitated by his alleged secessionist policies, then his father, Sheikh Abdullah, was guiltier, and this, raises the issue of desirability of the Beg-Parthasarathy Accord of 1975. If Farooq was, what the Congress claimed he was, then the responsibility of saddling the country with leadership of dubious credentials rests with Prime Minister Indira Gandhi. She was an equal partner in crime and the defence put forward by Jagmohan is too thin to be credible. Having said that, Farooq Abdullah's inability to control terrorism and apprehend antinational forces cannot be condoned and he has to answer a lot for the situation in which the State had landed. While the Government of India can be faulted for misreading the political situation in 1975 and not following democratic norms in dealing a very testing situation, Farooq Abdullah needs to be faulted for not showing commitment to defend the integrity of the country and living by the oath of his office when the first attacks began.

There was also more between the Prime Minister and the Chief Minister. Their relations had become strained after the alliance talk between the National Conference and Congress broke down on the eve of the 1983 elections. On the face of it the Congress could not come to terms with the changed equations where the latter had been marginalized by the National Conference after it had been brought back to power by it. The National Conference had been under so much of influence of the Congress leaders before independence that Sheikh Abdullah had risked rift in the Muslim Conference[227] to rechristen it as National Conference and gain countrywide acceptability and respect. It was also because of the bounty of the Congress that power was offered to Sheikh Abdullah on a platter at a time when the National Conference had been wiped out of existence. Even earlier, after the accession, the Ruler, Maharaja Hari Singh had been persuaded to hand over the reins of power to Sheikh Abdullah even though he represented only one region of the three remaining with India.[228] It had also been seen that without the towering presence of Sheikh Abdullah, the

National Conference had been reduced to a shadow of its former self. When it allowed itself to be merged within the national identity of Congress, this view was further strengthened. Congress believed that the National Conference shared the core principles of Congress, and therefore, was its extension in the princely State of Jammu and Kashmir, just as it had Praja Mandals etc. in many other princely states before 1947. It was, therefore galling for the Congress to see the National Conference defying it. Earlier, the Congress had not tried to assert itself too strongly because of Sheikh Abdullah, and his standing in the world was of such consequence that he could not be ignored. Indira Gandhi recognized this and hence, her disappointment with Sheikh Abdullah notwithstanding, she had never attempted to destabilize him even when she rued her decision of 1975. However, she was not prepared to accept this situation with Farooq at the helm of affairs, and, therefore, his hobnobbing with opposition parties outside the State became unacceptable.

However, political reasons apart, the then Governor, B.K. Nehru[229] is convinced that there were other reasons, more personal, that were the real reason for the uncompromising antipathy that Indira Gandhi had developed for Farooq Abdullah. While Nehru is partially correct, this was not the whole story. It is a coincidence that by 1983, pronounced centralizing tendencies had manifested in her personality, but the real change occurred when Farooq decided to join the ranks of the national Opposition to her.

In May 1983, fourteen important political parties of the country, all opposing Indira Gandhi, had committed themselves to an opposition alliance headed by the charismatic leader from Andhra Pradesh, N.T. Rama Rao[230] and Ram Krishna Hegde[231] of Karnataka. N.T. Rama Rao had just led the fledgling Telugu Desam Party[232] to a thumping electoral victory in the Assembly polls causing great deal of embarrassment to Indira Gandhi and injecting a new lease of life among the political opponents of Indira. These developments took place even as the poll campaign for the Jammu and Kashmir Assembly was approaching the end part. Finding time from his hectic schedule, Farooq Abdullah had not only attended the Conclave of Vijaywada but had declared that the next meeting of the Conclave would be hosted in Srinagar. This declaration indicated that the National Conference was no longer secure in its relationship with the Congress and hence its need to look for friends other than the traditional friend, particularly in the light of the breakdown of alliance talks for the 1983 Assembly polls. Moreover, there was the possibility of the Congress being once again replaced at the Centre by an Opposition Alliance. In that case it wanted channels of communications open with any new dispensation. But sight should also not be lost of the fact that it was the first time that the National Conference had reason to oppose Congress outside the State. Another possible reason for the moves of Farooq Abdullah could be the realization that Congress was no longer the dominant political power after suffering setbacks in a number of States. Thus, he probably wanted to be on the right side of the emerging powers. But the possibility of the National Conference gravitating towards other regional parties in the hope of enjoying greater autonomy cannot be ruled out since many of them were demanding more power for the states and less interference by the Centre.

As promised in Vijaywada, an Opposition Conclave was held in Srinagar in October 1983. The theme of the Conclave was Centre-State relationship, in pursuit of which the next Conclave at Calcutta (now Kolkata) in January 1984 specially focused on the central government's attempts to remove opposition governments not only in Jammu and Kashmir, but also Tripura, Andhra Pradesh, West Bengal and Karnataka. These apprehensions came true when a few months later, N.T. Rama Rao, in spite of his popular and legislative support was replaced as chief minister. These developments, which were later followed by Farooq's removal clearly indicated that there could not have been personal reasons for the removal of Farooq. The policy appeared to be to destabilize any government that seemed to be of significant threat to the Congress led by Indira Gandhi.

But there were other political observers, and one who had watched these developments from very close quarters, namely B.K. Nehru, who insisted on the personal reasons for the rift. B.K. Nehru being the Governor of the State, must have known, but even former Indian Prime Minister Chandra Shekhar[233] saw more than political reasons for what happened in the Valley. He was also a very active participant in the holding of the Conclaves. He was of the opinion that the relationship between Indira Gandhi and Farooq was 'complicated', and the latter would often claim that he was like a third son to Indira Gandhi. Chandra Shekhar was of the opinion that Indira's liking for Farooq was because of two reasons: he was likeable and could charm others when he so wanted, and also because she must have found him useful for her Kashmir policy. What she seems to have forgotten is that his father, Sheikh Abdullah, was a genuine friend of Prime Minister Nehru and yet he was uncompromising on the question of Kashmir. There were numerous examples when he had accepted a particular proposal of the Centre only to rescind on the pretext that his colleagues were not willing to go along, or, at other times, simply because he argued, it was against the interests of the people of Kashmir. His attitude was hurtful to Nehru but he never stopped being his friend. Indira Gandhi, however, was no Nehru, as many of the Congressmen and her opponents had discovered at great cost. Therefore, Chandra Shekhar was probably correct in analyzing the relationship between her and Farooq when he commented, 'one could say that socio-economic challenges and such were not the only factors behind the tense relationship between the Centre and the State.'[234]

In contrast, former Governor, B.K. Nehru was not only more forthcoming but categorical too on this subject.

> '...the very great...I can only say enmity, that arose against Farooq and Mrs. Gandhi and Farooq...I just have not been able to explain, except for an incident which is the only thing that I can possibly think of. In the elections ('83), Mrs Gandhi had come to the State, and her final meeting was in the Iqbal Park (Srinagar). When she was addressing that meeting, a certain number of men at the back of the meeting undressed and insulted her by showing her their private parts. This is something that happened, a lot of people did not notice, but she saw it, she never mentioned it, but I have a feeling that this was reported to her as being the doing of Farooq Abdullah. And that seems to have embittered her to such an extent that she simply could not think of him remaining in office. Farooq is a gentleman; he would never dream of doing this. It was only his enemies who could, like that idiot...G.M. Shah...Farooq says G.M. Shah did it. But to Mrs Gandhi it

> was reported by Mr Sayeed and Fotedar, these petty people, looking after themselves, and she believed them. That is the only explanation I can offer for the bitterness that arose. The fact that Farooq chose to join opposition had really nothing to do with her enmity. She did not like it...she would have preferred he joined her. But that was not the real cause. The real cause was that she thought that he had organized this personal insult to her. And, to womanhood, she was a very strong feminist. An insult to her was insult to her personally. It was then the complete lack of contact started and she decided to depose Farooq at whatever cost. I refused to do that because it was not only unconstitutional but it was politically highly undesirable and dangerous. So, Jagmohan was sent to do it.[235]

This is, however, was contested by Jagmohan who has given multiple arguments to justify the events and course of action that followed. In doing so he gently side steps the outrageous incident of Iqbal Park in 1983 by saying that Indira Gandhi's rally was '... violently disturbed and indescribably indecent.' This in itself does not mean that he considered the incident of no great significance. For the discernible reader it was a gentlemanly effort to not give too much of public importance to an undeniably embarrassing incident, particularly when a female was its target. So, whatever might have caused the rupture in their relationship, Indira was convinced that 'there were strong forces, both within and outside the country, which were bent upon "encircling" India and creating permanent headache for her in Punjab, Kashmir, North-East and Tamil Nadu-Sri Lanka area...She thought B.K. Nehru had become rather old, and certain forces of destabilization were taking full advantage of the fact. About Dr. Farooq Abdullah, she was both bitter and light hearted. She talked of his boyish, inconsistent and erratic ways. She thought that he was under the influence of some crafty men, and whenever it suited him, he would whip up communal and parochial emotions and promote "hate-centre" feeling. She was particularly worried about his extraordinary friendship with Sikh fundamentalists in Punjab.'[236]

Jagmohan further claims that 'She herself told me at the end of June that if Dr. Farooq Abdullah took effective steps against the disruptionists, she would, in the totality of the circumstances ignore his many other aberrations. His crafty friends, she thought, were taking advantage of his immaturity and egging him on to adopt a dangerous course which, besides bringing Muslim and Sikh fundamentalists together, would enable Pakistan to play its own game.'[237]

Katherine Frank, however, has succinctly described the unraveling of Indira Gandhi as the decade of eighties began.

> At the beginning of the 1980s India was threatening to deconstruct. Political upheavals rumbled in Assam, the Punjab and Kashmir. Throughout the country upper castes turned on Harijans, Hindus on Muslims, Sikhs on Hindus, Hindus and Muslims on Christians, and everyone on Tribals. The inclusive, accommodating nation that Nehru celebrated in all his books—especially in *The Discovery of India*, which Indira proofread when her father was in prison—seemed to be falling apart.[238]

This period turned fatal for Indira Gandhi and disastrous for the country. India was never the same again.

The 1983 elections turned out to be the beginning of a long and definitive road to perdition. To quote Jagmohan, 'At many places a large number of unaccountable ballot papers were found. In Zadibal constituency, for example, the National Conference candidate "secured" 90 percent of the vote polled even when in the hey-day of Sheikh Abdullah in 1977 the party candidate got 51 percent votes. The State Congress Chief, Mufti Mohammad Sayeed, bemoaned "This is exactly like Bhutto's 1978 Elections in Pakistan. It has no legitimacy. It is based upon fraud."'[239] These allegations and claims should be taken with a pinch of salt for there are rules that govern rigging of elections. Any booth, where there is a genuine contest, the possibility of rigging and booth capturing diminishes since the other party will resist. This results in violence by both the sides. However, booth capturing takes place when one of the contestants is too weak to resist and paves way for the other to cast votes on behalf of others. It ensures conversion of victory into landslide and the kind of examples proffered by Jagmohan keep happening wherever the congenial circumstances converge. That is why the neutral observers commented that Farooq Abdullah need not have indulged in such malpractices. But the rancorous battle and defeat had not been taken kindly by Indira Gandhi.

It was in these circumstances that Jagmohan came to the State as its Governor and no sooner had he arrived than events began to take a dramatic turn. By 1 July 1984, the Valley was rife with rumors of political upheaval and it was widely believed that the National Conference faction led by Ghulam Mohammad Shah, popularly known as 'Gul Shah', was planning to form government with the support of the Congress. The arrival of Jagmohan was a signal to this group to prepare for the strike. Craving for power, little did the Congress in the Valley and the Centre realize that it was playing with fire, and that it would initiate a process that would, with help from forces inimical to the country, gather such momentum that it would stream roll the political life that people knew. If the charge against Farooq was related to his failure to contain the secessionist forces, then it is hard to believe that the intelligence agencies had concluded that Gul Shah was the right person for such an important job in extremely trying circumstances. It is also hard to say if the Prime Minister was ill advised or she had developed such a strong aversion for Farooq Abdullah that she cared little for the price that will have to be paid by the country. But the fact was that everyday violence of the Valley could no longer be ignored.

The rumors doing the rounds crystallized on 1 July 1984 at 10.30 in the evening, when a group of National Conference MLAs and MLCs led by Gul Shah and Devi Das Thakur informed the Governor that they had withdrawn support to Farooq Abdullah and that their faction was willing to form an alternative government since the Congress legislature Party had decided to support them. Jagmohan claims that upon being informed of the development he asked his staff to ask them to return in the morning at 8.30 a.m. but they insisted that it was an urgent matter requiring immediate action since, they alleged, there was threat to their lives and the State police was under the influence of Farooq Abdullah and his supporters. Jagmohan further claims that he appreciated their apprehension that followers of Farooq 'with the connivance of the police, hooligans and criminals would be set upon us. We would be slaughtered, our houses would be burnt and our families harmed… (further, they requested) If you would like to see us only in the morning, let us enter the Raj Bhawan premises so that we are not attacked if the news of our gathering is leaked.'[240]

Inexplicably, even after sharing their apprehension, the Governor asked them to approach him in the morning though he re-scheduled the earlier time of 8.30 a.m. to 7.30 a.m. His claims notwithstanding, the general belief among the people of Srinagar and the Valley was that as requested by them, the National Conference faction was given shelter in the Raj Bhawan for the night. Another fact that cannot be ignored is that though this group had raised the issue of threat not only to their lives but their families and homes as well, the night had passed peacefully, neither the streets were taken over by the police supported hooligans and criminals nor were their homes damaged. It cannot be argued that somehow their plan had remained a secret throughout the night since the State capital and the Valley was already rife with rumors of the impending events. Looking at the fact that later the Valley indeed went through prolonged periods of curfew, it can be assumed that the phantom of danger to life and property was vastly exaggerated as was the perception that the police would be supporting Farooq Abdullah's 'workers, hooligans and criminals'. The fact was that the little time that was there for Jagmohan that evening was used to meticulously plan the next steps. Prabhu Chawla, writing for *India Today*, described the sequence of events relating to the dismissal of Farooq Abdullah in 1984: 'The shrewd administrator Jagmohan had ordered an elaborate security bando-bast before inviting Shah to take over as chief minister. Soon after midnight on July 1, when he was informed of the defections, the governor requisitioned over 2,000 armed men from the Border Security Force (BSF), the Central Reserve Police Force (CRPF) and other paramilitary units and even alerted the army. In fact, the swift and efficient dispatch of forces from faraway places such as Madhya Pradesh and Uttar Pradesh to Srinagar was clear evidence that the Centre was taking a more than routine interest in the whole exercise. Indian Airlines obligingly disrupted its schedules and ferried in the troops in four Airbuses and two Boeings.'[241] Jagmohan obviously had a mandate to remove Farooq Abdullah and he had planned accordingly.

What followed next constitutes a watershed moment in the troubled history of the State. Partisans of Jagmohan will argue that he did what was required to be done in the circumstances. Had he not removed Farooq Abdullah from office, the State would have irreversibly slipped not only into anarchy but also into the lap of secessionists. But Farooq Abdullah as well as neutral observers believe that the act was not only illegal but also pushed the State towards secessionism—the very thing that was sought to be avoided by Farooq's dismissal. The fact that the Gul Shah-led faction approached the Governor at 10.30 p.m., and the Governor asked them to come to him in the morning at 8.30 a.m. and then finally changed it to 7.30 a.m. does raise certain questions. Foremost among them being—had he already made up his mind that Farooq Abdullah had lost the majority in the House? If it was so then what prevented him from taking immediate action, particularly in view of the apprehension that Farooq Abdullah was indulging anti-national forces? Perhaps the truth was that he had already made up his mind but he wanted to be sure that all precautions had been taken to meet any eventuality.

The logic advanced by Jagmohan to justify the dismissal of Farooq Abdullah is a blatant attempt by him to place him above the rules of parliamentary democracy. In the morning he received the breakaway National Conference faction and one Independent that informed him that they had withdrawn support to Farooq Abdullah and Moulvi Iftikhar Hussain Ansari, the leader of the Congress Legislature Party also informed him that the Congress was willing to support Gul Shah to form a new Government. Jagmohan had by then made his decision. He wrote to Farooq Abdullah, 'I am satisfied that you no longer enjoy the majority support of the Legislative Assembly and have, therefore, forfeited the right to head the Government.'[242] In the P.S. of the same letter, Jagmohan recorded, 'We have since met and discussed the matter. You advised me to impose Governor's Rule under Section 92 of the J&K Constitution and keep the Assembly in suspended animation. I shall be grateful if you could kindly send me your confirmation in this regard in writing.'[243] To this Farooq Abdullah responded in clear words that he and his colleagues of the Cabinet were of the opinion that the Governor be informed that 'democratic traditions require that the question of loss of confidence should always be tested on the floor of the House' and added that 'I would on behalf of the Cabinet and myself advise you to immediately summon the session of the Legislature so that confidence of the Legislature enjoyed by me is demonstrated...If, however, you do not want to conform to this democratic method I on behalf of my Cabinet would request you to accept our advice of dissolving the Legislative Assembly so that we go back to our people'.[244]

On the other hand, Jagmohan has all along insisted that Farooq Abdullah verbally agreed to the dissolution of the Assembly, or more precisely, this is what he believes Farooq Abdullah said. He is also adamant in claiming that after he had asked Farooq Abdullah to resign since, in his perception, he had lost the majority, he should have resigned and was rightly dismissed upon refusal. In support of his argument, he has drawn upon the authority of Sir John Marriot, a British political-historian and politician[245], who observed 'Under no circumstances is the Cabinet entitled to demand dissolution of the Parliament from the Crown.'

Jagmohan also quoted Dr Eugene A. Forsey[246] from his book, *The Royal Power of Dissolution in British Commonwealth*:

> The enormous increase in the power of the Cabinet, and especially of the Prime Minister, raises the question whether the reserve power of the Crown to force or refuse dissolution may not be one of the few safeguards against dictatorship by the "leader of the junta" wielding for the moment the power of the office. The British Constitutional system was never intended to be a plebiscitary democracy, in which Parliament exists and debates only on sufferance, under threat of dissolution at any moment by the government in office. A system of that kind has certainly no right to the title of "parliamentary government", and it may at least be questioned whether it has any right to be called democratic.[247]

However, it appears that Sir John Marriot and Dr Eugene A. Forsey are probably the last to be resisting democratic parliament's struggle to make the King a titular and constitutional head and there is no convention or tradition from the English parliament to support the contention of both Sir John Marriot and Dr Eugene A. Forsey or the actions of Governor Jagmohan.

Moreover, this assertion flies in the face of the fact that the Crown is obliged to carry out the wish of the Prime Minister even if it is not supported by the Cabinet, the Parliament or the law. A case in point is the recent case of the year 2019 of the prorogation of the British Parliament by the Queen even though the advice of Prime Minister Boris Johnson was against the express wish of the Speaker and the Parliament and later declared unlawful by the highest court. 'The court is bound to conclude, therefore, that the decision to advise Her Majesty to prorogue parliament was unlawful because it had the effect of frustrating or preventing the ability of parliament to carry out its constitutional functions without reasonable justification,'[248] the court concluded.

It was said that the Parliament could not be thwarted from performing its duty of discussing the issue at hand. In the case of Jammu and Kashmir, the Governor, rather than the Assembly, had concluded on the basis of speculation and perception that the democratically elected government had lost the confidence of the Assembly. In fact, it was the Governor who had thwarted the Assembly from carrying out its duty and had arrogated to himself the power of the Assembly. In the case of British Parliament even the Speaker had opposed the prorogation of the House on the recommendation of the Prime Minister but the Queen had gone by the book and yielded to the recommendation. The British court had ruled that it was unlawful for the executive to have thwarted the right of the Parliament to discuss the issue. Farooq Abdullah had legitimately pleaded that the House was the proper forum for testing the strength of the contesting parties.

Jagmohan also defended his outrageous decision to give a month to Gul Shah to prove his majority by making the atrocious claim that his 'majority stood proved' (presumably on the basis of the claim laid by him and judged by Jagmohan). He innocently writes 'All that I asked him to do was to convene the Legislative Assembly within one month and seek a vote of confidence within that period.'[249] The Governor had forgotten to justify why he had given a month to Shah to prove his majority when he was not prepared to give Farooq Abdullah a day to do so. He had taken care to also record in his letter to Farooq Abdullah in which he had raised the issue of summoning the Assembly and said that he would like to assure him that Shah was invited to 'form the Government subject to a written undertaking that he would *again* prove his majority on the floor of the House within one month from the date of assuming office.'[250] But this was in the 1980s, before the political class realized the threat such partisan politics caused to the constitutional structure. It took few more such brazen acts of misuse of the office of the Governor before the Sarkaria Commission[251] recommendations and Court rulings brought an end to this politics. But that was still a few years away.

What followed was the bitter harvest of the competitive politics played out by the Congress and the National Conference with the BJP egging the Congress to take a harder stand against, first Sheikh Abdullah and then Farooq Abdullah. In this vitiated atmosphere every political move was suspect and motivated and paved the way for Pakistan to trigger an era of terrorism and separatism. By now, the involvement of Pakistan was so pervasive in the State that it could no longer be ignored and hence there is serious need to understand Pakistan, its ideology and its army that seriously believes that the ultimate responsibility of defending Pakistan's borders and ideology rests on its shoulders as has been explained in the earlier chapters. In a parallel development, fundamentalism in religion had begun to occupy considerable space in the political domain which was unwittingly whetted by the myopic policies of the Congress. Fundamentalism had become visible among the Muslim youth and with beards and skull caps becoming more visible, their number appeared greater than it actually was. It was only a matter of time before the reaction was set in the Hindu society and tilaks and other external marks of Hindu identity made public appearance.

In this, no mean part was played by the ever-increasing Indian Diaspora in USA, Canada and UK in particular. It probably began with the support of the Sikh immigrants to the Khalistani elements and as a reaction the Hindus too began to flaunt their identity and began rallying around causes that promoted Hindu nationalism. It was helped in no small measure by the increasing racism in USA, forcing large number of well-placed and affluent Hindus running the IT industry of USA to search for their roots in their culture, and proclaim their identity in public. The ill-advised reversal of the Shah Bano verdict invited a massive backlash which was soon followed by the campaign to build a Ram Temple in Ayodhya and finally the demolition of the Babri Masjid. The fact was that the Hindus were ready to assert themselves after almost 1,000 years of domination of the Muslims and, in the process, rewrite history.

In the charged atmosphere it was forgotten that this was precisely the fear shared by Allama Iqbal and Jinnah that made them demand the creation of a Muslim State and finally Jinnah settled for a Pakistan without fully comprehending its contours. The right-wing politicians and assertive thinking in India were actually validating Pakistan and India was on its way to becoming more and more like the mirror image of Pakistan. The period that followed, the beginning of terrorism and separatism in Kashmir, was a testing time for those politicians who believed that a middle ground had to be identified and accommodative politics and diplomacy was the only effective and less dangerous tool for bringing Pakistan to its heels. But the Hindus had realized the great power of their political rhetoric and sensed that the BJP was not just a challenger in few of the cow-belt states but could catapult itself into power at the center as well.

8

Erosion of Democracy

'Authoritarian politicians cast their rivals…unpatriotic, or a threat to national security or the existing way of life.'

—Steven Levitsky

Neither the State of Jammu and Kashmir was what it became after 1987 nor was Pakistan so resourceful in the Valley that it could make its cells work as effectively as they worked in the following years. Almost all experts of the subject agree that the State had come to terms with democracy, even if it was flawed in the earlier years. But it had an effective and functional democracy, more so between 1977 and 1982 and reasonably effective earlier during the Bakshi and Sadiq years. As a democratic State, it was no different from other States. In fact, greater threats to democracy had come from some other states.

The virus of defections had struck States like Uttar Pradesh, Madhya Pradesh and Haryana even before the 1970s had ended, and yet no stigma was attached to their democracies. Madhya Pradesh[252] had begun the era of political defections as early as 1967 when a breakaway faction of the Congress joined hands with dissimilar parties to form a coalition government. Haryana[253] soon picked up the thread and became so notorious that it came to be known as the land of '*Aya Ram—Gaya Ram*' (here comes Ram and there goes Ram, after one of the legislators—Gaya Ram—had crossed the floor multiple times during the day). Before Bahujan Samaj Party's Mayawati (2007-2012) tenure, no chief minister of Uttar

Pradesh had completed his or her tenure; such was the attrition rate. Jammu and Kashmir never displayed such unprincipled political opportunism. As far as secessionism is concerned, Tamil Nadu[254] had threatened secessionism but only for a while though it has remained there, even if just below the surface; Punjab[255] had returned from the precipice of separatism and terror and West Bengal[256] had toyed with revolution, again, only for a while. But Jammu and Kashmir had turned out to be different because of the peculiar conditions that allowed active entanglement of Pakistan in the politics of the State, the rise of religious fundamentalism, the changing political equations, hobnobbing of the State leaders of the ruling party with new partners at the national level and the concern it caused to the Government of India. In the process it was forgotten that the special status of the State demanded that it be arguably treated accordingly, something which the public opinion in the rest of the country was increasingly reluctant to concede. But first, we must talk about the changes that had occurred in the State in the wake of the return of Sheikh Abdullah and his impact on the politics.

Political commentators widely agreed that the elections of 1977 were the fairest but, worryingly, the political discourse had begun to change because of a number of influences and by the end of 1982, the more Sheikh Abdullah's successor found himself under assault from the central forces, the more he got pushed into politics in which the religious and the separatist card played a prominent role. However, democracy kept working, but as Sten Widmalm commented, 'the fact that democracy is working may not necessarily eliminate separatist demands; but on the other hand, it remains apparent that separatist voices did not receive much support when democracy was working during the late 1970s and the early 1980s.'[257] This was a significant observation.

It is to be noted that notwithstanding the State's history of disputed status and the mix of different languages and religious groups, ethnic peace prevailed during the 1970-1980s period. Development issues and popular sentiments of the period, even like regional discrimination, demonstrated that democracy was a shared and valued aspiration. To quote Widmalm again, 'Forces disloyal to the nation-state project may always be present in a functioning democracy, but the available evidence suggests that they attracted little support and that the level of violence can remain low as long as political freedoms remain intact and institutions are fairly stable.'[258] Political freedom and functional democracy often provides room for pragmatism and sometimes brings adversaries to a closer understanding and adjustment. In this context, it is pertinent to point out that in the late 1970s, there also appeared to be a political understanding between the National Conference and a faction of the Rashtriya Swayamsewak Sangh (RSS), and by extension BJP, so much so that in 1981-82, the former supported the latter in the Jammu Municipality.[259]

This fact apart, the preceding twenty odd years had constitutionally brought the state closer to the rest of the country. It was this integration that was threatened by the Beg-Parthasarathy talks and understanding. Dr Karan Singh alone stood out as one leader in the Congress who had reservation about the Beg-Parthasarathy Accord and explained it to Prime Minister Indira Gandhi in a communication. It is very revealing that even though he was a member of the Cabinet, he was not obliged with a copy of the 'detailed formulation arrived at between G. Parthasarthy [*sic*] and Mirza Afzal Beg,...I have not received this yet (he complained)...'[260] Regardless, he made some suggestions which, if followed, could have mitigated the continued imbalance among the three regions of the State. He also suggested a program for the rejuvenation of the Congress Party for there were early signs of the sloth and decay that had begun to set in its organization, leaders and workers, even before it had made an impact in Kashmir and spread the idea of Indian nationalism. To ensure that the Party was not demoralized by the return of Sheikh Abdullah, Karan Singh suggested that an equal share in the power structure be given to it, including the post of the Deputy Chief Minister. Unfortunately, none of this happened and Sheikh Abdullah was given absolute freedom to function. As a result, when the hour of reckoning arrived, the Congress was found woefully inadequate to meet the challenge.

Karan Singh pointed out to the Prime Minister that 'It will be unrealistic to deny that the people of Jammu and Ladakh have deep reservations with regard to Sheikh Abdullah, nor is this surprising considering the historical background as well as our own public stand for 20 years after the events of 1953…and it will not only be good…but also useful from the point of view of establishing the credibility of the new Government in those regions if certain safeguards are incorporated into the package which is being negotiated with Sheikh Abdullah.'[261]

Referring to the special geographical situation of Ladakh, he said that the 'best solution would be to adopt the pattern as laid down in the VI Schedule of the Constitution for Administration of Tribal Areas in Assam. Thus, while continuing to be an integral part of the Jammu and Kashmir State, this pattern of administration will place upon the Governor a special responsibility to ensure Ladakh's rapid economic development; will make the people of Ladakh eligible for reservations in services, admission etc. on a national basis from the quota set aside for the Scheduled Tribes; and will underline and preserve the special ethnic and political character of Ladakh, including the Leh and Kargil tehsils.[262]

Karan Singh also drew attention to the problems of the Jammu region and suggested that 'high-powered Regional Development Boards should be set up for the Jammu and Kashmir regions, which will ensure that development, and plan expenditure is equitably distributed and there is no unfair diversion of resources from one region to another. This was a recommendation of the Gajendragadkar Commission[263], and in fact, Sadiq Sahib had set up such Boards, but unfortunately, they have virtually remained defunct.'[264] He also reminded that the problem of the Scheduled Castes needed to be addressed by implementing another of Gajendragadkar Commission recommendations and 'extension of Article 335 of the Indian Constitution[265] to Jammu and Kashmir. This would go a long way to safeguard the interests of the Scheduled Castes who live only in the Jammu region.'[266] He also addressed the likely political-fallout for the State and the Congress party in particular.

The truth was that the regional imbalance and the pugnacious approach towards the Dogras had remained the hallmark of Sheikh Abdullah's policy. It was there when he was inducted in the Emergency Administration in 1947 and continued to be there till he breathed his last. He had learnt nothing during his years out of power as he was convinced of the righteousness of his policy. In 1968 too when he was trying to rebuild bridges with New Delhi, he had displayed the same blind conviction of his view. According to a written communication dated 3 January 1968 to Indira Gandhi, Karan Singh apprised her of a ninety-minute meeting between him and Sheikh Abdullah when the latter called upon him. During the meeting Sheikh Abdullah asked him about his views about the current political situation and the former told him that though the then status quo was not satisfactory yet whether some people like it or not 'Kashmir is in fact a part of India' and no action can be taken without convincing the people of India. He further pointed out that 'for two decades our official policy has been an increasingly closer integration between Kashmir and the rest of India, and that a whole generation of Indians had grown up to accept this premise. Any reversal would, therefore, require the most delicate handling of public opinion in and outside Parliament.'[267] When both of them discussed the Kashmir-Jammu problem, which according to Karan Singh was at the core of the issue, it was soon clear to him that for Sheikh Abdullah, Jammu meant the predominantly Hindu dominated area that specifically did not include the Doda district. This was a blatant attempt to reduce the Kashmir-Jammu conflict as Hindu-Muslim conflict which he had been trying to do even as Prime Minister of the State through his Revenue Minister, Mirza Afzal Beg when the Udhampur district was restructured on the communal lines.

Later, in the same month, Abdullah and his family had lunch with Karan Singh and the summary of the talks relating to the affairs of the State was duly reported by him to the Prime Minister in a communication dated 30 January 1968. When the issue of the necessity of India and Pakistan living in peace was brought up by Abdullah, Karan Singh pointed out that though desirable it was absolutely essential that the former realized that 'Kashmir had over the last twenty years got inextricably involved in two fundamental concepts in this country—national integrity and secularism. There was widespread apprehension that with the secessionist forces active in other parts of the country any breakaway as far as Kashmir is concerned would result in disaster. Also, because Kashmir happens to be the only Muslim-majority State in India, any such breakaway would immediately upset the whole delicate balance of secularism that we have been trying to build up since partition. I told him clearly that the tremendous dangers involved in both these respects clearly outweighed the advantages that might be expected to accrue from friendship with Pakistan at this price.'[268]

Subsequent years saw two parallel developments that derailed the narrative of the State. On the one hand, Sheikh Abdullah came back unrepentant and oblivious to the threats of future, and on the other the fire under the communal cauldron had slowly begun to burn in the whole country. In the State it manifested itself in various forms, beginning with the Resettlement Bill that accentuated the Jammu-Kashmir, Hindu-Muslim narrative, till, in later years, the Valley was almost completely purged of the Kashmiri Pandits for whom this had been a home since times immemorial. Power games played by various entities added fuel to it. In all these years, even as the warnings and suggestions of Dr Karan Singh became a cry in the wilderness and Sheikh Abdullah and other Kashmiri leaders remained deaf and blind to the growing resentment and anger in Jammu, the RSS, Praja Parishad, Hindu Mahasabha and later BJP, continued to harp on the theme of the removal of Article 370 from the Constitution. Dr Karan Singh, as has already been noted, had brought to the notice of the Prime Minister the dangers ahead and the possible solution in 1968, but apart from cosmetics, little was done. In the meantime, even though the National Conference under Ghulam Mohammad Sadiq and Mir Qasim had decided to merge its identity with the Congress yet it did little to change the attitudes of the Kashmiri leaders. This too, time proved, was a cosmetic change since it failed to address the basic problem of Kashmir and Jammu. The merger of the two parties notwithstanding, the Kashmiri leadership remained consistent in establishing its supremacy over Jammu. In this connection, Dr Karan Singh had warned when he wrote: 'As a Congressman, I am deeply disturbed at the fact that the Congress Party in the State—in the Valley, in Jammu as well as in Ladakh—is getting dangerously isolated from the genuine aspirations of the people. If the present situation is allowed to continue, there is danger that under stress the whole structure may collapse, thus causing a setback to the national interest.'[269] As it later turned out, the warning was prophetic as it not only harmed the national interest but the party too got nearly obliterated. Thus, the fractured legacy that Sheikh Abdullah left for his son Farooq Abdullah inevitably drew him into the vortex of a conflict, hatred and division.

Sheikh Abdullah left a State where religion and the status of the region was the only dimension of polarizing opinion and sentiments. This hardly favored peaceful democratic development. Compounding the problem, he had also left weak and fragile institutions that made the State vulnerable. The period had seen many development projects being launched with growing state funds and liberal central government financial support but unfortunately, they were all victims of apathy, inefficiency and corruption. This triggered accusations of financial irresponsibility against Sheikh Abdullah, his family and his administration. Such accusations had been conspicuous by their absence during his first term. He was also accused of exploiting the situation to increase the wealth of his family. This factor contributed a lot towards diminishing his stature in public eye, particularly the younger generation, and with his personal integrity under a cloud, his aura began to fade. He was now vulnerable to attacks and criticism from every quarter and particularly the youth was vitriolic in its comments. The institutions that he left were quite large but too soft and had degenerated into patron-client relationship with the government. Apart from this, Farooq Abdullah had inherited a fractured party set up. The rot had erupted in the open in 1978 when Mirza Afzal Beg was expelled from the party after being the right-hand man and close friend of Sheikh Abdullah for more than forty years. The senior Abdullah had already embarked on the road to establish his own dynasty and in the process had become the victim of the same tendencies that were already visible in Indira Gandhi.

Farooq Abdullah tuned out to be a much more complex character than his friends and opponents had bargained for. He could be many persons to as many people; a charming individual and an astute politician; a bit frivolous at times who engaged in lofty ideals the next moment. Initially he was warm to the idea of cooperation with the Congress but the Resettlement Bill had made that impossible, leading to intense rivalry with tragic consequences. It is to the credit of both the parties that after the events following the dismissal of Farooq Abdullah, they were still able to come together though by that time other developments taking place in the State and the country had begun to adversely influence the politics of the State.

After the dismissal of Farooq's government, if Indira Gandhi had thought that the central government will be able to bring the State back on to the desired path then she was sadly mistaken. For one, Gul Shah's government, which had replaced Farooq's under controversial circumstances in 1984, had proved to be absolutely incompetent. The two years of his rule, from 2 July 1984 to 6 March 1986, were marked by frequent incidents of violence which were aggravated by the general rejection of his government by the people. Much of the period was marred by extended periods of curfew and the typical Kashmiri acerbic humor described Shah as 'Curfew Shah'.

Two years is a long period, and during these years of Gul Shah's government, multiple anti-Indian forces had taken roots in the Valley and this raises the question about the role of intelligence agencies and the central government's functioning. Saudi fundamentalism had spread its tentacles, eating away the vitality of Sufi Islam, and Pakistani agents laid the ground for the tragic events that were to unfold at the ripe time. By August 1984, Indira Gandhi was disenchanted and she expressed her concern over the inability of the Shah Government to handle the increasing level of violence. By June 1985 the rift between the Congress and Shah's faction of the National Conference had come out in the open. There were reports of increased Pakistan-sponsored insurgency in the State; worryingly religiously defined groups began to take roots in the State. Newspapers reported that Islamic organizations, like the Jamaat-e-Tulba and the People's League, had increased their recruitment of young Kashmiris in the Valley, while in Jammu, Hindu organization such as the Shiv Sena had firmly established itself.[270] On the other hand, the Soviet invasion of Afghanistan had added a new dimension not only to the internal affairs of Pakistan but also Kashmir. The Americans had pumped in huge amounts of money and arms to train Mujahideens from all over the Muslim world, particularly, Afghanistan and Pakistan. The new militant face of Islam had begun to reveal its contours and soon the Valley was flooded with Mullahs from Bihar and Uttar Pradesh. Flush with Arab funds, the Wahhabi Islam began to take roots. Kashmiri Muslims, who were never categorized as martial, were becoming emboldened though still some way away from taking up arms. But mentally, they were becoming militant in their views. As a consequence, for the first time the extremist parties had begun to polarize the people on religious lines with greater success, forcing the Congress to finally withdraw its support to the Shah Government in March 1986, after which Governor Jagmohan imposed the Governor's Rule. It was during this period that Governor Jagmohan earned a name for himself as an administrator and also earned the gratitude of Jammu for this. Before the expiry of the six-month period, Farooq Abdullah reached an understanding with the Congress under Rajiv Gandhi to share power until the new elections could be held.

What followed was bizarre. Furious at the Congress-Farooq alliance, Gul Shah declared that he was willing to make an alliance with anybody, even Jamaat-e-Islami, BJP or Shiv Sena if that helped in defeating the Congress and Farooq's National Conference in the forthcoming elections. Not content with this, he declared that 'all Kashmiris are Pakistanis'[271], a statement that firmly shut the doors of mainstream politics on him. Another bitter truth of the period was that the politics of loose alliances, Governor's Rule and increasing intervention of the central government considerably eroded democracy in the State. It needs to be recalled that during this period Jammu and Kashmir was not the only State that flirted with the idea of separatism. Punjab was getting mired in the Khalistani movement and had to be pulled back from the brink by some astute maneuvering and firm handling in the coming years. Finally, its demand for more powers to the States had been referred to the Sarkaria Commission which had been set up in 1983 and this led to laying down some basic rules that guided imposition of

President's Rule and the rights of the States. In Assam, an accord negotiated by Rajiv Gandhi with the student leaders of the agitation brought the state back into the national mainstream. Secessionist movement of the Tamils had been resolved by settling the language issue no sooner than it had raised its head in 1965. The violent secessionist movement of the Tamils in Sri Lanka, led by Liberation Tigers of Tamil Elam (LTTE), had briefly threatened to encompass the Indian Tamils too but the assassination of former Indian Prime Minister Rajiv Gandhi by a LTTE suicide-bomber had changed the course of the rebellion. But in the State of Jammu and Kashmir, forces beyond the control of local actors were feverishly working.

To all this was added the idea of alliances which is not unknown to democracies and is ubiquitous in the Indian polity. However, the kind of alliance and cooperation that Rajiv Gandhi and Farooq Abdullah hammered before the 1987 election was so cynical that even the most hard-nosed politicians found it difficult to digest. It was not even a tactical alliance since such alliances are temporary in nature and are forged to defeat a common enemy. But in the State, there was virtually a two-party system with the National Conference and the Congress vying for power. Others were merely fringe groups, who had, at best only nuisance value or were safety valves that let off the steam of secession or religious extremism. The alliance was really an 'election cartel' meant to divide the constituencies and power before the election, and was, in fact what Dutch social scientist Arend Lijphart[272] calls an extreme form of 'consociationalism'.[273] In theory it means forging of a 'Grand Alliance' to keep at bay forces that threaten to create dangerous polarizations. In Jammu and Kashmir many observers at first welcomed this alliance since it appeared to be aimed against the communal and separatist forces. But in reality, this was not the case. This 'consociationalism' had assumed such a proportion that it had virtually taken the voter out of the equation.

The voters in the Valley were quick to sense the purpose of the 'Alliance' and no sooner did it appear thana 'strike' was arranged in the Valley by an organization that nobody had heard of until then. Jamaat-e-Islami led by Syed Ali Shah Geelani[274], Abdul Ghani Lone's[275] People's Conference, self-styled 'pro-autonomy' party that advocated the coming together of all forces opposed to the National Conference and Congress, and several other Islamic groups, who came under the banner of the Muslim United Front (MUF). The voter would not have been much affected by this alignment of sundry anti-India forces but when it was announced by the Congress and National Conference that they had agreed to share seats in the 40:60 ratio it was clear to the people that they had been taken out of the electoral process. This cartelization of election was too cynical and displayed contempt for the rule that democracy thrives on competition between parties of opposing ideologies and programs and where electorate makes the final judgment.

This cynical disregard for democracy was aggravated by the fact that the Alliance was marked by distrust and both the parties took the matters in their own hands to ensure that they won maximum seats. The irony is that the local leaders were aware of the huge contempt in which the people held them for this and, at least the Congress leaders, shied away from the people in the Valley. Yet the senior leaders insisted upon securing maximum seats from their quota. Even more ironical is that if the purpose of the Grand Alliance was to keep out radical forces from the mainstream, then the plan failed no sooner had it been announced. Consequently, the Muslim United Front emerged as the main opposition of the political cartel. In their greed to capture power it was forgotten that the main component of the MUF was the Jamaat-e-Islami, which was an outspoken opponent of accession of the State, and therefore unwittingly the Grand Alliance acted as a catalyst to the simmering discontent and anti-India sentiments. A more dangerous trend was that the MUF had blurred the distinction between the politician and the religious leader. Their religious identities tinged their political ideologies, which resulted in a political party that relied aggressively on religious dogma to solve the affairs of the State. For example, Maulana Ansari, the leader of the Shia Muslims in Kashmir, was one of the conveners. A the same time, two very different shades of religious leaders, Mirwaiz Qazi Nissar Ahmad of the Ummat-e-Islami[276] and Mirwaiz Mohammad Farooq[277], the chairman of the Awami Action Committee, who opposed the more radical element of the Jamaat-e-Islami, were also among the conveners of the MUF. Of these, Qazi Nissar had publicly endorsed the accession and truly believed the State to be part of India. Mirwaiz Mohammad Farooq too was not enamored of some of the policies of the MUF and criticized the communal tendencies and advocated unity of the secular, democratic and patriotic forces of the State. In fact, at that juncture, a paradoxical situation arose with diverse elements coming together, holding on to their contrarian views and yet presenting a united face. Analyzing the situation, Sten Widmalm opines that the diversity reflected the democratic environment that allowed differences and unity to co-exist.[278] The tragedy is that this environment did not survive for long and this inability of opposition forces to unite has constantly remained a serious problem for the separatists.

It was in this atmosphere that the Valley was living when riots broke out in the Anantnag district between Muslims and the Kashmiri Pandits. Considering that the infamous communal clash of 1931 was a one-way traffic, with Pandits being the sole victims, the situation in 1986 was the first of its kind where both communities indulged in violence in equal measure. Noted social activist, writer and political commentator Balraj Puri visited the place soon after the clashes and to the surprise of everyone found no evidence of the hand of the Jamaat-e-Islami, as believed by everyone.[279] On the contrary there were suggestions that since the riots that followed the Alliance did not appear to be spontaneous, they were the result of planned rumor-mongering and were, hence engineered under a conspiracy. The suggestion obviously was that the National Conference and Congress had conspired to engineer the riots.

The environment, before the polls, was already vitiated, first by the creation of a political cartel that wanted all others to be excluded from the fruits of democracy, and then, by the increasing polarization of Hindus and Muslims in the Jammu and Kashmir regions. Surprisingly, after taking all the political steps to win the mandate, neither Congress nor the National Conference was confident of victory and hence they both went out of the way to ensure that their candidates scored big victories. As it turned out, the 1987 Assembly elections marked a crucial turning point in the history of the State. For the record, among the winners, eight were Independents and of them four belonged to the MUF. The Grand Alliance won 87 percent of the seats but yielded considerable percentage of votes to its opponents in comparison to the combined total of the Congress and National Conference in 1983 when they contested against each other. The National Conference had then won 46 of the 75 seats and Congress 26 seats with 70 percent participation of the electorate and a total of 95 percent of the seats. In 1987, both the parties secured support from 53 percent of the electorate, 87 percent of the seats, and allowed others to get 35 percent of the votes but with only 10 percent of the seats. Clearly, in 1983 the voters had gravitated towards the Congress and National Conference whereas in 1987 the electorate had spread itself across a wider spectrum of candidates. It also needs to be taken into account that the timing of the formation of the cartel had left very little time for the opposition to organize itself into an effective electoral machinery. Looking at the increased share of the radical elements within four years, it is hard not to conclude that the deliberate and myopic attempt of the two major parties of the State to keep the fringe elements completely out of the picture had only succeeded in pushing more voters towards them.

The contemptuous Grand Alliance and the system did not stop at that as there were widespread reports that even when clearly winning, they went in for rigged elections. The overkill destroyed whatever sanctity was left of the elections with Abdul Ghani Lone becoming the most high-profile victim of the nexus between those who were wielding power and those who were tasked with conducting free and fair elections.

One explanation offered is that since the gargantuan alliance was assured of comfortable victory, even before the first ballot was cast, most of the watchdogs had made no effort to keep an eye on the polls. The case of Abdul Ghani Lone is a good example of this. A former Congressman, he had drifted away and formed his own political party—People's Conference—and was a candidate in 1987 from Handwara against the National Conference candidate. He complained that the counting of votes was disrupted by Deputy Inspector General of Police, A.M. Watali who is said to have arrived in a helicopter on the orders of Farooq Abdullah. He further claimed that he and his lawyer were hindered when observing the counting which was being influenced by the DIG. Upon approaching the High Court, all that the Court did was to summon all the ballots only to do nothing, though the easiest thing to do was to order a recount. Lone's was not an isolated case and there were many more such cases. Unconfirmed reports claim that Intelligence Bureau estimated that MUF might have lost 13 seats due to electoral malpractices. Among those of the candidates who lost was Syed Mohammad Yusuf Shah who contested from the Amira Kadal constituency in Srinagar. Disenchanted with the system and already radicalized, Syed Shah became one of the most wanted terrorists from the State under the adopted name of Syed Salahaddin.

This period is also marked by a combination of failures on the part of the system. There were few watchdogs and those that were there were reluctant to act in an independent manner. Even the High Court was reluctant in addressing the complaints. The government, on the other hand, was quick in circumscribing the freedom of the opposition parties and a number of MUF leaders were slapped charges for rousing religious sentiments of the people and demanding independence from the Indian Union. The cases were filed under the draconian Terrorist and Disruptive Activities (Prevention) Act (TADA) by the same DIG, namely Watali, who was involved in disrupting the counting of votes in Handwara. *India Today* reported that about two weeks before the polling, about 600 opposition workers were arrested from areas where the MUF, Independents and other opposition candidates appeared strong.[280] After the elections various complaints were lodged but neither the Government and nor the Courts or the Election Commission took notice. The consequences were disastrous for the State and the country.

Abdul Ghani Lone, who for most part of his life was a part of the democratic system and institutions too, was finally pushed to a situation where he became one of the leading voices of separatism. His life, indeed, encapsulates the various stages of transition that the State has undergone till he was killed by assassins in 2002. Recalling his experiences of the 1987 elections, he told Sten Widmalm in 1997: 'It was this that motivated the young generation to say "to hell with the democratic process and all that this is about" and they said "let's go for the armed struggle". It was the flash point. The thought was there, the motivation was there, the urge was there, the demand was there, and the opposition was there. The situation became ripe, and then a flash-point.'[281]

Many young men joined the armed struggle, men like Yasin Malik and Yusuf Shah, the former as a young student first became disenchanted with Sheikh Abdullah, and the latter, who began as a religious fundamentalist had forayed into electoral politics before joining the armed struggle. Yasin Malik became the leader of the JKLF and Shah came to be known by the name of Syed Salahaddin, after the famed Islamic hero of the Jihads. He went on to become the head of Hizb-ul-Mujahideen, a terrorist organization based in Pakistan and also headed United Jihad Council, based in Pakistan, whose goal is to annex Jammu and Kashmir to Pakistan. This came later, but the immediate fallout of the 1987 elections was that separatism supported by terror came to be seen as an attractive option by the youth of the Valley.

In the light of these developments, it is baffling to see that Jagmohan and some historians refuse to see any relationship between the arrival of terrorism with the contemptuous discard of the rules of democracy by the Congress and the National Conference with the Centre remaining a mute witness or supporting them by its silence. In Jagmohan's case, it is also a case of partial amnesia since nowhere in his book, *My Frozen Turbulence in Kashmir*, does he acknowledge the success of democracy, in spite of some aberrations during elections, during Bakshi Ghulam Mohammad's period or faster integration of the State and emptying of the Article 370 during Ghulam Mohammad Sadiq's rule. He mainly remains focused on himself. This explains why he fails to recognize the failure of the normal political process beginning with 1983 and reaching a crescendo when the unholy alliance of the National Conference and Congress in 1987 pushed hard line political thought off the political platform. He also forgets that the electoral process of 1987 was thoroughly corrupted and devalued under his watch and though he was so eloquent about the rigging of the 1983 elections, he maintains a stunning silence about 1987.

However, he makes a very interesting remark after Yasin Malik had escaped from custody in early 1990 when Jagmohan returned for his second term as Governor, this time as a nominee of the National Front Government. Lamenting the escape, he writes, 'It might have enabled me to talk quietly to Yasin, through an intermediary officer, and point out to him and other top functionaries of the Front, the escape route from militancy to elections and the road to power through legitimate means. It might have also helped me in isolating more fundamentalists, more ruthless pro-Pakistani groups like Hizbul Mujahideen [*sic*] and Sudents Liberation Front [*sic*].'[282] While making this quixotic but hypocritical claim, he forgets that he had been the Governor of the State for a long time and yet there is no evidence of his converting any of the hard-line terrorist or even thinkers to his views or even an attempt to do that. The State and Central Government reached this stage precisely because of the efforts made by them to keep the fundamentalists away from the State apparatus. MUF had been formed with the explicit goal of gaining significant voice in the State Assembly and the poll rigging too was resorted to with the explicit goal of denying them any space. It has to be acknowledged that with doors of representation shut, the fundamentalists found the route of secessionism and terror and grabbed it to achieve their goal, in the process renouncing any future participation in the constitutional democracy. While Jagmohan has been very vocal in condemning the Governments of India and the State and the Congress and National Conference parties for their failure to administratively rise to the challenge, he has turned a blind eye to the reasons of the disillusionment of the youth and then their turning to Pakistan for support.

Often, he harks back to the early years of the 1950s and the Article 370. He has devoted one full chapter in his book as to how the terrorists and separatists began to gain an upper hand. He begins the chapter by accusing, with some justification, some political elements who propagated the misleading and superficial claim that before Jagmohan returned as Governor in 1990, the situation under the National Conference-Congress Government was not as bad as it was portrayed. His account is largely accurate but his analytical mind does not find any mention of the Alliance that was sealed, when he was the Governor, with the sole purpose of keeping all others out of, not only power but also, the Assembly. The reader does not know if he had warned the Centre of the likely consequences because the ethical chicanery of the Alliance had robbed it of all moral authority, political and individual. The state of the administration is best described as suffering from paralysis and absence of will and in the words of Jagmohan: 'A force, an administration, that surrenders neither causes nor takes casualties.'[283]

In his book, Jagmohan has given a list of terrorist incidents that heralded and marked the beginning of the reign of terror. It began with the bomb explosion in a Maruti van parked at Lal Chowk in which eleven pedestrians, including a woman, were injured. He emphasizes the fact that the terrorists had not hesitated from injuring a Muslim female as if the bomb had the intelligence of making a distinction between a Muslim female and a non-Muslim female or for that matter males. The others to be injured were Muslims and equally innocent. But the bottom line was that the Maruti blast which shook Lal Chowk on 27 October 1988 was followed by an unending series of terrorist acts. By 13 July 1989 the terrorists had gained enough confidence and support to target a CRPF bus. Two died and 10 were injured. This attack was the first of its kind. Soon afterwards, on 17 July, the Jammu and Kashmir Liberation Front claimed responsibility of the attack. It also warned of more attacks. Close on its heels Hizbullah Islamia Jamhoria made a similar announcement adding a specific warning to 'traitors'.

On 20 July an explosion took place in the ladies' restroom of the Khayam cinema, indicating that the terrorists had also enlisted females among their ranks. But the situation began to slip out of hand when violence intensified in the month of August. The fact that Pakistan's Independence Day, 14 August, was celebrated with great enthusiasm and gaiety in the Valley and a general strike was observed the next day, on India's Independence Day, clearly showed lot of planning and penetration. 15 August was marked by protest demonstrations, burning of the tricolor, and hoisting black flags instead on private and public buildings. At night the street lights were switched off and even the State Secretariat was plunged in darkness. The domination of the terrorists had truly begun.

This was followed by a general paralysis that struck the State government. Marking a huge turnaround, on 8 September, the death anniversary of Sheikh Abdullah, the greatest of Kashmiri leaders of contemporary times, all that the National Conference could do was hold prayer meetings at the heavily guarded tomb. In contrast, the terrorists celebrated it as the *yom-e-nijat*—the day of deliverance. The mighty had truly fallen! The streets no longer hero-worshipped the 'Baba-e-Quam'. The signs were ominous and manifested on 14 September when Tikka Lal Taploo, the Vice-President of the Bharatiya Janata Party was gunned down. This was an assassination of considerable consequence and is variously read by the observers of the State. This killing, in fact, gave an insight into how some of the people interpreted it and, on its basis, formulated their response.

For Jagmohan, a 'signal had been hoisted for the Kashmiri Pandit community. It was at the mercy of subversives.'[284] The JKLF put it in its press release after the assassination, 'we will kill all those who say that Jammu and Kashmir's accession to India is irrevocable; we shall continue our armed struggle.' But Taploo's killing can be explained as the purge of all those who stood by India and since he was also a BJP leader, this message was underlined. The presence of a BJP activist, who advocated total constitutional integration without any conditions and abrogation of Article 370, was practically negligible. Yet by eliminating him, the message had reverberated far and wide. His killing was also the beginning of the communal narrative in Kashmir in modern times and soon thereafter 'martyrdom day' of Aijaz Dar, observed on his first death anniversary, indicated that the rising violence and militancy had political overtones. Aijaz Dar had been killed in a firing outside Srinagar's DIG Ali Mohammad Watali's residence. Watali was considered an active symbol of state authority but ironically, about two years later, four top JKLF leaders were arrested from his brother's house. DIG Watali, readers would recall was the same person who had arrived in a helicopter to allegedly ensure the defeat of Abdul Ghani Lone by disrupting the counting in 1987. He was also involved in slapping the draconian TADA law against a number of political workers at the behest of the Alliance government. Thus, clearly, the Taploo killing and so-called 'martyrdom day' of Aijaz Dar should be read as symbolizing the violent reaction of those who had been pushed out of the mainstream political space.

These incidents soon became routine and with the political and administrative system demonstrating all signs of paralysis of will, the State began to spiral out of control. In Jammu, the Government went on as if nothing had happened and in Delhi, the Congress decided to simply hitch its fate to the bluster of Farooq Abdullah. Politically, the terrorists had succeeded in rendering the Government superfluous. It was difficult to judge if a decision of the Government was designed to help the cause of the separatists or it was the result of total confusion and stupidity. A case in point was the arrest of Shabir Ahmed Shah of the People's League in an Intelligence Bureau operation near Ramban. Ideally, Shabir should have been taken to Jammu but for reasons not known he was taken to Srinagar under the directions of Director General Police, Ghulam Jilani Pandit. Shah's detention was followed by a four-day strike in Srinagar and other major towns and a number of public buildings were put on fire. With the head of the force committing such an error of judgment, there was little hope of the situation being confronted by the lower ranks. This was compounded by the fact that 'The Deputy Commissioner of Srinagar, Pardesi flatly refused to sign the warrant of detention of Shabir Ahmed Shah. The Deputy Commissioner of Anantnag also adopted the same attitude. The Advocate General did not appear before the court to represent the State. He tried to pass on the responsibility to the Additional Advocate General and the Government counsel. They too did not appear…(soon thereafter)…A large number of paid advertisements started appearing in the local newspapers, announcing dissociation with the National Conference and the Congress (I).'[285] This makes one wonder if the ire of the separatists directed towards those Kashmiris who were associated with pro-accession forces? Was the killing of Taploo because he represented the face of accession in the Valley and not only because he was a Pandit? Why were the

National Conference and Congress's Muslim workers no longer willing to identify their political affiliations? Was it not because they championed the accession of the State to India?

The situation was alarming indeed, and it needed a strong, firm and unwavering hand to deal with it. To those used to thinking and looking at things in binaries the action to be taken was as simple as the diagnosis appeared to them. Jagmohan was guilty of allowing himself to be guided by the binary nature of the problem for it did not cross his mind that ever since the National Conference was born the Kashmiri Pandits had been its supporters and that when Sheikh Abdullah returned in 1975 their loyalties were split between the National Conference and the Congress since their loyalties had become divided between the National Conference on the one hand and the Congress and, to a lesser degree, BJP on the other. The killing of Tikka Lal Taploo was not just because he was an office bearer of the BJP. (BJP hardly mattered and existed in the Valley and was of no consequence.)But he was a representative of those who stood against the age-old narrative of the Pandits not challenging the proselytizing Islamic view of Kashmir. The anger of the militants was also vented at those who had opposed the hardliners and kept them out of the political mainstream by hook or crook. This also explains why only the supporters of the National Conference and Congress felt the need to publicly announce their dissociation with their parent party. The electoral system, as practiced in the State, had throttled their political aspirations and, in failing them, had given rise to an unending cycle of violence.

The targeted attacks also assumed symbolic meaning when on 26 and 27 October, a complete strike paralyzed the Valley. These were the days that marked the accession of the State to India and the landing of the Indian Army in Srinagar. This left no doubt as to whose hand was behind these incidents. The Valley seemed to be drifting too far away from the time when it welcomed the Indian Army as their savior and also celebrated the martyrdom of Maqbool Sherwani in the face of invaders in 1947. It was also drifting away from the conclusion of British historian Alastair Lamb that had the plebiscite been held in the early years, the memories of the atrocities of the Pakistani invaders would have made the Kashmiris vote in favor of India.[286]

On 4 November N.K. Ganjoo, the retired District and Sessions Judge was gunned down. He was the one who had sentenced Maqbool Bhat to death on murder charge under the Enemy Agents Act. Amongst all this mayhem, the Union Government pretended as if everything was normal and announced holding election to the five Lok Sabha seats in the State along with the rest of the country. Another example of pushing party interests, even as the State was slipping out of control, is the inter- and intra-party squabbles with everyone trying to gain advantage out of the confusion that had engulfed the administration. Looking at the statements of the party leaders, it was hard to believe that these were coming from alliance partners. This had percolated down to the grass root workers resulting in the Chief Minister cancelling his visit to Badgam since he was to be accompanied by his ministerial colleague Iftikhar Hussain of the Congress. This is how distrust and dislike for each other had begun to affect the village-level worker and which needed to be addressed by the leaders. Unfortunately, neither Farooq Abdullah nor the Congress leaders had either the ability or the intent to do that.

As more and more violent attacks occurred, targeting the National Conference leaders and workers, the resentment against the Accord, from them, came out in the open. Farooq Abdullah was accused of abandoning the principles of the party which had considerable autonomy at the core of its philosophy. Resignations came thick and fast even as the administration went ahead with the preparations for the Lok Sabha polls. The polls, however, turned out to be a propaganda bonanza for the terrorists and secessionists. The day of voting turned out to be a curfew day. The cities remained deserted, and villages, sleepy but tense. At night complete blackout was observed and at one polling booth a TV set was placed with a placard announcing that the first who dares to vote can take it. At another polling booth, a coffin was placed as a warning to voters. The elections in the State have always been contentious and devalued due to the partisan conduct, but this election was the first where people were forced to boycott it for fear of death. The national and the international press had a field day.

Lok Sabha polls saw the ousting of Congress from the Centre

and the United Front came into power. From Anantnag, Mufti Mohammad Sayeed, who had broken away from the Congress and formed his People's Democratic Party, had been elected to the Lok Sabha. Being a part of the United Front and in order to give Kashmir representation in the Government, he was inducted as the new Home Minister by the V.P. Singh Government. The monumental illusion about the Kashmir unrest is clearly visible in the overtly simplistic grasp and solution to the challenge. Perhaps the government thought that having the first Muslim Home Minister, and that too from Kashmir on their side, will not only help the separatists in becoming part of the Indian mainstream but also give a sense of assurance to the Muslims of the rest of the country. But what followed was the exposure of democracy as a sham. Jagmohan compares the terrorists to the eagle whose appetite for kill is whetted by success. Emboldened, they committed an act of terror that was unthinkable not only in the society of Kashmir but also Islam.

Soon after Mufti Mohammad Sayeed had become the Home Minister, on 8 December 1989 the terrorists stunned the nation by kidnapping his daughter Dr Rubaiya Sayeed. For five days fear and gloom enveloped the people till five top terrorists—Hamid Sheikh, Sher Khan, Javed Ahmed Zargar, Mohammad Kalwal and Mohammad Altaf Butt—were freed. When the kidnapping happened, 20 prominent organizations condemned the act as un-Islamic. These included some religious men and scholars who were in Pakistan, including Maulana Fazal ul Rehman who was Chief of Jama'at-i-Ulme Islami and Kashmir's Mirwaiz Maulvi Farooq. The drift of the diabolical plan of the terrorists became public when the Chief of the Pakistan-based Jammu and Kashmir Liberation Front, Amanulla Khan, issued the threat to kill Dr Rubaiya if the demands were not met by the Government. Chief Minister Farooq Abdullah was of the opinion that though the Kashmiri terrorists had kidnapped a woman and taken her hostage, the Kashmiri culture would not allow them to carry out the threat since that would cut off their support in the society. The central Government however, put pressure on the Chief Minister to concede the demand. During those tense days, the Indian Home Minister ceased to be the Home

Minister of India and as father devoted all his energy and attention to securing the release of his daughter. Ironically, this was one time when Farooq Abdullah advocated a hard line and argued that a woman will not be harmed due to the pressure of the society. But finally, the safety of a VIP individual had taken precedence over the affairs of the State and the terrorists triumphantly walked free to the tumultuous welcome of the people. Governor Jagmohan has been unequivocal in condemning the State Government for being weak kneed and suffering from paralysis in his book, little realizing that many years later, as a Cabinet Minister of the Government of India under Prime Minister Atal Behari Vajpayee, the country would once again succumb under pressure and choose the freedom of passengers of Indian Airlines 814 flight in Kandahar after its hijacking in December 1999 and he would be party to that decision.[287]

The success in the kidnapping case acted as a tonic for the secessionists and the frequency and incidents of acts of terror increased manifold. Apart from bomb blasts and shooting, banks were looted and individual targeting too intensified. On 25 December a constable of the Armed Police was shot and then the communal angle surfaced with the killing of Prem Nath Butt, a noted journalist from Anantnag on 27 December. Many more such incidents began to be reported with greater frequency and were now interspersed with acts of arson. The targeting of those who were with the police or were ex-servicemen, as also the random shooting was clearly meant to discourage people from cooperating with the state machinery and creating general terror to erode the authority of the State.

The situation as it was emerging was just the kind of moment that Pakistan had been working for since 1953.

9

The Winter Chill

The traumatic moment becomes encoded
in an abnormal form of memory.

—Judith Lewis-Herman,
From Domestic Abuse to Political Terror

The autumn of 1989 had been ominous and the frenzied pace of events proved overwhelming. With winter, Chillai Kalan[288] arrived to settle down as the never-ending chill. No one anticipated what was to happen even as it tore asunder lives, destroyed centuries-old relationships and rewrote the history and culture of Kashmir. The people were prepared for an uneasy life which might be occasionally threatened but not for the upheaval that was to take place. Consequently, the snow that fell froze, and continues to remain frozen for the Pandit community; the icy winds have never stopped blowing for the Muslims either. Not only had the colors of maple leaves changed, as they do every season, but a good number of Muslims of Kashmir, even if briefly, morphed into hostile and coveting neighbors. The events that unfolded were all the more distressing and tragic since they happened at a time when the citizens had the protection of a constitution and there was no Sultan Sikander Shah[289] to torment and unleash terror, and yet, one of the biggest waves of Pandit exodus in post-Afghan history struck the Valley that year. The Valley has since been very nearly purged of them.

The warnings and targeted killings had begun in the month of

March 1989and everyone had the foreboding of the dark events that were to follow; but they continued to believe that like a bad dream they would pass, as they had passed on many earlier occasions. On 14 March 1989 a bomb blast claimed the first life of a Kashmiri Pandit when Prabhawati of Chadora tehsil was killed in a blast in Hari Singh Street in Srinagar. This was approximately seven months after the first blast had rocked Srinagar in July 1988. This blast had been very different since soon after the incident, it was common to see the conductors of the buses drawing the attention of the commuters with shouts of 'Sopore, Handowar, Upore'. In broad daylight aspiring militants were being solicited and invited to travel to 'Upore', meaning across the border!

The recruitment of militants was no longer a clandestine affair; it was being conducted in broad daylight, openly and on public roads. One can accuse the local police and intelligence of complicity, and hence turning a blind eye, but it is not known what the central intelligence agencies made of this and how they reported it to their superiors. Farooq Abdullah was still the Chief Minister and Jagmohan the Governor, but it is obvious that the former was suffering a series of mini paralytic strokes and the latter was content biding his time, in the hope that he might get a second term as Governor. Subsequently, after Rajiv Gandhi was ousted from power in 1989, Jagmohan was quite vocal in his criticism of the former Prime Minister. The reams of papers that he has written in later years, and has gone on to add, in his *My Frozen Turbulence in Kashmir* would have found universal approbation only if he had resigned in protest at the lackadaisical manner in which Rajiv Gandhi's government was dealing with an ever-deteriorating situation and ignoring his warnings and advice. His memoirs are remarkable for the complete absence of warmth and communication between him and his Chief Minister. The contours of their frosty relationship were more in the nature of adversaries ever since he had removed Farooq Abdullah from office in 1984 and that constrained their ability to cooperate for the good of the State.

Finally, he wrote an open letter to Rajiv Gandhi on 21 April 1991, long after he had failed to secure a second term with the Congress and after a very brief but disastrous second term in

1990 under United Front, when the relations between the two had soured. It was then that the bottled-up bitterness and rancor poured out in the open and he reminded the former prime minister that in April 1989 he had written, 'The situation is fast deteriorating. It has almost reached a point of no return. For the last five days, there have been violence, arson, firing, hartal, casualties, and what not. Things have truly fallen apart. Talking of the Irish crisis, British Prime Minister Disraeli had said: "It is potatoes one day and the Pope the next." Similar is the present position in Kashmir. Yesterday, it was Maqbool Butt; today it is *Satanic Verses;* tomorrow it will be repression day…'[290]

These were very strong words, but one presumes that this invocation of a very cavalier and arrogant comment of nineteenth-century British Prime Minister Benjamin Disraeli about the Irish struggle for independence was made without fully realizing the implication of it because the lowly potatoes had caused one of the biggest divides and migrations of that century, for famine had struck Ireland in the wake of potato crisis; and the Pope, had symbolized the struggle between the Roman Catholics and the Church of England. Because of the potato crisis, the relationship between Ireland and Britain was never the same. Both issues were of vital importance to the Irish Catholics as they triggered the secessionist movement. It did not strike Jagmohan that with passage of time, potatoes and Pope became the bedrock of separatism and partition of Ireland. After about seventy-five years of this statement Ireland was partitioned with the Catholic region becoming Republic of Ireland and the smaller one remained a part of Great Britain. Did Jagmohan really realize what he was implying by drawing upon the authority of an irascible imperialist British Prime Minister? Was he even aware of the numerous machinations that he had made in the nineteenth century to destabilize the Dogra State of Jammu and Kashmir? If he had not been carried away by the bombast and pungency of the words, he would have had a better understanding of history.

On 23 June 1989 pamphlets, distributed in Srinagar, gave warning to the women to strictly conform to the Islamic standards. The fundamentalists had now become so bold as to issue dictates to the society. The shrine of the venerated Muslim saint Baba Reshi in Gulmarg was gutted on 2 September of the same year. This more than anything else indicated that the shots were being called from across the border where Saudi money and influence had already radicalized society. Next month, the first collective threat to the minorities was sounded loudly, recalls Rahul Pandita. That year Eid-e-Milad-un-Nabi fell on 14 October and the faithful gathered in a massive crowd 'near Budshah chowk (square) in the heart of Srinagar, and from there, it marched towards Eidgah to the graveyard that had been renamed "martyr's graveyard". The onlookers cheered and showered *Shireen* (white sugary snack, traditionally showered on the marriage procession in Kashmir) on the marchers as if to welcome a marriage party. That evening, father returned home...and told (that) the crowd was shouting slogans that had shocked them. *Yahan kya chalega, Nizam-e-Mustafa / La sharqiya, Islamia, Islamia* and *Zalzala aya hai kufr ke maidaan mein / Lo mujahid aa gaye maidaan mein,* meaning; "What will work here? The rule of Mustafa / No eastern, no western, only Islamic, only Islamic", and, "An earthquake has struck in the realm of the infidels / The mujahids have come out to fight".'[291]

As the winter chill approached, there was uneasy calm among the Pandits. There were none too subtle hints about the changing relationships and often there were ominous remarks directed at them, sometimes warnings and at others loaded comments. But if the Kashmiri Pandits were hoping that what they were experiencing was hallucination then they were rudely brought out from their world of hope by the events of the night of 19 January 1990. This date will remain a part of their intergenerational memory, causing anxiety, regret, nostalgia, fear and anger. There is no reason at all to believe that the fear psychosis that was generated that day was provoked by anything that could be attributed to the Pandit community though it must be added that it had everything to do with the failure of the State and the Union Government. The events of that night set a pattern whereby the intelligence agencies have consistently failed in getting any information of any impending catastrophic turn of events or terrorist strike. This pattern has been complemented by the failure of the Governments to identify the persons failing to perform their duties or even inquiring into the causes of the failures. Since there has never been any acknowledgement, there has also been no accountability, therefore there has never been any punishment for anyone and things have just gone on as before.

At around 9 pm on 19 January 1990, 'loud and thunderous slogans of *Allah-u-Akbar, La Ila ha Illalullah, Islam Zindabad, Pakistan Zindabad* raised collectively by a multitude of humanity and relayed through powerful loudspeakers almost pierced the eardrums. These slogans were not new to Pandits in Kashmir... However the very odd hour, the tumultuous bang and intriguing spontaneity besides pressing loudspeakers into service, all spoke threateningly that a storm was brewing in Kashmir.'[292] The effect was electric and is vividly described by Kashinath Pandit: 'Suddenly, telephone bells began ringing loudly in the houses of most of the Kashmiri Pandits in Srinagar. Mobile phones had not been introduced then. Each caller on the other end of the line asked his relative, friend or the acquaintance whether they were all right. This question carried more meaning underneath its simple words.'[293]

Terror had truly arrived for the Pandits. On the streets of Srinagar, the monster of Islamic communalism was ruling the roost. Young and old, men, women and children had whipped themselves into a frenzy of religious passion and were yelling slogans of *hum kya maange—azadi, Pakistan Zindabad, Islam zindabad, la illah ilallah* and more threateningly, *azadi ka matlab kya, la ilah ilallah* and *Kashmir banega Pakistan*. Within no time the rugs, carpets and furnishings were out on the streets as the bonfire lit the sky and kept the bodies warm in the freezing night. Greater cause of concern for the saner eye was that the women and children were particularly boisterous and appeared to be in celebratory mood as if they had been anticipating this moment. In between the slogans, the loudspeakers from the minarets of the mosques blared a mix of revolutionary songs and readings of the Quranic verses. Alternately, the speakers would either praise Pakistan or narrate the stories of the heroes of early Islamic conquests along with the description of the paradise that awaited the *momins*—the pure ones—and the hellfire for the non-believers—the *kafirs*. The crux of the night was that there was no room for idolatrous and believers of dualism, and that the Pandits were living under the shadows of the guns of Pakistan-sponsored terrorists. But this was really oversimplification of what was happening. The failings of the Indian State and the national and State political parties had finally created a space wide enough for Pakistan to take advantage and unleash a cycle that it had failed to let loose earlier on many occasions.

The trauma of that night was too much to bear though persecution at the hands of Muslim rulers in the past was a rule rather than exception. The Pandit community of Kashmir loathes admitting but the only period when they enjoyed security and respect, except for the period of Zain-ul-Abidin or Budshah, after Kashmir passed into Muslim hands, was the one when it was ruled by the Sikhs and Dogras. The irrefutable fact beyond any debate is that their persecution had completely stopped since the Valley was ruled by a Hindu dynasty for a century from 1846 to 1947. The fate of Pandits before the Dogra rule is vividly described by Walter Lawrence in his book *The Valley of Kashmir* while writing about the rule of one of the Afghan rulers, Assad Khan: 'It was his practice to tie up the Pandits, two and two, in grass sacks and sink them in the Dal Lake. As an amusement, a pitcher filled with ordure would be placed on a Pandit's head and Musalmans would pelt the pitcher with stones till it broke, the unfortunate Hindu being blinded with filth.'[294] In another instance, during Atta Mohammad Khan's rule, he further writes: 'Any Musalman who met a Pandit would jump on his back, and take a ride.'[295] But that was in the distant past. In 1990 the terror unleashed was at a time when the country and the State had a constitution that guaranteed equality, secularism and social justice. A combination of safety and security provided by the Dogra rulers and the memory of the legends and myths of the past had instilled enough confidence in the Pandits to now be shocked at the turn of events. In such times of adversity, their strength came from the memories passed from generation to generation, about the infallibility of their Gods, with Shiva and Shivratri becoming the eternal fountain of faith, source of hope and the power of God.

The abiding myth of Shivratri has always given them strength, fortitude and will to live in hope and optimism. The snowfall on Shivratri was always special as it created the foundational myth about Lord Shiva, Kashmir and the Pandits. Since this festival falls in winter, snowing on that day can be easily explained away as part of a natural phenomenon of winter. Since children will be children, after the snow fell, they would make a snow figure of Lord Shiva and then horse around. Shivratri is also known as the festival of *Herath* and one of the legends informs us that to break the spirit of the Pandits, Jabbar Khan, an Afghan ruler, ordered that Shivratri be celebrated in the month of June-July so as to destroy the myth of snowfall on that day. It is said that the year when the Hindus of Kashmir were forced to celebrate the occasion during that summer, suddenly the weather changed and lo and behold, there was snow! Some say that everyone was in *Hairat,* so shocked that the Persian word *Hairat,* a miracle, became the name of Shivratri, which over a period of time became *Herath.* But it is also believed that *Herath* has origins in the Sanskrit word *Hara-Ratri,* the night of Hara or Shiva which over a period of time became *Herath.* Thus, the Gods and Goddesses were the limbs that had helped the Kashmiri Pandits to survive in hostile circumstances in the past.

But no one was prepared for what happened that night though there were early warnings since 1931 when the shops of Hindus were attacked and ransacked by the Muslims. However, Kashinath Pandit claims that 'an infuriated mob attacked and looted some shops of the Punjabi Hindus in Zaina Kadal, the hub of trade in Kashmir. Communal tension rose high and three Kashmiri Pandits are said to have been killed in the turmoil.'[296] After that, periodically communal tension and suspicion remained part of life and became the order of the day, particularly after Sheikh Abdullah came to power in 1947.

The history of the State between 1931 and 1947 has been of vain efforts of Maharaja Hari Singh to insulate it from the influence of the communal politics that had gripped the neighboring Punjab, from where it was spreading into the State, and contain these forces before they destroyed it. In the end, he had found these forces too formidable to be reined in. However, the Muslim violence against the Pandits had turned out to be a minor aberration and both communities embarked upon an era of cooperation when Sheikh Abdullah led his majority followers out of the Muslim Conference to form the National Conference with close links to the Indian National Congress. Both worked in close tandem and many of the Pandits with ties to the rest of the country supported it even during the 'Quit Kashmir' movement against the Maharaja.

Ironically, even this support turned out to be of no avail as Anantnag's Sarvanand Kaul 'Premi', a poet and a scholar, found out too late. His relatives had been urging him to leave the Valley but he was confident that no one will touch him since he had spent all his life with the Muslims and that as a seventeen-year-old, he had participated in the 'Quit Kashmir' movement against the Dogra Maharaja Hari Singh. 'After his retirement, he had taught for free for three months a year in two schools, one run by an Islamic and the other a Hindu educational society.'[297] On 29 April 1990, three armed men barged into his house bundled the valuables in a suitcase and asked Premi to carry it with them. Unable to see the plight of his father, his son too accompanied them. The next day they were found hanging from a tree, nail hammered into their foreheads. It can be said, and it is partially true too, that such barbaric acts were committed by terrorists who were not Kashmiris but the truth is that they always had local accomplices who at least collaborated with their new masters in perpetrating these acts. There are numerous other examples where the foul deeds have been done by local planners and also executed by them. The local population, the neighborhood in particular, or the political parties and leaders cannot be absolved of their culpability and they have to bear the cross of responsibility.

It is ironical that today most of the Kashmiri Pandit writers apportion blame to Sheikh Abdullah, among others, for their misfortune and claim that soon after assuming power he had warned the Pandit community to fully merge with the Muslim Kashmir or else leave. *Raliv, chaliv ya galiv*—merge, go or die.[298] However, the assertion is difficult to verify from independent sources and few would accuse Sheikh Abdullah of discriminating against fellow Kashmiris or willfully persecuting the Pandits. But discussing the persecution of Pandits in Kashmir, another author quotes

R.K. Sher, who writes that the beginning of the rule of Sheikh Abdullah marked another phase of Kashmiri persecution. 'There was no end to this persecution, of course not in the crude ways as was the case during the rule of the Sultans, Mirza Afzal Beg's advice to National Conference cadres was that they should not kill Pandits but find out ways and means by which their sources of sustenance is withdrawn and in this process they would steadily and slowly leave the Valley. This process was started in right earnest from 1950 and land reforms were implemented in quick succession for obvious reasons.'[299] Because of the antecedents of Mirza Afzal Beg, this accusation appears much more plausible. But it is interesting to note that in the Jammu region it is believed that it, particularly Rajputs of the region who enjoyed the privilege of owning lands and also, a few of them, *jagirs*[300], were the target of these reforms but in Kashmir similar grievance were being articulated by the Pandits. These reforms, it must be said, were of socio-economic significance which by their nature cut into the spheres of influence of the land-owning class. In this case, this class constituted of Pandits in the Valley and Rajputs in the Jammu region though the Pandits got away lightly since they also owned orchards which were exempt from the stipulated land ceiling. But behind all this stands the fact that till the Pandits were pushed to choose between India and the agenda of the National Conference, they had stood solidly behind Sheikh Abdullah and he, with them. It is only in modern times that the compulsion of choosing between the two opposing stands heralded distrust and mutual suspicion and ultimately enmity.

There are others who lament the absence of a Sheikh Abdullah in 1990 by recalling that he was the one who had given the slogan and mission of *Muslim Hindu Sikh Ittehad.*[301] Sheikh Abdullah was at that point in time the much loved and adored leader of the Kashmiris who held Pandit Jawaharlal Nehru in equal esteem. One a Muslim, the other Hindu—the perfect example of the much-touted syncretism of Kashmir, also called *Kashmiriyat.* In this context, Rahul Pandita also does not fail to point out that history records that on 2 November 1947 Sheikh Abdullah had recited Amir Khusro's Persian verse for Jawaharlal Nehru:

> *Mun tu shudam, Tu mun shudi; Man tan shudam Tu jaan shudi;*
> *Takas na goyad bod azeen, Mun deegaram Tu deegaree*
>
> (I am You and You are me; I am your body, You are my soul; So none should hereafter say, I am someone and You are someone else)

So, singing out Amir Khusro's Sufi verse, Sheikh Mohammad Abdullah had then turned to embrace Jawaharlal Nehru, Kashmiri Musalman to Kashmiri Pandit, in front of thousands gathered at Srinagar's Lal Chowk. But that was a long time ago and much had changed and the contract that was steeped in so much of emotion and commitment had been consigned to history. Both the leaders had evolved, and therefore changed, and apparently both had developed their divergent approaches to Kashmir after that brief but intense honeymoon during which Maharaja Hari Singh was sacrificed and compromises made on the Constitution of India to accommodate Sheikh Abdullah and the claimed aspirations of Kashmir. Their difference that evolved over time, are best described by Sheikh Abdullah himself in his autobiography when he says that both the stalwarts were pursuing and loved the same woman and wanted complete possession of her! The competition between the two was over complete possession of Kashmir.

Rahul Pandita also laments the fact that when Sheikh Abdullah issued the alleged ultimatum to Pandits, he had also forgotten not only the shared history and culture of Kashmiri Muslims and Pandits but also the fact that the Pandits had stood shoulder to shoulder with their Muslim brethren during the National Conference's struggle against the Dogra ruler.[302] Later, deprived of his home and environment, he also bitterly complains in his book about the hostile treatment that he suffered as a displaced boy in Jammu, forgetting that every community has a collective memory and that the Dogras too have suffered the trauma of suddenly losing power to the Kashmiris, Muslims and Pandits alike, in 1947, and that it had stood isolated and neglected then.

Post 1990, Kashmiri Pandits have also bitterly complained of the heat and humidity, the cobras, vipers and scorpions that they had to contend with in Jammu. Coming from the land of plenty, the shortage of water was also torturous for them. But that was the reality of the region they had come to for safety and anyone who comes there has to accept everything that comes with the geography and climate. Moreover, there were occasionally strained relations with the Dogras since with limited opportunities and meager resources the Jammu population was understandably resentful and unwilling to share them with anyone. In such a frame of mind, the less educated among them found the occasion to vent their accumulated anger and frustration of losing power and privileges in odious manner. But the bitter fact was that after their forced migration, the Kashmiri Pandits have periodically suffered selective amnesia. This was similar to when, after 1947, the Kashmiri Muslims and Pandits, with few exceptions, had joined forces in every confrontation with an outside force, including Dogras. This was understandable too, as long as the struggle was for maintaining an independent and distinct cultural and political identity, but now with the increasing involvement of Pakistan and Islamic fundamentalism for the annexation of the state by Pakistan and establishment of an Islamic society, the presence of the Pandits in the Valley had become an irritant that needed to be removed. Overtly, the over ground forces expected the Pandits to help them in their secondary goal of securing an autonomous State while the covert forces focused on the bigger agenda of Islamists. From the need to preserve ethnic identity, the struggle had become a fight to establish distinct Muslim identity. With the justifiable reluctance of the Pandits to struggle against India, the Muslims had found a reason to target the Pandits and create *Dar-al-Islam* after purging them.

The pain and frustration of becoming an exile in one's own country has been written by almost all the Kashmiri Pandits who could write books but the intensity, blurring the distinction between pain and anger, is best illustrated in the writings of Rahul Pandita's *Our Moon Has Blood Clots*. He describes the night of 19 January 1990 thus:

> Then the slogans ceased for a while. From another mosque came the sound of recorded songs eulogizing the Mujahideen resistance to the Soviet occupation of Afghanistan. The whole audio cassette played through and then the slogans returned. We were still

> wondering what would happen next when a slogan we heard left us in no doubt. I remember Ma begin to tremble like a leaf when we heard it. In Kashmir, every child is familiar with the slogan *Nara-e-taqbeer, Allah ho Akbar* but now a new and ominous slogan had become a part of sloganeering. In a well choreographed manner, a new slogan became part of the outpouring. *Assi gacchi pamu'nuy Pakistan, batav rostuy, batenein saan*—Kashmir will be converted into Pakistan *without* the Pandits but *with* their women—was a slogan that struck terror in every heart that heard and felt it.[303]

Since this was happening in Srinagar, where the Army Brigade headquarters was located in Badami Bagh and the Border Security Force (BSF) too was situated, therefore people hoped that at least the BSF will come to their rescue. None came because there were rules guiding the intervention of paramilitary forces.

The period is marked by a political vacuum with the Chief Minister Farooq Abdullah having resigned, but long before his resignation on 19 January 1990, since 1989, he had ceased to be an effective Chief Minister. His administration had been suffering a series of minor paralytic strokes till it had collapsed and as Chief Minister, he had abdicated his responsibility. Not surprisingly his resignation did not create any ripples on the streets of Srinagar. In New Delhi, with the Camelot of Rajiv Gandhi having collapsed, his government had been battling for survival during the run up to the 1989 Lok Sabha polls. The situation was grim before the polls and became grimmer after the defeat of the Congress. When V.P. Singh became the Prime Minister the logical thing for the new dispensation should have been to deal with Kashmir immediately in view of Pakistan's involvement. As it turned out, the political parties that had sunk their differences to oust Congress had neither any clue to the issue nor did it make any effort to form a committee or a group to urgently address the situation. Every account about the events in the Valley leading to the Lok Sabha polls points to the deteriorating situation in Kashmir and yet no one considered it serious enough to demand immediate attention. It appears that with the ouster of Rajiv Gandhi all the goals of the opposition had been achieved. Those Kashmiri Pandits who have written about the events leading to their exodus have few words of condemnation for this lack of concern, empathy, planning and strategy by the new Government. In any developed democracy, irrespective of the final outcome of an election, the political parties have a plan for resolving the serious issues and are on the job the moment they are entrusted power. Their countdown for the next polls begins from their first day in office. Not so in 1989, and the first week of 1990.

The United Front was too engrossed with the euphoria of victory. Therefore, the events that followed beg the question about the preparedness of a government that had planned and campaigned for correcting the wrongs of the preceding Government. Jagmohan had no clue about Dr Rubaiya Sayeed's abduction and release in exchange of dreaded terrorists till a call from the then Foreign Affairs Minister I.K. Gujral that roused Jagmohan from his sleep to ask him to attend an emergency meeting at Home Minister Mufti Mohammad Sayeed's house. This, and the throwing in of the towel by Farooq Abdullah no sooner than Jagmohan was appointed Governor against his express wish, tells us a little about the preparedness of the Government of India in general and in-coming Governor Jagmohan in particular. It can be argued that he was given very little time to prepare but by his own account, he was fully conversant with developments that took place during his short absence after the expiry of his first term. He had been away from the office of Governor only for a short period of 11 July 1989 to 19 January 1990. Moreover, since the terror activities had been taking place when he was Governor and he had been regularly sending reports to Centre and advising it about the urgent need to act, he must have had some roadmap about the action to be taken. On evidence, he had none, or perhaps he really wanted the Pandits to move out of the firing line so that the State could take some strong steps. But it is more likely that no one had any strategy to deal with the deteriorating situation.

One would imagine that the gravity of the situation should have prompted Jagmohan to utilize every moment from the time he was sounded about his appointment, in planning the action to be taken and the support that was needed. But that strategy did not unfold itself at that critical juncture of Kashmir. It is unbelievable that he, who by his own account, had been a very successful Governor in his first tenure not too long ago, and claimed that he was aware of how the situation was slipping, would reach Jammu without any preparedness. This was in sharp contrast to the meticulous planning with which he had reached Srinagar in 1984 when he had the mandate to remove Farooq Abdullah from office.

It is instructive to recall the meticulous planning that he was capable of and Prabhu Chawla had described the sequence of events for *India Today. (See Chapter 7 for more details)* This meticulous planner had arrived in Jammu in 1990withoutany plan or preparation; nor did he make any effort to redress the situation on taking oath on 19January1990. There is also no evidence to suggest that New Delhi had any strategy to deal with the fast-emerging situation or perhaps it was a crisis of leadership. Jagmohan did not even appear to be reacting to the events; on the contrary, it was felt that New Delhi and he were allowing matters to drift. If this was the case then one is left to wonder if there was a diabolical plan to force the Pandits out of the Valley so that with the resulting anger in the rest of the country supporting the use of brute force, separatist forces could be put down with a heavy hand. If this was so, it was too naïve a solution to a complex challenge. Alternately, an analyst can conclude that Jagmohan had no plan since grappling with the problems of this magnitude and complexity was beyond his capabilities. The United Front government had a vastly exaggerated assessment of his abilities. He needed a strong and decisive leader like Indira Gandhi to give him direction. Thus, both the Centre and the Governor were groping in the dark and living in hope rather than confidence in their action-plan.

It is also not known what brief he was given by the Home Ministry but by his own account as the BSF plane flew him towards Jammu his thoughts had been wandering in the past and were not on the present crisis. He recalls that he vividly remembered the events that had gone by from 3 February 1984, the day when Ravindra Mahatre, the Indian diplomat posted in Birmingham, UK was kidnapped and murdered in cold blood by the Kashmir Liberation Army to cause the latest outrage.[304] What is not known is if Jagmohan viewed the rising terrorist activities, and active and forced alienation of the youth, as a political and ideological problem or a purely law and order and administrative failure. What is known, however, is that the same evening as the Valley exploded with a hitherto unknown weapon of psychological terror, Jagmohan took oath as Governor of the State of Jammu and Kashmir in Jammu, and he took no action to douse the fire that had erupted in the Valley.

A person reputed as a man of quick decisions and actions did nothing that night and as the army and the paramilitary forces stayed put in the barracks, terror struck in hearts and minds of the Kashmiri Pandits. After the oath, Lieutenant General Gobinder Singh, the Northern Command Army Commander, apprised the new Governor of the deteriorating situation in the Valley, but he decided to wait. It is because of this that he is accused of letting the situation worsen so that the Pandits would migrate before strong steps were taken to punish the culprits. It has been suggested that Jagmohan feared greater reprisals against the Pandits if strong action had been taken when they were living there. Later, the partisans of Jagmohan, Kashmiri Pandits in particular, honestly felt that there was nothing that he could have done that night but according to Rahul Pandita's book, even as from 10 p.m. that night the phones of Raj Bhawan Jammu rang continuously praying for help. 'They (Pandits) whispered to him "Please ask the army to help us"...'[305] Obviously, the onus of calling the army or the paramilitary forces was put on the Centre though there is no account as to the efforts of the Governor to initiate this process. In contrast, in 1984 when Farooq was to be removed, he had not only requisitioned sufficient number of paramilitary forces but had also put the army on standby.

The next day Governor Jagmohan wanted to fly to Srinagar but because of inclement weather conditions he could not fly and therefore decided to go to the Civil Secretariat in Jammu where the major cogs of the administration were stationed.[306]Basking in the glorious memory of past administrative success, the Governor busied himself in meeting people, listening to their grievances while a fresh wave of offensive against the Pandits was being launched in Kashmir. In the Valley, an ominous development was taking place. Kashinath Pandit writes: 'The government was knocked out by a single night of defiance and revolt. Next morning not a single policeman was visible anywhere in the city. They had withdrawn to their barracks or hid in their homes. Administrative machinery collapsed, law and order crumbled. From the next morning viz. January 20, 1990, it was the rule of the mosque, the priests and Islamists.'[307] Simultaneously, a new development was taking place in the approach to dealing with the rising terror, but whether this had anything to do with arrival of Jagmohan, who carried the image of being a Hindu administrator in the wake of his takeover of Mata Vaishno Devi Trust during his earlier tenure, cannot be categorically stated. Expectedly, the paramilitary forces were enthused by his arrival. Thus, the challenge in the Valley became complex and bigger. The uncomfortable truth was that he was considered to be a counter weight to the Muslim dominated Kashmir and therefore a partisan.

Apparently, the paramilitary forces had been taking some action since morning as news reached Jammu Secretariat that large scale searches were taking place and about 250 suspects among the youth had been picked up from Srinagar's Chhota Bazar and Guru Bazar. Jagmohan narrates in his book that when he enquired about the incident, he was told that a few days earlier in the Guru Bazar area three personnel of the Central Reserve Police Force had been shot dead as a consequence of which the CRPF had carried out the search for the suspects and rounded up about 250 people of whom, after screening, 200 had been released.[308] But what followed the searches soon snowballed into an upsurge. Jagmohan is adamant that the searches were carried out on the orders of the former Chief Minister Farooq Abdullah on 16 January 1990 after a meeting at the Police Headquarters in response to the pressure built upon him by the United Front Government. But whatever led to those searches, which took place after Farooq Abdullah had resigned, the outcome was that later that day on 20 January 1990, the Kashmiris, men, women and children came out marching in protest at the highhanded manner in which they were conducted at night. There are two different versions of what followed. The CRPF version was that the small force near the Gawkadal was about to be overwhelmed and hence it opened fire killing 14 demonstrators.

The other version[309] claims that the fire was opened upon the demonstrators when, thousands of people, angry at the humiliating manner in which the searches had been conducted, reached the narrow bridge; the forces opened fire leaving no space for escape with many jumping into the Jhelum. From then onwards, this contested memory and interpretation of events became the norm in the Valley.

It is in this context that it needs to be remembered that there are about 1,100 mosques in the Valley and from all the mosques, the same kind of songs, verses and messages and slogans were relayed simultaneously the night before the searches. It could not be a coincidence. It was a sure sign that it had been meticulously planned and perfectly executed. The collective hysteria of the mobs had been whipped up and had torn apart the façade of liberal Muslim face and also announced the death of Kashmiriyat. If the State government had abdicated its responsibility long ago then the Central Government too was equally guilty now. As a result of the army and the paramilitary forces not doing what the Pandits hoped for, and as a consequence of the nightmare of the 19th January night, the Pandits decided to leave their homes and hearths for their safety.

Sometimes fiction describes historical events much more eloquently than history or political commentary does since it describes the emotions and thoughts that motivated the actions of the people at the given moment. History will only describe the dates and the sequence of events and also explain the reasons thereof; fiction provides the insight into what people in general went through as human beings as a consequence of those events. Kshama Kaul, in her novel *Dardpur*, has vividly brought out the exodus of the Pandits. Oscillating between hope and despair, even while assuring one another that they cannot abandon their motherland, the Pandit families made a beeline for the buses at dawn to take them across the Banihal to a safe zone. Others who could afford hired taxis, and still others allowed themselves to be herded into trucks with the instruction not to peep out of the tarpaulin covers. There is nothing to suggest that Governor Jagmohan suggested to them that they should migrate out of the Valley for a short period but there is also no evidence either that he tried to stop them from migrating or made alternate arrangements for them in the Valley. The process continued even after he had settled in his office. It should also be remembered that during a period of frenzy, people hope that once it has passed things will return to normalcy. However, when forced migrations take place with the objective of ethnic cleansing, normalcy becomes a victim, and the familiar normal never returns. It did not happen in 1947 in India or Pakistan, it has not happened in Palestine or in the emergence of Bangladesh, and it has not happened in constituents of the now disintegrated Yugoslavia and USSR. But all those tragedies happened and then passed, with everyone going their separate ways except in Kashmir. Even after the migration, a fair number of Kashmiri Pandits had chosen to ride out the storm with the support of well-meaning neighbors. But they became specific targets for the terrorists from time to time in the coming years till only a few thousands of the 15 percent that were there in 1947, remained.

19 January 1990 was the beginning of the terror for the Pandits and it intensified as the months passed. Every now and then it was punctuated by the wailings of the surviving family members of those killed, in the process striking terror among the other family members and the co-religionists, making them flee with or without their belongings. The targeted killings happened all over the Valley. The genial and meticulous professional, Lassa Koul, Station Director of Doordarshan, Srinagar was one of the first to be gunned down after 19 January when on 13 February he was visiting his old parents living in Bemina, Srinagar. After Tikka Lal Taploo and Justice Neel Kanth Ganjoo's killings, this killing had sent waves of terror among the Pandits and their migration became a steady stream. In downtown Srinagar's Chhota Bazar, a friendly neighbor of B.K. Ganju, a telecommunication officer, told him that he had seen his name at the local mosque in the hit list of those who were to be eliminated. Not knowing what to do and afraid of informing the police, Ganju and his wife spent a terrorized night. At nine in the morning on 22 March 1990 came the knock enquiring about him. His wife somehow managed to fob them off but they were tipped by someone outside and they rushed back into the house going

straight to the attic where he was hiding in a drum half filled with rice and shot him there.[310]

In April 1990, Hizb-ul-Mujahideen published a warning in the Urdu daily, *Alsafa,* for the Pandit community, telling them to migrate out of the Valley. Earlier in January also a similar warning had been issued in *Aftab*. The Pandit community had then chosen to linger and hope for things to get better. But then, as Siddarth Gigoo and Varad Sharma wrote in their book, *A Long Dream of Home: The Persecution, Exodus and Exile of Kashmiri Pandits*, 'One day, our neighbor, Professor Nilla Kanth Raina, a retired professor of history, was loading his luggage in a truck and about to leave with his wife for Jammu, when he was shot dead by his own students who had joined a militant group. Professor Raina was in his sixties at that time. We took his killing as a clear signal for the rest of us to leave.' The fate of the Pandits was also aptly described by Salman Rushdie in his book *Shalimar the Clown* when he wrote, 'Hindu community houses, temples, private homes and whole neighborhoods were being destroyed...Kill one, scare ten, the Muslim mobs chanted, and ten were, indeed, scared...Three hundred and fifty thousand Pandits, almost the entire Pandit population of Kashmir fled from their own homes and headed south to the refugee camps where they would rot, like bitter fallen apple, like the unloved, undead dead they had become.' Kill one, scare ten was a *mantra* that proved very effective.

The abduction, torture, gang rape and brutal killing of Sarla Bhat, a resident Nurse of Sher-e-Kashmir Institute of Medical Sciences sent a chilling message to all females who stepped out of their homes for livelihood and careers. A young woman in her mid 20s, Sarlais believed to have overheard a partial conversation between two doctors who were actively involved in terrorism. Abducted on 15 April 1990, her body was recovered four days later, clearly bearing the marks of torture and repeated rape. Attached to the body was a note claiming that she was an 'informer'. Her body was handed over to her father Shambhu Nath Bhat but he was barred from performing her last rites. He left for Jammu with the rest of the family immediately.

Earlier, on 1 April 1990, H.L. Khera, the General Manager

of the Government of India's public sector industry, Hindustan Machine Tools (HMT), was kidnapped and killed. On 6 April, Mushir-ul-Haq, the Vice Chancellor of Kashmir University and his Private Secretary Abdul Gani Zargar, who were sympathizers of the Pandits' plight, were abducted. Their bodies were found on 10 April. The kidnapping and discovery of tortured bodies was clearly a message of terror coupled with the nefarious design of hurting the economy and disrupting life. On 10 October 1990, Usha Kumari Koul and her husband who both worked in the HMT factory too were gunned down at their workplace. Not surprisingly, not only did the factory close down but the process of industrialization in the Valley received a setback.

The most brutal, heinous and inhuman fate was met by Girja Tiku in Bandipora. This young woman worked as a laboratory assistant in a school and was the sole breadwinner of her family. Terrified of the persecution and the killings, Girja and her family too had migrated from Kashmir, however, the rules for the government employees were such that she was required to be present in Bandipora every month to collect her salary. In April of that year, the situation had deteriorated so much that Girja's cousin, with whom she stayed during those short but essential visits to Bandipora, had told her to collect her salary, leave immediately, and not come back. While she did just that, the circumstances of her family brought her back in June only to find that her cousin too had migrated to Jammu. Thus, without any options, she stayed with a Muslim family from whose house she was picked by four men the following morning. She was never found. Her subsequent rape and murder on 11 June 1990 is the most devastating indictment of the governance under the watch of Jagmohan.

Years later, during a conversation the local commander of the terrorist group shared the fate of Girja with a resident of Bandipora. She was, he narrated, blindfolded and bundled into a taxi; then they had taken turns to rape her. 'As they were conversing with each other, Girja recognized the voice of one of the men who went by the name of Aziz. "Aziza, *chhetey chukha*?" Aziz, are you here as well? She asked. Aziz got worried. He knew that Girja had recognized him. So, in the final act of barbarism, they took her to the wood processing unit and cut her alive on a mechanical saw.'[311] While everyone is shocked and condemns the barbarity of the terrorists, no one has questioned how this rule of collecting the salary only from the place of appointment did not come to the notice of an efficient administrator like Jagmohan. Girja should never have been allowed to meet the gory fate that she did.

On 2 May 1990, Prof. K.L. Ganju, a lecturer in the Sopore Agricultural College, knew of the rising threat but continued to stay, reasoning with himself that since he had not wronged anyone that he knew, he would not be harmed. But that night turned out to be different. Even as he and his wife were joined by his cousin for dinner, four armed men barged into the house and asked them to accompany them outside. They were marched under the watchful gaze of the neighbors who dared not object.

Governor Jagmohan in his book has expressed outrage at the indifference of the neighbors. Then, either he possessed extraordinary moral courage or he was just unaware of the impact of terror or he was plainly trying to pin all the responsibility on the Kashmiri Muslims. In his book, while recounting the killings of Premi and his son, he acknowledges that the neighbors did try to intercede though he adds that it was but only 'mildly'. For whatever reasons, it was apparent that Jagmohan could not empathize with terrorized people living under the shadow of guns. People in Punjab have experienced terror and know it makes them act in extraordinarily abnormal manner, often bordering on inhumanity even among those who are its victims and are forced to see death being visited upon their family. But terror had truly arrived in the Valley.

The Ganju family was marched to the vicinity of a mosque on the banks of Jhelum and while Ganju was shot, his body kept in the mosque that night and then thrown away in the river, his cousin jumped in and swam to safety. Mrs Ganju is said to have been brutally killed and then tied to a stone and thrown in the river. Her body was never recovered.[312]

These killings are a few among the numerous that took place during those dark days and the exact numbers are still being debated. According to Kashinath Pandit, the State government has put the number to under 200. He claims that the reason for distorting the figures by the government agencies is that according to the Tokyo Convention, if the number of killed persons exceeds 200, then it falls under the category of genocide.[313] He goes on to note that the verdict of the National Human Rights Commission of India is that the Pandit killings are 'akin to genocide'.[314] However, according to a state government report of 2010, the number of Kashmiri Pandits killed was 219 in the region between 1989 and 2004. But according to a survey conducted by the Kashmiri Pandit Sangharsh Samiti, 650 were killed between 1989 and 2008.Panun Kashmir, a political organization of displaced Pandits has published a list of 1,341 Pandits who were killed after 1990. The debate goes on.

Other people who were involved in the happenings of the period have their own agenda. Illustrative is that of Jagmohan who has incidentally reproduced the experience of one Sudesh Kumar, then a law student, as a victim of terror in his book. It was published in the March 1990 issue of *Illustrated Weekly of India.* While Kumar was traveling in a Matador along with T.K. Razdan, an intelligence officer, terrorists accosted them and shot Razdan dead, took his body away to a mosque and after verifying his identity, threw his body on the road. The cremation of Razdan was done by the CRPF since his family was too terrified to come out and claim it. On another occasion, Sudesh Kumar merged with a crowd shouting anti-India and pro Islam slogans and joined them too, in order to escape being identified.[315] Terror indeed has no hue nor does it recognize the classification of religions but it causes extraordinary degradation of human beings. The Hindus of Kashmir were terrified but the Muslims too did not want to risk their life by displaying sympathy for their Pandit neighbors.

This incident defined the terrorism faced by the Pandit community in their homeland. In hindsight, one wonders at the naïveté of those who had issues with their identity with India and surely it is difficult to digest that they believed that sustained sloganeering and targeted killings would eat into India's resolve to maintain its integrity. Contrary to the quixotic hope of the separatists and terrorists, these acts only toughened the resolve of the country to defeat terrorism and the puppeteers who controlled the strings. It is true, as is desirable in a democracy, periodic attempts were made to politically address the issue but the next step always eluded as it depended upon the response. But as we have noticed in the chapters dealing with the ideology of Pakistan and its army's resolve to act as the guardians and protectors of that ideology, where the mere demonstration of the desire to resist India is considered victory, these acts became a part of their process. The broth has further been poisoned by the trans-national nature of jihad that had taken roots since 1979. Hence the tactics of the masters of the terrorists in Kashmir have changed from time to time. Purging the Valley of Kashmiri Pandits was part of that strategy though the negligible minority was hardly in a position to oppose the political designs of the Kashmiri Muslims. It is in this context that the persecution of the small minority of Kashmiri Pandits has not only been reprehensible and diabolical but also counterproductive since it failed to garner international support for the Kashmiri Muslims. It was rather acknowledged in world forums as being a sponsored tool of another country, instead of a Kashmiri struggle. Moreover, the forced migration of the Pandits failed to achieve the bigger objective of the trans-national Jihad too as it failed to trigger communal riots in the rest of the country and plunge India in a downward spiral.

With the passage of time, the separatist movement completely passed on to the Hizb-ul-Mujahideen, Lashkar-e-Taiba (LeT) and Jaish-e-Mohammad (JeM) from the home-grown leaders like Yasin Malik etc. and strings were being pulled from Pakistan by uncompromising fundamentalists. It was only a matter of time before individual killings gave way to community massacres. On 25 January 1998, Wandhama, a village in South Kashmir, witnessed the massacre of 23 Pandits, on 17 April 1998 Prankote witnessed a massacre of 23 Hindus, on 19 June of the same year, another set of 23 Hindus were killed in Chapnari. By 2000, the terrorists had become so bold as to attack the Amarnath Yatra and kill 30 pilgrims and the next year terror crossed the Pir Panjal to strike in Kishtwar and kill 19 Hindus. The atmosphere in the Valley was decisively no longer conducive for the Kashmiri Pandits and after the initial wave of exodus, the Pandits have continued to trickle out of the Valley.

However, what makes the fleeing soon after 19 January 1990 even more unfortunate and painful is that from the thousands of soldiers garrisoned in the Badami Bagh cantonment, the Government of India 'did not spare even one platoon of Indian soldiers to escort the fleeing fugitive.'[316] They were, effectively abandoned and left to their own fate.

In the times to come, some have criticized the Pandits for fleeing too soon, of not weathering the storm, for after the initial dilly dallying the Government of India would have come to their help and rescue. They cite the example of Punjab where targeted killings of Hindus had been taking place since the mid-eighties and except for isolated incidents no migration took place. It is true that at a number of places whole families moved out but such cases were isolated and too few and far between. For many of them it was triggered because the idea of moving to urban areas was already there. Moreover, it is not realistic to expect all communities to respond to a crisis in a similar fashion. The Kashmiri Pandits never had a history of collective defiance in the face of tyranny, therefore, it would be wrong to expect resistance when the only form of resistance ingrained was migration and to nurture their language, religion, life style and culture in alien lands. Alternately, they have evolved the concept of Kashmiriyat, which in reasonable times, has helped them live in peaceful coexistence. It also needs to be kept in mind that even during the times of benign rulers, few Kashmiris have returned to their motherland. Thus, the migration of the Pandits after 19 January 1990 has also to be seen in this context.

The conditions for the migrations in 1990 were entirely new and different from the earlier times. Whereas earlier many Pandits migrated because they were willing to plunge into the unknown times in the hope of rebuilding future while many had embraced Islam to save life, and or protect their properties, now all were united in the resolve to just save their lives. However, some among them had the advantage of being a government employee and hence were sure that their interests would be protected. This satisfaction apart, a long and dark future lay ahead of them.

10

The Churning

'Memories warm you up from the inside.
But they also tear you apart.'

—*Kafka on the Shore*,
Haruki Murakami

The effort to detract from the memory of the traumatic events of the night of 19 January 1990 notwithstanding, the night has now been embedded in the memory of Kashmir. It is, and will be forever, remembered and discussed as the watershed moment; while the Pandits will nurse the scars of the memory of the terror of the night and the beginning of their flight to safety to inhospitable environs, their counterparts among the Kashmiri Muslims would argue that it was the day when militant struggle for realizing their dreams began. In the process, both would struggle to recall the happier times when the syncretic culture of Kashmir was a model for plural societies.

Gowhar Geelani[317], who grew up to be a journalist, was in his early teens in 1990, but his memory is etched with images of protests that he believed, had the 'ring' of a freedom struggle. He will also vouch that it was a consequence of the latent desire of the Kashmiris for independence and against the alleged brutalities unleashed by the paramilitary forces. While recalling that period, he believes, that the slogans and songs that he heard on the night of 19 January, were 'perhaps the freedom songs.'[318] He vividly recalls that his generation grew up with the calls for revolt against

India from the loudspeakers of the mosques and the marches of the protesters. The most frequently heard was the poetic message of Hurriyat leader, Syed Geelani:

> *Khoon e Shaheeda rang laya...*
> *Fateh ka parcham lehraya*
> *Jago jago Subha hui*
> *Jaag utho a ahle Kashmir*
> *Haatho mai le kar shamsheer*
> *Badlo Jammu ki takdir...*
> *Jago Jago subha hui.*
>
> (Wake up, it is morning/the victory flag has been unfurled/ The whole Kashmir has woken up/ with swords in hands/ change the fate of Jammu)

Those who are convinced that the protesters were 'freedom fighters', do not grasp the sinister design and dream that these slogans conveyed. History will judge them as being either too naïve or complicit in unleashing terror on the Kashmiri Pandits and pushing Kashmir towards an abyss. The song was not only a call for violent and armed struggle for the secession of Kashmir but also for the subjugation of Jammu, a region which was historically and politically of no concern to the Kashmiris. This impression of the young Gowhar Geelani also resonates in the writings of many others though there are a few objective voices as well. He has few, if any, memories of the targeted killing of the Pandits. For him they might have happened in some other era, other world.

Thirty years after that day of 1990, this is how a journalist, Ahmed Ali Fayyaz, an eyewitness of that night and the morning after, recounted for the general news and opinion website *The Quint*:

> On the night of 19 January 1990, all hell broke loose in Kashmir—a place many think of as "Heaven on Earth". Several mosques in Srinagar played the Azadi slogans, asking the Indian security forces to quit: "aey jabiro, aey zalimo, Kashmir hamara chhor do" (*Aye you the powerful, the tyrannical—quit our Kashmir*). They didn't. Those who were in barracks and bunkers and at the borders were brought down to kitchens and bedrooms by

> the deafening chants. It triggered the exodus of the minority Kashmiri Pandits—who had started to move out in smaller numbers months prior. They call it "Holocaust Day".
>
> The following day, CRPF machine guns left over 50 Kashmiri Muslim demonstrators dead and scores injured in a peaceful procession at Gawkadal. Kashmiri Muslims remember 21 January as "the beginning of the genocide"—"the first massacre".[319]

There appears some confusion regarding remembering the day when Gawkadal incident took place. This is probably because of newspaper-dependent memory. Since the incident of 20 January was reported in the newspapers the next day therefore some sources erroneously remember 21 January, the dateline of the paper, as the day when the incident took place. Curiously, Fayyaz recalls slogans directed against the Indian State but not against the Pandit community. Thus, no sooner had the sinister plan to purge the Valley of the Kashmiri Pandits put into action, its orchestrators knew that the reaction from the State will also set in motion a counter-narrative that will alienate the younger generation from the Indian State. But significantly, within a span of thirty years one can notice the difference between the memory of Kashinath Pandit, Rahul Pandita (*See Chapter 9 for more details*) and other Pandits who migrated, and the memory of Ahmed Ali Fayyaz, a Kashmiri Muslim. One remembers it as terror; the other as a demand for vacation of their land by the Indian Army.

In *My Frozen Turbulence in Kashmir* Jagmohan has explained the searches (which allegedly were said to be the reason for the uprising) conducted in downtown Srinagar and which resulted in the firing by CRPF and killings at the Gawkadal bridge on 20 January 1990. His explanation is not very convincing but is a good starting point to understand how the world of the Kashmiris fell apart. Jagmohan squarely lays the blame at the door of Farooq Abdullah, who, according to him, after a long period of inertia woke up to the pressure of New Delhi and had consequently chastised the Police force for its inaction. He claims that as one of the last acts before resigning, he had ordered the raids and searches on 16 January 1990, three days before his resignation and that Jagmohan had no hand in it.[320] How the paralyzed administration of an ineffective Chief Minister, who had also resigned, could suddenly galvanize the police force into such an action after he had resigned remained unexplained. In any case, irrespective of whether the searches happened before 19 January or after, most people agree that the midnight raids and searches were indiscriminate and humiliating since a few women too were allegedly harassed.

Jagmohan also claims, with some grain of truth, that before his arrival as Governor for the second time in 1990, the Police and Administration had virtually ceased to exist. The impact of terror that had already set in is best illustrated by the fact that Jagmohan had wanted former Director General of Police, Peer Ghulam Hassan Shah, as his advisor and had secured his consent to be appointed after agreeing to give him the cabinet rank on the latter's request. Yet the next morning, Peer Shah had conveyed his inability to take up the assignment.[321] The Governor himself had experienced the pall of terror on his arrival at the Srinagar airport when on his way into the city, he had to control his urge to walk 'through the heart of the city and thus (walk) through the hearts of the people', as he had done in 1986 when the State was under the Governor's Rule. However, his 'instinct told (him) that things had changed and that such step would be extremely rash, almost suicidal.'[322] The fear of losing life had wisely inhibited him from putting his body on the line. Ironically, later in the book he castigates ordinary Kashmiris for failing to stand up to the gun wielding terrorists to protect the Kashmiri Pandits! (*See Chapter 9 for more details*)

It is hard to believe that the police of a terrified regime would be willing to carry out the orders of a Chief Minister who had demitted his office. It would be reasonable to conclude that with a new Governor in office, the CRPF would be enthused into action and it might have taken the token help of the local police to carry out searches. It should also be recognized that the Jawans of the CRPF had been itching to teach the Kashmiris a lesson after they had been targeted by bomb explosion and individual targeting and the apparent indifference of the Farooq Abdullah government. This force, drawn from various parts of the country, had no sympathy or patience with people who provocatively shouted anti-India slogans and defiantly made a pointed distinction between Kashmir and

India. This display of defiance riled the simple, uncomplicated and patriotic emotions of the personnel of this Force. Thus, there was also a clash between opposing forces, one owing loyalty to the country and the other to the secessionist cause of Kashmir respectively, in which violence and counter violence came to play a significant role.

Obviously, there are certain holes in the entire narrative, giving rise to speculation that the events were allowed to drift so that the Kashmiri Pandits could be removed from the scene before any action could be taken against the terrorists and their supporters. The news of the happenings of the 19 January 1990 and the sloganeering had reached everywhere, and it was infuriating for the nationalist sentiments, which are understandably dominant among the soldiers of the army and the paramilitary forces. The immediate result was even more dreadful than it could have been imagined.

The Pandits are unanimous in remembering the night of 19 January as the night when terror was simultaneously unleashed everywhere in the Valley, but some Kashmiri authors vaguely suggest that the trigger was the massacre at Gawkadal. The memory of those days is erratic for many and Basharat Peer, author-journalist from Kashmir, vividly remembers a number of his Pandit friends and recalls the uneasy feeling of finding the unoccupied seats of those friends in the classroom, after the school had reopened following the winter break. He does not recall anything about their ordeal but has vivid memory of experiences of Muslim boys at the hands of security forces. Perhaps it can be explained by the fact that Muslim boys remained there and therefore shared their experiences but he also has memory of how fear came to be the dominant emotion of the Pandit boys before their departure as also what happened to them though they lived in large numbers in south Kashmir. Though he felt their absence but beyond that they are not part of his memory. Does that mean that their presence or absence was only relevant to the physical occupation of the seats in classroom and they had no communication or emotional connect with each other? Or, was there more to it?

This selective memory of the events is made worse even by Jagmohan as he added to the confusion. By his own narration, the day after taking oath, that is, 20 January 1990, he 'went on working in the Secretariat (Jammu, since he had not been able to fly to Srinagar because of bad weather) and returned to Raj Bhavan late in the evening. The night that followed was the strangest night that I have ever lived. Hardly had I gone to bed when the telephones at my bedside started ringing, almost continuously. At the other end there were voices of alarm, of concern, of fright, sometimes muted voices of men too terror-stricken to speak.'[323] However, according to Rahul Pandita and Kashinath Pandith, the panicked phone calls happened the night before, when the Pandit community was collectively subjected to intimidation and terror. To be fair, Rahul Pandita was too young and remote to know what else was happening that night and surely what he later wrote has to be based on the memory of others, long after the event. But other Kashmiri Pandits are also of the same opinion, but whatever the date remembered by various sufferers, the facts remain unchanged.

In the light of this, some authors fail to reconcile the fact that the incident of Gawkadal took place on the morning of 20 January 1990, that is, after the trauma of the night of 19th had occurred and not the night of 19/20 January.[324] Apparently, the apologists for the events have been finding reasons to rationalize the reprehensible act of the night before. Ironically, most of them are ritualistically nostalgic about the social bonds and shared culture between the Pandits and Muslims where, unlike the rest of the country, they shared the same cuisine and culture in their everyday life. Thus, they appear to be suggesting in a roundabout manner that the Gawkadal march was a protest against the indiscriminate and dishonorable raids and searches of the homes during the night of 19 January 1990, and the rupture between Muslims and Pandits happened subsequently. Another victim of muddled thinking is Basharat Peer, a journalist and son of a provincial civil servant, who grew up with the dream given to him by his father to aspire for the Indian Civil Service (Indian Administrative Services).[325] This obviously is a good example of the most dominant aspiration of the Kashmiri educated classes aiming for upward mobility. This dream could not have been there without his father's empathy for the Indian State and the acceptance of the national symbols. Therefore, when Basharat

Peer writes: 'Despite...my ignorance about [the] political history of Kashmir I had a sense of alienation and resentment most Kashmiris felt and had against Indian rule. We did not relate to the symbols of Indian nationalism—the flag, the national anthem and cricket team...,' he is obviously not stating the truth.[326]

A schoolboy in 1989, Peer understandably has little appreciation of the developments of the past two decades. He is also not expected to recognize the changing face of Islam in the Valley nor how the developments in the rest of the Islamic world were shaping forces in the region. What is known from his writing is that he was struggling to reconcile the values that his father wished to inculcate in him with the outside world that was increasingly at odds with his father's world. In order to protect him from the new influence that seemed to be sweeping the young of the Valley, his father and grandfather had decided to send him to Delhi for his college studies. But in a candid admission of facts while reminiscing the early years of terrorism, Peer writes, that after the longest winter that year, that is 1990, 'Five of my classmates were not there. Along with killing hundreds of pro-Indian Muslims, ranging from political activists to suspected informers for Indian Intelligence, militants killed hundreds of Pandits on similar grounds but sometimes apparently without reason...*(he candidly concedes)* deaths had scared the Pandits and thousands, including my classmates and their families, had left the Valley by March 1990 for Jammu, Delhi and various other cities and towns.'[327] After having expressed his lack of empathy for the Indian symbols and alienation from the Indian state as reason for the killings of political activists, intelligence workers and other people owing loyalty to India, he attributed the same reason for the killings of the Pandits. By his admission, they were a scared lot. Barring few exceptions, none dared oppose the regional political party or aspiration. But Peer is not forthcoming in explaining their killings. Were they killed because they had begun to stand by the Indian symbols or, were they killed because they were Pandits and the Islamic agenda had decided to purge the Valley of all *kafirs?* Peer does not offer any explanation.

In the final analysis, what unfolded from 1989 onwards was religious cleansing which almost became a competitive sport between the various splitting and merging groups of the terrorist organizations. The aims of this nefarious exercise were multiple, first, to promote Islamist agenda of establishing a society that is governed by *Shariat* law, second, to bring Kashmir under the ambit of Pakistan, and third, to create religious reaction in the rest of India to divide it along communal lines. It is obvious that this was less a Kashmiri agenda and more of Pakistan, but the fact remains that the Kashmiris allowed themselves to be used as a tool by Pakistan.

Therefore, this 'egg or the hen' debate about what triggered the events from 1989 draws our attention away from the meticulous planning of the Pakistani agencies as well as the colossal failure of the Indian agencies to anticipate and pre-empt them. Were the Indian policy makers not aware of the fact that Pakistan was a revisionist State that was determined not to give up on its goal of annexing Kashmir and were the intelligence agencies not prepared for a new approach by Pakistan to incite the local youth? Had Jagmohan, who was Governor of the State till a few months before the volcano erupted, not sufficiently warned the Centre of the possibilities? The last question has been answered by him in considerable detail in his book. His report to the then Prime Minister Rajiv Gandhi were there but from the correspondence released by him they were general in nature with hardly any actionable information. It is also possible that because of Jagmohan's perceived prejudice against the Muslims, the Centre erred in not taking his warnings too seriously! But the bitter truth is that either the intelligence agencies were so incompetent as to be clueless of the events that were to unfold or they allowed things to drift till finally everything had erupted in the open when in every nook and corner of the Valley, the voice amplifiers had simultaneously come alive with songs of valor of the jihadis of the past and unmistakable warnings and threats to Kashmiri Pandits that suggested a carefully planned strategy, executed with precision. If the intelligence agencies did not get a whiff of it, then it was a criminal oversight that should have been severely punished.

There is also need to objectively understand Jagmohan. No one credits him with political acumen since he was a quintessential administrator and a good one at that. His protestations notwithstanding, when he first arrived in Jammu and Kashmir as Governor in 1984, he had come with a clear-cut brief from the then Prime Minister Indira Gandhi. He duly obliged by removing Farooq Abdullah, the democratically elected Chief Minister, in a ham-handed political operation. But readers could not have failed to notice that he had done his best out of a bad operation by his meticulous planning and deployment of forces to face the aftermath, as Prabhu Chawla the journalist pointed out. But did he understand the State? Hardly, is the answer. Gul Shah, a man of dubious credibility, had been hoisted upon the State as Chief Minister and during the time that he stayed in office, much of the time, curfew had been clamped in the Valley. It is also now known that the Pakistani cells found a favorable climate to flourish during Gul's rule. There is little doubt that Farooq Abdullah had made serious errors in his career but Jagmohan has been so intent upon transferring all the guilt on to him, and as a bonus, on to the Congress because of his soured relations with Rajiv Gandhi, that he goes on to accuse both of instigating not only the Gawkadal tragedy but the violence that followed.[328] Of course, his best period as Governor was between March 1986 and November 1986 when the State was ruled under the Governor's Rule. It was during this period that he earned goodwill, particularly of Hindus by taking over the administration of the Mata Vaishno Devi shrine, Katra and providing fair and responsive administration. But even then, he was known for his efficient administration rather than political acumen.

It is unfair to claim that Kashmir was plagued only by inefficient and corrupt administration and not by contesting politics between the state and Centre, inter-regional rivalries, competing political aspirations and degradation of the democratic institutions. India, in fact, should have been more vigilant of Pakistan since it knew, that the latter had tried invasion in 1947; it had used the ploy of sending in the infiltrators in 1965 in the belief that their mere presence in the Valley would rouse the people against India: on both occasions it had failed and it should have realized at Tashkent and other international platforms that, 'you cannot get at the Conference table what you have lost at your chosen forum i.e. battle field', as celebrated lawyer, activist and writer A.G. Noorani had spoken bluntly during the Islamabad Literary Festival, 2017.[329] Therefore, learning from each failure and revising its strategy after each failure, it had devised a new strategy whereby it took full advantage of the disenchantment of the local youth with the kind of democracy that was practiced in Kashmir, widespread corruption and the failure of Sheikh Abdullah and his successor Farooq Abdullah, to deliver on the unrealistic dream of 'Kashmir' that they had given to the youth. All this while, the government agencies remained oblivious to the forces that were biding their time to strike.

The different phases of Kashmir since 1947 have demonstrated the tenacity of Pakistan even though all its attempts to reopen the Kashmir issue at the international forums have met with failure. Where it has succeeded since the 1980s is in inflicting wounds on Kashmir that have left it scarred beyond recognition. In this it took full advantage of two parallel developments in the region. Just when the Kashmiri youth felt disillusioned with India and the State leaders after Sheikh Abdullah's compromise with Indira Gandhi in 1975, the Soviet Union had invaded Afghanistan that ultimately led to its implosion and fragmentation, triggering the historical animosity among various ethnic groups of former Yugoslavia and the resultant civil war. How deeply the events in the Muslim republics of Soviet Union impacted Kashmir is best illustrated by the frustration expressed by Jagmohan when he saw on the night of 20 January 1990 Doordarshan's special telecast about the 'ethnic' revolt of Azerbaijan and the 'Romanian Liberation'. He was incensed at the timing of the telecast (coinciding with the events of 19 January 1990) as it was misread by the Kashmiri youth which too was getting ready to rise against the State. Obviously, it was an example of the misreading of the situation and Kashmir by Delhi, Jagmohan felt.[330] Clearly, the United Front led by Prime Minister V.P. Singh had little or no appreciation of the currents and undercurrents of the situation in Kashmir, with his Kashmiri Home Minister Mufti Mohammad Sayeed being of little use.

After the abject capitulation of the government in securing the release of his daughter, two years later, the Jammu and Kashmir Students Liberation Front (JKSLF) repeated the act by kidnapping Nahida Imtiaz, the daughter of the prominent parliamentarian

Safiuddin Soz. There are multiple versions of how her release was obtained but Hein G. Kiessling, the author of *Faith, Unity, Discipline: ISI of Pakistan* asserts that the then 'Prime Minister Chandra Shekhar was forced to ask his counterpart Pakistan's Nawaz Sharif for assistance in the release…This request was humiliating for India.'[331] However, this is contested by local sources that claim that the release was secured by the state police by taking the brother of the leader of JKSLF hostage.

By 1990, the same author says, more than thirty militant political religious organizations had flourished in the Valley. Initially 'their attacks were directed against bars, cinemas, beauty salons, video shops and the like. The women in the Kashmir Valley were soon forced to be veiled. Fanatics attacked unveiled women with ink or acid.'[332]At the same time, Pakistan was greatly energized as its Inter-Services Intelligence (ISI) had played a crucial role in the defeat of the Soviet Union. In the process, the ISI came to own the victory over the Communist superpower and also became too powerful to be controlled either by the government or its parent organization—the army. Pakistan, however, was waiting for just this kind of an opportunity that had opened up in the Valley. Not surprisingly, the first phase of militancy was largely dominated by the foreign Mujahideens in which the Kashmiri youth played the role of apprentices after which, with the guidance of their Pakistani handlers, they moved towards taking control of the operations. The transformation that took place among the youth is best described by an *India Today* report written as early as 15 January 1990:

> Earlier, there was sullen anger. Now, there is violent fury. Once, youth used to throw stones at buses. Now, they hurl sophisticated plastic explosives at government offices. They used to be called the "angry boys". Now they are hailed as Mujahidin (freedom fighters). Yesterday, they masked their faces to wave flags.
>
> Today they do that to brandish Kalashnikovs. Six months ago, a police picket was enough to scare mobs in downtown Srinagar. Now, it takes two machine-gun-fitted armoured cars. From a valley of tears Kashmir is swiftly climbing up a separatist hill marked by the jagged rocks of militancy, blind hatred and bloodshed.[333]

In this early phase the dominant force and ideology was that of Jammu and Kashmir Liberation Front (JKLF).[334] It is more appropriate to say that this is the mother organization of all the militant and terrorist groups, but it primarily drew its support from people belonging to the State, the Pakistan occupied region of the State and among those who were settled in the UK as well. Its ideology was the reunification of the divided regions of the State and also to strive for an independent State. Notwithstanding the fact that JKLF has only Muslim members, it is notionally secular. It continues to assert till this date that a secular and independent Kashmir, free of both India and Pakistan is its eventual goal. Theoretically, it also advocates the return of the Pandits to their homes in the Valley or in safe enclaves though it is also accused of the first killings of the Pandits. Despite having received weapons and training from forces supported and patronized by the Pakistani military, the JKLF regards Pakistan as a 'force of occupation' and carries out political struggle against it in Pakistan-occupied-Kashmir. The killings and exodus of the Pandits was not on its agenda till the gun culture transformed its members. Kashinath Pandit, a respected historian from Kashmir, is willing to accept that 'in the training camps, these JKLF gunmen were not strictly told to unleash terror against the Kashmiri Pandit community as a whole. But being [a] young Muslim indoctrinated with fundamentalist ideology and with deadly automatic weapon called Kalashnikov in his hands, [he] wanted a target. Maligned Kashmiri Pandit was the sitting duck.' He goes on to say that Amanullah Khan, the founder of JKLF, explained the culture of using the Kalashnikovs against the Pandits during a conversation he had with him during a seminar in the European Parliament in Brussels in 1992 He said 'boys back to Kashmir with weapons became uncontrollable. They attacked Pandits because Pandits did not join the armed struggle. The truth is that this conspiracy was shrouded in such secrecy as not to let even the parents and family members of the *Jihadists* know where they had gone and what their objective was.'[335]

At an ideological level, a dispassionate and objective assessment of the JKLF would reveal that it had not deviated too greatly from the policies of Sheikh Abdullah of the early years of 1950s except the fact that Sheikh Abdullah desired an independent State with the independence being guaranteed by both, India and Pakistan. In case Pakistan was not amenable to it then he preferred settling with a special status within the Indian Republic. In all political discourses and elections after returning to power in 1975, securing the pre-1953 status had been the dominant platform both for him as well as Farooq Abdullah. But the younger generation felt that Sheikh Abdullah had deviated from this dream that he had given to Kashmir and had not only succumbed to the temptation of power in 1975 but had also failed to get his demands fulfilled by the Centre. Therefore disillusioned by him this generation expressed its disappointment and disapproval quite openly. It must also be again emphasized that Jammu and Kashmir had enjoyed considerable degree of sovereignty before 1947 and the common people of all the regions proudly announced their separate identity. This was true of Muslims as well as the Hindus and Sikhs. This began to change when the Hindus of the Valley began to break rank from this common identity after the country's independence and its accession to India because they realized that with the umbrella of a Hindu king gone, they were to be at the mercy of the Muslim majority. The latter, unfortunately displayed all the signs of a force that had found in the changed circumstances, a chance to be assertive and rule the State after many centuries as the Sultans had done. Muslims had also become greedy of power and impatient of the control of Delhi. The fears of the Pandits of majoritarianism were similar to those expressed by Sheikh Abdullah on behalf of the Kashmiri Muslims to Nehru while demanding constitutional guarantees for Kashmir's autonomy.[336] This was at odds with what the JKLF boys expected of them.

This dream of an independent State was thus originally given to the people by Sheikh Abdullah, and his covert hobnobbing with world powers to achieve this goal was not unknown to the people. However, since he apparently gave up on this dream after he had been removed from power for a long time, the younger generation chose to boldly strive for their desired goal of a united and independent State. By then, the Palestinian exertions and resistance offered by Yasser Arafat and his organization, Fatah, had grabbed the attention of other people struggling for independent recognition. Armed struggle appeared a viable option to the Kashmiri youth too. They had seen that armed uprisings against the imperialists had brought freedom to Algeria and Vietnam. Inspired by such trends, a group of young men got together to get organized as the Jammu and Kashmir Liberation Front (JKLF). It is not without significance that the first branch of the JKLF was established in 1987, the year when the youth concluded that democracy in the State was rigged in such a manner that the constitutional institutions were not made available to those not owing allegiance to either the National Conference or Congress.

The JKLF was, in fact, an offshoot of the UK chapter of the Plebiscite Front. Maqbool Bhat is often credited as being its co-founder along with Amanullah Khan who was born in Gilgit, studied in Srinagar and immigrated to Pakistan in 1952. Bhat was born in Kupwara and had also immigrated to Pakistan after studying in Srinagar. The duo had earlier formed the Jammu and Kashmir National Liberation Front (NLF) in the late 1960s, along with Hashim Qureshi. The group carried out the hijacking of Ganga, an Indian Airlines plane flying from Srinagar to Jammu, in January 1971, and diverted it to Lahore. The Pakistan government returned all the passengers and crew to India, and subsequently tried the hijackers and several members of the NLF on charges of being Indian agents. Khan was imprisoned in a Gilgit prison during 1971–72 and was released after protests broke out. Maqbool Bhat was released in 1974, and he crossed over into Indian-administered Kashmir where he was arrested on a bank robbery charge. Earlier, before crossing over to Pakistan, he had been charged with the murder of a person from the CID in Kashmir and had been awarded a death sentence. Upon his return, after his arrest, the case was reopened and the Supreme Court of India restored the earlier death sentence. It was in connection with this case that he was hanged in Tihar Jail in 1984.

Amanullah Khan had moved to England, where he received the enthusiastic support of the prosperous British-Mirpuri community. Soon, the UK chapter of the Plebiscite Front was converted into the Jammu and Kashmir Liberation Front (JKLF) in May 1977.

It also formed an armed wing called the National Liberation Army. Amanullah Khan took charge as the General Secretary of the JKLF the following February. With the active support of the British Mirpuris, the group expanded rapidly, setting up branches in Pakistan, Denmark, Holland, Germany, France, Saudi Arabia, United Arab Emirates and the United States. It had also organized well-attended conventions in Birmingham (1981) and Luton (1982).

On 3 February 1984, members of the National Liberation Army had kidnapped the Indian diplomat Ravindra Mahatre in Birmingham and demanded the release of Maqbool Bhat as ransom. Amanullah Khan was named as the interlocutor. Unfortunately, the kidnappers, upon instructions, shot the diplomat and India executed Maqbool Bhat six days later, turning him into a martyr and a rallying point that gave the JKLF the visibility it had lacked earlier. A British court convicted two members of the JKLF for the killing of Mahatre, and Hashim Qureshi and Amanullah Khan were expelled from the UK. By now, the hanging of Maqbool Bhat had turned him into a martyred hero and consequently the JKLF consolidated itself, with the young Yasin Malik playing a leading role. The militancy of the early years was dominated by it but simultaneously Pakistan realized that JKLF's emergence was a threat to its own plans. In Pakistan occupied Jammu and Kashmir, a large number of people were Mirpuris, Soodhan Rajput Muslims, and those who had migrated from the Jammu region. Few among them wanted to merge their identity with Pakistan and most were drawn to JKLF with the dream that they would be reuniting with its other half and creating an independent State. Since this did not serve the interests of Pakistan, and with various trained Jihadists available in Pakistan after the withdrawal of the Soviet Union from Afghanistan, JKLF was soon infiltrated by them and in many places the terrorist activities were appropriated.

This was further facilitated after Yasin Malik and others had returned disillusioned from Pakistan, having also realized that the life of Muslims in Kashmir as part of India was much better than their counterparts in Pakistan occupied Jammu and Kashmir. It had also dawned upon Yasin Malik and his associates that Pakistan will never allow them to realize their dream of independent Kashmir and will reduce them to second rate citizens like the Mohajirs of Karachi, the Balochs and Pashtuns. Through the Islamist infiltrators in Kashmir, their masters in Muzaffarabad had also been giving information about them to Indian security forces so that those owing loyalty to JKLF could be eliminated. Thus, by 1994, Yasin Malik was ready to come back to the democratic mainstream where differences and demands could be negotiated. It is ironical that much to its consternation, the intelligence agencies of Pakistan had by then also assessed that Yasin Malik and the JKLF had considerable influence over the Pakistan occupied Jammu and Kashmir, and were, therefore, a threat to their designs. So, efforts were exerted more vigorously to whittle down the influence of the JKLF. There was no better way than by indulging in greater violence in order to discredit the JKLF and demonstrate whose writ runs in the Valley.

The disillusionment of Pakistan with the JKLF had begun as early as 1991 and consequently many terrorist organizations had surfaced. One of them was the Al Jihad Force (AJF) which announced its arrival with the kidnapping of a French engineer working with the Dhulhasti Power Project in Kishtwar in December 1991. Since this project was on the river Chenab, it was obvious that the deed was meant to serve the interests of Pakistan as it had been objecting to all power projects on Chenab which was part of the Indus River systems, the waters of which were shared according to the Indus Waters Treaty.[337]Four months later, the engineer was rescued from Anantnag by a rival group, the Hizb-ul-Mujahideen. This incident was a proof of the multiple masters and puppets indulging in the State with each one of them pursuing their own agenda. On the Republic Day, 26 January 1992, a rocket attack was launched on Lal Chowk. It was followed by another such attack on the Bakshi Stadium, Srinagar on 15 August, which was the venue of Independence Day celebrations. It was after this that a series of abductions and killings of the foreigners coming to Kashmir took place. Abductions, hostages for ransom and killings became a common instrument of terror in the Kashmir Valley. After Dr Rubaiya Sayeed's abduction in December 1989, it became the primary tool used by the militants to pressurize authorities into releasing their jailed colleagues. In this, foreigners were more vulnerable and fruitful targets since their abduction brought international-media attention too. In March 1991, two Swedish engineers, working at the Uri project, were kidnapped near Gulmarg by the Muslim Janbaz Force. Its demand was that Amnesty International and Asia Watch, two western non-profit NGOS, send human rights investigators to inquire allegations of rape, torture and murder. However, the hostages escaped unharmed after 97 days. In June 1991, a militant group, Pasdaran-e-Islam, tried to kidnap six Israeli tourists from the Dal Lake area in Srinagar. However, in the skirmish, two militants and one tourist were killed.

In June 1993, Harkat-ul-Ansar kidnapped two British nationals, Kim Housego and David Mackie, from Gulmarg. They demanded that security bunkers be lifted from around the Hazratbal shrine. The hostages were freed after 17 days and handed over to local journalists in south Kashmir after the government conceded their demands. On 4 July 1995, a hitherto unknown outfit called Al-Faran kidnapped four foreign tourists, two Americans and two Britons near Pahalgam. They demanded that 21 jailed militants, including four chiefs of different outfits, be released. However, one American hostage escaped.The same outfit kidnapped one German tourist from Zojibal in upper the Pahalgam enroute to the Amarnath cave on 8 June. The militants struck again in Zojibal area on 9 Julyand took captive a Norwegian tourist, Hans Christian Ostero, a performing artist. Later, he was found brutally beheaded.

Two years later, Kim Housego wrote about his experiences as a hostage and the gamut of emotions that he experienced as well as his reaction upon knowing about the barbaric execution of Hans Christian Ostero on 4 February 1997 in the English paper, *The Independent:*

> My abductors, I later found out, were members of the Harkat-ul-Ansar (HUA), the Movement of the Supporters of the Prophet, a militant Islamist group fighting to unite Kashmir with Pakistan. Not the largest group operating in the Kashmir valley, it is nevertheless reputed for its ruthlessness—and also its resources, drawn from businessmen in Pakistan and the Middle East. It was originally founded in Faisalabad in central Pakistan in the early 1980s to help Afghan Mujahidins fight the Russians. Its

> leadership, by no means clearly defined, is based in Muzaffarabad, the capital of Pakistan-occupied Kashmir…It is claimed that the HUA receives direct support in weapons and training from the Pakistan army's Inter-Service-Intelligence (ISI), which wields significant influence over the group. However, the ISI denies any connection…It seemed that the killing of Ostero had opened a new chapter in the group's handling of Western hostages…The year before they presented us with souvenirs on our release. Now they had shown a very different face.
>
> It was in Anantnag that David Mackie and I had been released on June 23, 1994. Two days before, large crowds had taken to the streets angrily protesting at the murder of Dr Quazi Nissar, the religious leader of south Kashmir. He had been a key figure in the negotiations over our release. David and I did not know it at the time, but he had put himself at risk as a secret intermediary between the HUA and my father. As a moderate political leader, he felt obliged to intervene. Three days later he was murdered. In retrospect, his killing probably did not result from negotiating our release. But the possibility still haunts me…What I have learnt from all this? That all the parties to the hostage drama—militant groups, governments, embassies—have their own objectives and priorities. Sometimes these tie-in with the release of the hostages and sometimes they do not. The wider political issues at stake, such as curbing international terrorism or strengthening US-Pakistan relations, overshadow the governments' preoccupation with the life of any one hostage. As my father says: "In the end, it's only the relatives who really care about the lives of those held."[338]

The traumatic experience of not knowing what fate awaited him and the realization in hindsight how close he was to death and what price a man of God had paid for his humanitarian effort to secure his and David Mackie's release had taught the young man not only about how terrorists functioned but also about how politics was played out at the local and international level. But one thing that stood out was the fact that the strings of terrorism were being controlled and pulled by the ISI of Pakistan.

The civilian killings that had begun with the targeting of State symbols and its agencies, had soon in the hands of Pakistani controlled agencies, deteriorated into indiscriminate killing machines of, first the Pandits and those loyal to the symbols of India, and then foreigners. It was clear that the militant movement of the Kashmiris had now become a movement controlled by Islamist fundamentalists who, since the experience of Afghanistan, enjoyed killings and the display of power over the innocents. Thus, the JKLF suffered not only splits but also relegation with, first the Hizb-ul-Mujaheedin and then the Lashkar-e-Taiba (LET) and Jaish-e-Mohammad (JEM) taking the center stage. The JKLF was supported and based in PoJK in its early stages but gradually as it appeared that its success could pose a challenge to Pakistan's illegal occupation of some parts of Jammu and Kashmir, Pakistan withdrew unreserved support. For Pakistan, in the absence of any other alternative, this was an acceptable option as long as it was a headache for India. But once it found sufficient number of volunteers for conducting clandestine operations in the Valley, it wasted no time in propping these new elements to counter the influence of the JKLF. The combination of these forces created the darkest period in the history of Kashmir. Soon, not only was the Valley plunged into darkness but the Islam-driven operations also crossed over the Banihal to strike terror in the Poonch, Rajouri, Reasi, Doda and Kishtwar. These were the same areas where, as Prime Minister of the State, Sheikh Abdullah had injected the element of communalism by carving out constituencies based on religious identities. The chickens had finally come home to roost and since now it was discovered that Sheikh Abdullah and his son had joined hands with India, the new generation turned on the legacy of Sheikh Abdullah and made the Abdullahs a legitimate target.

The cycle of killings of militants, civilians, army and paramilitary forces that was to begin then is yet to come to an end. In the meantime, it has passed through multiple and distinct phases. The first, between 1990 and 1996 when at times everything appeared to have gone out of control for India but the Government still succeeded in holding Assembly elections and bringing back the democratic government in 1996 by the untiring efforts of the bureaucracy in giving good governance and the security forces in keeping terrorism under prolonged periods of control. It was during this period that the new generation developed selective memory of post-1947 Kashmir and seriously began to believe in a separate and communal identity. In this the All Parties Hurriyat Conference (APHC) played a significant role though there were isolated voices that questioned a leadership that asked sacrifices from others without putting themselves or their families to any kind of risks.

Apart from the Hazratbal standoff and the Charar-i-Sharif tragedy, this period was also marked by the Ekta Yatra of BJP leader Murali Manohar Joshi[339]. This Yatra began from Kanyakumari with the avowed goal of hoisting the national flag a Lal Chowk on 26 January 1992 to mark the Republic Day, and provide an appropriate response to the secessionists. That was a time when a number of changes had been taking place in the Indian polity. A much-weakened Congress party had been hobnobbing with the Hindu communalists after its defeat in 1977. It had found that not only was its caste Hindu vote base slipping but even the Muslims could no longer be said to be its 'vote bank' because of the rising number of communal riots. In addition, the scheduled castes and backward classes too had begun to flex their political muscles, having found new messiahs. To recalibrate the political equations, Rajiv Gandhi had overseen the opening of the locks of the disputed Ram Mandir in Ayodhya. When Narasimha Rao became the Prime Minister, he went a step further and seemed to be appropriating the Hindu agendas of BJP. Many believed that the Ekta Yatra[340] had the tacit blessings of Prime Minister Narasimha Rao. But probably the truth is that the Hindus had begun to consolidate themselves and had begun to assert their identity after the Shah Bano judgment—which they considered as an act to appease the Muslims—was overturned by a constitutional amendment initiated by Rajiv Gandhi. Thus, after the Hindus had been galvanized by the Rath Yatra of Lal Krishna Advani[341] in 1990, the Ekta Yatra—which was apparently secular since the goal was national unity and integrity—was announced by Murali Manohar Joshi, a senior member of the Bharatiya Janata Party. In reality it was a none too subtle campaign by the Hindu India to send a message not so much to Pakistan as to the Muslims of India in general and Kashmir in particular.

From the beginning of the Yatra, the perception was that

Narasimha Rao's government was subtly encouraging it and that is why no attempt had been made to stop it during the long march. By the time it had reached Delhi, countless enthusiasts had joined it. Thousands had joined the Yatra from the southern states and in their innocence arrived poorly attired only to be shocked by the discovery of the inadequacy of their preparations in the face of the harsh winter conditions of the north. Meanwhile, the wintry weather had become intolerably inclement with rains and blockages on the Jammu-Srinagar highway. It was apparent that the organizers of the Yatra had failed to anticipate problems and consequences of a frenzied mob reaching the Valley. It was then that the possible complicity of the Congress became apparent when Atal Behari Vajpayee was prevailed upon to step in and he succeeded in holding back the multitude.

Many years later, Zahoor Malik of *Kashmir Times* recalled those events:

> The Governor's administration at that time had ruled out permission to thousands of BJP workers to reach Srinagar for security and law and order reasons. Finally, the bad weather and unpredictable condition of Srinagar-Jammu highway helped. But BJP supporters were adamant on reaching Lal Chowk and thought that the administration was deliberately stopping them in Jammu. It was finally left to Vajpayee to pacify the agitated party workers and he did it very effectively.
>
> Addressing a rally in Jammu, Vajpayee had said, "Nobody in the administration wants to stop us. Even the Governor Sahib wants that we should reach Lal Chowk and hoist the national flag. But weather is not permitting us. It is not possible for all of us to go there in such bad weather conditions particularly when the condition of the road is unpredictable and not good. Now it has been decided that Joshi sahib and other leaders will go to Srinagar and will unfurl the national flag at Lal Chowk."[342]

In fact, the government provided all facilities to Joshi and a few others to fly to Srinagar, hoist the flag and then hurriedly get back to Jammu with the news of the mission accomplished. Not much publicized at that time, but a significant element of that Yatra was that the organizational responsibility was on the shoulders of a young Gujarati leader by the name of Narendra Damodar Modi. What everyone had also missed was that though skillful in organizing the Yatra, Mod displayed poor judgment about how it would end and how the consequences would be handled—a trait that was to remain a hallmark of his leadership in later years. Finally, when everything was about to spiral out of hand in a bloody showdown, it was left to the wise and mature head of Atal Bihari Vajpayee to find an acceptable denouement.

Reacting as an ethnic Kashmiri, this incident was more passionately described by Badri Raina in an article written in *Seminar*, where he admitted that he was like Frantz Fanon[343] 'he simply cannot be objective about history. I can easily empathize with the perpetual bind Fanon expresses, especially after what I can only describe as the recent custodial rape of the valley; the invading posse of Murali Manohar Joshi was, after all, in connivance not just with the Congress party but open and protective state patronage. The conquering flag was implanted at Lal Chowk to the menacing accompaniment of bared, phallic bayonets.'[344]

Raina staunchly believes that the killings that took place during that period were because of the takeover of militancy by the Hizb-ul-Mujahideen at the behest of the Inter-Services Intelligence (ISI) of Pakistan to weaken the unity of Kashmiri ethnicity by effecting communal killings. He points out that for every Pandit killed six Muslim lives too were taken per day by the bullets. He also points out that by the end of the first quarter of 1992, when the peak of Pandit killings had passed, there were still about 5,000 Pandits living in the Valley, protected by their ethnic but Muslim brothers.[345]

During that period, in November 1993, another flash occurred when the Hazratbal holy mosque, along with civilians who had come to the mosque, was taken over by a group of militants owing loyalty to the JKLF. After a long-drawn-out affair, the low-level leader of the militants finally surrendered but it was marred by a bomb blast in Srinagar city during the celebrations, killing eight civilians. It was one of the longest sieges marked by absolute lack of coordination among the various wings of the government. The following year, in the month of August, the security forces put up sand bag bunkers around the Hazratbal mosque. Later, after a prolonged confrontation over the setting up of the bunkers, the government buckled and removed them. By this time, Pakistan's Directorate of Military Operations, which was directly monitoring the Kashmir insurgency had concluded that the 'insurgency spirit was depleting' and, therefore, to give a fillip to 'home grown' insurgency it facilitated the induction of '*mehman mujahids*' (guest Mujahids).[346]

However, the most painful and challenging terrorist activity during that period was the occupation and burning of the Charar-i-Sharif, the final resting place of the most revered saint of Kashmir, Nooruddin or Nund Rishi, the founder of the Rishi[347] philosophy in the Valley. The takeover of the shrine in 1995 by Pakistan-based Sunni terrorists, belonging to the Harkat-al-Ansar group, came as a huge disappointment since the Valley had gone without curfew for six months and the government was toying with the idea of holding Assembly polls when Mast Gul-led group of terrorists rudely shattered the deceptive peace. It was a group that was made up of terrorists owing loyalty to both Harkat-al-Ansar and Hizb-ul-Mujahideen, and that looked towards Pakistani handlers for guidance and directions. The strategic location of the Charar-i-Sharif made it an ideal place to infiltrate and escape from the harsh winter and was routinely used as such. In December 1994 too, they had been trickling into the fair-sized town for sanctuary.

By March 1995, when their presence became known and the takeover of the shrine complete, the government feared its destruction and offered a free passage in April, which the Harkat-al-Ansar elements were willing to take but were over ruled by the terrorists belonging to the Hizb-ul-Mujahideen. They had been told by their handlers to stay put. By then there were about 75 of the most hardened terrorists in the shrine. The terrorists had been well armed and also well equipped to handle explosives and since they belonged to the fundamentalist faith of Sunnis, the Government of India and the State were wary of any hasty step since it was feared that the terrorists will have no compunction in putting a shrine to a saint to harm. Therefore, the negotiations revolved round convincing them of safe passage. This was a situation that was embarrassing for the Government and it was a rare opportunity for the APHC to not only aggravate the embarrassment but also appear to be the sole voice of the Valley.

Finally, when the terrorists escaped, in controversial circumstances after lighting the shrine on fire, not only the government but the APHC too faced flak, since it had been demonstrated that not only did it not have any control over the foreign based terrorists but it had failed to convince them to spare the most cherished of the Valley shrines. However, the APHC managed to remain in the limelight when it led in the rejection of the offer of the Government to rebuild the shrine. Instead, Muslim organizations of the world met in Mecca and raised funds to route it through the APHC for its construction. But for some time, it remained an ineffective organization in public eye as it was seen to be more interested in playing politics rather than look after the interests of the people. The reputation of the Government too had suffered with the daily news trickling out about the various organs working at cross purposes with confusion prevailing everywhere. The inability to take a firm decision and absence of credible intelligence were the most visible failures.

In between, there have been quiet phases when signals for peace and development have been unmistakable and during one of these phases, after recovering from the ignominy of Charar-i-Sharif fiasco, assembly elections were held in 1996. An important development, of the years before the 1996 elections, beginning with 1994, was the emergence of those militants who after crossing over to Pakistan had been disillusioned by the movement since they saw that while the people living in the occupied part of the State lived in poverty and backwardness, the Kashmiri youth was being used by Pakistan for the ultimate goal of annexing Jammu and Kashmir. On their return from Pakistan, some of these militants joined hands with government forces to form armed militia by the name of Ikhwan-ul-Muslmeen headed by Mohammad Yusuf Parray, better known as Kuka Parray, to resist terrorism. He was joined by Yusuf Ahmed Shah and Liaquat Khan and their joint effort yielded in eliminating a large number of terrorists, mostly foreigners. Much maligned, this group needs to be seen in the frame of the larger movement of Kashmir where different routes have been taken to find a respectable solution to it. This had brought instant reaction from the Pakistani Army which assessed that the Kashmiris were 'tending to stay away from the insurgency and tending to return to their normal lives.'[348] Finally, after the ill-fated 1987 elections, democracy was restored in 1996. This phase began with 1996 and ended in 2002 when the people voted on the issues of governance and for the first time inflicted electoral defeat on the National Conference.

11

Reclaiming Democracy

'Men are not prisoners of fate,
but only prisoners of their own minds.'
—Franklin Delano Roosevelt

Politically, the events of Kashmir, beginning with the night of January 1990, had threatened India of dire consequences. The V.P. Singh government in Delhi, living on the support of BJP, had proved to be singularly inept in handling the emerging challenges, particularly in Kashmir where Dr Rubaiya Sayeed's abduction episode had exposed the soft nature of the Indian State. In fact, the government of the day did not even show a semblance of understanding the State and its problems. Not surprisingly Pakistan took full advantage of the situation and not only accelerated the terrorist strikes to create more confusion but also piled diplomatic pressure on India.

In 1990, after the deposition of Benazir Bhutto as the Prime Minister of Pakistan, late General Zia-ul-Haq's protégé Nawaz Sharif was elected the Prime Minister and with it began an era of brutal killings and terrorist activities in the Valley. It was not surprising since Nawaz Sharif was a product of the Islamist right wing. It was during this period that the '*Kashmir Banega Pakistan*' slogan became the war-cry of Pakistan. But before her dismissal, Benazir Bhutto had drummed up the issue of Human Rights violations by Indian security forces in the Valley. She had called on 4 February 1990, an urgent conference of Pakistan's political leaders on Kashmir situation and announced 5 February as a Solidarity Day with Kashmir. It was during this campaign that Benazir referred to the slogan her father Zulfikar Ali Bhutto iterated—of waging a 'thousand-year war' against India to claim Kashmir. Since then, the day is still being observed in Pakistan. Within the next five days, the Pakistani Parliament passed a resolution which rejected Jammu and Kashmir's accession to India and even demanded a UN resolution for it. This Kashmir policy was further carried forward by the new Nawaz Sharif government and 'despite several proposals suggesting bilateral talks by PV Narasimha Rao; Bhutto government, which was then in the good books of US, was successful in internationalizing the Kashmir Issue.'[349]

These developments had taken some time in crystallizing. According to late Satinder Lambah, former High Commissioner to Pakistan and later Special Envoy of Prime Minister Manmohan Singh, for the back-channel parleys with Pakistan, even Pakistan was taken by surprise by the developments of the 1980s in Kashmir but was then quick to exploit the situation. Lambah quotes Ahmed Rashid, a journalist and best-selling foreign policy author in Pakistan. Soon, President of Pakistan Ghulam Ishaq Khan was bold enough to repeat the earlier slogan of Kashmir being the 'unfinished agenda of Partition'.[350] Soon after, Benazir's ouster, Nawaz Sharif, the new Prime Minister resumed the rhetoric and chanted the slogan that reverberated in the Valley for some time—*Kashmir Banega Pakistan.* (Kashmir will become Part of Pskistan) It must be acknowledged that the most critical phase of Kashmir militancy had to be dealt by Narasimha Rao. To begin with, the challenge was caused by Pakistan's assistance and active involvement with Kashmiri militants and the support given to them by *jihadi* organizations. These included the United Jihad Council headed by Syed Salahuddin, an umbrella organization of fourteen small groups active in PoK, including Al-Badar and Tehrik-e-Jihad. Apart from them, organizations like Lashkar-e-Taiba (so-called army of the pure), Harkat-ul-Ansar and Hizb-ul-Mujahideen too were active and supported by Pakistan.

At this point the stock of Pakistan was high in the western world, having helped in dismantling the Soviet Union. This was the beginning of the most serious diplomatic challenges posed to India and it raised Kashmir persistently and with vigor. During this period when Benazir was back as Prime Minister in 1993 (this time Nawaz Sharif having been removed by the army) Pakistan tried to canvass support for its plan to put India under sanctions by the United Nations. Benazir's policy was to work towards diluting the Simla Agreement and put more emphasis on the UN Resolutions on Kashmir. It also needs be remembered that ever since the pivotal role played by Pakistan in USA's fight against Soviet occupation of Afghanistan, the relations between the two countries were particularly friendly and the sole super-power, after the demise of the Soviet Union, was eager to help Pakistan. As a result, plans were afoot to put a Kashmir resolution before the UN General Assembly. Additionally, and more worryingly for India, 'this resolution came in the backdrop of increasing attempts by the US to term the Kashmir issue as "dispute". New Delhi was alarmed when in May 1993 John Malott of US State Department followed by Robin Raphael visited India and during the talks, they termed Kashmir a "dispute". However, what really rang the bell was September 1993 reference of "Kashmir dispute" by US President, Bill Clinton, in his UN General Assembly address and New Delhi felt that there was an international coup to dislodge the Indian government from Kashmir. Emboldened by this, the Organization of Islamic Countries too began seeking visas to send a fact-finding mission to Kashmir. Pakistan which was the member of OIC cried oppression of Kashmiri Muslims at the hands of Indian Army.'[351] India had valid reasons to believe that in its keenness to reward Pakistan for its help against the Soviet Union, the western world had ganged up to engineer an international coup against India. Even the European Community had passed a resolution supporting right of self-determination to Kashmir on 12 March 1992. Not to be left behind the 'Swedish Parliament expressed its "deepest concern" on the human rights situation in Kashmir. It also attracted backing from British Parliamentarians like Lord Avebury.'[352]

It was indeed an alarming situation for India, particularly because Prime Minister Narasimha Rao was not known to possess the resolve of an Indira Gandhi though he was widely respected for his erudition and understated style of functioning. Quietly he let loose a flurry of activity to counter Pakistan's resolution; and the Indian parliament unanimously passed the Kashmir Resolution on 22 February 1994. The resolution read:

> On behalf of the People of India, the Indian Parliament firmly declares that:
>
> The State of Jammu & Kashmir has been, is and shall be an integral part of India and any attempts to separate it from the rest of the country will be resisted by all necessary means; (b) India has the will and capacity to firmly counter all designs against its unity, sovereignty and territorial integrity; and demands that (c) Pakistan must vacate the areas of the Indian State of Jammu and Kashmir, which they have occupied through aggression; and resolves that (d) All attempts to interfere in the internal affairs of India will be met resolutely.

Just after five days of this resolution, Pakistan, on 27 February 1994, moved to the UN Human Rights Commission and tabled the resolution through OIC that condemned India for violation of human rights in Kashmir in Geneva. If the resolution had passed, India would have been put on UNSC economic sanctions. But Rao used all his persuasive skills to put together a team that the world could not have ignored. Faced with challenges on several fronts, 'he flew from Davos (where he was attending World Economic Forum) to Germany. He formed a team of delegates all carefully chosen to represent India. He chose Atal Bihari Vajpayee, then opposition party leader to represent India at Geneva. The delegation also included Salman Khurshid, E. Ahmad, National Conference head Farooq Abdullah and Hamid Ansari. To counter Benazir Bhutto's personal presence, Rao sent his reformist Finance Minister Manmohan Singh who was a known figure at UN. At such a juncture, it was important that no move could go wrong. It was also the time when the leaders from across the party lines and religions came together to defend the country...Rao's masterstroke of including Muslim delegates turned out to be effective in dismantling the claims of oppression of Kashmiri Muslims in India. Furthermore, Rao even sent Hurriyat men to UNHRC as non-governmental presence. New Delhi called six ambassadors who were influential with OIC member countries and other powerful Western nations.'[353]

Emissaries were also sent to Tehran and even Atal Bihari Vajpayee used his personal and BJP's influence on the UK-based Hinduja Group that enjoyed considerable clout with the Iranian establishment. According to Lambah, when the Pakistan resolution was to come up, the Foreign Minister Dinesh Singh was not keeping good health but when apprised of the developments he insisted upon taking a trip to Tehran. An Indian Air Force plane took him to the Iranian capital where Foreign Minister of Iran was surprised to find him undertaking travel and work in his poor health condition. During the talks Velayati informed him that the Chinese Foreign Minister Quin Qichen too was in Tehran and the Indian counterpart would like to talk to him? Dinesh Singh said he will think over the offer and informed him that he was carrying a letter from his Prime Minister for President Rafsanjani. After reading the letter, Iranian President assured him of careful consideration of the matter. Later, Dienesh Singh also met the Chinese Foreign Minister where he emphasized that the Indo-Pak relations could best be handled under the provisions of Simla Agreement. Quin Qinchen's response appeared encouraging. 'At the airport, when Dinesh Singh was departing from Tehran, Velayati held his hand and informed him that the President had instructed him to say that India's interests would be kept in mind…The seeds of Pakistan's withdrawal of the resolution were sown during Dinesh Singh's one-day visit to Iran, which was to be his last diplomatic initiative as he passed away a few days later.'[354]

To cut a long story short, on the day of Resolution, most of the countries that Pakistan expected would favor the country had backtracked. Indonesia and Libya withdrew support to the OIC Resolution, Syria escaped saying it would reconsider the revised draft. Even China, which was well on its way to economic resurgence after liberating its economy from State control did not want to jeopardize its trade and business with India because of the vast potential of its markets. On 9 March 1994, the final day, Iran asked for revised resolution after consultation. Having lost two biggest key players—China and Iran, Pakistan withdrew the resolution by 5 p.m. that day. Thus, a major crisis was averted. But this in no way meant that India and Kashmiris had ensured respite from the ever-increasing Pakistan sponsored terrorist strikes.

Undeterred by the failure at the international forum, Pakistan continued to pile pressure through the *Mehman Mujahideens* who carefully chose targets to derive maximum publicity for the atrocities in order to impress upon the international community the need to take notice of Kashmir. As the date for the Amarnath Yatra neared, the terrorists sounded a deadly warning for the Yatra with two blasts in Jammu. The first, on 20 July 1995 killed 16 people and injured 45; the second, on 26 July, killed a yatra pilgrim. The responsibility for the 20 July killings was owned by the Harkat-ul-Ansar, the Valley's most feared militant group and dominated by foreign militants, and it also issued a note of caution: 'The blast is a warning to the people and officials against associating themselves with the yatra.' This was a clear indication of the Islamist agenda trumping over the Kashmiri movement for separatism.

These blasts had followed the 5 July abductions of five foreigners from Pahalgam by Al-Faran group which many believed was the same as Harkat-ul-Ansar. The hostage crisis, together with this latest warning, kept Kashmir on the boil. The abductions of the foreigners had been roundly condemned by not only all the separatist groups in Kashmir, including Hurriyat leaders, but also by the Amnesty International and Organization of Islamic Countries (OIC). This, however, had little effect on the Al-Faran group. The ineffective role played by the Hurriyat once again proved that it had little or no influence on the foreign terrorists. The local police, that had been so successful in securing the release of two British hostages, Kim Housego and David Mackie in 1993, were also of no help. According to Ramesh Vinayak, a journalist with *India Today*:

> Efforts to find an intermediary, though, are hamstrung by the militants' threat. At first, the police chief of Anantnag, Mohammad Amin Shah, was asked to establish contact with the Al-Faran. Incidentally, Shah had played a key role two years ago in the release of two British hostages Kim Housego and David Mackey [*sic*] by soliciting the help of Qazi Nissar, the Mirwaiz of south Kashmir. Shortly before the release of the Britons, who

> had been held in captivity by the Harkat-ul-Ansar, Qazi was shot dead allegedly by a pro-Pakistan group.
>
> His intervention in the crisis was said to be one of the reasons behind the killing. This time, however, when Amin Shah tried to contact some locals known to have close links with militants, no one dared to come forward. Shah believes "Qazi's killing is acting as a deterrent".[355]

Many believed that the Government's apparent reluctance to show any initiative in resolving the crisis was a deliberate attempt to denigrate the separatist movement. Prominent among the critics was Abdul Ghani Lone, a leader of the Hurriyat who said: 'The Government is deliberately prolonging the crisis so as to portray the Kashmiri movement as a terrorist campaign.' Meanwhile, four countries—UK, USA, Germany and Norway (whose citizens were the victims of the abductions)—among others, got together and approached the separatist leaders but to no avail. The fate of the hostages remained shrouded in mystery with no conclusive evidence of their killings either.

The Jammu blasts had taken place amidst this crisis. But Narasimha Rao was determined to bring back the democratic process and made a tactical move at a time when the people of the State too had got weary of the prolonged cycle of blasts and killings. Importantly, the Charar-i-Sharif and the Pahalgam's hostage issue had proved that the Hurriyat and other separatist groups who claimed to be influential among the people had actually no influence or control over the terrorists. It was apparent that rather than being an indigenous movement for independence, it was run and orchestrated by Pakistan based terrorists who were driven by the philosophy of fundamentalist Islam. The world, in fact, was playing with fire by not looking at it in the right perspective.

Thus, most of Narasimha Rao's tenure was marked by persistent efforts of Pakistan to create conditions in Kashmir that facilitated international intervention and thereby settlement of the issue in its favor. Significantly, the near withdrawal of the authority of the democratic institutions in the Valley during the early phase of terrorism had instilled confidence not only among the Pakistanis but also the Kashmiris that a 'final' settlement was on the card.

It was in this phase during which the Kashmiris excised from their memory, the attack, rape, plunder and killings by Pakistani raiders in 1947 and the gradual acceptance of the democratic provisions offered by the Indian Constitution. It was as if the clock had been reset with Pakistan occupying larger space in Kashmiri consciousness than its role in history called for. Emboldened, the Pakistan-based terrorists had committed the unthinkable outrage of the burning the Charar-i-Sharif. However, this setback had not deterred the bureaucracy from working with a renewed vigor under the leadership of the Governor of the State, General (Retd) V.K. Krishna Rao. The unintended consequence of the desecration of the shrine was that even Hurriyat lost face as it was exposed as a dummy group since the Pakistani terrorists had refused to be seen to be influenced by its leaders.

As a consequence of democracy having been put in abeyance, the State had gone without representation in the Lok Sabha since 1991. But because of the efforts of the bureaucracy in bringing about some normalcy, the State was once again able to conduct the Lok Sabha polls along with the rest of the country in 1996. Incidentally, the main Kashmiri party, the National Conference stayed out of it after overplaying its hand by demanding that the 'sky is the limit' assurance be first redeemed. Much before the country went for polls, Prime Minister Rao had been quietly working on resolving the issues and had publicly declared on 4 November 1995 at 'Burkina Faso, formerly called the Republic of Upper Volta, that Sky was the limit as far as the demand in Kashmir for autonomy was concerned. "From a long distance away from home, I am addressing an appeal through this statement to the people of Jammu and Kashmir, at a time which could well turn their destiny once again in glorious manner, so as to make that lovely land a peer to paradise—*jannatnishaan*, as it has been called for centuries".'[356] This statement, according to 'autonomy-wallas' in Kashmir, outlined his package and set the stage to fulfill his commitment to the people of Jammu and Kashmir that 'short of azadi', 'sky is the limit'.

The statement of Narasimha Rao was an attempt to appease the Kashmiri secessionists and to induce the people of Kashmir to take part in the democratic processes. Predictably, as was expected of the Congress, the statement did not address the issue that faced the people of the Jammu province and Ladakh region that wanted to merge their identity with the larger Indian identity or carve a separate identity of their own. However, even at that time, there were observers who looked at the offer skeptically as it was no different than what had been offered by Indira Gandhi in 1975. Later it was to be repeated by Rajiv Gandhi in 1987. Atal Behari Vajpayee too or even Dr Manmohan Singh made similar offers. Writing about Prime Minister Rao's offer, in *India Today*, Inderjit Badhwar, commented, 'From his statement that the sky was the limit as far as the negotiations on Kashmir's autonomy are concerned, Rao did a turn around to categorically assert that he would not go beyond what is called the 1975 position—the accord between Sheikh Abdullah, after he was released from his long prison term, and Mrs Gandhi. By this, he simply rubbed salt into the gaping wound that is Kashmir.'[357]

Obviously there were contrarian views in the Indian media too! For much too long Sheikh Abdullah had drummed the idea of autonomy as the pre-1953 model of relationship between India and the State so well that it had become embedded in the public memory. Anything short of that was considered as sell-out and surrender. Scared of losing ground to the extremists, the National Conference leadership too echoed similar sentiments and continued to make promises that were impossible to deliver in an India that had made integration of Kashmir and secularism integral to its idea of India.

In the same article, written in 1995, Inderjit Badhwar also asked the question: 'Can the clock ever be turned back, especially after so much bloodshed over the past seven years? Certainly not through recourse to the 1975 status, for that year is etched in the minds of most Kashmiris as a time of treachery, calumny and the virtual negation of the spirit of Article 370 of the Indian Constitution that was supposed to guarantee Kashmir an autonomous status within the Indian Union.'[358] But the same can be said of the rest of the country. The sentiment about complete integration of the State with the rest of the country is so strong that no government can survive by making the concessions that a section of the State's leadership demands. Thus, political leadership in New Delhi has at various times made grand announcements in hope of buying time and then hoping that a fairly representative government in the State will succeed in mollifying the people and wean them away from secessionism. Unfortunately, in this tug of war between two ideas, the Kashmiri leadership has been consistent in not preparing the people for acceptance of their destiny by merging with the Indian constitution. One can understand the aggressive posturing of Sheikh Abdullah and his lieutenant Mirza Afzal Beg after 1953 but a careful perusal of events and history shows that even as late as 1974 when the Beg-Parthasarathy talks were in advanced stage before the 1975 Accord, the Kashmiri mindset had not changed a bit. Sheikh Abdullah had sent his son Farooq Abdullah to Pakistan-occupied-Kashmir to gauge the reaction of the Kashmiris living there in the wake of those talks. Farooq is said to have made a public speech in Mirpur wherein he assured that 'nothing short of independence would be acceptable to Kashmir.'[359] This obduracy has been the bane of Kashmir as it rules out a compromise and as time passes, the rest of the country too becomes rigid in its insistence on complete integration with the constitution.

The political reality by 1995 was that the Kashmiri militants were fast losing steam, with the average life of an armed militant being two and a half years after which he was either killed by the army or the police or someone else from a rival militant organization on the promptings of their handlers in Pakistan. The 'boys' had realized that not only time was running out on them but the ISI and Pakistan had no intention of escalating violence to a point where an Indo-Pak war is triggered to enable Kashmir to gain independence just as the 1971 Indo-Pak war facilitated the freedom of Bangla-speaking East Pakistanis. Pakistan, in short, was in no position to deliver them the '*azadi*' that it had promised. For five years the Kashmiris had suffered violence and were now in a hopeless situation since their political class, including Farooq Abdullah, had gone silent because of fear. He had left the Valley soon after his resignation as chief minister on 19 January 1990 and had settled with his wife in England. Most of the politicians left in Kashmir were not sure about themselves and consequently Delhi was groping in the dark to identify anyone who was willing to talk and deliver on peace and normalcy. As part of this exercise, one by one, leading militants were released from jails with the last big name to be released being Yasin Malik. The issue after this was of conducting negotiations with someone who could deliver on the understanding that they would reach. The choice was difficult since the Rao government was not very keen on opening any dialogue with Farooq Abdullah since the Prime Minister did not trust or like him.[360] It was in these circumstances that Shabir Shah[361] had been identified as the man who could be negotiated with as he also enjoyed considerable influence over the militants, both over ground and underground. Known as the 'Headmaster' among the militants, he was thought to be the ideal person for replacing Farooq Abdullah and his National Conference.

Shabir Shah, readers would recall, was the same militant who had been arrested from Ramban in 1989 but was inexplicably taken to Srinagar instead of Jammu. It had caused a near rebellion in the Valley and no one from the prosecuting agency was willing to file the case in any court. In addition, the Valley had suffered a complete shutdown till he had been released. He, for the record, had been courting arrest since 1968 when he was only 14 years old and was among those who had formed the People's League to protest against the ongoing talks between Beg and Parthasarathy in 1974. He had been so frequently put behind bars that the Amnesty International had declared him a 'prisoner of conscience'. The Government of India had come to the conclusion that since he was the only person of substance among the militants who had not been to Pakistan and was therefore free from the influence of the ISI, he could be trusted to deliver a peace plan to the people. The 'Headmaster', so called because of his seniority among the militants, was respected by them and generally, no one except Sheikh Abdullah had spent more time in jails than him in the Valley. In addition, since he was not under the control of the ISI of Pakistan, he had earned the respect of all categories of Kashmiris. As far as Delhi was concerned, Rao had succeeded in putting democracy back on rails in Punjab in 1992 by holding Assembly elections and was, therefore, keen on restoring it in the State too. With this in view, Shabir Shah was released in 1995.

He, however, dithered, unable to make up his mind or, perhaps, afraid of taking guard and facing the consequences of an electoral battle. But the truth, according to A.S. Dulat, is that when Prime Minister Narasimha Rao made that famous offer of 'the sky is the limit' to Kashmiris from Burkina Faso in 1995, he was addressing it to Shabir Shah. Inexplicably, Shabir Shah wavered even when the Assembly elections were announced because 'he thought that Narasimha Rao's offer of the sky was for Farooq and the National Conference to draw them in and thereby legitimize elections.'[362]

Farooq Abdullah too had heard the message and as Shabir Shah dithered, he knew that if he stayed out any longer from the political scene then he and his National Conference would be wiped off the pages of history. Earlier, however, contrary to his offer, the Rao government did not follow it up by holding the Legislative Assembly elections in the State when the General elections were called in 1996. This was done by his successor government led by Prime Minister H.D. Deve Gowda a little later but in the same year. The Assembly elections were held again after 1987.

The matter was also compounded by the fact that following Narasimha Rao's announcement from a foreign forum that 'sky was the limit', Farooq Abdullah raised the stakes by demanding a commitment that the pre-1953 autonomy of the State will be given back. Failing to get an assurance, National Conference boycotted the Lok Sabha polls. It was a little later that Farooq Abdullah realized that the Government of India had made up its mind to move on without waiting for him. It was only after this that National Conference jumped into the election fray.[363]

Post elections, after a massive win, it was in an atmosphere of optimism and belief in turning a new page that the National Conference and Farooq Abdullah moved towards apparent reconciliation with Jammu and the national ideas. The people had suffered a lot during the period in which many innocent lives were lost, the Valley had been nearly purged of the Pandits and a generation lost due to militancy, curfews, blackouts and closure of schools. Jammu too had suffered not only from the trickledown effect of terrorism but also the futility of continuing a state of confrontation with Kashmir, particularly after Farooq Abdullah had promised to go into the issue of regional disparities and autonomy also, and find a solution to it. Theoretically, this took care of the fault lines that had plagued the Valley since long but the National Conference had taken the words of Rao on face value and therefore, promised the Kashmiris autonomy. Little did Farooq realize that even if the Congress had been voted back to power in the Lok Sabha and Narasimha Rao continued as Prime Minister, he had never meant that the 'sky' that he promised as the limit was anything but the provisions of the 1975 Accord between Indira Gandhi and Sheikh Abdullah. Farooq, on his part, extended his hand of reconciliation to Jammu and Ladakh and announced an Autonomy Committee to go into all the issues concerning regional disparities and appointed Dr Karan Singh its Chairman who, it would be recalled, had been raising this issue with successive Prime Ministers, beginning with Jawaharlal Nehru. So, on the face of it, the Committee allayed suspicions of the Jammu and Ladakh regions and therefore with Dr Karan Singh as the Chairman, there was a message of genuine commitment to the cause. Other members of the Committee were Mohiuddin Shah, Abdul Ahad Vakil, Abdul Rahim Rather, Piyaray Lal Handoo, Bodh Raj Bali, Moulvi Iftikhar Hussain Ansari, Kushok Thiksay and Sardar Teja Singh. Subsequently, after Dr Karan Singh resigned as Chairman on 31 July 1997, Mohi-ud-din Shah was appointed as the Chairman.

But no sooner had the Committee been constituted than Dr Karan Singh realized that the National Conference had neither learnt nor forgotten anything during this extended period of agony of the State. The convergence of Karan Singh and Farooq Abdullah, before the elections to the State Assembly—which was seen as a landmark in Kashmir politics with many believing that the traditional rancor and mistrust between the two families had been buried—was too superficial. With the age-old positions and demands being reiterated by it, the National Conference had laid the ground for renewal of old battles. The introductory remarks of the report that was finally produced were enough to give the message that no solution was in sight. It began by reminding that right from 1919, the future of India was seen as a Federal State. In fact, it quoted the Simon Commission (that was unambiguously rejected by the Indian National Congress) that said: 'Apart together from any question of an ultimate Federal Union between the Indian States and British India, there are, we think very strong reasons for the reconstruction of the Indian Constitution on a Federal basis. It is only in a federal structure that sufficient elasticity can be obtained for the Union of elements of diverse internal condition and the communities at very different stage of development and culture.' It then went into detail on how Article 370 came to be incorporated, without touching the circumstances that necessitated it and in the exercise of which a large number of provisions of the Indian Constitution were made applicable to the State and recommended that the word 'temporary' be deleted from the title of part XXI of the Constitution of India; and, that the word 'temporary' occurring in the heading of Article 370 be substituted by the word 'special'. Clearly, the National Conference of the 1990s wanted to renegotiate Article 370 and expand its demands and restrict the scope of the Article.

Outrageously, the Report recommended that the relationship between the State and the Union be confined only to the subjects conceded to the Union under the Instrument of Accession and matters in the Union list, which were not connected with the three subjects of Defence, External Affairs and Communications and or ancillary thereto should be excluded from their application to the State. Further:

> b. All modifications made in Article 246 in its application to the State subsequent to the 1950 Order should be rescinded.
>
> c. Article 248, 249, 250 and 251 whether applied in original or substituted modified form should be omitted in relation to the State.
>
> d. As in 1950 and 1954. List 11 (State) and List 111 (Concurrent) of the Seventh Schedule should not be applicable to the State.
>
> e. Article 254 be restored to the position it had in its application to [the] State in 1954.
>
> f. Article 262 and 263 which were not applicable under 1950 Order but were subsequently extended to the State should cease to apply.

There port also recommended that the right to conduct the elections should be taken out of the purview of the Election Commission of India and reverted to the State Legislature and recommended changes in the Emergency Provision (Article 352 to 360) to add that 'request for concurrence of the Government of the State shall be subject to whatever decision the State Assembly may take within two months of declaration of emergency and failing any such decision, the proclamation of Emergency shall be deemed to have been revoked.' The Report also wanted that Article 355, 356, 357, 358, 359 and 360 should be made non-applicable to the State of Jammu and Kashmir as was the position in 1954 and the State taken out of the purview of the Supreme Court and the Comptroller Auditor General of India. The long and short of the Report was that the integration of the State Constitution with the Indian Constitution that had taken place be reversed and the 1953 situation be reinstated. It was apparent that nothing had changed and the State had renewed the battle and that it cared neither for the history of the country nor the system that it had evolved, and nor for the overall wellbeing of the people of the State. The misery and tragedy of the past years meant nothing to the National Conference and that for it the funeral processions of the dead youths were an acceptable form of macabre politics.

Thus, the die had once again been cast. Consequently, there was little hope of reconciliation and, therefore, peace. This is how the situation lingered as the term of Farooq Abdullah moved in the second half. The bottom line was that nothing had changed; he continued to promise autonomy of the pre-1953 era, knowing full well that no Union government could do that and survive the anger of the people of the country. He did not even see that the country had changed and the vast majority had begun to resent what they perceived as Muslim appeasement. A new, more vigorous and assertive majority was taking shape. Oblivious of the opinion of the majority, the National Conference also ignored the demands of the regions of Ladakh and Jammu. Ladakh had been given some autonomy by way of the constitution of an autonomous district council—the Ladakh Hill Development Council. But the communal agenda of the National Conference had so perverted the issues that even Kargil demanded and got a separate Council for itself and in the process triggered a backlash from the Young Buddhist movement in Leh. Thus, the stage was set for the Buddhists of Ladakh to demand secession from Jammu and Kashmir, but not India. In India, the Ladakhis found a security that they craved for from the Kashmiris as well as the Tibetans.

One might wonder why the National Conference has remained so focused on the Autonomy aspect of the problem, but a careful analysis would reveal that by convening the Constituent Assembly of the State, Sheikh Abdullah had effectively rejected the UN resolution calling for a plebiscite to determine the accession of the State. He was aware of the fact that with the passing of each year, Pakistan was capable of vitiating the atmosphere thereby making the outcome not so certain since large regions of the State were not only under the occupation of Pakistan but also Muslim and communalized. For a few years the demand for plebiscite was supported by Sheikh Abdullah, particularly after he had been deposed and arrested but that was because he had to use it as a tool to challenge the Union government. He, the National Conference and his successors have, therefore, been comfortable with the autonomy given by Article 370. In later years, whereas the separatist groups and Hurriyat revived the demand for plebiscite, the National Conference has remained focused on Article 370 and regaining of the ground that might have been conceded by the governments headed by Bakshi Ghulam Mohammad, Ghulam Mohammad Sadiq and Mir Qasim.

In the meantime, when terrorism became the order of the day, all separatist political parties, 26 in number, came under the umbrella of the All Parties Hurriyat Conference (HPHC), which made plebiscite their core demand. When Assembly elections were held in the State in 1996, a quiet effort to find points of convergence with Pakistan was already taking shape, first when I.K. Gujral as Foreign Minister met Nawaz Sharif and then later when both again met as Prime Ministers in 1997. Since Gujral was born and brought up in what became Pakistani Punjab, as was Sharif, it was easy for the two to communicate and express the desire to have peace. Both knew that it was Punjab that had borne much of the evil consequences of Partition and also knew of the need to rekindle the bonds of trade and commerce between the two countries. Therefore, a right earnest effort through the backchannels as well as officials was made. Unfortunately, Gujral was politically unstable and therefore he had to give way to general elections and the formation of the BJP-led Vajpayee government. It was during this phase that the Lahore bus trip of the Indian Prime Minister took place. However, since the military and the hawks were not on board, the Kargil misadventure of the Pakistani Army derailed the peace initiative.

Farooq Abdullah and the National Conference were aware that the Union government wanted an early resolution to the Kashmir situation and, as Narasimha Rao had shown, no politician or party was a pariah for achieving that goal. The backchannels had established contacts with everyone in Kashmir, including the Hurriyat. The Kargil setback notwithstanding, Vajpayee was determined for a breakthrough and communication with the Hurriyat had been established. The Hurriyat too had modified its demand to also include autonomy as part of the discussions. In fact, in real earnestness, a three-track communication had been opened by India and Pakistan to find a common meeting ground. At one level, the civil society was actively involved and at another, the Foreign Ministry officials were in communication. In the State, the government had also opened up channels with Hurriyat, which in turn was also consulting and updating its contacts in Pakistan. It was in these circumstances that the fears of getting marginalized made Farooq Abdullah place the Autonomy Report in the Assembly for approval. Radha Kumar, who later became one of the interlocutors of Dr Manmohan Singh's government, opined: 'Whether deliberately or unintentionally, Chief Minister Farooq Abdullah almost closed the Hurriyat window when he placed his State Autonomy Commission report before the assembly and introduced a resolution calling for restoration of autonomy under the original Article 370.'[364] The resolution was passed by the assembly on 26 June 2000 and sent to the Centre.

Understandably, the Union Cabinet rejected the resolution though initially, both Prime Minister Vajpayee and Deputy Prime Minister Advani were only cautious and not averse. Vajpayee had said that it was 'within the domain of constitutional validity' and the Advani hedged by saying that it would be placed before the parliament. RSS, the parent body of BJP, and the Shiv Sena, its coalition partner, both declared the resolution as a document of secession. It was in these circumstances that the Assembly resolution came to be discussed in the Lok Sabha on 26 July 2000 and Madhavrao Scindia of Congress made an incisive discourse on the subject, condemning the report as well as attacking the Prime Minister for opining that it was 'well within the domain of constitutional validity'.

> This is attempting to put the clock back again. It is going back not just to the pre-1953 situation but going back to the 1950 situation. There is talk here of articles 355, 356 and 358, should be made inapplicable in the State as was the position in 1954. There have been constitutional amendments in the Parliament, again with the full concurrence of the State Assembly. We are talking of the pre-1953 situation. I think that Shri Abdullah will have to look a little more closely at those autonomy recommendations before he says that he is not necessarily asking for a pre-1953 situation because a number of those very fundamental and important recommendations pertain to the State and the Centre in such a way that it would go back to the pre-1953 situation. In any case, whilst talking about going back to 1953 situation and wiping the slate clean, are we not, in a way, obviating, violating and annulling article 370? The Congress Party is committed to article 370. There are parties which are today and even earlier been talking about removal of article 370. The Congress Party believes that article 370 should remain. But when you talk of going back to pre-1953 situation, you yourself are violating article 370. What did article 370 say?...Article 370 in effect says that all the subjects that were covered by Instruments of Accession that is Defence, External Affairs, Communication and residual ones were to be implemented after consultation with the Jammu and Kashmir Government. Parliament could implement them after consultation. Article 370 then goes on to say that as far as the remaining subjects are concerned, you must take the full concurrence of the Jammu and Kashmir Assembly. This is clearly laid down in the Constitution. Whenever any Act or any provision was extended to Jammu and Kashmir, both the principles of consultation, as far as three items

> that came under the Instruments of Accession were concerned and positive concurrence as far as the rest were concerned, was always undertaken. I am not even re-mentioning that. Sheikh Abdullah in 1975 by signing this Accord in effect totally ratified it in a way…All I am trying to say is that the National Conference and Farooq Abdullah asking for the slate to be wiped clean are tacitly and indirectly themselves hitting at article 370.
>
> …It is because they want to say that whatever article 370 legitimized in those 30 or 40 years should be pushed under the carpet. Let us start again. So, they themselves are violating article 370. I would like them to pay a little attention to this. In fact, in many aspects…Shri [Farooq] Abdullah is asking for much more than his father asked for. It is not possible to get into a time capsule and go back in the space of time and erase everything that happened earlier.
>
> …Specially what does the Autonomy Resolution mean? It would have meant—among other things the more important provisions are—that article 356 would not apply to Jammu and Kashmir. But the Prime Minister says this is within the Constitution. It would have meant that the Jammu and Kashmir Assembly would have the final say on the central role not just in cases of internal emergency, but in cases of external emergency too. But the Prime Minister says that this is within the Constitution. The President and the Parliament's role in Jammu and Kashmir would be curtailed because here they talk of articles 246, 254, 355, 356 read with 358 and 359. The Parliament would not be able to amend any constitutional provisions in the State. The Supreme Court and the Election Commission would have no say in Kashmir and the Comptroller and Auditor-General of India would not scrutinize the State's finances.[365]

Clearly, with two-third majority in the Assembly, Farooq Abdullah was convinced that since he had made an electoral promise to his people, he was making a just demand by asking for the return of the 1952 equations of State powers whereas neither Narasimha Rao, nor Deve Gowda or Atal Behari Vajpayee had ever intended to go beyond the line drawn by the Indira Gandhi-Sheikh Abdullah accord of 1975. The 'sky is the limit' of Narasimha Rao, or 'anything within the Constitution' of Gowda or later, the heart pleasing promise of Vajpayee—'*insaniyat, jamhooriat aur Kashmiriyat*'—was the same as the 1975 accord and none of them could have gone beyond that limit without risking their political capital. While Farooq Abdullah might argue that the people had again reposed their faith in National Conference because of the promise of autonomy to the people of the State then it needs to be also stressed that if a political party makes unrealistic promises that go beyond the scope of the country's constitution, then the whole country and its aspirations cannot be held hostage to it. The National Conference made a promise to the people of the Valley without consideration for the rest of the country and then wanted that it be bailed out by the Government of India by conceding its demand.

But there were other constraints too in the State that exposed the hollowness of the 'autonomy' refrain. It was the realization of these constraints that made Farooq Abdullah back track on the subject. The consistent efforts of the National Conference, beginning with the restructuring of the Udhampur district by the first Sheikh Abdullah government on communal lines, had also found its echoes in the recommendations of a member, Mohammad Shafi, who suggested that the State be redefined as a collection of Muslim, Hindu and Buddhist majority regions. Clearly this was to create communal enclaves and destroy the unity of the State. But the hollowness of the report was better defined by Ladakh than Jammu that had been vocal about it since the times of Sheikh Abdullah. As the secessionist movement took roots in the Valley in the 1990s, Ladakh became vocal about its neglect and demanded that it be given the status of a union territory. In fact, as the secessionist movement was gaining strength in the Valley, the Buddhist Ladakh demanded its 'secession' from the State of Jammu and Kashmir! But since Ladakh had two distinct areas, Leh and Kargil, equally divided as Buddhist and Muslim, respectively, the regional grievance soon developed into communal strife. Unrest in Ladakh had been brewing for a long time, but the Autonomy Report aggravated it and soon Leh and Kargil and Doda and Jammu were drifting towards ethnic strife. Realizing the dangers ahead 'Farooq put the autonomy report on a back burner. Vajpayee's administration, under pressure from its own party and allies, and with a larger goal of involving the Hurriyat in autonomy talks, was happy to let the issue rest.'[366]

Meanwhile, Pakistan had gone through internal turmoil after the Kargil war, with the culprit usurping power by executing a military coup against the elected government of Nawaz Sharif. But this period influenced perhaps by the Good Friday Peace Deal in Ireland also saw an interesting development among the Irish Diaspora. Most of secessionist movements the world over have been funded and fueled by the Diaspora and Ireland was no exception. But it dawned upon them that while they had migrated from their motherland and had rebuilt their lives, they were supporting and funding a cause which was regularly claiming human lives and destroying homes while they were safely tucked away in their safety zones. Finally, when this wisdom dawned, the Irish Diaspora stopped funding and instead exerted pressure to strike a deal. In the case of Jammu and Kashmir, a large number of people of Kashmiri origin had settled in Europe and USA, particularly Britain. It was their support that kept the secessionist movement going for a number of years for they used their finances and influence to keep the issue alive in the world media and forums. But by the time the Kargil conflict was at its peak, a rethinking of beliefs had already started in Europe and Farooq Siddique, a diaspora Kashmiri and founder of Council for Independent Kashmir, announced at the Hague Appeal for Peace conference that 'guns and violence should be replaced by dialogue'. He also accused the Hurriyat of turning a blind eye to the violent crimes being committed in the Valley by the foreign fighters.[367]

Initially, this did not have any effect on General Musharraf who had taken over as Chief Executive of Pakistan after the coup as he doubled down in his defence of the Kargil conflict during his first press conference. He announced that 'Kashmir cannot be sidelined' and that the Kargil offensive was within the 'framework of Kashmir'. He admitted that Pakistan was under intense pressure from the US and European administrations because of the nuclear program and the sanctuary that Islamic groups enjoyed in Pakistan. Aggravating the situation further for Pakistan was that as a condemnation of the military coup, it had been suspended from the Commonwealth membership. But, he asserted, whatever was needed for Pakistan, will be done. Following the Kargil war, the level of violence had sharply increased in the State and during the 1999-2000 period, on an average seven lives were lost in army-militant confrontations.

Soon after the Musharraf press conference, the Lashkar-e-Taiba called a three-day convention where President Tarar and Musharraf too were invited. At the convention, Hafiz Saeed called on the guerrillas to increase the terrorist attacks in the State while the Pakistani Army intensified cross border firing that not only facilitated the infiltration but also inflicted casualties. New 'hit-and-run' tactics were adopted by the Pakistani Army and soon Border Action Teams consisting of 15-20 soldiers became a regular part of the Pakistani Army. But this heightened activity had a downside too. Emboldened by the establishment's support, the Islamist also started choosing targets in Pakistan. Attacks intensified on the US embassy, American Culture Centre and the offices of the United Nations. This was happening at a time when the economy of Pakistan had dwindled as a consequence of sanctions imposed post nuclear tests. India too had been the subject of sanctions but it was not impacted as seriously as Pakistan had been. It was in these circumstances that Musharraf was forced to look for ways of engaging with India.

The Vajpayee government, all this time, had continued to explore various channels for peace: it continued to work for a breakthrough with the terrorist groups as well as the Hurriyat leaders and the government-to-government level. Finally, it was the Indian Army and the militant group Hizb-ul-Mujahideen that found a way forward when its commander Majid Dar announced unilateral ceasefire in the same year, 2000, when the autonomy report was under discussion in the Parliament. Hizb-ul-Mujahideen, the most powerful Mujahideen Group operating inside the Indian side of Kashmir announced a unilateral ceasefire on Monday, 24 July 2000, at a news conference on the outskirts of Srinagar, the summer capital of Jammu and Kashmir.

This was also noted in Pakistan and soon a retired Lieutenant General, Sardar J.S. Lodi, wrote in a defence journal of Pakistan: 'Abdul Majid Dar chief commander of Hizbul Mujahideen said, "we want to show the world that we are not hard-liners and we are flexible in the search for a solution."'[368] Majid Dar was at pains to reject the accusation that the insurgency in the State was completely controlled by the Pakistan based militants and asserted that the decision making was in the hands of local people and all the field and sector commanders were local militants. In fact, he appeared at the press conference in the company of three local commanders. The Prime Minister welcomed the announcement as did his Deputy Prime Minister and Home Minister L.K. Advani. The Home Minister too went to great lengths in justifying the decision of the government to accept the peace offer. 'Many may not be aware that the Hizbul members, though pro-Pakistani, are mainly Kashmiris,' he said and added, 'We have no hesitation in talking to our own people, even though they may have strayed into the path of militancy.'

The ceasefire was to be followed by unconditional talks which would not exclude Pakistan, and, in the meantime, the Indian Army, the paramilitary forces and the State police would not indulge in reprisals. These steps were to be implemented within three months of the ceasefire and accordingly, Dar crossed over from his base in the Pakistan held areas. Appropriate instructions were issued to the field commander of the Army and Fazal Haq Qureshi appointed negotiator on behalf of Hizb-ul.

According to Radha Kumar, two unfortunate developments stymied the peace process which was well on its way. First, the ISI is said to have developed second thoughts and second, since Hurriyat had not been taken on board, it took offence. The second development was a bit of surprise since Qureshi was a member of the Hurriyat though not a member of the seven-member executive committee. In an interview with Radha Kumar on 14 August 2000, he told her that he would have taken Hurriyat into confidence but for the fact that he was sworn to secrecy by Dar.[369] At that point, Hurriyat was being chaired by Abdul Ghani Bhat who promptly wrote a letter of protest to Jamaat-i-Islami head, Hussain Ahmed.

The consequences were immediate. Within a week of the announcement of the ceasefire, Lashkar-e-Taiba attacked a pilgrim base camp at Pahalgam, killing 30 people, including pilgrims, shopkeepers and porters. This was followed by the killing of seven residents and 19 laborers from Bihar and Madhya Pradesh in

Anantnag and five members of a family of a person accused of being an informer. Across the Banihal, in the Doda district, terrorists killed 22 and then another eight members of a village defence committee in Kishtwar. Though these killings started on a Monday and continued through to Tuesday, in all claiming 80 lives, they came to be known as the 'Bloody Tuesday' deaths. Naturally, these put a question mark on the credibility of Majid Dar and all kinds of motives were attributed. His explanation to the Hurriyat that he only wanted to prove that the guerrilla fighters were not extremists but fighting as no other option was left, was not good enough for the extremist Hurriyat leader Syed Al Shah Geelani who derided the whole exercise as 'drama'. 'On November 19 one of Dar's closest aides…Khurshid Ahmad Zargar, a one-time veterinary surgeon who operated as the head of the Hizb in the south Kashmir region under the alias Asad Yazdani, told a group of journalists that while he understood that "the armed movement brought the Kashmir issue out of cold storage, at the same time we accept the gun alone is no solution to the problem." [He added] "We want organizations such as the Jaish-e-Mohammadi, Lashkar-e-Toiba [*sic*] and Harkatul Mujahideen to work under the local leadership."'[370]

As a consequence, the Pakistan based chairman Yusuf Ali Shah alias 'Salahuddin' intervened and announced that he was taking charge of the negotiations and demanded that the only formula to be negotiated will be of acceptance of Kashmir as a 'disputed' area at the international forum and which involved the governments of India, Pakistan and Hurriyat. The Islamabad correspondent of the Press Trust of India (PTI) report of 8 August 2000 published in the daily *The Tribune*, said: 'Pakistan-based Hizbul Mujahideen militant group withdrew its unilateral ceasefire in Jammu and Kashmir this evening, accusing New Delhi of not responding positively to its call for tripartite talks involving Pakistan to settle the Kashmir issue and directed its field commanders to resume their operation in the state.

'We withdraw the unilateral ceasefire…We direct all the commanders and the Mujahideen in the field to break the ceasefire and go ahead along with target-oriented mission,' Hizbul's supreme commander Syed Salahuddin said at a press conference…'India has failed to respond categorically to our offer of peace and has dillydallied in giving peace a chance. India intended to tie the affair in a bilateral dialogue, which is not acceptable…Kashmir tangle can be solved only by a just negotiating process involving all three parties—Kashmiris, India and Pakistan,' he said.[371]

It was very obvious that the ISI had once again stamped its authority. Consequently, Majid Dar was also expelled from Hizb-ul leading to an intense in-fight that claimed over 200 lives of Yusuf Shah and Dar's followers. With Pakistan-based Islamic militia opposing the peace initiative and Hurriyat and the Jamaat-i-Islami also shunning Majid Dar, he was no longer in a position to lead the negotiations. Finally, within two years, Dar too was eliminated. *The Outlook* reported, 'Former Hizb-ul-Mujahideen, Salar-e-Ala or chief commander, Abdul Majeed Dar, was shot dead by unidentified gunmen in the Noor Bagh area of Sopore township in north Kashmir when two gun-wielding youth barged into his ancestral house and fired indiscriminately, killing Dar on the spot and critically injuring his mother and sister.'[372]

In the bloody unraveling of the terrorist groups, the overriding negativity of the Hurriyat, and mutually competing Kashmiri leaders, what is often ignored is that there was a large constituency within India too that was averse to any peaceful negotiations with the terrorist groups. The Indian Parliament, since 1991, had been deeply polarized, more so since BJP secured election victory in 1999. The 'Bloody Tuesday' killings of nearly 80 people in terrorist attacks and the contentious autonomy proposal of Farooq Abdullah had already created a toxic atmosphere in a deeply divided country. But even then, Dar had not given up on peace plan, and therefore, changed tactics to win over the support of Hurriyat. Radha Kumar claims that he 'spent the next six months visiting Hurriyat leaders to canvass support. As a result, renewed backchannel efforts yielded a new plan to get a peace process going in Kashmir. The Hurriyat would call for, and get, a unilateral ceasefire by the Indian Army. Hurriyat members would then visit Pakistan to seek a reciprocal ceasefire from the United Jihad Council that Shah headed.'[373]

The unilateral ceasefire announced by the Army was hugely popular in Kashmir and people welcomed it with celebrations. However, this time dissension within the Hurriyat became the stumbling block since the Jamaat-i-Islami representative in the Hurriyat, Syed Ali Shah Geelani opposed the call for a reciprocal ceasefire by the militants. Meanwhile, Jamaat-i-Islami and Hizb-ul insisted that Geelani be included in the delegation that was to go to Pakistan. Earlier it had been proposed that only those who were involved in the backchannel negotiations with India and Pakistani government should be part of the delegation for Pakistan. The Geelani demand was too much and consequently the Pakistan visit was canceled and once again the peace proposal fell through. The downside of the cessation of counter-insurgency operations of the forces was that the terrorists used the period to rearm and regroup.

Before the term of Farooq Abdullah ran out of time, the Government of India made one more big effort for peace. This opportunity came when General Pervez Musharraf, after having come to power following a coup in 1999, called for talks 'anytime, anywhere'. Vajpayee and Advani decided to give peace another chance and the Track II and semi-official channels were activated to explore common ground and on finding sufficient reason for talks it was decided to hold a summit at Agra in July 2001. Unlike at Lahore, the Kashmir issue was not put on the back burner but was there up front. As always, Pakistan wanted India to recognize that Kashmir was the central issue between the two countries. India had always refuted this contention but this time it was decided to concede this demand but in return India wanted Pakistan to eschew violence or support for violence in Kashmir and rest of India. Pakistan was unwilling to give this undertaking, resulting in the failure of the summit at the last minute.

The sides gave their own reasons for the failure. On return to Islamabad, Musharraf claimed that he and Vajpayee had agreed for a joint declaration but it was sabotaged at the last minute by the hawks within Indian Cabinet. He claimed that they were alarmed by the prominence given to Kashmir in the declaration. On the other hand, India's Foreign Minister, Jaswant Singh, claimed in the Lok Sabha that the 'Pakistan establishment until the last was not clear itself because the establishment had not been taken in full confidence by the President of Pakistan himself.'[374] Prime Minister Vajpayee further elaborated this in the Parliament: 'We did not succeed to make the Pakistani delegation agree that cross-border terrorism should find a mention in the declaration. They went a step forward and termed it as freedom struggle. This was totally unexpected of them and this is where the atmosphere of negotiations got sullied.'[375]

A close examination of the peace efforts will reveal that while India participated in them wholeheartedly and with the support of almost all major segments of the society, it was Pakistan that suffered from schizophrenia, and a section backed by its army worked overtime to wreck peace efforts. Since 1990, buoyed by its success in its role to drive out the Soviet Army from Afghanistan and trigger dismantling of the Soviet Union, it made the State of Jammu and Kashmir its main theater of terrorist activity in India. According to a detailed note circulated by Ministry of External Affairs of India on 20 May 2002, its sponsored activities have caused a 'loss of about 27,000 lives in the last 11 years. The number of weapons and other military hardware recovered in anti-terrorist operations could equip several battalions of a modern Army. During the decade long Pak sponsored terrorism in J&K, in over 51,000 terrorist incidents around 27,000 persons including about 9,700 civilians and over 3000 Security personnel have been killed. The terrorist violence caused extensive damage to private and public property, with large number of people, particularly minority Hindus, being forced to migrate from the Valley. Even foreign tourists have not been spared. Terrorists posed a serious threat to Aviation Security as they resorted to hijacking to achieve their demands. With the decline in local militancy, pan-Islamic "jehadi" [*sic*] outfits have come to dominate seeking to destroy the secular fabric of the State. The complexion of militancy has undergone a change with focused attacks on Security Forces (SF). Suicide attacks are on the rise. A systematic effort is being made to tarnish the image of security forces by whipping up allegations of violation of Human Rights even though terrorists have shown no concern for the human rights of their victims.

'...Terrorist's attempts to target the State democratic apparatus was reflected in their poll boycott threats issued in the wake of announcement of Parliamentary, legislature and in the last few years and culminated in the October, 2001 attack on the State legislature building. The threat to Census enumerators and attempt to disrupt could also be seen in the same light. Grass roots political workers have continually been targeted by the terrorists.'[376]

It was in these circumstances that Farooq Abdullah's government moved towards completing its term with nothing to show. It had been marked by periodic killings by the terrorists and retaliatory action by the security forces with the most outrageous massacre taking place on 20 March 2000 in Chittisinghpura on the eve of President Clinton's visit to India. In between, it was also punctuated with peace efforts, both back channel and at the official level. But the truth was that all too often the Kashmiri leadership had put itself into a corner because of the unrealistic dreams they had fed the people. Soon thereafter, the controversy regarding the killings of five 'terrorists' in an encounter with the army broke and there was another round of finger pointing and shifting of blame. This, combined with little improvement in matters of administration where the old style of nepotism amidst accusations of corruption in public life flourished, the State moved towards holding the next polls for electing a new Assembly.

12

Peace Efforts—2003 to 2008

'Peace cannot be kept by force; it can only be achieved by understanding.'

—Albert Einstein

By the time 2002 elections were to be held, a few realities had dawned upon the people. They had grown weary of and fatigued by more than a decade of violence in which Kashmiris had lost an unacceptably high number of lives, and this had been working against the incumbent party. The tragedy of death had knocked at almost every household door, directly or indirectly, and the National Conference, which had lost an exceptionally high number of its front-line leaders and *karkuns* (workers), had raised the stakes for Kashmir unrealistically high by promising them pre-1953 autonomy but had miserably failed in coming good on its promise. The two-third majority in the Assembly had been of little use. On the contrary, it had aggravated divisions and animosities not only among the three regions of the State but also intra-Kashmir region. By insisting upon its pre-1953 status it had only thwarted peace initiatives. There were times when observers suspected the Farooq government of sabotaging peace talks by clandestinely disclosing the name of some key player in the peace efforts, thereby facilitating killing.

Tragically, Kashmir had few options. Shabir Shah had long run out of steam and was in such a pessimistic frame of mind that he was convinced that all his electoral efforts would be fruitless. By the time of 2002 elections were to be held 'Shabir had missed the bus.' Even then, Prime Minister Vajpayee's point man in Kashmir, A.S. Dulat 'had a long chat' with him 'to persuade him to contest, but he said, 'What can I do single-handedly? I can at most win one seat. If I had more people, I could win probably three seats. And it is decided that Farooq Abdullah or his son Omar will become the chief minister.' I told him he was wrong, but he did not listen.'[377] Despondent, Shabir could not see that though he no longer enjoyed the kind of position that he had in the 1990s, in Kashmir nothing could be taken as given. Having failed to stand up when destiny beckoned him in 1996, he drifted away into history to ultimately become dependent on the financial help from ISI. Dulat has rued the time invested on him but also acknowledges that the experience of talking and handling as complex a character as Shabir had given him the experience and confidence to bring in many other militants on to the dialogue table, notably Hashim Qureshi and Abdul Majid Dar.

Another factor that played a critical role prior to 2002 Assembly elections was that the National Conference had chosen to join the BJP led National Democratic Alliance (NDA) that was in power in Delhi, and its nominee Omar Abdullah had become State Minister for Foreign Affairs from July 2001 to October 2002. This was a major shift from the historical animosity between National Conference and BJP. It could also be interpreted as Dr Abdullah's repetition of the same mistake that he had committed while entering into an alliance with Congress to buy insurance against machinations of New Delhi against Srinagar in 1987. It can also be explained as a regional party's admission that it is difficult to survive in government without support of the central government. However, the period of this dalliance was marred by the Gujarat communal riots and killings of Muslims. The backlash among the Muslims was said to be one of the reasons for the defeat of the National Conference in the Assembly 2002 polls since it had aligned with BJP, the party allegedly responsible for the killings of about 2,000 Muslims there. The National Conference was thus duly punished by the people during the polls mainly for the widespread maladministration, charges of corruption and failure to deliver on promises but also for its dalliance with BJP in Delhi. No progress had been made on the much-publicized autonomy, state as well as regional, and this had weighed heavily against it.

Meanwhile, the Peoples' Democratic Party (PDP) had been formed in 1999 when Mufti Mohammad Sayeed, a long time Congressman and at one point in time, a chief ministerial candidate of Congress in 1977 when Congress withdrew support to Sheikh Abdullah's government, had broken away from it. He had realized that Congress was no longer in a position to compete for victory and that it would remain in the supporting cast. Moreover, the national goals of the Congress were often at variance with the state party and a constraint in the politics and political ambitions of the State leaders. Additionally, South Kashmir, from where Mufti came, had become the hub of militancy and because of the familial and social equations of Kashmir no active politician could afford to be seen to be hostile to the militants. Convinced that there was no space for his ambitions in the Congress, he had broken away. He also realized that while the armed forces, by the nature of their training, were prone to using tough measures in dealing with the militants and their sympathizers, it was up to the politicians to provide the 'healing touch' and this became the main mantra for his and PDP's election campaign. PDP was made of those who were disillusioned with the Congress and National Conference and the election results threw up surprising results. The National Conference was reduced from 57 seats in 1996 to only 28, way short of majority. Congress improved its tally to 20, gaining significantly in Jammu where the Jammu Mukti Morcha, backed by the RSS demanding trifurcation of the State, cut into the BJP votes to reduce it to only one seat. But the surprise package of the elections was the PDP which won 16 seats in its first ever electoral battle. The electorate had not given a clear mandate to any party but since the defeat of the National Conference had primarily been a loss of confidence of the Kashmiri voters in the National Conference, and since PDP was instrumental in defeating it in the Valley, the Congress chose to lend support to it to form an alliance government with it and other smaller groups. Thus, Mufti Mohammed Sayeed finally fulfilled his ambition. This alliance had in fact been dictated by the poll results since otherwise the State would have had to be put under Governor's rule. With BJP ruling at the Centre, Congress grabbed the chance to form government with both hands.

The unexpected alliance between PDP and Congress opened up new possibilities. With Vajpayee-led BJP at the Centre, it was the first time that the two nationalist parties were on the same page as far as Kashmir was concerned. Even more significantly, also onboard was a regional party that many were convinced had close connections with the separatists and terrorists. Pakistan, however, was slow to recognize that fortuitous circumstances had thrown open a window of opportunity. Perhaps it was skeptical because of the most unexpected coming together of these parties who should have been, following the traditional wisdom, at each other's throat.

As far as Prime Minister Vajpayee was concerned, he finally decided to give one more chance to everyone to get the peace process going. This third move, by a leader who represented the traditionally hostile face to Pakistan, was made in 2003, and observers would not fail to notice that the timing was politically very risky for him and his party. The next year, in 2004, the general elections in the country were due and any betrayal, like the one he suffered after his Lahore bus journey, would prove catastrophic. Playing a high-stake game, in April 2003, he gave a call for peace with Pakistan. Significantly the call was made from Srinagar and when one of the reporters asked him if the talks with Hurriyat would be within 'the ambit of Indian constitution', he answered that the talks will take place within the ambit of humanity (*insaniyat ke daire mein*). He elaborated this in the Lok Sabha on his return by saying, 'I assured the people of Jammu and Kashmir that we wish to resolve all issues, domestic and external, through talks. I stressed that gun can solve no problem, brotherhood can. Issues can be resolved if we move forward guided by the three principles of *insaniyat, jamhooriyat aur kashmiriyat* (humanity, democracy and Kashmiri oneness).'[378]

This phrase was electrifying and Vajpayee became an instant hero in Kashmir. Spoken with the customary conviction and passion of an orator, it was very assuring and optimistic. It was clear that Vajpayee wished to go beyond the binaries and traditionally stated positions. He was aware that without breaking from the mould there can be no peace, either within Jammu and Kashmir or India and Pakistan. Knowing his party and the RSS, he was also aware that if this breakthrough was not achieved by someone from this stable then it was a mountain too high to climb for anyone else. If he succeeded, not only would he be in a good position to get his party back in power but also leave an indelible legacy behind him. A careful analysis of his statement would reveal that the words chosen were not just for lyrical or emotional impact but were the result of a very carefully planned move. He had sidestepped the issue of the talks being within the ambit of the Indian Constitution or not, for otherwise he would have had to expend all his energy in balancing the two opposing forces in the State: the one seeking autonomy, and the other, advocating that Article 370 was invalid and wanting complete integration. The politicians and political parties who remained bogged down in this quagmire, forgot that the Article had gone through almost 100 amendments and any peace agreement would have again made an amendment imperative as otherwise it would not have been valid. If the Article were to be altogether abrogated then too an amendment would have to be made. By his *insaniyat* phraseology, Vajpayee had sidestepped the contentious debate and had also given Hurriyat a perfect cover for entering into talks.

Credit should also be given to Pervez Musharraf who, after the infamous Kargil aggression, had made the effort to bring peace to the subcontinent by making to the failed Agra summit in 2001, and was yet not deterred by the failure and disappointment, sending feelers to India. Radha Kumar writes, 'Vajpayee's offer was made possible, at least in part, by quiet feelers from Pakistan over the first three months of the year. A delegation of Pakistani MPs in March 2003 bore a message from Musharraf that his government would no longer aid cross-border infiltration, and would not attempt to prevent or impede Indian counter-insurgency efforts, including border fencing and surveillance. 'We will look the other way'.'[379] True to the promise, Pakistan did not impede the border fencing, but for internal consumption, it did make noise at the UN by drawing a parallel between what India was doing and what Israel was doing on the West Bank of Gaza. Pakistan also announced ceasefire in

November and the protestations at the UN notwithstanding, the ceasefire held.

Two significant achievements of this period were the accelerated activity at South Asian Association of Regional Countries (SAARC) and the creation of the South Asian Free Media Association (SAFMA). Together, they recognized that it was advisable not to wait for the political differences and conflicts to be resolved and jump to economic and trade cooperation and exchange of ideas not only among the civil societies of the two countries but also among the media so that the rhetoric of the media is tempered. Consequently, India and Pakistan were able to roll over their differences and strike South Asian Free Trade Agreement. This resulted in regular arrival and departure of traders and also frequent exchange of ideas among the media persons. On the political front, backchannels were activated and Musharraf went to the extent of declaring that he was willing to leave the UN resolutions on Kashmir behind and move on provided India agreed for the talks. His formula was to focus on those solutions that were acceptable to both rather than wasting time and increasing hackles by focusing and debating on the unacceptable solutions to any of them, or the Kashmiris. This approach resulted in breakthrough on the trade and commerce front, thereby creating a new constituency that found peace fruitful. Proposals regarding the gas pipelines from Iran and Central Asia through Pakistan to India were floated and discussed. There were also proposals for cross border openings between Mumbai-Karachi, Rajasthan and Sindh at a few more places. Civil society groups in India and Pakistan became active in which representatives from Jammu, Kashmir and Ladakh interacted with the activists from across the LoC representing Muzaffarabad, Mirpur, Gilgit and Baltistan. The trade and commerce lobby, supported by the media helped in creating a large section that rooted for peace and cooperation. Both, the Indian and Pakistani Punjab, Sindh and Rajasthan were particularly excited since they had been closely connected by history and culture. But even more significant was the emergence of new middle class in India. Driven by the enormous breakthrough that India made in software, it had created a very confident middleclass whose ambition and world perspective was different from the earlier generation. It was eager to grab the emerging global opportunities where the Indian, Bangladeshi and Pakistani identities came to be subordinated to the shared South Asian identity and legacy. Even from Pakistan, a new generation looked to the future that did not obstruct them from exploring new options. Whereas the earlier generation of Pakistanis settled abroad would aggressively argue that if the UN could interfere in Serbia, Kosovo, Bosnia and East Timor then why not in Kashmir, now most had mellowed down to accepting that perhaps lowering of volume of rhetoric and holding talks for peace and development was a much more acceptable route to resolving differences. It is unfortunate that, unlike the diaspora of two Irelands, Indian and Pakistani diaspora opened this window of opportunity only narrowly and briefly. Had both exerted pressure, as the Irish diaspora had done, the period between 2000 and 2008 was the most conducive period for settling the issue once and for all.

Vajpayee's efforts did bear fruit and by early 2004 Hurriyat had held two rounds of talks with Deputy Prime Minister Advani who was believed to be a hawk in the government. This time there were no dissensions among the separatist leaders, and the hot-heads in Pakistan too had been held in check. Musharraf had committed that Pakistan 'would not allow any part of its territory under its control to be used for terrorist activities against India'. This offer was considered sincere since it was made from Islamabad thereby eliminating the possibility of denial.

In December 2003, Musharraf and the Pakistani Army were shocked by the Islamist guerillas attempt to assassinate Musharraf. It was a clear signal that the terrorists who had been sheltered by Pakistan had grown too big not to think and act independently, and that, they had their own agenda to pursue. In another development, Geelani had broken away from the Hurriyat, making space for the middle path for the others, and unlike earlier occasions, this time the Hurriyat talks had the tacit support of Pakistan. As a confidence building measure, Hurriyat demanded freeing of the political prisoners. Advani too responded favorably and released 69 prisoners and also ordered screening of 500 more. The other demand of Hurriyat was concerning the human rights violations and Advani assured that the forces will be functioning with a human face. In another related development, the Hurriyat had insisted upon having direct talks with Advani. They made it clear that since Advani was a 'Hindu hardliner' therefore there was purpose in talking only to a person who had the potential of wrecking any deal brokered by some interlocutor who had no decision-making powers of his or her own. Thus, Vajpayee and his National Security Adviser Brajesh Mishra had succeeded in creating a situation in which hawks of both sides were on board. Buoyed by the success, and at the peak of his popularity the Prime Minister and BJP confidently called for general elections in May 2004, six months before the scheduled period since the government had slated the next round of talks for June. But the unexpected defeat and coming to power of Congress-led coalition, United Progressive Alliance (UPA), upset the applecart.

Fortunately, Dr Manmohan Singh-led UPA continued the peace process on assuming office and went ahead with the scheduled talks with Hurriyat. Radha Kumar, who was already a part of the Track II diplomacy, claims that Dr Singh, on assuming office asked Vajpayee if he would act as the Indian government's special envoy to head an India-Pakistan-Kashmir peace process. There is no doubt that had Vajpayee agreed to the proposal it would have greatly accelerated the process and would have been a great booster for all concerned as that would have demonstrated the united resolve of India to forge peace and would have also recognized the seminal contribution made by Vajpayee's '*insaniyat ke daire mein*' statement that had been made in Srinagar.[380] The utilization of the services of a former President or Prime Minister for attaining a higher national cause is not unknown to modern history. It becomes a statement not only of united intent of a nation but also an acknowledgement of continuity. UPA's Foreign Minister Natwar Singh also met former Foreign Minister Yashwant Sinha and Advani to canvass support. Radha Kumar, who was actively involved, claims in her book that she had already interacted with Dr Singh in 2000 when Vajpayee wanted Congress on board the peace mission. He had then whole heartedly cooperated and was instrumental in muting the Congress criticism and had lent support. She says that on behalf of Dr Singh, she had taken the offer to Brajesh Mishra who was enthusiastic and was disappointed when Vajpayee turned it down. It is not known if Vajpayee turned down the offer because he had read the change that was taking place in the RSS and BJP and had no desire for a showdown with the emerging hard line and fanatical forces who had concluded that the thrust of their organization should be to capture power and institutions on their own if their vision of Hindu Bharat was to be realized. The treatment given to Advani in subsequent years when he praised Jinnah for his Constituent Assembly speech in Pakistan on 11 August 1947, is ample proof of how the new forces had begun to dominate the BJP.

Meanwhile, the talks between Centre and Hurriyat appeared to have come to a dead end when the latter took umbrage to the statement of Home Minister Shivraj Patil that talks would be held only within the scope of the constitution and Mirwaiz Umar Farooq accused the government of not being sincere. The rest of the year drifted on the peace front in Kashmir but finally in February 2005 the breakthrough arrived when Indian and Pakistani foreign ministers announced after talks in Islamabad that the road connecting Srinagar with Muzaffarabad would be reopened. This road had been closed since the War of 1947-48.[381] Symbolically and emotionally, the opening of this road was of immense importance for the Kashmiris on both the sides of the LoC. After the Lahore bus, this move was already on the Vajpayee-Sharif table but had been put off by Kargil and subsequent events. That was at a time when the National Conference was ruling the State but when PDP-Congress government assumed office, chief minister Sayeed had taken up the matter with Vajpayee. The significance of this was enormous since it was a loud announcement of the BJP at the Centre and Congress in the state that they were both on the same page. Finally, when the bus service was announced, there was a Congress-led alliance at the Centre and Congress-supported alliance in the State. Understandably, Sayeed went to town claiming all the credit and putting up billboards all over the Valley. On the eve of its launch some terrorists did try to disrupt it but the schedule went ahead and it was noted by an observer that the 'opening of the road can be considered the biggest Kashmir-centric confidence-building.'[382]

There was, however, a departure from the Vajpayee years since the Hurriyat had not been involved in the negotiations to open the road. Perhaps it was a mistake as that would have been an effort towards presenting a united face of Kashmiris. All that would have happened is that Chief Minister Sayeed could not have taken all the credit for its opening but it would have kept the Hurriyat on the right side. Thus, once again a misstep had happened and the Kashmiri politicians had come out in the open with their competing ambitions and rivalries. There is no doubt that the Hurriyat would not have objected to the move. With the Srinagar-Muzaffarabad bus service on its way, the next diplomatic step was again taken by Musharraf who came down to Delhi on the pretext of watching an Indo-Pak cricket match scheduled in Delhi on 17 April 2005 but used the occasion to discuss opening of more routes in Kashmir and elsewhere. It was clear that economy had become a priority.[383]

When a devastating earthquake ravaged PoK in November 2005, compulsions of the circumstances opened new opportunity for cooperation. The worst affected areas were located in such remote and difficult to access areas that not only the international aid agencies but also Pakistani help groups were finding them difficult to reach from the Pakistani side. Some of the areas were such that they could be better approached from the Indian side rather easily. India offered help and proposed opening routes to Poonch, Mirpur and Muzaffarabad but the Pakistani Army feared that it would make these areas vulnerable to the influence of Indian intelligence agencies. But since the shortest route to the quake-hit areas was from the Indian side therefore the international aid agencies pressurized Pakistan to open those routes for humane reasons. Finally, when Pakistan did open the Mirpur-Jammu route for help there was such large throng of people that Pakistani authorities had to use tear gas to hold them back. Indian aid also poured in but Pakistan obstructed it on the ground that the Indian labels were meant to influence the people! India responded by agreeing to remove all the Indian labels that identified their Indian origin.[384] India also offered helicopters for ferrying the sick and the injured and dropping food and medicine but President Musharraf said that they were welcome but without the Indian pilots, because of certain 'sensitivities.' India did not pursue the matter further, and Pakistan had to finally depend on US helicopters and NATO forces for rescue work.[385]

By now Hurriyat too realized that staying away from the peace efforts was counter-productive and it found the perfect excuse to get back into the picture when Dr Manmohan Singh's government made it abundantly clear that it had all the intentions to pursue the three-track formula of the Vajpayee government. Abdul Ghani Bhat, one of the leaders of the Hurriyat took the initiative to prevail upon others to give the effort a try. Consequently, in June 2005, a seven-member Hurriyat delegation left for Pakistan-occupied-Kashmir, consisting parts of Poonch, Mirpur and Muzaffarabad. Hurriyat was joined by Yasin Malik representing JKLF though he travelled separately. In India, in contrast to the silent support that Congress lent to the efforts of Vajpayee, BJP was strident in its criticism of the government for allowing the Hurriyat to go to Pakistan without Indian passports and also lambasted Pakistan for allowing them to enter without Indian passports. BJP also expressed the apprehension that the Srinagar-Muzaffarabad bus service would be carrying passengers without passport thereby opening up possibilities of inimical forces entering India for terrorist activities. But the Hurriyat delegation continued on its mission and very significantly an appeal for ending violence was made by Hurriyat and JKLF from Muzaffarabad. The delegates also visited Islamabad and met with opposition to its effort from Lashkar and Jaish-e-Mohammad terror groups. In Islamabad Yasin Malik, who was still considered a hero in PoK and was extremely popular, had a public spat with the Information and Broadcasting Minister of Pakistan Sheikh Rashid at a press conference. On return, speaking on behalf of the delegation, onc of the Hurriyat leaders said that during the visit they had done all the talking to the Pakistani leadership and that they also intended to do the same with the Indian leadership. He claimed that the visit had established the credentials of the peace efforts and of those involved in it.[386]

Dr Manmohan Singh's government continued to involve the civil society groups as well as backchannels though the expected support did not come from the BJP which had in the first place started that process. In fact, Dr Singh had simply carried on the process that Vajpayee had started. But unfortunately, new forces had emerged within the BJP and the former Prime Minister had been increasingly marginalized within the party. The revisionists had begun to take control of the party no sooner had BJP lost the elections in 2004. According to A.S. Dulat, Vajpayee's point man in Kashmir, when he went to meet him after the unexpected poll reverse, and wondered what had happened, Vajpayee, according to a recorded conversation of Dulat, laughed and said that even the Congress did not know what had happened and how it had won! But on further reflection he simply added that perhaps they (Vajpayee's BJP) had erred in Gujarat. He was, of course, referring to the Muslim massacre in that State under Narendra Modi in 2002 and the refusal of the party to take action against him. But unbeknown to Vajpayee and also L.K. Advani, as seen by the unfolding of events, churning had been going on in the BJP too. While Vajpayee's comments were part of a private conversation, Advani had crossed a RSS redline when he visited Karachi, the city of his birth and early education, and during his visit to the mausoleum of Mohammad Ali Jinnah, he praised the Quaid-i-Azam of Pakistan as a secular politician who had delivered that largely forgotten speech in the Constituent Assembly of Pakistan, espousing the secular credentials of the new state. It had created a furor in India, particularly in the RSS and soon thereafter he was made to resign as the President of BJP. Soon thereafter, the results of the churning were becoming more assertive when Jaswant Singh, a BJP stalwart, who had his roots only in the political philosophy of BJP and not RSS, wrote a book on Jinnah and praised him and blamed Nehru for Partition. But he aggravated the tension by also making critical remarks about Sardar Patel. The book was immediately banned by Chief Minister Modi in Gujarat! In the light of these developments, it is not surprising that BJP refused to cooperate with Dr Manmohan Singh on his peace efforts.

Dr Singh was also hampered by voices of dissent on his Pakistan policy within the Congress too but Sonia Gandhi, the Congress president and UPA chairperson's unstinted support helped him to focus on the effort rather than look for his flanks. Therefore, carrying forward the dialogue with Hurriyat he not only offered the hastening of the screening of political prisoners who could be released but at the second round of talks also announced the redeployment of 40,000 troops away from the civilian areas. Mirwaiz Umar Farooq also exuded optimism and declared that soon there would be a formal mechanism for conducting dialogue. As a result, for the first time after the violence broke out in the Valley in 1989, the number of such incidents fell below the 1990 level. 'Total fatalities declined from the high of 4,507 in 2001 to 1,810 in 2004 and further to 1,116 in 2006. Civilians killed in crossfire fell from over a thousand in 2001 to around 350 in 2006.'[387] The Mirwaiz was still the chairman of the Hurriyat for the second time when these developments took place and he was full of praise for the Indian government for talking to the Hurriyat and recognizing it as a political entity. He declared: 'Kashmiris must be masters of their own fate. Self-rule and autonomy are two different things. Autonomy is within the framework of the Indian Constitution. Self-rule is not.'[388]

It was clear that the Hurriyat had moved away from the rigid position that it had adopted in the past and was ready for a solution that could also be acceptable to both India and Pakistan. This shift in the stand was not appreciated by the Islamist elements in Pakistan as well as some who were also present in the Valley. They did their best to wreck these efforts by following their tried and tested formula of targeted killings and the Mirwaiz was the object of several failed attacks. It must be said that he displayed remarkable physical and moral courage by refusing to be cowed down and unlike many, did not leave the Valley and the country for safety. His staying the course of negotiations was all the more laudable since his father had been a victim of the bullets of those who had always opposed peace efforts. There were other terrorist killings meant to derail the peace process. Notably, an army establishment in Akhnoor became the target of a *fidayeen* attack on 22 July 2003. Eight security force personnel, including a Brigadier, were killed and 12 others were injured. This was the highest ranked casualty in Jammu and Kashmir.

Undeterred, the government at the centre and the state continued in their confidence building measures. It is another matter that Dr

Manmohan Singh, true to his immensely understated style did not make any loud attempt to take credit for the small steps that were taken and Mufti Mohammad Sayeed, true to the breed of politicians, hogged all the limelight and the credit. Dr Singh was content to work quietly and therefore the optimum use of the Track II diplomacy and civil society efforts took place during this period. However, this period was also marked by the killings of those militants who had been disenchanted by the machinations of Pakistan and had returned home from across the border with the intent to turn a new page. Many of them had been used by the security forces in the counter-terrorist activities and were accordingly rehabilitated. Prominent among them was a group led by Pakistan trained Kuka Parray who laid down arms on return and offered cooperation in fighting terrorists. Thus Ikhwan-ul-Muslmeen was formed in 1994. It is believed that 300 to 500 Ikhwanis, as they were known, were recruited in the J&K Police and about 150 of them lost lives fighting terrorists. A few like Kuka Parray became part of the mainstream and Kuka Parray got elected to the State Assembly in the 1996 elections. Some of them, including, Kuka Parray, were also accused of extortion and running their own fiefdoms. In 2003, he was shot dead by the terrorists, and his killing, and of his associates gave suspicion of revenge killings under the patronage of the State. There is little doubt that Mufti Mohammad Sayeed's rule had marked a near normalcy after more than a decade of strife but it was also marred by the killings of Kuka Parray and some of his supporters who had helped in eliminating terrorists and establishing some kind of normalcy. It was rumored that he had helped in the elimination of those militants and separatists who were based in South Kashmir and were supporters of Mufti.

As the year 2005 was approaching its end, it was time for Sayeed to hand over power to a Congress nominee as chief minister. Understandably the PDP was reluctant to do so. Goaded by forces that contended that the much publicized 'healing touch' of Sayeed had brought the state back from the brink and therefore it would not be wise to rock the boat at that juncture. It was also contended by Kashmiri leaders that the construct of the state demanded that only a Kashmiri be its chief minister, and that, since Congress will have to choose a candidate from among its legislators from Jammu, therefore, the historical animosity will come in the forefront and destroy the peace and normalcy process that was going on. But Congress was not prepared for any change in the power sharing formula between Congress and PDP and chose Ghulam Nabi Azad as its candidate for chief minister and he took the oath of office of chief minister on 2 November 2005 as the seventh chief minister of the state. This period of jockeying and assumptions was marked by heightened terrorist activity and in one of the attacks a former Minister of State for Education, Ghulam Nabi Lone was assassinated, PDP leader Ghulam Hassan Mir critically wounded and Mohammad Yusuf Tarigami, the Marxist leader wounded.

But soon thereafter, the tenure of Azad stabilized. Contrary to the fears that being a Jammu politician his roots will prove a baggage for his office, his efficient and responsive administration coupled with the fact that he was from Jammu, became an asset for him. Under his leadership, the historical fault line between the two regions seemed to have ironed out. Importantly, it hammered home the point that if democratic institutions are allowed to function and if they are reasonably strong then the separatist tendencies get weakened and can be absorbed in the democracy. As Chief Minister, Azad continued to provide a responsive and sympathetic government. In a short time, Azad had created a new constituency for himself not only in Jammu but also the Valley and Ladakh. He turned out to be bold enough to create new districts, something that he did in a coalition government, and which, many before him had failed to do as chief ministers with massive majorities. He created eight new districts, four each in Kashmir and Jammu regions thereby addressing their aspirations in an even-handed manner. These were legitimate demands waiting to be fulfilled since long. Along with the creation of new administrative and revenue units, Azad also announced the setting up of a new delimitation commission so that in view of the rising population and the need to rationalize them according to the geography, 25 percent more Assembly seats could be added. These decisions went a long way in assuaging the feelings of political discrimination in the Jammu region. In doing so he had been careful not to give the impression of the balance of power shifting against the Valley.

The year 2007 had come on an ominous note with militant activity and encounters occurring more frequently. Two militants were killed by security forces in Sopore on 1 January 2007 and four more were killed in the Udhampur district on 4 January 2007. Thirteen individuals, including 10 militants and two soldiers, were killed in clashes in the Kupwara district on 28 June 2007. Two soldiers and nine Islamic militants were killed in clashes in Tangmarg on 2-3 October 2007.On 11 October 2007, five soldiers and two civilians were killed in an explosion at a military camp in the township of Pattan. This went on in December too and the transnational jihadists, as a mark of boldness or proof of their Pakistani handlers' design behind these activities, decided to spread their area of operation beyond the State boundary when they were suspected of killing seven soldiers at a military camp in Rampur in the state of Uttar Pradesh on 2 January 2008. This was obviously a part of the broader agenda of creating communal tension outside the State to initiate Jihad.

The Confidence Building Measures (CBMs) that had been given a fillip by Dr Singh, and were supported by Sayeed, continued during Azad's time, both within the divided parts of the State, and between India and Pakistan. Soon there appeared a significant breakthrough when India and Pakistan agreed upon the gas pipeline project from Iran and possibly Central Asia. Considerable progress was made on the trade and business front and new opportunities opened up in both the countries. The journalists were permitted to freely travel not only in the two countries but those from the State were allowed to travel in the divided parts of the State though not yet to the Gilgit-Baltistan region. Prior to this agreement, the media-persons belonging to Jammu and Kashmir were particularly barred from visiting PoK. In contrast to Mufti Mohammad Sayeed, Azad was a low-key politician who was not too eager to hog all the credit. This was partly because of the Congress culture where it was customary to pass on all the credit to the central leadership but it proved to be a blessing since the CBMs and the State was no longer the focus of attention.

Whatever progress that took place during the Vajpayee days and the early years of Dr Singh were made possible 'because there was rare confluence of political and civil society inputs on the Indian side, and a rare confluence of military, political and Kashmiri inputs on the Pakistani side. The years 2004-2006 had seen a flurry of Track II meetings and conferences that brought together Kashmiri leaders from the two sides of the Line of Control... To have Farooq Abdullah, Abdul Ghani Bhat and Sajad Lone at the same table with leaders like Sardar Qayyum from across the Line of Control, discussing a peace process proactively instead of combatively, was in itself a huge confidence-booster. It freed the Hurriyat leaders to speak openly and in their own right about the next steps they would like to see.'[389]

Pursuing the process, Dr Manmohan Singh set up a round table conference of representative from the civil society, regional and Kashmiri political platforms. The intention was brain-storming and finding a way forward to forge durable peace and permanent settlement of issues. The Hurriyat leaders stayed away from these parleys though they kept discussing through the back channels that were appointed by the Prime Minister. Unfortunately, the Hurriyat measured the success of the efforts by their meetings with the Prime Minister. The Track II negotiators failed to convince them that the significance of a meeting with the Prime Minister assumes importance only if a major announcement has to be made. Moreover, Hurriyat did not grasp the time constraints that are there on the Prime Minister of a country like India that has complex and multiple problems and challenges waiting at his table.

The year 2006 also saw some hectic activity after Mirwaiz Umar Farooq declared that elected political leaders and civil society must be involved in the talks. This led to a meeting of the Prime Minister with the Hurriyat leaders. Forces inimical to peace struck back and the Mirwaiz's uncle was killed as a message to the Hurriyat to stay away from the talks. Speaking to the media, Hurriyat clarified their absence from the round table meetings by saying that though they were not against such meetings where a host of people representing various groups were meeting yet none of them was in a position to take a decision whereas Hurriyat wanted to confabulate with only those who had the authority to take a decision. Readers would remember that during the Vajpayee era, they had insisted upon talking only with Advani because of his reputation of a hardliner who could wreck any settlement if he was opposed to it. This stand notwithstanding, the Hurriyat leaders were believed to have agreed to attend round table conferences and according to Prime Minister Dr Singh, 'The round table conference process was developed to enable all segments of Kashmir's political groups the opportunity to join hands with the Centre to look at the problem. It is my regret that the Hurriyat, despite promises, did not come for talks.'[390]

The boycott of the round table conference was a retrograde step and proved to be an obstruction in developing internal harmony but notwithstanding this hiccup, in the meantime, considerable progress had been made by the diplomatic efforts of India and Pakistan, both at the Track II level and the official level between S.K. Lambah, former Indian ambassador to Pakistan and Tariq Aziz, a confidant of President Musharraf and National Security Adviser. The most significant outcome of these talks was that while India agreed on the need to reduce military from the civilian areas, Pakistan realized that confidence building measures would remain empty words if cross border infiltration and terror was not curbed. Accordingly, the Indian Army transferred many of its duties, like manning the check posts, to J&K Police and the CRPF and Pakistan also brought down the level of infiltration. During daytime, there was minimum presence of the army in civilian areas.

While the broad contours of the discussions have since come out, Kasuri's narrative in his comprehensive tome—*Neither Hawk Nor Dove*—provides rare insights into how Pakistan handled the talks and worked towards sorting out contentious points. Kasuri writes that Aziz met Lambah over a dozen times quietly in places such as Dubai, Kathmandu and Bangkok. On his return, Aziz would then present a draft of the discussions at a meeting convened by Musharraf at his Rawalpindi residence which included Kasuri, the ISI chief, Ashfaq Kayani, (who would later succeed Musharraf as army chief) the foreign secretary, and the president's chief of staff. After making amendments, Aziz would be given a draft of issues to take up with S.K. Lambah, who in turn took them to his principals in Delhi. It was during this period that considerable progress was made in securing greater peace.

According to a report of Raj Chengappa in *India Today*, though Lambah has been very reserved about the details of the back-channel activities, he did say that one of the reasons the talks made so much progress is that the two countries decided to focus on the 'core' issues of terror and Kashmir, and not go into other outstanding issues such as Siachen, Sir Creek and bilateral trade. It also helped that Musharraf, apart from being president was the army chief, and that the ISI was fully on board so that there was a rare military-civil convergence of purpose. Lambah confirmed to *India Today* that 'I got a confirmation directly from the top-most level of the Pakistan Army regarding their support for what was being discussed in the Back Channel.' Significantly, during the Back-Channel negotiations, Pakistan did not push its maximalist demand of referring the dispute to the UN for a plebiscite or for third-party intervention. Both sides also had tacitly agreed that there would be no redrawing of the borders and that any future agreement should ensure that the LoC acted as a border between the two countries.[391]

It was during these talks that Kasuri acknowledged that containing cross-border terrorism was a prerequisite from India's point of view and unless that was addressed, no progress was possible. It was in the wake of this realization that Pakistan launched its much publicized 'De-radicalization, Disengagement and Rehabilitation' (DDR) program. Figures also reveal that during this period the infiltration was contained though for obvious reasons it was claimed that it was because of the effective measures taken by the Indian security forces.

Among the most contentious issues under discussion was the demand by Pakistan for self-governance of Kashmir that had always been viewed by India as a ploy to loosen Delhi's grip on the Valley. While Pakistan argued that PoK had its own constitution, legislature, judiciary, prime minister and president, India had changed the status quo in the Valley by bringing the whole system under its constitution. But when India brought up the issue of Gilgit and Baltistan that had been part of the State of Jammu and Kashmir till 1947, but had been integrated with the Pakistani constitution, Pakistan argued that this was because these regions, including the Northern Areas of Hunza, Chilas etc. had revolted against the Dogra Maharaja's rule and had expressed their desire to be a part of Pakistan. But more importantly, Pakistan baulked on this issue because, over the years, it had systematically separated the two areas from each other. The Northern Areas had become its strategic soft-spot as it adjoined China's Xinjiang and was important not only because of its proximity to Central Asia but also because of its strategic interests with China. In fact, it was through the Karakoram highway that Pakistan had a direct land access to China, its all-weather friend.

Hitherto, all talks and negotiations had taken place in complete secrecy but since it appeared that both countries were close to a settlement, there was need to ensure that nothing appears suddenly in public. India after all was a democracy and people needed to be convinced of any change in stance. The people of India had come to live with the fact of the integration of Jammu and Kashmir with it and any shift would need to be convincing to the emotions as well. Moreover, the fact that the BJP and RSS had traditionally demanded the removal of Article 370, any alteration to the status that suggested loosening of integration, would be impossible to accept. In view of this, those involved in Track II considered the time opportune to take the public into confidence. The proposed policy was disseminated for public consumption by eminent diplomat G. Parthasarathy and Radha Kumar under the title 'Framework for Kashmir Settlement' by Delhi Policy Group, 2006. This group was also of the opinion that Musharraf too should be urged to make the Aziz-Lambah talks public so that people across the border are also prepared to accept the shift from the traditional position. By pushing this in the public sphere those involved in the talks and negotiations also hoped that Musharraf's actual commitment would also be tested. Dr Manmohan Singh had already demonstrated his seriousness by ensuring that the military was considerably withdrawn from the civilian areas and the duties at the check posts were handed over to the Police and CRPF. Pakistan, however, needed to be evaluated.

The peace process had the wholehearted support of the international community too, though the US and Bush administration spoke in two different voices in India and Pakistan. It was largely due to its heavy dependence on Pakistan for keeping the supply lines open to US-led NATO forces in Afghanistan. But since the 9/11 attack, the US had begun to view terrorist acts in new light. Now all terrorist activities, whether in Afghanistan or in Jammu and Kashmir, were considered acts of terror and the hard reality was that the new approach of the Pakistani government had not deterred certain forces from carrying out terrorist acts in both the countries. Supporting them were the people who controlled the ISI. But post 9/11, there was a global shift in perspective and for the first time, in 2006, the European parliament's foreign affairs committee released a report that indicted Pakistan for its role in the armed conflict in Jammu and Kashmir and also denying democracy in PoK and Gilgit-Baltistan.[392]

This report had annoyed and angered Pakistan, particularly the terrorist groups. They roundly criticized it and accused the European Union of prejudice. In any case, these groups had become vocal against the peace efforts for they believed were convinced that Kashmir was very close to seceding from India. The concessions offered by India were construed as marks of weakness. Just when it was evident that considerable progress had been made in the peace process things began to go wrong though earlier also a number of attempts had been made to derail the peace process.

On 11 July 2006, at peak rush hour in Mumbai, a series of bomb blasts rocked the local trains, killing 209 commuters. On 8 September 2006, Malegaon in Maharashtra suffered bomb blasts in which 40 people lost their lives. The New Year saw more such incidents. On 18 February 2007, the Samjhauta Express, the Indo-Pak rail link, was victim to bomb blasts, killing 68 people including 43 Pakistani citizens, 10 Indians and 15 unidentified. On 7 March 2007, Varanasi's Sankatmochan Temple and the Cantonment Railway Station were rocked by bomb blasts yet again, killing 28 persons. Obviously, there were forces that were desperate to thwart the peace process and unleash communal riots. These acts of terror began building an atmosphere in which any peace proposal involving Pakistan began to look like an act of betrayal of the national cause.

At the State level, the position of various political parties and groups was articulated with great clarity. The National Conference focused only on the human rights violations and more autonomy and the BJP strongly advocated nothing but complete integration with India. Panun Kashmir, representing Kashmiri Pandits who had migrated from the Valley and were settled mostly in Jammu and Delhi, also supported the BJP's point of view and were so vocal in their bitterness that it appeared to be goading others to extract revenge on their behalf from Kashmiri Muslims. BJP though, had influence only in the Jammu region with no voice in the Valley. There were minor parties like the Jammu and Kashmir National Panthers' Party (JKNPP) and CPM, and both were in favor of status quo. In Ladakh, there was the newly constituted Ladakh Union Territory Front, and as the name suggested, favored complete integration with India and possibly severance of all links with both Jammu as well as Kashmir. While the National Conference championed autonomy, its rival in the Valley, the PDP favored 'self-rule' which appeared closer to secession. There were serious talks about opening the Kargil-Skardu, Jammu-Sialkot, Turtuk-Khaplu, Chhamb-Jorian, Gurez-Astore-Gilgit, Tithwal-Chilhan and Jhanger-Mirpur routes. While there were dissensions at the political level, the general public was enthused by these proposals.

The year 2007 also saw the resolution of the Baglihar Dam on the river Chenab. The 1960 Indus Waters Treaty had given Pakistan the exclusive right to the western rivers of the system, that is, Chenab, Jhelum and Indus, but it had also given India the right of use of these waters for run of the river projects and storage of up to 1.6 MAF. The acute power shortages had compelled the country to take up hydro power projects in the State on a priority. Pakistan had objected to the Indian proposal to construct a dam on Chenab for generating power for domestic use and there the matter had rested till India decided to approach the World Bank for arbitration in 2005. In 2007, the arbitrator announced the verdict in favor of India. But the year was also lined with dark clouds. In an ill-advised move, President Musharraf on 3 November 2007 suspended the Constitution of Pakistan, sacked 15 Supreme Court judges and 56 judges of the provincial High Courts and also put the then Chief Justice of Pakistan under house arrest. This consequently aroused the anger and frustration of the civil society leading to massive demonstrations, and eventually his resignation and trial for high treason. The demonstrations that followed were supported by the Islamists too. Ever since the attack of the Pakistani Army on the Red Mosque in Islamabad that had resulted in hundreds of deaths of Islamist clerics and religious students of the *Deeni Taliban*, these elements had sworn enmity against Musharraf. The terrorists and Islamists who had been nursed in Pakistan all these years had become the proverbial Frankenstein's monster and it had turned on the State of Pakistan making it a target of these forces, largely consisting of Taliban and their supporters. They had found safe refuge in the Federally Administered Tribal Areas (FATA), now part of Pakhtunkhwa, a haven from the pursuing US and NATO forces. However, by then the US had developed drones and frequently used them to target the Taliban in these areas; the bombings claimed several innocent civilian lives. It is believed that for every terrorist killed in drone attacks, ten civilians too were also killed. The Americans called these deaths 'collateral damage', incensing the people even more. The Islamists had consequently found willing allies in Pakistan and soon the Pakistani Taliban had come to haunt the Pakistani Army too. In contrast to the developments in Pakistan, Jammu and Kashmir was witnessing a rare era where the focus was on governance and development. Azad's administration had begun a period of reconstruction when suddenly every advantage had to be surrendered because of an ill-thought and ill-timed decision.

The outgoing Governor, Lieutenant General (Retd) S.K. Sinha, controversially allotted land to the Shri Amarnath Shrine Board on the Baltal-Holy Shrine route. The local residents felt that it was a step towards usurping their land and livelihood since they provided tents, ponies and guides to the more than 2,00,000 pilgrims every Yatra season and now they feared this would be taken over by outsiders. Soon it morphed into fears of encroachment on the autonomy of the state as well as a subtle attempt to change the demography. The PDP gave an ultimatum to the Congress to withdraw the land allotment. Once again, this crisis brought out the deep-rooted fault line between the two regions as there was a counter-reaction in Jammu. In the Valley, it also triggered a violent agitation against the land allotment and also paved the way for foreign elements to once again play a role in the communal killings. On the other hand, the counter agitation launched in the Jammu region galvanized the Hindu forces that polarized both the regions. The fault line between Kashmir and Jammu was fully exposed and all the good work that Azad had done was consigned to the dustbin. The fact that Jammu virtually blockaded supplies to the Valley aggravated the fears of the Valley of being left at the mercy of Hindu communalism. This once again revived the memory of the natural connectivity of the Valley to the plains via Muzaffarabad. Finding Azad dillydallying over the ultimatum and the National Conference applying pressure, Mufti and the PDP withdrew support to the Congress, leading to the fall of government. Finally, when the storm did blow over and the Assembly elections were held again, the National Conference made a comeback and once again formed a government, now in alliance with the Congress. This time Farooq Abdullah bowed out of the State politics to make way for his son Omar Abdullah as Chief Minister.

This was soon followed by an outrageous attack on Mumbai on 26 November 2008. The well-trained Islamist terrorists had boldly taken the sea route to land near Mumbai and target the Chhatrapati Shivaji Station, Taj Hotel at the Gateway of India, and the Jewish Chabad House. The attack, planned by the Lashkar-e-Taiba in coordination with their handlers from the ISI, consisted of a group of ten well-armed and well-trained terrorists. In all, 175 persons, including nine terrorists were killed. The tenth, Ajmal Kasab was caught, tried and executed by the law agencies. The attack lasted four days. This siege, killings of people of multiple nationalities and the reign of terror over the financial capital of India, turned the public opinion decisively against Pakistan and any peace effort. The peace efforts after this just limped till it was completely overwhelmed by hard-line nationalists on both the sides of the border. For the State, the immediate concern was of holding the Assembly polls. It had tried and tested new political combinations to untie the Gordian knot but the well-entrenched templates governing the real and supposed ambitions of the Kashmiris made it flounder.

13

Hope and Despair

'He who has never hoped can never despair.'
—George Bernard Shaw

In 2008, elections to the Assembly were due. Since Azad had done a reasonably good job of giving a responsive government, the PDP feared that the credit for its achievements, including those by Mufti Mohammad Sayeed, would go under Azad and the Congress's name. Therefore, the PDP was said to be reluctant going into the election under Azad's leadership. The expected blow, however, did not come from the PDP but the Governor Lt Gen. (Retd) Sinha, who in one of his last acts as Governor, on 26 May 2008, reached an agreement with the government of India to transfer 99 acres or 800 *kanals* of forest land to the Shri Amarnathji Shrine Board (SASB) on the Baltal-Holy Shrine route to set up temporary shelters and facilities for Hindu pilgrims. When this happened, the two month-long annual Amarnath pilgrimage had begun, but on 22 June protests started in Ganderbal, which fell on the route to Baltal from Srinagar and was one of the two base camps for the Amarnath pilgrimage. The protests against land allotment spread across many parts of the Kashmir Valley. The local residents felt that it was a step in usurping their land and livelihood since they provided tents, ponies and guides to the more than 200,000 pilgrims every Yatra season and now they feared this would be taken over by outsiders. Soon these apprehensions morphed into fears of encroachment on the autonomy of the State as well as a subtle attempt to change the demography.

On 25 June counter protests began in Jammu against the government in general and separatists, in particular. As expected, the PDP, which was always suspected of having links with the secessionists, threatened to quit government if the allotment was not canceled, and not getting satisfactory response, withdrew support from the Azad-led coalition government. After the fall of the Azad government on 8 July, the new Governor, N.N. Vohra soon after taking over, revoked land allotment to SASB and the protests ended in the Valley. However, they continued in Jammu, now against the cancellation of the land allotment. The police opened fire on protesters. In the Valley, the government had responded by clamping curfew, disabling the internet and mobile services in the hope that in the absence of communications, the protests would die. But they only grew and about 70 protesters lost their lives. The gains of the past few years were lost amidst the communal agendas, slogans, stone pelting and defiant processions.

In Jammu, on 8 July, the Shri Amarnath Yatra Sangharsh Samiti (SAYSS) was constituted to spearhead agitations for restoration of land to the SASB. 'There is a great deal of anger among the people of Jammu. Even the army seems to be unable to contain the anger of the people, said Mr. (Arun) Jaitley,' according to a report published in *Economic Times*. 'Referring to the upsurge among the people, the BJP leader said that despite blocking off all SMS services, people have come out to protest. He also spoke of the continued atrocities on the media. The party has also condemned the restrictions on media persons, arguing that it was against healthy democracy. The BJP has also suggested that a team of the National Human Rights Commission visit Jammu and investigate human rights violations by the security forces.'[393]

Clearly, a message and warning had been given by the protests and counter-protests in Kashmir and Jammu. Jammu had for far too long witnessed the eruption of periodic bouts of protests in Kashmir and seen the governments buckling under them. It was no longer prepared to do so now and the government needed to be fair to both regions. But it was also deeply offended by the fact that while the fears of Kashmiris were imaginary(according to Jammu), the government had rescinded an order that was meant to provide facilities to the Hindu pilgrims coming from all over the country only during a particular period. The Kashmiri agitation was seen as an agitation against Hindu religion and community, and, even more offensively, it had been done under the cover of Article 370 which the rest of the country now wanted abrogated. At a political level, this was one of the more glaring examples of Muslim appeasement.

Later, when the Assembly elections of 2008 were conducted under the shadow of these circumstances, the electorate in the Valley reposed faith in the leadership of the oldest Kashmiri party to a certain extent. It did not get a clear mandate but it emerged as the largest party in Assembly with 28 seats and had to form a government in alliance with the Congress with 17 seats. The PDP won 21 seats which were not sufficient to form a government in alliance with the previous partner, Congress. The people were clearly divided in their preferences. But significantly, the BJP made rapid strides post the Amarnath agitation with 11 seats, that is, 10 seats more than its 2002 tally. These had been won from the Jammu region and at the expense of the Congress. An analysis of the vote distribution also revealed that the votes had begun to be polarized in constituencies consisting of mixed electorate. These elections had also been held under the shadow of the Mumbai attacks apart from the devastating Amarnath land allotment controversy and violent agitation in the Valley and Jammu. Apparently, democracy had triumphed over both the events and the people were determined to move on in a democratic manner. But also clear was the mutually hostile position of Kashmir and Jammu that had worked in favor of the BJP and it was also clear that the gains of the BJP would be at the cost of Congress and that sharper the divide between the two regions on the communal lines, the better it would be for it in constituencies where the PDP and National Conference were in matching strength. It was a portent for the things to come and the template set by Indira Gandhi in 1983 was about to be perfected and marshaled by the BJP. That was the year when the Resettlement Bill had sharply divided the Jammu and Kashmir regions on communal lines in favor of the Congress and National Conference respectively, with the avowedly communal parties, like the Jamaat in the Valley and BJP in Jammu, getting wiped out.

In the National Conference, the baton of leadership had changed hands with the mantle falling on the young shoulders of Omar Abdullah who became Chief Minister at the age of 37 years of age. It was a very favorable time for him to take charge as the armed conflict in the State was at a historical low. Fatalities had fallen to 541in 2008 and 375 in 2009 as well as in 2010. The number of civilians killed in crossfire was well below 100, at 69 in 2008 and 55 in 2009.[394] With the change of the helmsman, there was great optimism in the State as Omar had worked in a corporate sector before joining politics and had been a Minister of State for Foreign Affairs in the Vajpayee government. It was expected that he would bring in the efficiency of the private sector and also the larger vision of the world. In other words, with a young and fresh face of Omar, oozing the typical charm of the Abdullahs as also the modernity of times, it was the perfect time for peace-building and making a clean breast with the hitherto style of administration that was dependent upon favoritism and corruption. Unfortunately, he found it difficult to reconcile the two different worlds: one that existed and involved dealing with human problems and ambitions that could not be dealt by simply passing on a direction, and the other that worked in an impersonal manner with computers and mobile phones. Having spent much of his life away from the State and being pitched into the murky world of local politics, he was not really ready for the responsibility that had been thrust upon him. In addition, there were the challenges posed by the machinations from across the border. Each new and fresh initiative in the State brought response from the Pakistani handlers of the militants and sporadic militant activities and encounters kept occurring.

Omar began with a call for continuation of the peace process and this was welcomed by the Hurriyat and the JKLF. Perhaps both hoped that he had come without the baggage of the past and, therefore, was really sincere about it and, for the first time there was a possibility of these two groups, who had never agreed on anything, of coming together on a table. Hitherto, both had argued that the state government had no role to play in the negotiations since the conflict was between the union government and the pro-independence and pro-Pakistan groups in Kashmir. But this newfound opening was closed as soon as it had been opened with an alleged rape and murder of two women by security forces in the Shopian district of south Kashmir on 1 May 2009. This time violence erupted in the rural areas of south Kashmir and army pickets were subjected to stone throwing all over the Valley. For close to two months the agitation continued in which 12 lives were lost and 1,000 were injured. It was left for the CBI inquiry and a team of doctors from AIIMS, New Delhi to exhume the bodies and determine that rape had not been committed. Meanwhile, the young Chief Minister had given permission to the Police to tap the phones of the local doctors who had initially conducted the post-mortem, and it had recorded a conversation between the doctor and a member of the Majlis Mashawarat, the organization that led the agitation, in which the doctor confessed to the truth that rape had not taken place.[395] Apparently, the first medical report of rape had been doctored! Within the first year of his administration, Omar had realized the complexity of the situation and the challenge of adhering to the traditional loyalties and beliefs and doing the right thing as a chief minister. In these contentious times, nothing was what it seemed and his path was strewn with deceptive and well camouflaged pitfalls.

Before the year had ended, Omar had also experienced another dimension of terrorism in which killings took place of suspected 'informants' by the terrorists. This was a tool that was frequently and effectively used by the terrorists in the year 1989-1990 when the objective was to send a warning to all those forces in the civil life and administration who owed loyalty to India and its constitution. During the early years of insurgency this had forced the Pandit migration and the 'looking the other way' by government officials as well as the workers of main political parties. But now terrorism had assumed a different dimension in which the 'Mehman Mujahids' would force themselves on the nomadic Gujars and isolated homes for hospitality. Often those giving shelter would later be picked up by security forces for interrogation. Thus, many among them would inform the forces of the presence and location of these terrorists, leading to encounters and their killings. To deal with this threat, the terrorists had chosen to eliminate all those suspected of being 'informants'. In April of 2009, Reshma Begum, 65 years old was shot dead; on, 30 May, a young man Sahibuddin was killed; three days later, 26-year-old Nageena Akhtar was shot. In July, another young woman, Parveena was killed. Later that month, Mohammad Aslam Awan and his three-year-old son, was killed. Such targeted killings continued till the year had ended.

Meanwhile, Dr Singh's government had continued its peace efforts by renewing the peace talks with Hurriyat and the JKLF. Home Minister Chidambaram spoke of the government's determination to continue 'quiet talks and quiet diplomacy' and Dr Singh repeated during the 15th ASEAN Summit in Thailand the offer to engage with all sections to find a practical and pragmatic solution. The next day, Abdul Ghani Bhat, the acting chairman of Hurriyat welcomed the Prime Minister's offer. Significantly, he added that there would be no conditionality since dialogue and conditions don't go together. This was followed by the Mirwaiz's call for withdrawal of troops from the Valley and Chidambaram responded by announcing troops cut and around 30,000 troops were moved out of the Valley. Unfortunately, at this point, Geelani had broken away from the Hurriyat to form Tehreek-i-Hurriyat and was in open confrontation with the Hurriyat.

The point of difference between the two was that Tehreek wanted withdrawal of troops, repeal of draconian laws like Armed Forces Special Powers Act (AFSPA), and release of all prisoners before talks are held while the Hurriyat treated them as CBMs to be negotiated. According to Radha Kumar, the Chidambaram-Hurriyat backchannel 'had progressed to discussing the core elements of permanent peace settlement, building on the set of ideas that the Singh administration had developed through Aziz-Lambah in 2006-07. On the Hurriyat side, talks were chiefly conducted by Fazal Haq Qureshi…[he] had led the 2000 Hizbul ceasefire talks and was growing to be recognized as one of the dissidents' most credible negotiators.'[396] Though the Chidambaram-Hurriyat and Chidambaram-Malik (JKLF) talks were being held in utmost secrecy, somehow these got leaked and Praveen Swami of *The Hindu* published a report, leading to the killing of Qureshi by a local guerrilla in December.[397] It was suspected that someone from the intelligence had leaked the news with the objective of derailing the talks.

Things went downhill after this. Pakistani politicians rejected the progress made under Musharraf because he had usurped powers and therefore all his actions were illegal. Even the new Prime Minister Zardari went back to the times of harping US mediation. The atmosphere was further vitiated by the discovery that the Muzaffarabad-Srinagar bus service was being used by the ISI to smuggle agents in. One such agent had married a woman from Surankote, the wife of a local Lashkar commander who was in prison, in order to ensure frequent permits to enter the state for visits. This is how things continued till everything exploded once again in 2010. On 30 April 2010, trouble came from unexpected quarters yet again. It had nothing to do with any act of commission or omission by the state government. The Indian Army killed three young men, claiming that they were armed militants from Pakistan planning an infiltration bid from across the Line of Control at the Machil Sector in Kupwara district of Kashmir.[398]This was at first accepted as one of the routine incidents on the LoC. However, the local villagers claimed that the men, who were actually daily wagers, had been lured with promises of army jobs by a counter-insurgent and former special police officer of the Baramulla district, Bashir Ahmed Lone. He had conspired with army officials to stage an 'encounter' in order to win cash awards. The claim of the army blew in its face when police investigation revealed that the three were indeed residents of the Nadihal village of Baramulla district. The police investigation also revealed that they were killed in a fake encounter by the army, who had lured them out on promise of providing jobs and cash. Subsequently, the bodies of the three were exhumed from a graveyard at Kalaroos and investigated; it confirmed the police findings.

As the news of the fake encounter spread, public protests broke out in Baramulla, Kupwara and Srinagar. The army immediately ordered an inquiry and later, the Court Martial awarded life imprisonment to commanding officer Dinesh Pathania, Captain Upendra, Havaldar Devender Kumar, Lance Naik Lakhmi, Lance Naik Arun Kumar and Rifleman Abbas Hussain who were alleged to have staged the fake encounter to claim cash rewards and promotions. Later, in 2015, the accused challenged the Court Martial proceedings before the Tribunal's Principal Bench at New Delhi.25 July 252017, the Tribunal suspended life imprisonment of the accused. It cited the attire of the civilians killed in fake encounter to suspend the sentence. 'The fact that the accused persons were militants who have infiltrated across the border or were crossing over to the other side cannot be ruled out because they were wearing "pathan suits" which are worn by terrorists,' read the order of the Tribunal! After the Tribunal order, the State government led by Mehbooba Mufti examined whether it can challenge the Tribunal order. The government, however, chose not to challenge the suspension of the punishment of the accused before the J&K High Court or Supreme Court. The families of the victim continue to wait for justice.[399]

The Machil incident had once again brought the issue of the AFSPA under public glare and National Conference demanded that not only should it be repealed but the peace talks with Hurriyat be immediately revived. Prime Minister Dr Singh stressed that 'the government policy is to protect human rights of the people even when dealing with terrorism. The security forces in Jammu and Kashmir have been strictly instructed to respect the rights of civilians. We will act to remove any deficiency in the implementation of these instructions.'[400] But this had no impact on Kashmir and the two Hurriyat factions came together to give a call for strike.

In such an environment when people started believing that innocent civilians had been killed in stage managed encounters, on 11 June 2010, protests broke out against these killings in the downtown Srinagar. Police used massive force to disperse the protesting youth during which a teargas shell killed a seventeen-year-old student, Tufail Ahmad Mattoo, who was returning home after taking tuitions and was playing cricket at the time when he was hit.[401] This incident also happened at an opportune time for the secessionists as there were reports that a high level meeting of the United Jihad Council in Muzaffarabad, chaired by General Hamid Gul, former chief of the ISI had taken place where it was decided to give a vigorous push to militancy in the Valley to invigorate

Jihad until Kashmir was free from 'Indian occupation'. It was also reported that about 40 acres of land near Muzaffarabad had been bought by the Lashkar to set guerrilla training centers. Fresh recruitments had been made from among the residents of Gilgit and Baltistan for this purpose. This land could not have been bought in that part of Kashmir since no resident Pakistani could purchase land in any part of Kashmir, therefore, giving rise to the belief that the Pakistani Army and government must have been instrumental in its purchase.[402] This meeting had taken place as early as 10 February 2010, indicating to the deep planning for such an agitation that rocked the State. By March, the Military Intelligence had warned that Pakistan was up to something 'big', without being able to specify it, and even the Home Ministry got reports that there was 30 percent increase in infiltration across the border and the LoC. The figures showed that from 342 recorded incidents of infiltration in 2008, the number had risen to 499 in 2009. The violent summer of 2010 had indeed, been warned. How strong was the planning and network of the conspirators is best illustrated by the fact that throughout the agitation the main point-man of the agitators, Masrat Alam could not be arrested and only Geelani and Mirwaiz Farooq were put under house arrest.

After the high-level meeting of United Jihad Council in Muzaffarabad, most of the planning must have been done and then the Jihadis must have been waiting for some incident to ignite the fuse. One might wonder what might have motivated the Jihadis for invigorating the secessionist movement at this particular time. It will not be too farfetched to conclude that after witnessing Chief Minister Omar Abdullah's ways of handling the crises 2009, leaders and handlers of this movement must have thought that here was a chief minister who oscillated between the two worlds of Indian nationalism and Kashmiri nationalism and, therefore, could be pushed into situations that would diminish the credibility of state and the union government. The resultant instability would swing even the fence sitters, swelling the ranks of the protesters.

Omar Abdullah, it was apparent from his handling of the Shopian 'rape and murder' case, was a man with dual identities and loyalties. It was his insistence that had led to the complete exposure of the concocted allegations in 2009 though he was consistent in demanding reduction of troops from the Valley. The champions of secession had in 2010 found a just cause to agitate. It had exposed the deeply flawed, cruel and ruthless nature of some in the Indian Army that could go to any length, even exterminating Kashmiri lives, for promotions, awards and financial rewards. The death of young Tufail Ahmed Mattoo, an accident as it was, was, for the Kashmiris, proof of the diabolical use of violence and force by it. The Valley, in short was ready to rebel.

Outraged by the atrocity, people came out on to the streets where their most potent weapons were stones. The lanes and the by-lanes became their allies that drew the forces into them only to be pelted with stones from the rear too. Protesters demanded that India must 'quit' the Valley and for the first time an agitation came to be completely dominated by Geelani-led Tehreek-e-Hurriyat which launched a protest-calendar. The widespread support can be judged by the fact that after the 'calendar' was announced in downtown Srinagar to a select group of journalists, it was meticulously followed. 'Campaigners' were told to organize social boycott of those policemen and their families who obeyed the government orders to quell protests.

The weekly protests calendar read:

25 June: Kashmir shutdown
26 June: *Koncet Nazilu* (special prayers)
27 June: writing 'Go India Go' on walls, streets and social media sites
28 June: boy students' protest
29 June: girl students' protest
30 June: protests after Friday Maghrib (sundown) prayers
1 July: march to Pathar Masjid (the National Conference headquarters)
2-3 July: complete shutdown

The common factor of all these protests was the stoning of the security forces though it was called non-violent. Those who failed to adhere to the calendar were severely punished as the enforcers of the protests were armed with sticks and stones. Praveen Swami,

The Hindu correspondent reported: 'In one bizarre incident, a group of women travelling for a wedding in north Kashmir was lashed stinging-nettle.'[403] No town was immune to this agitation, with Srinagar, Anantnag, Sopore, Baramulla etc. becoming battlegrounds. Even the peasantry was drawn into the conflict and broadly, among the youth, two categories could be clearly made out. The first constituted of the jobless educated class and the other, from the rural areas, who had dropped out of school or whose education had been interrupted by the two-decade long militancy that was marked by closure of schools, curfews, black-outs due to fear of either the insurgent or the forces knocking the door or extended periods of rising uncertainty. This class had received little education and was more influenced by the Islamic and insurgency propaganda that was more readily available. Later, Omar Abdullah explained that a survey of about 200 stone-throwers had revealed that 60 percent were those whose both parents were uneducated and they themselves had dropped out of school education at the middle school level.[404] With militancy having affected all aspects of economic activity, these ill-educated young boys were not even able to work in the orchards and therefore were easy target for those who were offering money on a daily basis for stone-pelting.

Radha Kumar quotes in her book that a British psychiatrist, Justine Hardy, who worked in Kashmir to study the impact of violence on minds before the agitation, told the media that the young men she treated were in despair at seeing no future. Their anger, she said, sought a physical outlet or, as a young man put it to her, 'It will explode inside me, it will really kill me.'[405] The employment scene in the State was really bleak. First because the peculiar conditions existing there were a dampener on those who wished to invest, and secondly, and more importantly, for Kashmiris a job is only a government job because that alone gives security with pension for life after superannuation. It was estimated that in 2009 there were more than 5,00,000 unemployed in the State. Omar had also lamented that even when investment was wooed for the Valley, the violence, curfew and suspension of internet and communication channels soon drove them out of it.

Stone-pelting had indeed thrown up a new challenge. In

December 2010, Masrat Alam, the person who became a familiar name during the summer agitation, confessed that he received Rs 4 million (forty lakhs) through the Tehreek to fuel the stoning protests, thereby confirming the allegations of the security forces that the stone-throwers were paid for it and that they got Rs 500 per day.[406] The bulk of these funds were received from across the border and there was gross misuse of the Srinagar-Muzaffarabad bus for this and other allied activities like drug smuggling to generate money from local sources. In the retaliatory firing, after the persistent stone-pelting, the security forces killed about 120 Kashmiris, the largest number till date in any agitation. In addition to these casualties, 537 civilians were injured along with 1,274 CRPF troops and 2,747 state police personnel. The streets of the cities and towns appeared more like the scenes from the Palestinian 'Intifada' rather than the 'paradise on earth' that literature had described the Valley to be. The anger at the concoction of the Machil encounter and the tragic killing of Tufail Ahmad Mattoo was compounded by the burning of the Holy Quran in USA at the time of 9/11 commemoration. Now religious affront by the Christian USA poured oil on an already burning situation and a Missionary school and a government building were burned down. The State government of Omar Abdullah responded by clamping curfew all over the Valley, which soon aggravated the already difficult situation. *The Hindustan Times* wrote that the curfew was a 'collective punishment' and it tested the patience of the people since they ran out of even 'milk, vegetables and baby food'.

While stone pelting became a norm, these accusations only riled the forces drawn from all over the country and many among them retaliated with vengeance. During the agitation, there were two very significant responses. The first was from Yasin Malik, the leader of the JKLF, who accused Pakistani militants of subverting the Kashmiri struggle,[407] a charge that was also made by the Home Minister P. Chidambaram.[408] Malik had for long been chafing over the direction that his struggle had taken and the Home Minister articulated what was being widely believed in the intelligence circles.

But the response to the unrest by Kashmiri Pandits, who had left the Valley indicated to the rise of a force that was to play a significant role in the hardening of 'Hindu' India's attitude towards the Kashmiri Muslims. Kashmiri Pandits had in the meantime recovered some of their poise after the trauma of forced migration, and were bitter and demanded a forceful response to the militants in particular and Kashmiri Muslims in general. They met with Indian finance minister Pranab Mukherjee and asked that there be no dilution of the Armed Forces (Special Powers) Act that applies to Kashmir, a demand that was also supported by the State government. Their leader Ramesh Manvati, belonging to Panun Kashmir, stated: 'The security forces must be provided the constitutional protection as they are playing crucial role in preservation of the country's sovereignty. 'The Kashmiri Pandits also staged a *dharna* in Jammu stating that no solution of the problem was possible without including them in any dialogue for the solution.[409] There is little doubt that Mukherjee was the senior-most minister in the government but he was not holding either Defence or Home portfolios. The fact that the Pandit leaders called upon him arouses the suspicion that it was a blatant attempt to appeal and polarize leaders and opinion makers on communal lines since he too was a Brahmin. It was another portent of the direction which public opinion was taking.

From India's point of view, the agitation happened at a very inopportune time since the Union Government had begun to implement reforms of far-reaching consequences in the Valley. In October 2009, Home Minister Chidambaram had announced that the government was working towards sending the army to the borders or the barracks and hand over all internal security to the State police with CRPF as a back-up. In November Chief Minister Omar Abdullah announced the same and revealed that the State police was also being trained by the army to take up the more challenging role of dealing with insurgents.[410] This was confirmed by Defence Minister Antony, who also claimed that the situation in Kashmir was improving.[411] The then Army Chief, General V.K. Singh went to the extent of saying in June 2010, when the agitation had started, that 'bold and far sighted steps' were urgently needed to control the situation in Jammu and Kashmir: 'I feel there is a great requirement for political initiatives that take all people together.'[412]

This refreshing approach of the Army Chief had rubbed on to his field commanders who also talked about the 'battle to win hearts and minds'. This made a huge difference towards resolving conflict within the society. The Chief Minister also responded to the calls being made upon him and he did try his best to galvanize the administration, interact and mobilize the civil society, intellectuals and professionals, as well as also constituting ministerial committees for Baramulla, Anantnag and Pulwama that would work with citizen groups to restore normalcy and protect the livelihood of those who had been severely affected by the agitation. But there is often a gap between good and honest intentions and delivery of the same. The culture of sloth, nepotism and corruption had been so intrinsically woven with the culture of administration and politics that the best efforts of the young but inexperienced Chief Minister failed to break it. Not too far into the future this was to seal his fate and open a new chapter and unexplored territory. The agitation, stone-throwing and deaths also exposed the cruel and heartless side of Kashmir politics. The PDP in general and Mehbooba Mufti in particular, appeared to be almost gloating at the erosion of Omar's authority and credibility even as the death toll of the Kashmiris mounted. The tragedy was treated as if it was the National Conference's concern and the PDP was just a bystander even though the worst affected areas in stone throwing and deaths were those that were PDP strongholds in south Kashmir. The least that the PDP could have done was to interact with the civil society and together provide a healing touch.

The prolonged agitation convinced many intellectuals that India had lost the plot and had begun to rethink about continuing to hold on to a people who erupted in protest more frequently than ever before. By mid-September, the Prime Minister called an all-party meeting to discuss a way out. Consequently, Home Minister Chidambaram led a thirty-member delegation which was boycotted by the Hurriyat though it sent a memorandum reminding the assurance that Prime Minister Nehru had made in the Parliament promising not to hold Kashmir if the people were unwilling. The Hurriyat leaders, Geelani, Mirwaiz Farooq and Yasin Malik, did meet a select band of leaders who approached them in their independent capacity. After the delegation's return, an eight-point program was drawn to restore confidence in the Valley. These included, among others, appointment of interlocutors, release of students and youth arrested for stone-pelting, review of all the cases of Public Safety Act (PSA), dismantling of bunkers and check-posts from residential areas in particular and towns in general, special task forces for Jammu and Ladakh etc. It was at this point that the JKLF released a press statement accusing Pakistani militants belonging to the Jamaat-ud-Dawa of 'hijacking' the Kashmiri cause and seeking to subvert the 'indigenous movement'. The Jamaat-ud-Dawa responded by launching a mass-contact program consisting mainly of non-Kashmiris in PoK. The agitation and the renewed efforts of Pakistan through its so-called 'non-state actors' effectively froze the Indo-Pak peace efforts. The same happened in the intra-Kashmir efforts because of the belligerence of the Hurriyat.

The agitation served the cause of Pakistan and the PDP well for it damaged beyond repair the reputation of Omar Abdullah as an administrator. Ironically, he was also branded as a collaborator in the eyes of Kashmiris. But it also created such adverse reaction in the rest of the country that most of the people not only became antagonistic to the Kashmiris but also against Muslims at large. The process of 'othering' of the Muslims seemed to be complete. Omar Abdullah, on his part, did little to assuage the feelings of the people, taking for granted the forbearance of the Kashmiris and continued in the same vein till the Assembly elections which were about to be held.

After a Cabinet decision in June 2014, the Justice Koul Commission was instituted to investigate the unrest of 2010, almost four years after it had taken place. 'Two years after Omar failed to win a second term to the office, [the] Justice Koul Commission submitted a scathing report to incumbent Chief Minister Mehbooba Mufti, recommending, among other measures, to avoid deploying the Central Reserve Police Force (CRPF) on the streets during protests to avoid untoward incidents like civilian killings'.[413] The report also nailed the problem that afflicts the State's political system which is ridden with internal rivalries, where political leaders are willing to cut their own noses in order to spite their rivals. *Firstpost* commented that 'While the Opposition parties led by Abdullah's

National Conference (NC) sought a debate on the 2016 agitation on the first day of the Budget session, (when the report was presented) Chief Minister Mehbooba Mufti, armed with the findings of [the] Justice Koul Commission, instead trained guns on NC, demanding a debate on [the] 2010 agitation which brought the Valley on the brink of anarchy. In the process, both forgot that collectively their respective administrations were responsible for the deaths of more than 220 people in agitations of 2010 and 2016.

'The senseless bickering and blame-game in the House comes at a time when the Valley is yet to come out of the trauma suffered under one of the longest curfews and worst crackdowns on civilian population in recent memory where more than 8,000 people have been put behind bars to restore a semblance of 'normalcy' on the streets. Instead of discussing ways and means of ensuring that the mistakes committed both by Abdullah and Mehbooba are not repeated in coming days, months or years, the two leading regional parties of the Valley, (National Conference and Peoples' Democratic Party) with their cheap theatrics have ensured that there will be no end to the dance of death on the streets of Kashmir'.[414]

In a way, Mehbooba Mufti was right in her demand since the unrest of 2008, 2010, and the one which followed in 2016 post Burhan Wani killings (*See Chapter 14 for more details*), are interlinked and of long-term consequences. The Amarnath land allotment agitation of 2008 which had brought out in the open the fatal fault line in the construct of the State had only accentuated with passage of time. The anger that had been simmering in Jammu since 1983 boiled over when the Kashmiris opposed the land allotment to the Shrine Board in 2008. Notwithstanding the fact that the allotted land was forest land and its use could not possibly be legally altered, but once the government had done it for the convenience of the Amarnath pilgrims, the Hindus of Jammu and beyond took the opposition to it and, the reversal of the land allotment, as an affront to the community. On the other hand, the feeling among the Kashmiris—that the Government of India through the Governor had unraveled a plan for changing the demography of the Valley—fanned by the politicians became firmer. Moreover, the feeling of injury to Jammu sentiments, that is, the Hindu sentiment, was shared by most of the country from whence came the bulk of the security force, including CRPF. These hard feelings and mutual suspicions played a major role during the 2010 unrest as well as the one that was to follow in 2016.

The unrest of 2010 and its inept handling had irretrievably damaged the reputation of Omar Abdullah. The grapevine too had played its part though it must be said that no one was to be blamed for his dwindling fortune but he himself. His administrative immaturity played a part but his partiality to the mobile and the social media played a greater role in building his image of an indifferent politician. Culturally, India and the south Asian countries expect the politicians and ministers to be hands-on public servants. Therefore, using mobile as an administrative tool is not appreciated by them and is considered to be a mark of indifference and disinterest since the personal and human touch is missing from the communication. That is why Omar's next four years after 2010 just rolled by with him having nothing to show for his achievement. The State Autonomy issue remained where it was and he also failed to convince the Government of India to withdraw the Armed Forces Special Powers Act. As a consequence, the major promises of the National Conference remained unfulfilled, with great disappointment being focused on the continued implementation of the AFSPA, which thwarted the efforts of the State government, police and the civil society from bringing the recalcitrant elements within the security forces to face criminal proceedings. These unaddressed demands have remained the main demands of the Kashmiris. It was obvious that he would be at a disadvantage during the scheduled Assembly polls of 2014.

However, a bigger disaster, not his doing and not manmade, struck him about two months before the polls. Natural disasters unravel social and political construct of a society and challenge the government and administration in an embarrassingly awkward manner. The summer of 2014 had been as summers had usually become in the Valley—streets abuzz with tourist activity, and in the rural area, peasants busy with their tasks of everyday life. But September brought in an extended period of rains that resulted in the worst floods in living memory. With the natural flow of the water, including Jhelum River, flowing northward from south, almost every drop of water from the slopes of the north-facing Pir Panjal range flows into Srinagar on its onward journey to Baramulla, before flowing into Pakistan-occupied-Kashmir, and then descending to the plains of Pakistani Punjab. Years of unplanned growth in the urban areas had gobbled up much of the floodplains and wetlands and blocked the canal system that took care of excessive waters. The resultant flood affected more than 2 million people in the Valley and apart from the losses that they suffered many remained marooned for days without access to the essentials of life. Hundreds of villages and large parts of Srinagar remained inundated bringing unprecedented misery. The administration, it was alleged, largely remained paralyzed with all the relief work being done by the volunteers of the civil society.

This disaster highlighted the social struggles and the inherent inequities produced by the political system. To the scholars, abrupt disruption of normal life gave a deep understanding of the shocking structure of the Valley. The effect on the political fortunes of Omar Abdullah was not apparent but, like in all disasters, '...The relationship between state and society, tested under duress, becomes transparent in the public domain. [Importantly] The spontaneous rise of voluntarism, the dysfunctionalities of the State, the hypocrisy of the powerful, and the opportunism of the politicians are all briefly and viscerally evident in the nakedness under conditions of emergency,' a study said.[415] In fact, Omar Abdullah had frankly confessed that during the first twenty four hours there was no government and it took him days to get back to his ministers who probably had been busy rescuing themselves and their families from the water logged Srinagar city. 'One of the main criticisms against Mr. Abdullah's government is that it did not sound out a warning or began evacuating people when the meteorological forecasts had predicted a long spell of unending monsoon rains. When the floods struck, the authorities, by their own admission were also stranded, and the government went into a limbo. Public anger has risen after reports surfaced that his ministers and families were evacuated first and moved to Jammu and Delhi.'[416]

Many said it was ironic that Abdullah had tweeted that there was 'nothing to panic, we will reach you, I promise'. But 'then he abandoned everybody,' said Shujaat Bukhari, the now slain editor of *The Rising Kashmir*. 'This has been a complete failure of his government. Even a week after the floods, people are stranded without food and water in central areas of the main city of Srinagar. That's how bad things are.'[417] Once again, Omar Abdullah had demonstrated that good intentions are not enough and they needed to be backed by deed and action. None came from him when they were most needed by the people.

The two scholars, Venugopal and Yasir concluded in their study that, 'the State government remained a mute spectator…[and] the national media used the floods as a platform to paint the Indian army as the saviors…[but] the army was actually busy in rescuing the non-locals and tourists…the police appeared on the scene only when the dust had settled.

'The floods confirmed the widely held views of the people. First, it provided evidence that the State government was ineffective and that the central government does not prioritize them. Secondly, it confirmed the widely held perceptions that the Indian media is hostile to them, that it willfully distorts the reality of what happens in Kashmir. Thirdly, it reinforces the belief that their safety and wellbeing rests within elements of Kashmiri society itself.'[418] Thus in public perception the State government, the Government of India and the national media had all failed the people of the Valley but redemption was found in the display of public spiritedness of the youth and generosity and benevolence of the people. The boatmen of Dal Lake and the Jhelum made untiring efforts to not only to rescue people but also provide them with the daily necessities. In a nutshell, it was a disaster of epic proportions with nearly 200 dead, but the failure of the government only helped in firming of the already existing opinion that Omar Abdullah's government had to be ousted not just because of the misery caused by the floods but because of his general inability to get the desired results for the people.

14

The Unraveling

'We decided to never look back.
The problem was that we never really looked ahead.'

Before the State Assembly polls, the Lok Sabha elections too were due in 2014 and the writing was on the wall for the Congress and its allies. The second term of Dr Manmohan Singh had been marred by ever rising number of scandals involving alleged corruption in high places. Scandals, beginning with the issue of black money allegedly stashed in foreign banks; and the allegations that engulfed the auction of the Indian Premier League (IPL) to Commonwealth Games held in 2010; coal and 2G spectrum auction and allotment; Adarsh Housing scam in Mumbai; to the sale of S-band spectrum by ISRO without competitive bidding that sucked in even Dr Manmohan Singh since the space program was under his direct control, had rocked the Parliament which had been virtually brought to a halt by persistent opposition. The opposition had sensed a kill and the media had been unsparing in its criticism with the electronic media getting hysterical and shriller by the day. The UPA had, in fact, begun to fall apart in public eye from the year 2011 when Anna Hazare launched his agitation against corruption in Delhi. By then the scandals involving spectrum allotment and coal block allocations had already made headlines and nothing that the government said in its defense appeared credible. A large number of Congress ministers were said to be involved in these scandals. The Comptroller Auditor General's report had minced no words in pointing out the 'loss' that had been caused to the exchequer. Nothing that the government said would make the critics hold back their fire.

Anna Hazare, a simple man of modest traits but professing Gandhian virtues, appeared from the obscurity of a never-heard-before village in Maharashtra and instantly caught the imagination of the civil society. He was projected by the media as a knight in shining armor having the wherewithal to dispel the darkness that had engulfed Indian polity. It serves no purpose now to argue that the agitation was a conspiracy hatched and executed by the BJP and the RSS and that Anna Hazare was the creation of the media at the behest of some politicians. Influenced by Anna Hazare, people from all walks of life came to Delhi in the summer heat to express their discontent and desire to purge public life of impurities. Dr Manmohan Singh was truly exposed for his naïveté in politics and with the Congress not being able to put up any credible defence, the forthcoming elections were lost even before they had been fought. With even the most credible and reliable of Congressmen as Chidambaram being accused of corruption, there was really no hope for it. No one believed that Dr Manmohan Singh was involved in corruption but he was successfully projected as an ineffective Prime Minister who was too helpless and naive to keep his roguish colleagues on a leash. With each passing day, the ineffectiveness of the Prime Minister was projected with the implied message that India needed an effective Prime Minister who had a political constituency of his own so that no non-government actor gave direction to him. Obliquely, this meant that the strings of Dr Manmohan Singh were being pulled by those who were non-government power centers. Dr Singh's case was not helped by Rahul Gandhi, the presumptive-heir of the Congress party, when his public condemnation of a governmental decision taken by no less a person than the Prime Minister forced the government to reverse it! The hand of Sonia Gandhi in government decisions too was visible since the post of UPA Chairperson was created for her to provide her with access to governmental consultations, legal and constitutional. These did not go down well with the public, particularly after scandals of the UPA came to light through the media.

The BJP had, in fact, begun to position itself for ousting Congress from its perch soon after its second successive defeat in 2009. It had unexpectedly lost the Lok Sabha polls of 2004 but was more surprised by the loss in the 2009 polls because of multiple reasons, including the incumbency factor, which was supposed to go against Congress, and for the fact that for the first time it was being led into a poll by a non-charismatic leader who did not even qualify to be called a politician. But even more significantly, there were clear signs that the tide was turning against the Congress because of the continued terrorism in Jammu and Kashmir and escalation of Jihadi terror attacks outside it. Therefore, while the BJP was still stuck in the Advani or his version of alternative for leading it during the 2014 poll, the RSS think tank had already begun to boldly float the name of Narendra Modi, the then long serving Chief Minister of Gujarat as the next prime ministerial candidate by 2011. On 13 September 2013, the BJP formally declared him as the prime ministerial face of the party for next year's polls.[419] Shockingly, what was perceived as a mill around his neck had been deemed to be an asset of great value by the RSS and its affiliates.

For many people Modi's name evoked memories of the 2002 Gujarat riots and the killings of more than 2,000 Muslims. Many believed he was complicit though the Enquiry Commissions and courts had given him a clean chit. He was not a politician the western world was eager to welcome and even though a chief minister of a state that had a fair share of adoring diaspora in the US, he had not been granted visa by it. Many other countries had similar reservations about him. But what many observers felt was weakness, was indeed strength, according to many more.

What had gone unnoticed was that the long years of insurgency had taken a toll on the forces and the paramilitary, with hardly any state remaining that had not received bodies wrapped in tri-color. The national media and the regional media in greater detail, brought cremation ceremonies of the fallen heroes into the homes and slowly anger had built up against the perpetrators of terrorism, who were primarily viewed as Muslims. It was a pan Indian phenomenon. Since, the terrorists were Kashmiri Muslims, supported by Pakistan and Pakistani-based terrorists, and had struck even in places far away from Kashmir, the anger and resentment had built up against the Muslims in general. The fact that the Al-Qaeda and the Taliban had been carrying out terrorist strikes across the globe, Muslims in general came to be seen as the bane of mankind. The idea of a global Islamic State had already been floated, with the Islamic State of Iraq and Syria (ISIS) as its visible manifestation. It had almost overrun Iraq and Syria. Buoyed, the Islamic warriors had begun to dream of re-establishing the Caliphate. The world opinion, including in India where Muslims had ruled for a thousand years, had turned against it. As mentioned earlier, India had remained a land which had, since the medieval ages, held their ground against the complete conversion to Islam. This had rankled fundamentalist Islamists who wished, even now, to convert it as the *Darul Haram*—the land where Islam rules. That is why India was of special interest to international jihadists.

Amidst this growing discontent towards Islamist extremism, much of the Indian population also noticed that prior to 2002, Gujarat in general and Ahmedabad in particular, used to be plagued by communal riots. But after the 2002 riots, in which the State and the Chief Minister were blamed, there were no riots. Thus, it stood proven that a person of Narendra Modi's resolve alone could deal with Jihadists, Kashmir as well as Pakistan. Gujarat under him was also a State that did not hit the headlines over corruption allegations. Meanwhile, the Congress was lurching from one scandal to another and the 'Radia tapes'[420] had completely exposed how easily the decision-making in the government was manipulated for personal gains and influence. The Congress, indeed, had decayed and was crumbling, literally begging to be freed from the responsibility of administering this complex country any longer. Not surprisingly, it was routed at the polls.

Prime Minister Modi began his term on a very positive note by inviting Pakistani Prime Minister Nawaz Sharif to his oath taking ceremony, raising hopes of a peaceful resolution of all disputes. It has been known for a long time that more than the Congress, it is the BJP that has a better chance of arriving at a mutually agreed settlement with Pakistan as the fiercest opposition to any peace can come only from BJP in India. But the day when new ministers attended their first day of office, the cat was out of the bag when, in a moment of enthusiasm, the Minister of State in Prime Minister's Office (PMO), Jitendra Singh from the Udhampur-Kathua constituency of Jammu and Kashmir, announced to the media that Article 370 would be abolished.[421] He was ticked off by the Prime Minister for the public comment and after that no one in a seat of responsibility in the government made such a public comment again. But there was no doubt in anybody's mind that this was high on the agenda of BJP/RSS and was only a matter of time. It had also been put in the BJP's election manifesto, therefore, Jiitendra Singh's ticking off came as a surprise.

In Pakistan, the army had not appreciated the peace overtures and suspected that Nawaz Sharif was once again on his road to peace with India; it increased ceasefire violations manifold. According to Home Ministry figures there were 583 violations against 347 in 2013 and 112 in 2012. More worryingly, the violation did not just involve exchange of fire by the troops posted at the border, but heavy and persistent shelling of villages, even across the international border, gave the conflict a new dimension. By the year 2015, this had affected 2,15,110 families and many among them had to flee their homes. The shelling had partially or fully damaged 193 houses.[422] This was the time for the new government which had a Prime Minister who had boasted of possessing a '56 inches chest' and who had promised a robust and muscular response, to retaliate and prove India's 'muscularity'. Accordingly, a 'massive retaliation' took place all along the Jammu and Kashmir border. But the escalation proved counter-productive as Pakistan too responded in kind, putting the border residents to great hardship. The local news and social media brought the miseries of the residents to public domain. A number of villagers from the border areas had to be evacuated and put in relief camps. Thus, the Modi administration's attempts at giving 'befitting response' backfired as the human cost was too high to bear to make Pakistan desist from cross-border infiltration and terrorism. There the matter rested till, later in the year, the Assembly elections for the State were due.

To be fair to Omar Abdullah, he and his government had no role in triggering the agitation of 2009 and 2010, as well as the tragedy that came with the floods of 2014. In 2009, in fact, Omar Abdullah had been so partial to justice that his insistence had led to the discovery of the whole conspiracy of the separatists that rubbed them the wrong way. The blame for the 2010 agitation and resultant deaths, squarely lay with the rogue elements in the Indian Army, and, the flood were a result of natural calamity and bad governance of the previous governments. But Omar was the Chief Minister of the State and therefore bore the responsibility of the fall-out of all the three. The two agitations were inter-related in the sense that they were the symptoms of the deep-seated malaise that was afflicting the State. Forces inimical to India were resourceful, unscrupulous and exploitative and were well managed from across the border. To combat them, the State and the union needed totally committed people. Together, the two agitations had damaged the state government and exposed the changing attitude of the personnel of the security forces. Pushed to the brink, the personnel revealed that they were not immune to the centuries old biases and prejudices that had become a part of the collective memory and had now become active. The daily confrontations and periodic bouts of violence and spewing of anti-India propaganda in Kashmir had begun to elicit hard and violent response in almost every State.

By the time the floods struck Kashmir in 2014, Omar Abdullah's administration had lost much of his credibility because of multiple reasons. The general perception was that he had allowed security forces a free run during the protests of 2010 thereby establishing his anti-Kashmiri attitude. His reputation, or whatever remained of it, took a big hit during the floods. For much of the time, the administration was completely out of action, and initial rescue work was left to the local boats people and the army. Omar Abdullah could never shrug off his culpability after that though the main reason for the flooding was that over a long period of time the flood-plains of Jhelum had been colonized and wetlands encroached. Unauthorized colonies and housing projects had mushroomed and the canal system, developed by the Dogra rulers to meet such an eventuality, had been allowed to fill with silt for reclamation. To cap it all, the abdication of duty by the administration during the floods and non-fulfillment of promises made by him haunted him and not surprisingly, he lost the elections in 2014. The results threw a huge surprise in general but significantly turned the tables on the Congress. The fate of Congress and BJP was almost reversed from that of 1983 when the Hindu vote of the Jammu region had supported the Congress and not the avowedly Hindu party BJP. In 2014, the voter had decided to no longer play hide and seek with their latent intentions and voted for a party that openly professed to be champions of the Hindus. As a result, while in the Valley PDP was the clear winner, the Congress was wiped out. In Jammu too the Congress was routed and the defeat virtually left no trace of it.

The PDP had secured 28 seats, the National Conference 15 seats, the Congress 12 and the BJP 25 seats. However, neither PDP nor BJP was a clear winner but PDP emerged as the largest single party and the only one to have a realistic chance of forming a government. Both the Kashmiri parties could have come together to form a government but that would have completely eroded whatever base the National Conference had in Jammu region, and since the Congress did not possess the numbers to help either PDP or the National Conference to form the new government there was a long period of stalemate. Despite the seats won from Jammu, as expected, BJP had drawn a blank in the Valley, and there was a considerable swing in favor of the PDP there, yielding a rich harvest of seats for it. The overall share of vote percentage was almost equal with PDP getting 22.7% of the votes cast, the National Conference getting 20.8%, the Congress 18%. But the surprise was for BJP that secured 23% votes. Almost the entire vote bank consisted of votes from Jammu. It had secured all its seats from the Jammu and Ladakh region. The major reason for this success was the consolidation of the Hindu vote in its favor and heavy divide in support for the PDP and National Conference in Jammu region in seats with heavy Muslim presence. The results had been announced on 23 December 2014 but till late February 2015 there was a stalemate in the talks for forging a government.

Finally, on 24 February 2015, BJP President Amit Shah and Mehbooba Mufti announced that the PDP was entering into an alliance with the BJP and will be forming a government with Mufti Mohammad Sayeed as the Chief Minister. 'A Common Minimum

Programme (CMP) covering contentious issues such as Article 370 of the Constitution that grants special status to J and K and the controversial AFSPA is the basis of the alliance of the two parties which will enable BJP to come to power for the first time in the sensitive state,' a newspaper report said.[423] The announcement sent shock waves since abrogation of Article 370 was the bedrock of BJP's policy in Jammu and Kashmir and one could not imagine BJP compromising on it. Similarly, its abrogation when it was in an alliance with the PDP, would not only bring opprobrium to the PDP but also completely erode its support base and make its leaders targets for the ire of the people and guns of the militants. Also, withdrawal of the AFSPA was the core demand of the PDP, which BJP could not have conceded without losing ground not just in the state but the entire country. Even a layman could see that the only glue that was binding them together was the lust for power by putting aside their core principles. The BJP wanted power so that it could make deeper penetration in Jammu and also keep their workers in the driver's seat in administrative matters. But PDP was all set to lose face since this alliance was driven by opportunism and greed. It had negated all that the Valley hitherto stood for. In fact, the Valley would have preferred a coalition of PDP, National Conference and Congress to this one but politics does indeed make strange bedfellows.

The thought of BJP and PDP coming together was beyond the realm of imagination at that point in time as both had bitterly fought each other. But stunning the political Pundits, the hitherto unimaginable alliance between the avowedly nationalist champion of Hinduism—BJP—and the PDP—which championed autonomy for the State and flirted with the separatists—was forged. They had entered into an alliance of convenience based on what was called an 'Agenda for Alliance', which many denounced as unholy. On the face of it, this was an ideal situation since two opposing viewpoints had come together, and theoretically it could be hoped that while working together both will respect certain boundaries and shed some of the hard stances adopted earlier. Working together for the common good would also make them realize the limitations of each other's politics. But more importantly, the optimists thought, it gave hope of isolating the separatists and making others accept the hard reality of the coming together of apparently irreconcilable forces. Mufti once again took the oath of the office of chief minister with the BJP nominee, Nirmal Singh, being appointed as the Deputy Chief Minister. Once again, in a democracy, PDP and BJP, like National Conference and Congress in 1987, had plotted capturing of power by taking the will of the people out of the equation. They, in fact, had gone a step further in tearing into smithereens the mandate of the electorate since both parties had been at each other's throats during the election campaign.

On the face of it, this was an ideal situation. The Congress had been pushed out of the frame with heavy defeats in Kashmir and Jammu regions. Even its stronghold, Ladakh, had been breached and vanquished as the BJP cashed upon anti-Kashmiri sentiment there and had also promised it of UT status, if voted to power. This worked to its advantage. But beneath these apparently revolutionary changes the only thing that had really changed was that the Congress had been replaced by the BJP and the National Conference by the PDP. Now the situation was that the hard-line BJP was in command at the Centre and also sharing power in the State. Understandably, the people of Jammu too, fed up with the secessionists and continued terrorist acts, had decided to give that party a chance that boasted of a determined and strong-willed leader in Narendra Modi. The fact, however, was that BJP and PDP had entered into a mutually prickly and poison laced embrace. The power sharing arrangement in the State had not gone down well with the people of Kashmir and it appeared that the PDP had exhausted all its political capital by banking upon the hope that the BJP will yield on the issue of autonomy and repeal of AFSPA. The BJP, on the other hand, was able to keep its party cadre in control by the exercise of power for its supporters in Jammu which, incidentally, was a first for them in the State. On the face of it, the State in general and the Valley in particular appeared to have reconciled to the situation and remained so even after the death of Mufti and the election of his daughter Mehbooba Mufti as Chief Minister. But any student of the Kashmir problem knew that a share in power by the leaders was not what the people had been told was their goal. The aspirations raised among the Kashmiris and Jammu region were high but mutually irreconcilable. The stooping of the PDP to grab power evoked memories of 1975 in the Valley when Sheikh Abdullah had allegedly let the Kashmiris down by returning to power after making huge compromises. If that was a letdown then the alliance of the PDP with BJP was an act of perfidy for which there was no remission and penitence. Pakistani agencies too had been smarting, because of the apparent somersault and political stability and were working overtime to prop new forces to challenge the PDP and BJP. Meanwhile, the Pakistani Army had chosen to raise the temperatures at the LoC and the international border, and Jammu and Kashmir, as usual, was the focus of this new brinkmanship.

This continued even as mid-2015 approached by which time it had become abundantly clear that the Sharif administration and the Pakistani Army were once again on a collision course and that the India policy was the bone of contention. In July, Modi and Sharif had met on the sidelines of the summits of the Shanghai Cooperation Organization (SCO) and BRICS (Brazil, Russia, India, China and South Africa) at Ufa in Russia and had pledged to conduct counter terrorism measures with each other's cooperation. It was decided that the two countries will follow a two-step strategy to achieve their goal. The first was to create conditions conducive for dialogue through cooperation about counter-terrorism and de-escalation of tension on the LoC; and second, cooperation on the International Border and resolve conflicts over Kashmir, Sir Creek and Siachen. This pragmatic understanding brought strong reaction from Pakistani opinion makers and the army, forcing the Nawaz Sharif government to ask India to put the two steps together in which Sartaj Aziz, the National Security Advisor (NSA) of Pakistan would hold parallel talks when he visited Delhi. Therefore, when Aziz arrived in Delhi in August 2015, he sought to meet Ajit Doval, the NSA of India and S. Jaishankar, then Secretary Foreign Affairs, and at the same time, hold talks with the Hurriyat. Accordingly, he invited them for exchange of views as the Pakistani officials had frequently done in the past, but to his consternation, the Indian government objected, resulting in calling off of the talks.[424]

Clearly, the Modi government had signaled a departure from the earlier policies of Vajpayee and Dr Singh. During the Vajpayee era, the Hurriyat was found useful in bridging the gap between the government and the representatives of Pakistan. Hurriyat had the dual purpose of communication within Kashmir and sending the message across. This would clearly draw lines which the Government of India was not prepared to cross. Dr Singh's policy was similar and therefore his administration too ignored the meetings of Hurriyat with visiting Pakistani representatives. It was apparent that a new set of ideas was overtaking government's decision-making in which the predominant view questioned the relevance of Hurriyat as a stake holder in Kashmir. This change in policy was also in violation of the 'Agenda for Alliance' between the PDP and BJP as talks were pivotal to moving forward. Earlier during the Vajpayee era, Mufti Sayeed had prevailed upon the then Prime Minister but now, more than a decade down the line, the decision makers as well as the decisions were undergoing churning and change. It was a slow process but the change was relentless.

In Delhi, the government had decided to up the ante about implementation of the BJP agenda. Cow slaughter and beef eating was a part of it and had been put on high priority. The fallout was felt in many states where vigilante groups emerged resulting in lynching, in some cases on mere suspicion. The fact of its effect on economy and rendering many jobless was another matter but of least concern to the government. But Chief Minister Mufti was the one who had to deal with the worst kind of fallout. Ironically, there was already a ban on cow slaughter in Jammu and Kashmir and Kashmiri Muslims traditionally did not consume beef; but making it unlawful became an emotive and divisive issue and then one day, legislators came to blows over it in the Assembly.[425] An Islamist, Asiya Andrabi[426], the woman who has been in the frontline of not only promoting fundamentalist Islam among women but also every anti-India move, and heading the Dukhtran-i-Millat[427], publicly slaughtered a cow to show her defiance; and, an independent MLA, Rashid Engineer, hosted a beef party. As the issue snowballed in the State, once again a clear divide between the Jammu and Kashmir regions became apparent. The Jammu bench of the

J&K High Court directed the government to implement the ban order whereas the Srinagar bench struck down the ban as unconstitutional. With communal passions rising, the government approached the Supreme Court for direction and it suspended the earlier order of implementation of the ban for two months.[428]

Often, it appeared as if the Union Government was suffering from muddled thinking. Knowing Pakistan well, as also the limitations of an elected government there, Prime Minister Modi had extended a hand of friendship to Sharif by inviting him for his oath ceremony. But then soon afterwards, he had a change of heart when the Pakistani Army raised the temperature at the border. Modi's resentment at not getting appropriate response was also reflected in the domestic affairs. Post the 2014 floods, Modi had liberally offered aid for the rescue and relief work but unfortunately for almost a year the plans for rehabilitation remained stuck in the bureaucratic maze. Finally, he announced a grant of Rs 80,000 crores (800 billion) which included connectivity and infrastructure development and, therefore, his visit to the Valley in November 2015 was eagerly awaited. The liberal grant had raised expectations of more steps following the financial part. Mufti hoped that it would be complemented with some political initiative so that the coalition could make a new beginning with renewed efforts for a dialogue with the Hurriyat. Thus, hopeful, the Chief Minister referred to the peace process during Modi's address at the Sher-e-Kashmir stadium but was shocked to be rebuked by him and be told that he did not need any advice on Kashmir.[429] This was considered a mark of arrogance emanating from power and added to the alienation of the Kashmiris. It also signified his frustration at not getting the desired response from the Kashmiris and Pakistan.

Soon after this, Mufti died in January 2016 and his death was followed by an audacious attack by Pakistani terrorists not in the State but in neighboring Punjab where an important Air Force station was located at Pathankot. The attack outraged the whole country and Sharif acknowledged that it was carried by the Jaish group and also promised action. The Indian Government went to the extent of giving access of Indian witnesses to Pakistan's Federal Investigation that was allowed to enter the Pathankot Air Base for its own investigations but it came to nothing. On the contrary, the government faced heavy criticism for having provided access to the enemy to one of the most sensitive Air Force Station in the country. Meanwhile, with the death of Mufti, there was a political crisis in Jammu and Kashmir. His daughter and President of the PDP, Mehbooba Mufti, was extremely sensitive to the callous manner in which her father had been treated by Modi and the BJP. It was a steep fall from the halcyon days when Vajpayee and Dr Manmohan Singh were the Prime Ministers and, therefore, she was reluctant to take over the reins of the government. She was also aware of the loss of her party's credibility in public eye because the agreed agenda between the alliance partners had been reduced to a meaningless piece of paper that exposed the party leadership's greed for power. With dwindling public support, she feared her party will be decimated. Therefore, it took three months of hectic parleys and backchannel negotiations before she was made to agree to become the chief minister. The BJP was eager not to lose the opportunity of exercising power for as long as possible in the hope of consolidating its hold on the Jammu region.

Thus, once again, principles were sacrificed at the altar of convenience and greed of power, and this is how things were at the beginning of 2016 which turned out as one of those years when the Valley was sun-bathed and the weather gods benign. Tourists from all over the country were too eager to visit the 'heaven on earth'. The urgency in hospitality and hotel industry was electric and could be felt even in the air. The housekeepers were busy preparing rooms as impatient guests restlessly waited in the lobbies. Handicrafts of all kind and fruit sellers were doing brisk business and all through the day and evening the boulevard was agog with the chattering and excitement of the people. There was hardly an Indian language or dialect that could not be heard on the busy roads and places of tourist interest. The ruins of the temples of Awantipora, being on the roadside, were abuzz with tourists and at Gulmarg long queues for the Gondola rides could be seen. Kashmiris were happy because of the liberal spending of the tourists and they in return came back excited and happy at discovering the genial and hospitable nature of the Kashmiris that gave no hint of the pain and suffering of a generation raised and brought up under the shadow of guns, violence and death. But this was the tourist season when everyone dependent upon it has to work for the hard times when cold winter with its *Chillai kalan* and *Chillai khurd* periods bring life literally to a halt. But unknown to the tourists, underneath this busy and happy exterior, the lava of discontent was simmering. Even as the taxi drivers ferried their passengers from airport to hotels and tourist destinations, the conversation would occasionally veer towards 'the conditions' in polite enquiries by an inquisitive outsider. The driver in return would volubly speak of a young sensation in south Kashmir who was adept at using social media, was always ahead of the government agencies, a young militant who was elusive. The enthusiasm with which his escapades through the security cordon were narrated pointed towards an unconcealed adulation and pride. There were unmistakable signs of unease that was simmering beneath the calm and the hope that the people in the streets were pinning on.

In the uneasy new phase, the Valley waited in suspended anticipation of some momentous happening to explode. And, when it came, it brought an abrupt and ugly end to the sunny summer of 2016 with the killing of Burhan Wani, the young terrorist so eulogized by the people. Home grown, he and his group were not controlled by any outside agency, and this added to their aura. Unlike Yasin Malik and his JKLF, Burhan Wani and his friends had neither crossed over to Pakistan for training, nor were they known to have received any financial aid from across the border. Burhan Wani's emergence had ushered a new phase in militancy as well as the Government's hardline response. The image the BJP had built during the run up to the 2014 Lok Sabha polls was of a party that was strong and uncompromising on national defence issues and had repeatedly promised to deal with militancy in Kashmir with an iron hand. This image of Prime Minister Modi as a determined and uncompromising leader was being eroded by the evasive presence of Burhan. The news of his presence and disappearance challenged and taunted the security forces of the Tral region in south Kashmir.

As was expected, Burhan was finally gunned down by the security forces. What followed his killing introduced a new phase that had new meaning for different sides of the conflict. The BJP Government was convinced that to build a better future, steps for a clean break with the past needed to be taken. The militants, on the other hand, believed very strongly that by now there were too long and broad a stretches-of-graves of the Kashmiris for the Indian Army to cross, and the Government of India to reach out to the people and succeed. The bottom line was that the people of Kashmir appeared to have drifted too far away from the modest demand of maintaining the sanctity of the constitutional guarantees provided to the Kashmiris by the Indian Constitution. The drift became a dilemma for the Government of India: should it cajole or browbeat the Kashmiris into giving up on that dream and instead embrace the future that awaits it as an emotionally integrated unit of the Indian Republic? After Burhan's killing, journalist Gowhar Geelani traveled to Tral to understand the 'phenomenon', and discovered that: 'Almost every second household had a story to narrate… For them, Burhan had found a new way of fighting against the injustices towards Kashmir at a time when militancy was perhaps at its lowest ebb. He infused fresh life into an otherwise declining armed rebellion. His USP, as I understood it, was that he instigated Kashmiris to think beyond Pakistan. With his bravado, he effectively conveyed the powerful message that Kashmiris can rise against New Delhi without seeking Pakistan's "diplomatic, political, moral or financial" support, thus renewing and invigorating the indigenous strain of Kashmir's rebellion.'[430]

The Government of India, the Indian Army and other Security Forces have been battling Pakistan-backed militancy in the Valley since 1989. Pakistan has trained the ideologues of this militancy, provided religious and armed training and money in the hope that whenever the militancy reaches the end that it desires, the people of Kashmir will be ready to secede from India and integrate with Pakistan. But it does maintain the façade that it is for the upholding of the right of the people of Kashmir to decide what they want for themselves. This has been happening in different forms since the 1950s. Thus, Ghulam Mohiuddin Karra[431] was propped by Pakistan to challenge Bakshi Ghulam Mohammad in the 1950s in the belief that being a senior member of the National

Conference he still commanded loyalty and following of a large section of Kashmiris. However, soon thereafter, when Bakshi had released Mirza Afzal Beg, the trusted lieutenant of Sheikh Abdullah, from custody, Pakistan had found him as a more effective tool and financially helped him with his Plebiscite Front.[432] But even when Pakistan had been banking upon Mirza Afzal Beg, it had not entirely given up on Karra and had extended him enough support to keep his movement against India alive. It, at least, created some people who remained disgruntled against the Indian State. It was only in the 1980s that Pakistan realized that a combination of fortuitous circumstances, created by the rise of transnational jihad, western need to finance this jihad to combat Soviet presence in Afghanistan and shortsighted machinations of the Government of India and the State leaders had given it an opportunity to experiment with a new strategy of 'bleeding India by a thousand cuts'. Code named 'Operation Tupac',[433] it promised to be a low cost but very effective tool against India. After the new phase beginning with 1989, those who took up arms against India, mostly jihadis trained by Pakistan, ironically with American aid, gradually became an inspiration for the local youth since they were dying for their cause and they collaborated with the Pakistanis in the hope that when they do succeed, they will be realizing their dream of an 'independent' Kashmir. But such Kashmiris who believed that they could use Pakistan have usually been neutralized, sometimes by parallel leadership created by Pakistani agencies or by the rival groups, who mysteriously get information about their whereabouts, and quite often by the Indian security forces.

In such a scenario, the life and death of Burhan Wani was a milestone. He came from an educated, upwardly mobile, middle-class family. His father, an M.Sc. in Mathematics, was the Principal of a senior secondary school. His grandfather was a retired government servant having served the State government as an Assistant Director, Planning. The family was said to be ideologically aligned with the Jamaat-e-Islami, which, however, according to his father, did not deter Burhan from dreaming of joining the Indian Army when he grew up.[434]

Burhan, the second son in the family, was like any other boy of his age and generation in Kashmir. Handsome and fussy about himself and obsessed with cricket, he was drawn towards militancy, it is said, when he witnessed his elder brother being thrashed by soldiers over some trivial issue. Humiliated and disgraced by the encounter, Burhan who was with his brother, seethed in anger and resolved to avenge it. For his young mind the disgrace was not just his personal experience: it was an everyday occurrence, often and randomly at the hands of arrogant and ill-educated soldiers or some evil-minded officer. Maybe this story is concocted to build the myth around him, but it can also be true since some soldiers are indeed capable of behaving like a force of occupation. This incident drove Burhan, only of fifteen years age then, away from home into the forest to arrange arms to begin his short romantic journey. He joined the Hizb-ul-Mujahideen, though by the mid-2000 this organization had all but withered. He infused new life into it with his innovative use of the social media.

Radha Kumar notes: 'He was not particularly notable as an armed guerrilla; according to Jammu and Kashmir police force, he had been implicated in the murders of two sarpanches and three troops over the course of six years. But he was adept at social media, posting selfies in military fatigues complete with gun, recording speeches calling for azadi and establishment of caliphate. Fair and brown-eyed, with the slightly chubby cheeks of an adolescent, his social media campaign was a hit amongst the Valley's unemployed and partially educated youth, who were, as in the rest of India, in sizeable demographic.'[435]

However, as hero worshiped as he was by the general populace, his venture into aggressive militancy resulted in his family getting directly entangled in terrorism. His elder brother was pursuing a post graduate degree when he had left his home with the excuse that he was going for a picnic, on a pleasant day after cooking biryani. But he was killed by the forces. He was, in fact, said to be going to the Tral forest, the guerrilla stronghold in south Kashmir, to share the dish with his younger brother when he was allegedly picked up by the army. Obviously, the security agencies were either on his trail or someone had tipped off the visit to Burhan. The army said that he had been killed in an encounter but this was vehemently contested by the locals.

For about seventeen months, till the killing of Burhan Wani in June 2016 both, the BJP and PDP, had few political challenges except the silent indifference and contempt of the people. However, anger and fury erupted no sooner had the news of Burhan's death spread. The mourning of his death was spontaneous and massive. Thousands of mourners marched towards his village in Tral using multiple roads. Eyewitness reports said 'They were seen on the Srinagar-Jammu highway, and on the streets, lanes and by lanes of Tral, Awantipora, Pulwama, Pampore, Shopian, Kulgam, Kokernag, Anantnag, Qazigund, Srinagar, Sopore, Pattan, Baramulla, Bandipore, Ganderbal et al.'[436] There were various reports about the attendance at the funeral—the numbers were anything between 30,000 to 3,00,000—with the common desire to grieve over the 'martyrdom', and offer '*khiraj-e-aqeedat*'—glowing tributes to their 'hero'. It is said that the police exhausted the tear gas shells and therefore resorted to pellet-guns. But their use turned out to be lethal though the experts termed it as non-lethal. Kashmir had never been this angry before and the PDP-BJP government was caught off guard. 'The state's security grid grew nervous, unable to stop the swelling crowds that had formed a sea of protesters. They resorted to the tried and tested tricks like firing bullets and pellets indiscriminately at unarmed protesters, hitting most of them above the waistline. News of the brutal crackdown further exacerbated an already tense situation. Kashmir was on the boil…The cycle of killings had resumed.'[437] The government also blocked the mobile phones and internet services in response, as it had become the standard response of the government whenever faced with protests. There is no data or study to prove or disprove its effectiveness but it can also be presumed that blocking or censoring communications has never paid dividends for any government. Ironically, this was the same tactics which was adopted by Omar Abdullah's government in 2010 and was roundly condemned by late Arun Jaitley, the finance minister and one of the key advisors of Prime Minister Narendra Modi.

Chief Minister Mehbooba Mufti's response created a challenge of its own, more to her than the State. Not being able to decide what to do, her response created a rift between Delhi and the Valley.

In an ill-advised statement, she said that had she known that the police operation was against Burhan Wani she would have stopped it. This caused great anger among the troops who had given enough warnings and chance for him to surrender. In total disarray, her appeals to the civil-society, religious organizations and dissidents to intercede and stop the mayhem were completely ineffective. Her direction to the MLAs of the PDP to go to their constituencies and appeal for peace fell on deaf ears for they feared for their own safety if they went among the people.[438]

By now, the alliance government seemed to have lost the plot and legitimacy though it must be said that it was the cumulative effect of decades of history. After nearly three decades of insurgency, it was crystal clear to everyone that the Indian security forces had broken the back of the Pakistan-sponsored militancy a number of times. But each time the political establishment had failed to capitalize and build on their success. They not only used an unrealistic dream to shore up their political fortunes but also fed the youth with a dream that was packaged in the romance of sacrifice, heroism and vindication of all the 'sufferings of ages past'. In his death, Burhan became the third hero for those Kashmiris who nursed the dream of an independent Kashmir. The first was Maqbool Bhat who was hanged in February 1984 in Tihar Jail and the second, Ashfaq Majeed Wani,[439] the young and educated 'commander-in-chief' of the pro-independence JKLF who was killed in an encounter with the security forces in March 1990. It is said that his funeral too had attracted thousands of mourners. But the death of Burhan became an important reference point in the militancy of the Valley. Unlike Ashfaq Majeed Wani's, his insurgency was indigenous and without any support from Pakistan. As subsequent developments proved this was but another phase in the insurgency since gradually Pakistani agencies once again established control over it. But this phase brought many more young people into its fold than ever before.

It would be a gross and misleading understatement to believe that a single incident of his brother's humiliation had transformed a normal boy into a defiant militant. He became the romantic and charismatic hero as a result of years of glossing over the problem of the Kashmiri identity and the sweeping of the issues under the carpet. This has created such a huge logjam that few remember how the State and the country reached where it finds itself today. Successive governments have contributed in making it what it is today. India had the option of honestly implementing Article 370 and to leave the rest to the seductive advantages of a successful democracy. Separate flag, constitution and system of governance are not unknown to modern democracies and they work seamlessly with the Union government as long as the basic tenets of democracy are enshrined in their governance model. Moreover, if good administration and satisfied polity had been built then its presence would not have made any difference. Very early during the life of the Republic it had become abundantly clear that while Pakistan was unable to build either democratic institutions or even respect the ideals of democracy, India was determined to occupy its destined place among the liberal and democratic nations of the world. However, there were some issues that arose because the residual challenges of accession remained unaddressed and it allowed the idea of independence to survive and grow. History teaches us that ideas can be made superfluous by making an alternate idea work more effectively, on the other hand, the more it is suppressed by the use of greater force the more it gets a life, strength and momentum of its own. The governments do not acknowledge the fact that the use of paramilitary and military forces in the Valley has only succeeded in pushing the youth on to the road of militancy. This was emphasized by the Justice Sanjay Krishna Koul Commission report instituted by Omar Abdullah to go into the agitation of 2010 as well as Deputy Inspector General (retired) Watali, who in an interview to *The Telegraph* said, 'militancy was still a low-key affair in 1989 with only a 100-odd youths wielding guns, but the decision of the Farooq Abdullah government, on the Centre's prodding, to use the "military option" changed everything. The CRPF was deployed and civilian casualties began to mount, angering more and more people.'[440]

But going back into the challenge of secessionism in India, Sten Widmalm has made a powerful case for healthy democratic institutions in his short but significant book, *Kashmir in*

Comparative Perspective: Democracy and Violent Separatism in India. He contends that it is clear that to neutralize the secessionist forces one needs to look at the cause of such demands and then address them. In Jammu and Kashmir, the Governments of India and the State ignored the Plebiscite Front and hoped that it would just vanish one day and expected the people to accept its complete merger with the rest of the country. This was coupled with the flawed elections and the rampant charges of corruption, nepotism and maladministration. In his autobiography, Dr Karan Singh expressed his deep disappointment when an otherwise committed and enlightened democrat like Ghulam Mohammad Sadiq too failed to deliver fair Assembly elections in 1967 as Chief Minister.[441] To this was added the insult of depriving the Kashmiris of their regional voice and local platform when the National Conference was merged with the Indian National Congress. This was in stark contrast to what happened in Tamil Nadu. At the time of Independence, the Nehru government had inherited the demand for a separate 'Dravida Nadu'. It was first aired on 1 July 1939, a year before the demand for Pakistan was made. This demand had remained alive when India attained independence but Widmalm stresses that 'separatist demands and turbulent political climate at this crucial stage of development, when democracy was being introduced, did not lead to widespread attempts to overthrow the democratic system, from either the central government or the state parties. Political institutions seem to have functioned in Tamil Nadu to such extent that democracy continued to be the accepted form of government. In other words, loyalty to the political system survived, because channels for voice and exit remained open. This is reflected in the intensity of debate, where radical opinions were freely formulated and new parties were formed which offered voters a wider choice of representation and several channels for expression of opinion and discontent. Maybe the standard of internal democracy in parties such as Dravida Kazhagam was no better than in the National Conference in the late 1970s and early 1980s, but at least political alternatives were allowed to develop freely. At this time Nehru also maintained his secular approach to politics and this continued in Kamraj's (the then Chief Minister of the state) policies. This trend was broken by Indira Gandhi in Jammu and Kashmir in 1983, which aggravated the situation there.'[442]

Moreover, the 'divide and rule' policy of the British had meant that the Muslim League had advanced its 'two nations' theory and had got it accepted. Their success had encouraged not only the Sikhs and Harijans to demand a separate state but when the elections for the 1967 Assembly inflicted a crushing defeat on Congress and brought Dravida Munnetra Kazagham (DMK) to power the perspective of the hot-headed Tamils changed. Ever since, the Congress has become an appendage of one or the other faction of the Dravida parties and with this the secessionist demand of Dravida parties has died down. Before that a serious challenge was posed by the Tamils in 1965 when contrary to the assurance given by Nehru to Annadurai, the Dravida leader, that English will not be replaced by Hindi as a link language, Lal Bahadur Shastri's government had announced after a year of Nehru's death that Hindi will become the official language. This was in accordance with the Constitution of India which had retained English as a link language for only 15 years. Hindi had been announced only after the expiry of that period but the southern state had been rocked with widespread riots and deaths for two months. These protests died only after it was announced that English will remain the link language as long as the southern States wanted.

Contrary to this flexibility in the south, the Centre had been trying to forcefully impose its will on the Kashmiris and every contrary voice was treated as a threat to national sovereignty. It was the desire for uniformity and hegemony that had tried to wipe the National Conference out of existence by merging it with the Congress. On the face of it, the merger looked as if the State had finally merged its identity with the rest of the country but in hindsight it can now be said that it was a colossal blunder since it took away a part of Kashmiri history and identity and deprived the opportunity for powerful regional voices to be heard. How skin deep this merger was, was exposed by Sheikh Abdullah who, upon his return in 1975, revived the National Conference, invited all those who had joined Congress to return to the fold of the National Conference and then proceeded to decimate the Congress in the Valley in the elections of 1977. The Congress has never really recovered from that blow.

Then there were apparently insignificant sentiments that were born and grew into rallying points. Kashmiris as one unit have supported Pakistani cricket and this touches irrational and crazy heights when it plays India. For an Indian this is humiliating and provocative but it calls for introspection. It is, in fact, a symptom of our failing to instill the idea of India in the hearts and minds of the people of Kashmir who continue to give precedence to their religious identity. People do not identify with new identities at the word of command; they happen when advantages are felt and experienced. The Government of India should have reined in the ambitions of small people in Congress in the 1980s, and at the state level Sheikh Abdullah should have been fairer to Jammu and the Hindus of the region. If he had not pressed the divisive Resettlement Bill, things would have been different.

It is appalling to note that the generation that grew up post 1980, have only a selective memory about post 1947 developments. Consequently, secessionist memories occupy a space that is much larger than it deserved. The case of Tamil Nadu, where the language, culture and history flow uninterrupted since ancient times, is an example. In contrast, in Kashmir, over the years conditions were being tailored for a Burhan Wani to come and mark his place in history. All these years have instilled a belief among the Kashmiris that they have the power of the argument, that their grievance, cause and demand is just; and that, India may have the physical power to hold them down but it does not have the argument to do so. The three decades of militancy has seen many developments and the transition and the transformation of the Kashmiri youth from timid and inhibited to bold and daring, is remarkable. Today the army personnel do not dare travel without following standard safety procedures as if they were in enemy territory. Gone are the days when a young Captain could take to the steering of his jeep and drive from Baramulla to Jammu enjoying the cool air. This change did not happen overnight. Today the series of agitations and confrontations have brutalized and hardened them into people who can go into a battle with stones in hands, if not guns.

15

Redeeming a Pledge

'I say let the world go to hell, but I should always have my tea.'
—Fyodor Dostoevsky

The protests post Burhan Wani's death were remarkable for their changed nature and the rampant use of pellet guns by the security forces. They were different because they engulfed the rural Kashmir on a large scale for the first time, drawing the raw emotions and energy of the peasantry into the conflict. In response, the security forces routinely resorted to pellet guns till the damage done by the flying pellets outraged the global conscience. By using the Israel imported weapon on the Kashmiris, the BJP government had equated them with the Palestinians battling for survival against the US-supported Israel.

This change in approach went unnoticed in the country, or perhaps, its silence wholeheartedly supported it! Ever since the Second World War, a contentious definition of violence and its perpetrator has become part of the modern political culture. In the process, a new definition of terrorist, where only the 'non-state actors' could be termed terrorists and never the state, became an established norm. Thus, the Americans were never branded terrorists for N-bombing of the civilian and non-combatant population of Hiroshima and Nagasaki, or bombing to a rubble other cities and civil populations of Japan. Similarly, the bombing of the civilian population of Dresden by Britain during the Second World War, or the devastation of North Vietnam by USA through bombing and use of napalm bombs, or for that matter in more recent times, the USA hostilities in Iraq and Afghanistan, has never been termed as terrorism. None of them has been condemned by historians. Interestingly, even Pakistan thinks that it is at the receiving end of such a narrative. Lieutenant General Asad Durrani, former head of ISI, but currently blacklisted by the Pakistani Army, opines that the discourse about terrorism and terrorist changed decisively after the 9/11 attack on American soil. Thereafter, 'only NSAs (non-state actors) could be called "terrorists", although states on the "wrong side", Pakistan and Iran, for example, but never India or Israel, could still be hauled up for "sponsoring terrorism"... Consequently, terrorism as a label is now an invaluable instrument of state policy.'[443] The fact that domestic media in India had equated the Kashmiris with Pakistan and Taliban would have gone almost unnoticed but for the shrill voices of TV anchors who found the prime hour as a new platform where their histrionic talents could be displayed, and it soon became the new normal.

During that summer, more than ever before, it appeared that Kashmir was finally lost even as the condemnations of the brutalities of the security forces came from across the political spectrum. Of course, the BJP was the only party whose conscience remained unmoved, even after the photograph of a young child, pock marked and blinded by stray pellets of the gun, was flashed across the world or that of many young people blinded in one or both the eyes by the flying pellets became all too frequent. The world had come a long way from the 1972 photograph taken by Nick Ut of a 9-year-old naked girl running away from the horror of the Napalm bomb![444] That single photograph had shaken the conscience of USA and soon afterwards, a chorus of protests against the American involvement in Vietnam led to an end of that involvement. But the 'pockmarked and blinded by pellet guns' photographs failed to similarly rouse India's conscience. However, the matter of pellet guns did reach the doors of the Supreme Court where a bench of Chief Justice T.S. Thakur and Justice D.Y. Chandrachud, although they just demanded an assurance from the Government of India that 'pellet guns will not be used indiscriminately and excessively' and then let the matter rest.[445] Later, in 2020 this matter once again came up before the courts and 'in a relief to security forces operating in the union territories of Jammu and Kashmir and Ladakh, the Jammu and Kashmir High Court refused to ban the use of pellet guns for crowd control during protests in the region.'[446]

The effect of the pellets was devastating and *The New York Times* that covered the 2016 protests and use of pellet guns, captioned its report 'An Epidemic of "Dead Eyes"'. It also noted: 'The stone-throwing crowds have no political leaders, put forward no specific demands and metastasized with alarming speed. Around 60 civilians and two members of the security forces have been killed; on each side, thousands have been wounded.'[447] Explaining the gun, *The Times* commented: 'The name can make them sound like toys, but pellet guns cause very real injuries. Since 2010, pellet guns have reportedly killed 14 people in Kashmir, according to Amnesty International. "The Indian forces call it a pellet gun, but it is a pump action shotgun," says a spokesman from the Omega Research Foundation, a U.K. based charity that monitors military technologies. The only difference is the type of ammunition: a cartridge with up to 500 tiny lead pellets, which disperse in all directions when fired. They are commonly used by hunters. "The ammunition is not designed for crowd control," he says.'[448] These guns are liberally used by the Israelis but they have no compunction and they do not mask their malicious glee in blinding or killing the Palestinians with their government, legislature, law and judiciary protecting them.

Saiba Varma, an assistant professor of anthropology at the University of California, San Diego, United States wrote:

> The lack of empathy in the face of mass Kashmiri suffering exemplifies how deeply embedded the logic of dehumanization and demonization of the "other" has become in India's majoritarian Hindu public. Kashmiri Muslims are the "other" whose pain and suffering is suspect, because their very humanity is suspect. Not recognizing the humanity of the suffering other has become an emblem of xenophobic and nationalist governments globally—it is the same story from refugees who were recently [Trump era]teargassed by the American border security force to civilian protesters in Gaza who are killed in broad daylight after being labeled 'dangerous' to the Israeli security state.

> Instead, images of injuries have sparked a debate around the pellet gun. The Indian government and the Supreme Court have both condemned the "excessive use" of pellets in Kashmir but there has been little engagement with the reasons for their use or the protests themselves. Instead, military experts and public opinion have suggested using "innovative" non-lethal weapons such as PAVA shells, or chilli-based munitions. This flowering military imagination suggests that Kashmiri bodies may become grounds for experimenting with yet more "non-lethal weapons." What goes unquestioned is the broader strategy of permanently blinding and mutilating civilians.[449]

For the PDP, these were testing times. The more people died or were hurt the more its base eroded and it was exposed as a party of power-hungry individuals who had compromised their principles and betrayed their people. In the process, it *was* complicit in the killings of the youth. The BJP, however, did not see the problem in its handling of Kashmir and addressing the party convention in 2019, India's then Defence Minister Nirmala Sitharaman made a bold and false claim. 'We have not had one major terrorist attack in this country after 2014,' she said. Quite contrary to the reality, for 'in 2018…Kashmir saw the highest fatalities in terror-related violence in a decade with 451 deaths, according to the South Asia Terrorism Portal (SATP).The last time this toll was exceeded was in 2008 when Congress held power.'[450] In addition, there were quite a few bold and major attacks, for example the Pathankot Air Force station and the Uri army camp where 17 soldiers were killed.

The stark reality was that this is how the alliance had drifted into 2018 when a heinous crime that should have been dealt with by the police in a routine manner, tested the BJP and the judicial process. In January 2018, an eight-year-old Muslim Gujjar girl was found raped and murdered in a village in the Kathua district of Jammu, the stronghold of BJP. Her body had been found in a nearby jungle, six days after she had gone missing. Initially, the local police, comprising of the residents of nearby villages, tried to cover it up but the crime was too heinous to be brushed aside in a routine manner and soon when a Special Investigation Team was formed, gruesome details came out. The suspects, from the local village were arrested after some dilly-dallying. Since the Gujjar girl was Muslim and the suspects and the whole village Hindu, it soon assumed communal color reflecting the fault lines that had existed all along but had now got accentuated since the socio-economic causes had already build up confrontation between the two communities in Jammu region. This soon snowballed into an issue on which almost the whole of Hindu Jammu stood behind the accused against the Gujjars, with the activists of the civil society demanding justice, ranged on the other side. Since BJP was part of the government, pressure mounted on it to help out the accused to such an extent that it appeared that the BJP too would be splitting on the issue. The case nevertheless went on, the prosecution stuck to its version of events, produced evidence and later secured conviction after the case had been transferred out of the state following higher court's intervention. During this period the Hindu lawyers in large numbers displayed the audacity of trying to prevent the prosecution from filing the case in the local court, giving an indication of the kind of Indian society this country could nourish if majoritarianism was allowed to rule.

The confrontation between the Gujjars and the Hindus had been building and was a consequence of the socio-economic changes that development had brought. Some role had also been played by terrorism, which had made the nomadic Gujjars one of the most vulnerable and frequent targets, of both, the terrorists as well as the security forces. The emerging changes had thrown up challenges to the government and the society they lived in, and both had been found wanting.

Traditionally, the Gujjars would descend to the plains with their livestock just after the farmers had harvested their paddy and maize crops. Farmers would usually keep a part of their land uncultivated during the *rabi* season and allow the Gujjars to occupy it for the winter sojourn along with the livestock. The dung thus left in that part would mature into organic manure for the farmer to use for the next crop when the Gujjars had departed for higher and colder reaches of the mountains. While in the plains during the winter months, their females would usually ferry milk to the nearby markets in towns for sale while the men folk tended to their herd. But development and government schemes had modified this lifestyle since they bought three-wheeler vehicles to transport milk, and since the men drove them, the women no longer needed to go to the market and be ogled at by lecherous men. Terrorists, who crossed the porous international border and then treaded through to the mountains, would also often become unwelcome, but unavoidable guests, in the Gujjars' *deras* (temporary abodes).Often the security forces came to know of this and then they were treated as accomplices who provided shelter, food and then accompanied them to a point from where they could cross over the mountain ranges to Doda or Kishtwar. Caught between two ruthless forces, they desired to live a settled life and since the mountains were no longer safe and practical, particularly during the winter months, they tried to settle in the plains. In this they were encouraged by all governments thereby giving the settled local population, reason to resist their permanent settlement since it threatened the demographic change in favor of Muslims. This fault line fully played out during the confrontation between the two communities over the rape case. The conviction of the accused had further embittered the Hindus and BJP began to fear its support base slipping.

By June of 2018, the BJP realized that it was on the verge of paying a heavy price for having a share in power with the PDP and bailed out of it, declaring that 'continuing support to PDP was untenable'. The BJP said that Mehbooba Mufti's government had failed to contain militancy and radicalization of youth in the Kashmir Valley. No journalist reminded it that it was a PDP-BJP government and that both partners needed to share the failure collectively. 'The situation in Kashmir Valley has deteriorated... radicalization is on the rise,' Ram Madhav, the BJP general secretary and in-charge of Jammu and Kashmir, declared in New Delhi.[451] This was preceded by a ceasefire during the holy month of Ramzan but it was marred by the killing of a noted journalist Shujaat Bukhari, editor of *The Rising Kashmir* and an army jawan on his way to his home on annual leave. Obviously, the BJP could not have approached forthcoming Lok Sabha elections, which were to be held in 2019, under these circumstances. With the folly of an alliance with PDP fully exposed, as a first corrective step, it called off, what observers had dubbed, 'an unnatural alliance'. The year passed with BJP making up its mind about what it wanted to do in the State. It was evident that it had decided that political business can no longer be conducted on the pattern it had been till now but it continued to bide its time. The Government of India too did not give any clue and prepared for the General Election for Lok Sabha without taking a call on Jammu and Kashmir.

The pre-election picture was not very encouraging and appeared that the BJP had lost considerable ground. The economy had begun to slow down, agriculture was facing a crisis, unemployment was rising and the opposition parties were poised to exploit the situation after the ham-handed demonetization and unplanned implementation of the Goods and Service Tax (GST), but more worryingly, the image of BJP as an uncompromising party on national security issues had been damaged. Contrary to the claims of the BJP government, terrorist attacks, whether in Jammu and Kashmir, in the North-East or the Naxal-affected tribal areas, were alarming. For a while even Punjab was sucked into the vortex of terrorist attacks when in July 2015, three gunmen sneaked across the Ravi towards Dinanagar, gunned down citizens before attacking the Police Station in Gurdaspur district. In another attack, the Pathankot Air Force base was targeted in January 2016 and five soldiers were killed. In Jammu Kashmir, apart from the regular attacks and encounters, terrorists attacked the Mohra army camp on 5 December 2014, in which 11 security forces personnel had been killed. Another attack took place on an army base in Uri, on 18 September 2016, in which 17 soldiers were killed. On 3 October 2016, in a terror attack in Baramulla, one Border Security Force (BSF) soldier was killed, and in another incident, on 29 November 2016, Nagrota became the target in which seven soldiers were killed. According to a 5 February 2019 reply in the Lok Sabha, the government admitted that six terrorist attacks were reported between 2014 and 31 December 2018, nationwide, in addition to the 1,708 attacks in Jammu and Kashmir, 2,442 in the northeast and 4,969 attacks by Maoists. It was almost as if the terrorists and their handlers across the border were goading the Prime Minister. With both, India and Pakistan, having become nuclear countries, it was almost a guarantee to Pakistan that India will not risk a nuclear war and if it did then the international community will intervene and stop not only an all-out war but also put Kashmir on the table as a dispute that needed to be sorted with international intervention. Non-action or hollow loud noises were eroding the credibility and political capital of the Prime Minister.

The sheen of Prime Minister Modi had indeed begun to wear thin when in a suicide attack, a car, laden with high explosives, rammed into the convoy of the paramilitary forces near Pulwama in Kashmir, on 14 February 2019, killing 40 paramilitary soldiers. The audacity and the ferocity of the attack outraged the whole nation and with clever maneuvering, the government and the media focused the attention of the nation towards the tragedy, arousing nationwide anger. This helped in deflecting questions about the intelligence failure of the multiple agencies active in the state, and they were never asked from where or how so much of dynamite was procured without their getting a whiff of it; or, if they had any prior information then how it was disseminated. Satya Pal Malik, former Governor of the State, raised the question as to why the convoy of the paramilitary forces was not provided with air facility when they were to move in large number and why the convoy route was not sanitized before the movement and link-roads closed for all other traffic while it was passing. But like on earlier occasions, no questions were asked by the government and the accountability too was not fixed. However, the political leadership knew that the country was less interested in enquiries to fix responsibility for intelligence failure and more in teaching Pakistan a lesson. So 'in the early hours of 26 February, 12 Mirage-2000 combat jets of the Indian Air Force (IAF) armed with Israeli Precision Guided Munitions (PGM) also SPICE 2000 and Crystal Maze Mk2, called AGM 142 Popeye PGMs, retaliated by taking off from their airbase on a crucial mission, cloaked in secrecy. The multirole fighter aircraft flew over Himachal Pradesh and Kashmir before crossing into Pakistani airspace and striking the largest training camp of the JeM in Balakot inside Pakistan's Khyber Pakhtunkhwa.'[452] Thus, along with the destruction of the largest training camp for terrorists in Pakistan, an unspecified number of terrorists and their commanders too were claimed to have been eliminated. While the attack was taking place, the Pakistani Air Force too scrambled and launched a strike against the Indian targets but they failed to hit the target and were chased away. During the attack an Indian fighter was downed and Wing Commander Abhinandan Varthman captured, but in captivity he won the hearts of Indians by his exemplary cool behavior and dignified conduct. In another incident, when the forces were on high alert, even as the aerial combat with Pakistani Air Force was going on, an Indian helicopter was shot down in friendly fire by the air defence unit and it fell near Budgam, Kashmir, killing all its six occupants. In sharp contrast to the Government of India's non action over the Pulwama intelligence failure, a court of inquiry was duly constituted by the Indian Air Force, which found five of the Air Force personnel responsible for negligence and Air Chief Marshal A.K.S. Bhadauria admitted it was a 'big mistake'.[453] This inquiry and appropriate punishment to those responsible is in stark contrast to the Pulwama terrorist strike, where death of 40 security forces soldiers almost led India and Pakistan, two nuclear countries, to war and yet no effort was made to find how it happened and why the intelligence failure took place though a number of alleged culprits have been arrested by the National Investigation Agency (NIA) and even now, more than four years down the line, arrests are being made.

The Balakot attack had decisively proved that nuclear arsenal did not necessarily guarantee deterrence when the stakes are raised too high by any one of the parties. For much too long Pakistan had been testing Indian patience, since 1999, to be precise, with its irresponsible behavior in sending terrorist across the border for targeted suicide and *fidayee* attacks in the belief that their own nuclear capability would remain a deterrent for India. With no space to maneuver in domestic politics, Prime Minister Modi chose to raise the stakes by the Balakot attack. It was a bold move and President Trump supported it by saying that India was justified in taking this action in response to Pulwama and many other such attacks. By making an open airstrike in Pakistani territory and not PoK, India had now put the responsibility of escalation squarely upon Pakistan. For long, Pakistan had been on the terror watch list of USA and world bodies but it had not paid any heed; on the other hand, ever since India limited its Kargil war to its strategic interests in the region, and exercising exemplary restrain during the 2008 Mumbai terror attack, the world opinion knew that India was the victim and the more responsible nuclear power. Now when India had finally retaliated, the world stood by it. India's patience had paid rich dividends in the end. As far as domestic politics was concerned, the Prime Minister had won a jackpot!

The Balakot strike reestablished the image of Prime Minister Modi as a strong man in whose hands the security of India was safe. Notwithstanding the fact that Pakistan possessed nuclear weapons, the strike had forced Pakistan to rethink its approach to Kashmir and India, since now India was willing to strike first, if so provoked, and also risk nuclear strike. Internationally, barring China, Malaysia and Turkey, Pakistan stood isolated as its role in promoting terrorism had long been exposed. Politically, within the country, it yielded rich dividends as national security and Pakistan occupied the center stage, pushing the economic turmoil and multiple failures of the BJP in the background. This proved fortuitous and the BJP secured a landslide victory, winning 303 of the total 543 Lok Sabha seats, the highest that the BJP had ever won. The BJP-led alliance, the National Democratic Alliance (NDA), had won 353 seats. With a majority of its own, the BJP had freed itself of all the shackles and was now free and ready to comprehensively implement its political ideology. It had always demanded that a Uniform Civil Code be enforced in the country and now, soon after the second term of Prime Minister Modi started, it got an opportunity to do the next best thing by bringing in a Bill on 30 July 2019 that banned and made 'Triple Talaq' among Muslims illegal and punishable. The Prime Minister had signaled that he meant business. This move yielded rich dividends for the BJP: on the one hand it won the support of liberal Muslims, particularly women who were at the receiving end of an obnoxious practice, and on the other hand, it satisfied the appetite of vast majority of Hindus who wanted to teach Muslims a lesson.

But the main priority, and test, of the BJP was dealing with the conundrum of Jammu and Kashmir. At the core of its philosophy was the abrogation of Article 370 and Article 35A of the constitution. In its opinion, the special status granted to Jammu and Kashmir was not only a hurdle in its complete integration but also the reason to remain emotionally segregated from the rest of the country. The separate constitution and flag of the State also riled the BJP but it had not been able to do anything for lack of complete support in the Parliament to make necessary amendments during the period of 2014-2019. Now, the huge majority after the 2019 Lok Sabha polls gave it the opportunity to fulfill its long-cherished dream.

To briefly recall, Article 370 of the Constitution of India was adopted as a 'temporary provision' on 17 October 1949 since the question of accession of Jammu and Kashmir was under the consideration of the Security Council of the United Nations. It gave special powers to the state of Jammu and Kashmir, lawfully authorizing it to have its own constitution which, in turn, also gave it a separate flag. Only the provisions of Article 1 and Article 370 of the Indian Constitution applied to the state. But the contentious Article was the only route through which the Central Government could apply to the State any law passed by the Parliament of India. As a result, if a central law or any provision of the Constitution or part thereof, other than the three subjects surrendered to it under the Instrument of Accession, were to be applied then it needed 'consultation' and 'concurrence' of the State Government. Similarly, Article 35A of the Constitution of India introduced through a constitutional order in 1954 authorized the state legislature to define 'permanent residents' of the State. Those defined as permanent residents were entitled to property rights, employment, scholarships and other social benefits in the state. The validity of this Article had been challenged in the courts and in April 2018, the Supreme Court of India had ruled that notwithstanding the term, 'temporary' used to describe it in the Constitution, Article 370 had attained permanency since the State Constituent Assembly, which was empowered to alter the Article, had ceased to exist.

After the 1954 order, 47 Presidential orders were issued between 11 February 1956 and 19 February 1994, making various other provisions of the Constitution of India applicable to Jammu and Kashmir. All these orders were issued with the 'concurrence of the Government of the State' without any Constituent Assembly.

The effect of the Presidential orders issued between 1954 and 1994 had been to extend 94 of the 97 subjects in the Union List (the powers of the Central Government), and 260 of the 395 Articles of the Constitution of India to the State of Jammu and Kashmir. The remaining subjects were those for which the State Constitution had its own corresponding and identical laws. In fact, way back in 1964, responding to a motion for the abrogation of the said Article, Home Minister Gulzari Lal Nanda had argued that 'Article 370, whether you keep it or not, has been completely emptied of its contents. Nothing has been left in it.' He was referring to the process of implementing central laws through Presidential orders after 'consulting' the State Government and securing its 'concurrence'.[454] This argument, however, had never satisfied the right wing which wanted the abrogation accompanied by considerable sound and fury.

With this precedent, to overcome the legal challenge raised by the Supreme Court judgment of April 2018, the Indian Government chose to render Article 370 as 'inoperative' even though it continued to exist in the constitution. On 5 August 2019, a presidential order was issued—the Constitution (Application to Jammu and Kashmir) Order, 2019—which superseded the Constitution (Application to Jammu and Kashmir) Order, 1954. Elaborate security plans were made before the revocation of the status by the Ministry of Home Affairs. Thousands of paramilitary security troops were moved into Jammu and Kashmir. On 2 August, the Indian Army also said that the Pakistani Army and terrorists were 'planning to upscale violence' and would try to 'target the Yatra' which was going on. The Government of India notified students and tourists, both local and foreign, to leave Jammu and Kashmir and it was ensured that they left by physically searching each and every hotel, guest house and tourist bungalows. The Valley was rife with rumors and it was feared that Article 370 was about to be abrogated. The stealth, deception and secrecy with which the Government moved is best illustrated by the fact that on 3 August, Omar Abdullah said that Governor Satya Pal Malik had 'assured him there was no initiative in progress to dilute Article 35A of the Constitution, start delimitation or trifurcate'[455] of the State. In the end, it turned out to be a war that was declared by New Delhi on the Kashmiri people and therefore all rules of engagement had been suspended.

On 4 August, security forces were equipped with satellite phones in central, north and south Kashmir. Thereafter, a total communication blackout was ordered, shutting down cable TV, landlines, mobile phones and the Internet. Doctors and district administrators were advised to remain on standby. Prior to the 5 August revocation announcement, Section 144 and curfew was imposed in all the three regions of the State i.e. Jammu, Kashmir and Ladakh. The lockdown was far more intense in the Kashmir region and shops and clinics were closed, as were all educational institutions. The government lifted Section 144 and curfew and reopened schools only in some parts of Jammu region from 10 August 2019. But Kashmir remained in lockdown conditions.

Before issuing the Presidential order, the Government had flown additional security forces into the Valley to secure every inch of Kashmir. In a single stroke, the State Constitution was made 'inoperative' and the State was brought under the Constitution of India. The President, it was argued, had technically issued the order with the 'concurrence of the Government of State of Jammu and Kashmir'. This in effect meant the concurrence of the Governor of Jammu and Kashmir since President's rule had been imposed at that time in the state. Ironically, the order was issued using the third clause of Article 370, which authorized the President of India to declare the article inoperative with exceptions and modifications, if recommended by the (now non-existent) State Constituent Assembly to do so. To circumvent the legal issue of the non-existent State Constituent Assembly, the President used the Clause (I) of Article 370, which conferred him with the power to modify the Indian Constitution on subjects related to Jammu and Kashmir. He first added a new clause to Article 367, which dealt with interpretation of the Constitution. He replaced the phrase 'Constituent Assembly of the State' with 'Legislative Assembly of the State' and since the state legislative assembly had been suspended, the order said that any reference to the legislative assembly will be construed as a reference to the Governor of Jammu and Kashmir and since the Governor was an appointee of the Central Government, therefore, the Indian Parliament would now function for the State Legislative Assembly!

For a democratic polity, unprecedented and unheard-of measures were resorted to by the government to ensure that no media report could be filed. Journalists became the special targets and most of them complained of not being able to file their reports. It was only the *Times Now* news channel, whose editor Navika Kumar was to claim that its reporters had been filing reports without any hindrance to which veteran journalist and former adviser to two Prime Ministers, H.K. Dua, dubbed the channel as 'conformist' and alleged that the channel and other sections of the media looked like it was 'afraid of the government'.[456] But then Navika Kumar argued that her channel could not be criticized for the reports of its correspondents not being curbed by the authorities because, 'As far as *Times Now* is concerned, we have taken a position that removing Article 370 is a welcome step,' she said, referring to the reason for the unhindered reporting by its correspondents. 'We are not ambiguous about the stand we take.'[457] The implication was obvious that only that media will be allowed to work and report that presents only the Government's point of view. Moreover, since the cable news and all other communications had been cut off in the Valley, the permission to *Times Now* to file reports meant that the channel was not bringing news to the residents of the Valley but addressing the rest of the country with pro-government news and opinions about situation in Kashmir.

This kind of news and communications blackout had not happened even when Emergency was clamped in the country in 1975 by Congress Prime Minister Indira Gandhi. Ironically, during that period, routinely dubbed by the BJP as a black chapter in the history of the republic, current Prime Minister Narendra Modi and Defence Minister Rajnath Singh as well as Arun Jaitley, the 'go to man' of Prime Minister Modi in the earlier ministry, had opposed the Emergency and most of its leadership had been jailed. The government also took into custody the three former Chief Ministers, Dr Farooq Abdullah, Omar Abdullah and Mehbooba Mufti and another 400 political leaders of various denominations. To ensure that there was no possibility of any political opposition and unrest, about 4,000 political activists too are said to have been arrested to be later released on the condition that they will not criticize the government. 'Government officials have defended the clampdown, which has included the detention of at least 300 politicians and activists, as well as the addition of tens of thousands of soldiers in a region that was already one of the most militarized in the world. They rationalized that the measures were necessary for the security of the state's population'.[458]

Facing widespread criticism, India's Foreign minister S. Jaishankar defended the clampdown saying that this was done to prevent an outbreak of violence and civilian casualties, citing the unrest caused after the death of militant Burhan Wani in 2016.'He said that it was not possible to stop communication among militants without putting the entire region under a blackout…[and] justified the restrictions on phone and mobile services in Jammu and Kashmir saying that it was needed to stop communication between terrorists.'[459] He further added in an interview with *POLITICO* magazine in Brussels, that the internet and telephone outages were needed to stop the activation of 'terrorist assets' and to prevent 'people who are doing violence to contact each other…How do I cut off communications between the terrorists and their masters on the one hand, but keep the internet open for other people? I would be delighted to know,' Jaishankar added.[460] He forgot that this tactic was used earlier during the 2010 and post Burhan Wani unrest, and yet not only scores of civilians had lost their lives but the unrest had gone on for months. He also forgot that Arun Jaitley, senior leader of BJP, had also castigated the then government in 2008 for the communication clampdown under which the state had been placed during the Amarnath land allotment row.

The Government of Jammu and Kashmir defended the curbs, stating that the restrictions on internet access, among other restrictions, were imposed to preempt the disruption of public order by various 'anti-national' elements. It said that the misuse of data services and internet by 'terrorists' to conduct terrorism and to incite people by spreading fake news necessitated such restrictions and assured that they will be gradually reduced. The bottom line was that the BJP achieved in doing what it had resolved to do under the leadership of Dr Shyama Prasad Mukherjee almost 70 years ago, soon after Article 370 had been incorporated. Few political parties would go to such lengths to redeem a pledge it made, particularly when it has meant jumping into unknown territory, but then it can be said that an irredentist streak, and all that it means and stands for, is reflected in BJP and is very strong and that for irredentists, gesture and symbolism is much more important than the substance. For the BJP, the clock seemed to have stopped and Indian history was restarted from 1950 onwards.

After making Article 370 inoperative, the next political step was to dismantle the State of Jammu and Kashmir and bifurcate it—both into Union Territories. Thus, a State that was created brick by brick by the toil and blood of the Dogra armies in the nineteenth century, and had survived the scheming of the champions of imperialism in British Parliament, finally came to a tame end. It was also conveniently forgotten that if Ladakh was an integral part of India today, it was because Jammu had made it an integral part of the State of Jammu and Kashmir, and therefore, by extension, it was part of India. With it becoming a Union Territory, this was another leap into the unknown for no one could be sure of the reaction of Pakistan, to a lesser degree, and China on a much larger scale. How the two units, now UTs, will evolve was also not known. By and large, it was known what course Jammu will take but with the mutual hostility of Leh and Kargil in Ladakh, the danger was that the move will accentuate the communal divide in those regions.

The creation of Ladakh as a Union Territory was obviously met with boisterous joy in Leh region where the Buddhist population was in majority but gloom descended on Kargil. With a Muslim majority, it was unhappy since it was about to lose its preeminence in the new political construct. Many decades ago, when Sadar-i-Riyasat Karan Singh made his maiden trip to Ladakh in 1952 and saw for himself the isolation and poverty of the region, he had submitted a detailed note to Jawaharlal Nehru for paying special attention to the development of this strategically important part of the country.[461] The Dogra rulers had remained contented by letting the Ladakhis live their traditional lifestyle without interference. But after 1947 when cataclysmic changes had taken place in the State and its neighborhood, Ladakh too demanded change and modern development. That need had remained largely unattended and except for minor concessions and defence needs-driven development, the neglect and indifference had remained unchanged.

In Jammu, the people generally welcomed the move since they believed that the Article 370 had bred arrogance among the Kashmiri leadership making them immune to the needs and demands of others. However, it rued the fact that it had been downgraded from a State to Union Territory. Many also felt disappointment at the continued relationship with Kashmir because they were conscious that at the core of the Kashmir problem was conflict—political, socio-economic and religious—between the two regions, which had remained unaddressed. Representatives of the Kashmiri Hindu community, who were displaced from the Kashmir Valley as a result of ongoing violence was ecstatic and welcomed the move and expressed the hope that members of their community, estimated to be numbering between 2,00,000 and 4,00,000 people will be able to return though how that will happen, no one knew.

The Gujjar Bakarwals, Sikhs, Valmikis and West Pakistan refugees too, who were all victims of Srinagar's discriminatory laws, celebrated the revocation of Article 370 and 35A. In the rest of the country also the mood was euphoric among the people though there were odd voices of protest. The Congress, under whose aegis the Article had been negotiated and authored was divided on the issue, with a word of strong opposition and condemnation coming from Punjab's Congress Chief Minister, Amarinder Singh. He argued that a wrong precedent had been set and it was a threat to the federal character of the Constitution for now any State could be put under President's Rule and then the central government could assume the powers of the State legislature thereby authorizing the Governor to even reorganize the state without reference to the people. In Jammu and Kashmir, the Congress appeared to be in sixes and sevens with the Kashmiri leaders stunned but opposing the move. In Jammu, Dr Karan Singh cautiously and conditionally welcomed it, hoping that soon the statehood would be restored.

A widely acknowledged historian and commentator, Ramchandra Guha commented, 'This action of my government disturbed me because of its harshness, and because of how widely it was welcomed among the public at large. For many Indians, the troubles in Kashmir over the past few decades had been entirely caused by Pakistan, which bordered the state, claimed it as its own, and had in pursuit of its own agenda fomented three wars against India while sending a steady stream of terrorists into the Valley. If there was a secondary villain for this section of the Indian (read Hindu) public, it was the Kashmiri Muslims, for not adequately showing their gratitude to India for the special privileges that had been granted them, and for the sin and crime of having purged the Valley of the Hindu residents (known as Pandits) who had once lived there. Therefore, this abrogation of Article 370 was seen as a slap in the face of Pakistan, and a justified slap on the face of the ostensibly pampered Kashmiris too. On social media, raucous Hindu majoritarians exuded a naked triumphalism, some exulting in the possibility of owning homes overlooking lakes in the Valley, others indulging cruder fantasies of possessing beautiful Kashmiri women.' Guha also wondered: 'The timing of the government's clampdown on Kashmir was also strange. Narendra Modi had just been re-elected with an impressive majority; at a time when the faltering economy needed urgent attention, and foreign investment was not forthcoming, why risk adverse international publicity by such a draconian measure? Was, one wondered, the action driven by majoritarian hubris, by the desire to rid India of its only Muslim-majority state?'[462]

Legally, a number of petitions were filed and the Supreme Court clubbed them together. Petitions were also filed against the draconian curbs on the communications but even after months the apex court had failed to help the citizens secure their fundamental right though in one judgment it did acknowledge that access to internet did constitute fundamental right. Most of the cases continue to be pending and Faizan Mustafa, Vice Chancellor NALSAR (National Academy of Legal Studies and Research) University of Law, Hyderabad had sounded a note of gloomy warning when he commented that, 'No one can predict what will be the outcome of the legal challenge in Supreme Court, but our experience has been that when you have governments with massive majorities, courts stay away from political questions. When there are coalition governments, they assert their power little more and I have a feeling that when it comes to their own powers, they jealously guard them. But when it comes to constitution, citizen's liberties, same kind of anxiety is not demonstrated by the courts. So, at best the court will refer this question to the constitution bench and the matter will be decided after 2-3 years, by that time it will become redundant.'[463]

It took more than four years for the Supreme Court to take up a matter that was not only vital for a large section of the society but also had great bearing on the federal characteristic of the Constitution. Even a habeas corpus petition for 82-years-old Safiuddin Soz, a Congress leader, suffered repeated deferments in the Supreme Court. It is not too long ago that even a postcard was taken up urgently and treated as a Public Interest Litigation by the Supreme Court of India!

The constitutionality of the reorganization of the State was even more controversial. Mustafa had argued in the same interview and questioned that, 'before 5th of August, you had Article 3(1) one exception created for Jammu and Kashmir which said 'concurrence' is needed of the Legislative Assembly. Not 'ascertainment of views'. So, when was before 5th of August, this bill referred to the Legislative Assembly? After 5th August, it [Jammu and Kashmir] becomes an ordinary State and like any other State, views of the Legislative Assembly are to be ascertained. Now 'views' are not 'powers.' There is a distinction between views and powers. Parliament can exercise the 'power' on behalf of the Legislative Assembly. But here public expression of 'views' of peoples representatives of that state must come to public fore.' In this context, 'just recall about Telangana. The bill was referred in 2013 December to Andhra Assembly. [Eighty-four]...members in Assembly, 54 members in Council participated. [Nine thousand]... amendment bills were moved. They rejected it. Still Parliament enacted the Law. But there was an expression of views. There is a difference between individual's freedom of speech which is subject to reasonable restrictions and Parliament or Assembly's privilege to speak which is absolute.'[464]

But as Faizan Mustafa suspected, in these times, when the parliament is dominated by one political party and there was widespread sentiment pervading in the country that Kashmiri Muslims needed to be taught a lesson, the hope of getting redress at the hands of the courts was remote. A former Director General of Police, Ashok Bhan, of the State reflected that 'the adjournments of petitions challenging the validity of the constitutional changes as well as hesitation in holding the executive accountable in habeas corpus petitions, restrictions on media and the internet, are being perceived as denial of legitimate legal remedies.'[465] During the past few years, the judicial pronouncements have tended to validate the actions of the State rather than give protection to an individual from its highhandedness.

***

Finally, after fifteen days of sitting by, the Constitutional Bench consisting of five judges and headed by Chief Justice D.Y. Chandrachud, delivered its judgment upholding the scrapping of Article 370 on 11 December 2023. The Court held that the 'declaration issued by the President in the exercise of the power under Article 370(3) is a culmination of the process of integration. Thus, we do not find that the President's exercise under the Article 370(3) was mala fide.' The court also rejected the contention that Article 370, though temporary, had assumed permanence, as found by another Supreme Court judgment of 2018. It concluded that it was a temporary provision meant to bring the State gradually into the fold of the Indian Constitution. It held that the Article prevented the residents of J&K from being treated on par with other citizens of India.

The Court however, disapproved the manner in which Article 370 was amended as it had amended Article 367 to achieve its purpose. In other words, it had used the provision of one Article to alter another. Yet, the bench decided that since the Union Government had assured the court that statehood would be soon restored, therefore, there was no need to go into the reorganization of the State and creating two Union Territories.

There is little doubt that except for Kashmir, the whole of the country has welcomed the judgment and Dr Karan Singh, speaking to *The Indian Express*, advised the people of Kashmir to accept this decision and move on to focus their energies on the forthcoming elections. But the moot question is, are communities so orderly that they accept the changing circumstances with the same sense of acceptance with which they accept changing weathers? One is man-made, and the other, by Nature. One can only hope that somehow peace and normalcy return but with the manner in which the delimitation exercise has been held and amendments introduced, one suspects that the next stage of confrontation is being prepared for. The fact that every inch of Kashmir has the presence of security forces indicates to a neutral observer that the Government does not have the confidence to allow normal life in the Valley to return. The Government claims that life is back to normal and as evidence claims the elections to the local bodies have been held ever since the abrogation of Article 370. But the number of votes cast belies the claim of normalcy. While it is true that there has been a manifold increase in the footfall of the tourists, it is because a vast majority of the Kashmiri population have no choice but to bite the bullet and entertain the tourists since it is their livelihood and tides them over during the bleak months of winter.

Kashmir is deeply hurt and offended and the silence of the people should not be taken as a sign of acceptance of the new normal. The truth of Kashmir today should worry those for whom nationalism and country are not words to be used for only whipping emotions and scoring political points. The ordinary Kashmiri, particularly the youth, is drifting away from India. The warning of former DGP Ashok Bhan needs to be taken seriously and not contemptuously brushed aside in the mistaken belief of the security forces being in total control. Bhan says, 'There is a surge in local recruitment to terrorist ranks in south Kashmir. An overwhelming majority of terrorists killed in the hinterland are local youth, some of them having joined terrorist ranks in the past few weeks or months. They are 'gravely hurt' at the loss of the special status. Such misgivings need to be discounted and reversed. Leaving this for the uniformed forces to handle alone, through restrictions, arrests and detentions, is fraught with dangerous consequences… There is a menacing disquiet in the air. It is time to redeem the situation through political and administrative outreach. In a political vacuum and in the absence of a vibrant civil back-up, the forces face a daunting challenge. They can only bring terrorist violence down to manageable levels and make the situation conducive for political outreach. Peace will remain elusive if these measures are not taken.'[466]

Moreover, no one should be carried away by the fact that militants have a very limited life before they are eliminated, for they are the sons and brothers of the local residents and their deaths at the hands of the security forces reinforces the opinion that they died for a cause. This distances them further from the idea of India.

16

Ladakh

'He who climbs upon the highest mountains laughs at all tragedies, real or imaginary.'

—Friedrich Nietzsche

Understandably, the Independence Day of 2019, after becoming a Union Territory, was marked by Ladakh as its 'first Independence Day'. The Ladakhis were clearly alluding to their long and checkered history, sometimes as an independent state and at others a satellite state, but also underlining its resentment against Kashmir as well as the Dogras, who in the first place had denied them their independence in 1834. But digging a little deeper into the history it reveals that on the international stage, Ladakh, more than Kashmir, has been the subject of dispute, less between two major civilizations that lie towards its east and south—China and India—but more between the competing ambition of independence of the Ladakhis and the hegemonic tendencies of the Tibetans, with whom it shares not only the borders but historical, religious and cultural ties. With the mainland of India, however, its ties go back deep into history and culture.

There is not much information on Ladakh before the tenth century CE, yet there are certain inscriptions in Brahmi character belonging to 200 BCE which furnish substantial evidence of Ladakh's association with India right from the second century BCE.[467] It is said that around 250 BCE, Ladakh came to be ruled by Litsaby (in all probability of Lichhavi) race[468]. In another account he is said to belong to 200 BCE, and might have been banished from his homeland.

Lichhavis professed belief in *Swasti*, from which they derived their names of *Swastikas*. Cunningham writes that the very fact that *Swastikas* migrated from India and settled in Tibet can be estimated from the nomenclature, which was assigned to them in Tibetan. Being the followers of, what scholars like to call *swastika*, the Indian symbol, and what the westerners call the mystic cross, the Lichhavis believed in the doctrine of eternal annihilation after death, from which they derived their Tibetan name of *Mu-stegs-pa*. The Lichhavis also called themselves *Tirthakara*, or 'pure-doers' and the synonymous name of *Punya*, 'the pure', was carried with them into Tibet, where it was revered for ages, and continues to survive as *Pon*. Ladakh's relations with India also persisted under Asoka, credited with the introduction of Buddhism in Ladakh. After the third Buddhist council,[469] Asoka sent missionaries to the distant lands including Ladakh for the propagation of the Buddhism and August Hermann Francke, a German Tibetologist, believes that this was not just a religious mission; it had political motives too.

The proof of political connectivity of Ladakh with India becomes more evident during the reign of king Kanishka under whom it was included in the dominions of Kushana Empire, which comprised of a considerable part of the Indian subcontinent. The fact that Ladakh was part of the Kushana Empire is also substantiated by the famous Kharosthi inscription of Uvima Kavthisa found near the K'a-la-rtse (also spelt Khaltse) bridge on the Indus. Though the chronology of the Kushanas has never been satisfactorily settled, the inscription proves that in the first or second century CE, lower Ladakh was included in the Kushana empire. In addition, not only are the Brahmi and Kharosthi inscriptions found at a number of places but there are a number of Sanskrit names and words that were in vogue indicating to the close affinity between the two. About the post Kushana period in Ladakh, Francke writes:

> As regards politics, Western Tibet or Ladakh, did not come under the Chinese, when the power of the Kushana declined. It was apparently governed by local chiefs, whose names have been occasionally preserved in inscriptions and tales. Thus, at

> Khal-tse according to a Gupta inscription, a certain Satya-wati (or Shrimacharpati), and according to oral reports, fifty or sixty miles higher up the Indus *valley*, a certain Suryawati are mentioned.[470]

It is only from eighth century CE that we come to know that Ladakh came under the suzerainty of Tibet. This fact is substantiated by a glimpse of this region that we get in the travels of Hui-Ch'ao, a Chinese pilgrim who made the journey from India to Central Asia in 727 CE. He mentions three kingdoms lying to the north-east of Kashmir, which he describes as follows:

> Under the suzerainty of Tibetans…The country is narrow and small, and the mountains and *valleys* very ragged. There are monasteries and monks and the people venerate faithfully the three jewels. As to the kingdom of Tibet to the East, there are no monasteries at all and Buddha's teaching is unknown; but in the [three above-mentioned] countries the population consists of Hu, therefore they are believers.

The same source tells us that Ladakh was inhabited mainly by the people of non-Tibetan stock (Darads) who had embraced Buddhism, whereas in Tibet proper, Buddhism was not yet popular.[471]

A number of accounts indicate that during the second half of the eighth and the first half of the ninth century, Ladakh, being a peripheral state, must have been under the loose suzerainty of Tibet. But the political suzerainty of Tibet notwithstanding, the main cultural component of Ladakh was very much Indian in disposition and this influence was especially transmitted via Kashmir. During this period Buddhism had penetrated deep beyond the Zoji-la, as shown by the Sarda inscriptions at Dras and Chigtan which seem to go back to a period 700-1200 CE. 'The rock engravings in deep relief found at various places of [Kargil] Zanskar, Dras and Mulbekh certainly exhibit the influences from Indian form of Buddhism. The best known is the Bodhisattva Maitreya [Chamba] at Mulbekh, dated 8th century CE and in style they are purely Indo-Gandhar. Consequently, at the beginning of the tenth century, Buddhism was in a flourishing state in Western Ladakh (roughly the present Kargil district). The decline of Buddhism especially in north India may have resulted in the immigration into Ladakh of large number of Indian Buddhist monks who brought with them their own traditions of iconography and worship. This immigration further strengthened the cultural and religious links between Ladakh and Indian subcontinent, which may have been maintained for more than a thousand years from the 2nd century BCE to the 12th century CE-well into the period of rule by an originally Tibetan dynasty and even after.'[472]

Ironically, despite these strong and close cultural ties, Ladakh was often subjected to invasions by Kashmir. It is possible that revenue or trade disputes led to these invasions and they are recorded by Kalhana[473] who wrote in his *Rajtarangini*[474] that Ladakh (Tibet) was conquered by the Kashmiri ruler Lalitaditya (699-733 CE). According to Aurel Stein this claim is based upon the historical fact since it is recorded in the Tang Annals, that an ambassador from Lalitaditya's court visited the imperial court of China, where he distinctly claimed for his master victories over the Tibetans. Lalitaditya was said to have blocked all the five great routes leading to Tibet and had also entered into an alliance with the Chinese against their common foe—the Tibetans, who had by then established a strong and influential empire, which was powerful enough to lead an aggression westwards and Lalitaditya would have endeavored to be secure against this danger with the help of a Chinese alliance. Ironically, the visit by Lalitaditya's envoy to the Imperial Court of China is interpreted by Chinese as a mark of Kashmir's submission to China and the gifts as a tribute of a subordinate king. However, history does not record that Lalitaditya established his rule over Tibet after conquering this region but it can be surmised that because of its difficult access from Kashmir and the fact that the Zoji-la Pass remained closed for almost six months in a year, it would have fallen on the periphery of Lalitaditya's empire and hence difficult to effectively administer. The region, therefore, continued to be ruled by Tibet during all those years.

After the collapse of the Tibetan monarchy after 842 CE, Tibetan suzerainty in Ladakh ended. It was the collapse of the Tibetan monarchy that gave rise to independent Ladakhi kingdom. According to the Tibetan chronicles, a break-away prince from Tibet, dPal-gyi-mgon of Nyima-Gon dynasty, or as some others call him Sklde Nyimagon, was the earliest ruler of the kingdom of Ladakh. He had fled Lhasa to Ngari in western Tibet or eastern Ladakh and settled at Maryul, the original name of Ladakh, where he married the daughter of a local chieftain who gave birth to three sons. He was the real founder and organizer of the Ladakhi kingdom. This has been the foundational truth of Ladakh which has found echoes in subsequent history, including the important and landmark treaty of 1684 between Tibet and Ladakh.

The chronicles of Ladakh also give the list of the 13 successors of dPal-gyi-mgon who ruled Ladakh. The first son, Paldegon, ruled over Maryul (Ladakh), second son Tashigon ruled over the area around Mount Sangpo (Zanskar and Spiti) and the third, Detsugon controlled the area of Guge, with Mount Kailash as its capital. The three regions symbolize the water, mountain and grassland. This is how it remained till the sixteenth century when a local chieftain, Bhagan of Basgo, overthrew the earlier king of Ladakh and established his own dynasty, Namgyal. His successors, Tashi Namgyal and Tsewang Namgyal consolidated the Ladakh kingdom between 1555 and 1595 and extended the borders up to Nepal. Successor of Tsewang Namgyal, his eldest son, Jamyang Namgyal ruled till 1616. Although a Buddhist, he married a Muslim princess from Baltistan, the daughter of the ruler Ali Sher Anchan. In due course, the princess, Gyal Khatun, gave birth to a son named Singge Namgyal meaning 'the lion king' in 1570. Ladakh history considers him the greatest king who gave decisive historical turn to its history which finds echoes in the contemporary disputes that afflict its borders.

Among all these developments, rulers of the Ladakh kingdom were always keen to have cultural ties with the Indian subcontinent and there are numerous references to make this fact evident. This was more so because they were wary of Tibetan cultural influence since they considered it to be just a step away from the political influence and intervention. For instance, the inscriptions of king Lha-bla-ma-ye-shes'od of Guge (1025 CE), who resided at mTho-lding, state that the king was not happy with the Tibetan influence on the Buddhism in his dominions, and resolved to purify it by bringing it into contact with Indian-Buddhism. Therefore, he sent

21 young monks, to Kashmir and distant parts of India to receive instructions in Sanskrit and philosophy and he himself invited 13 Indian pundits (monks) and secured their services. The king had, in addition, heard of the famous Buddhist monk, Atisha, who was residing at the monastery of Vikramasila in Magdha and sent an embassy to him with a large quantity of gold and invited him to Guge. The monk, however, was not inclined to come and it was only after considerable persuasions that he finally agreed.

It is apparent that after Lalitaditya, as the dark period engulfed the Indian mainland, political connectivity betweeen it and Ladakh too diminished and for the next few centuries, Ladakh's ties with the Indian subcontinent remained more in terms of religion, culture and commercial rather than political. This changed again from twelfth century onwards, and we learn from the *Rajatarangini* of Jonaraja, that the *rgyal-bu*, Rinchana, a Ladakhi chief usurped the throne of Kashmir and ruled there from CE 1320-1323. Rinchana also married Kota Rani, the daughter of Ram Chandra, the Prime Minister of king Suhadeva (1300-1320 CE) of Kashmir and also founded a town Rinchanpura after his name.[475] According to Jonaraja, Rinchana not only established peace and order in Kashmir after the devastation caused by Zulju the Mongol but also proved to be an able administrator. The very acceptance of Rinchana as a ruler by the people of Kashmir and his praise by the local chronicler exhibits the bond which people of both the regions had mutually shared. The cultural and commercial ties, shared over the centuries, are well known since Kashmir had brisk trade relations with Ladakh and the regions beyond Ladakh from times immemorial. Political confrontations between the two regions too were not uncommon, presumably over trade disputes since craftsmen of Kashmir have always flourished when there is uninterrupted trade between Kashmir and Ladakh and beyond and have suffered when it is disrupted.

Consequently, after the establishment of the Sultanate in Kashmir, Ladakh was frequently subjected to invasions of the sultans of Kashmir. The first Sultan of Kashmir to conquer Ladakh was Shihabu'd Din (1354-73). Along with Ladakh, he also conquered Gilgit, Dardu (Skardu) and Baltistan.[476] From Jonaraja's

Rajatarangini, we find that Ladakh was made to submit by Sultan Zain-ul Abidin (1420-1470 CE) too. Immediately after his accession, Zain-ul Abidin led an expedition against Tibet including Ladakh.[477] From Jonaraja's account one can infer that Zain-ul Abidin marched as far as Guge (Goggadesa as it was also called). It seems that Shey was also sacked in the course of the invasion, where the Sultan saved a golden statue of Buddha from the hands of his soldiers (in Sayadesa.). The name Sayadesa may stand for the present Shey as well as for the whole of Ladakh, of which Shey was the capital in olden times.[478] In 1451, Baltistan was again conquered by Adham Khan, the eldest son of Zain-ul Abidin. In 1483, Ladakh had to again face an invasion from Kashmir and Sultan Hasan Shah (1472-1484) sent a force to subjugate Ladakh and Baltistan. Both had reasserted their independence after the death of Zain-ul Abidin, while the Kashmiris emerged as victorious in Baltistan, in Ladakh they had to face a severe defeat.[479] This period brought much uncertainty since for nearly two centuries Ladakh was subjected to the raids and invasions from Kashmir. This indicated the resolve of Kashmir rulers as well as the defiance and resilience of the Ladakhis and it can be presumed that there were unequal arrangements over the tribute as well as the trade conditions. Matching the frequency of the trade caravans on the Lhasa-Leh-Srinagar was the alternative route to India from Lhasa-Nepal-Patna, a route that could easily be favored by Tibet to reach out to Indian mainland markets.

In 1545 C.E., Mirza Haidar Dughlat, a Chagtai from Kashgar who later became the Governor of Kashmir, invaded and conquered Ladakh but his hold was only tenuous, so in 1548, he again launched a large-scale operation conquering 'little Tibet' (Baltistan) and 'Great Tibet' (Ladakh), as they were also known and appointed governors for his new dominions, Mullah Qasim, for 'little Tibet' (*Tibet-i-Khurd*) or Baltistan and Mullah Hasan for 'Great Tibet' (*Tibet-i-Kalan*) or Ladakh. Again, this rule turned out to be nominal; in any case every trace of it vanished after Mirza's death in 1551 C.E. The persistent efforts of the rulers from Chak dynasty notwithstanding, the impact of their invasions never had any enduring influence because the Ladakhis, whenever they found the opportunity, reasserted their independence.

This was a period in which major developments affecting the course of Ladakh and sub-continental history was made. The Mughal interest in Ladakh left an indelible mark and rewrote the relationship underlining the political and economic underpinnings of both. In fact, the Mughal showed a keen interest in the subjugation of Ladakh especially after the conquest of Kashmir because of the several important reasons, not the least being the shawl industry of Kashmir, which was the most income generating industry as the Kashmiri shawls were in great demand in the foreign lands and fetched high prices. But the wool for the hand-weaving of these shawls primarily came from Tibet and therefore the trade routes needed to be secured for the uninterrupted supply of *pashm*, the raw wool needed for *pashmina* shawls. Jahangir informs in his *Tuzuk-i-Jahangir*: 'The wool for shawl comes from a goat which is peculiar to Tibet.'[480]

French traveler Bernier has explicitly remarked that the finest shawls of Kashmir were made from the wool which was imported from 'Great Tibet.'[481]In order to ensure a continuous supply of the *Pashm* or the sheep wool, Mughals always tried to exert their authority upon the region of Ladakh. Second important reason for the Mughal interest in Ladakh was that Ladakh was an important mart on the trade route from Kashmir to Central Asia and China, which further signifies the commercial importance which was held by this region. The last reason, but not the least, this region was also known for the production of gold. Leh and Kargil were the entrepôt where traders and their caravans gathered from the Indian subcontinent, Tibet, China and central Asia. The Mughal chroniclers, right from Mirza Muhammad Haidar Dughlat to Inayat Khan, provide interesting information about the extraction of Gold in Ladakh and Tibet. For instance, Abul Fazl records the availability of the gold in abundance in the Tibet: 'Although gold is imported into Hindustan, it is to be found in abundance in the northern mountains of the country, as also in Tibet. Gold may also be obtained by the Saloni—process from the sand of the Ganges and Indus, and several other rivers, as most of the waters of this country are mixed with gold…'[482]

And the first initiative to bring this region under his control was taken by Mughal Emperor Akbar. Abul Fazl informs us that both Ladakh and Baltistan submitted their allegiance to Akbar and frequently sent gifts to the Mughal court as a mark of tribute and Akbar adopted a conciliatory policy towards them: 'One of the occurrences was the sending of an ambassador to Tibet. When the sound of the world conquering armies reached that country, the rulers thereof had not the courage to come personally to the sublime court. They remained in bewilderment. As they showed obedience by continually sending presents, M. Beg was sent to 'Ali Rai the ruler of Little Tibet and Mulla Isfahani and Mihtar Yari to the ruler of great Tibet.' Soothing and encouraging words were written to them.'[483]

A matrimonial alliance was also made between the Mughals and the ruler of Baltistan, and the daughter of the ruler of Balitstan was married to Prince Salim. Tibet's subordination to the Mughals continued during the reign of Shahjahan too. We are told by Inyat Khan, author of the *Shahjahanama*, that the rulers of Tibet, most probably Baltistan, occasionally sent the tributary offerings to the Mughal emperor Shahjahan: 'On the 7th of Ramzan 1043 (7 March 1634), a tributary offering from the Abdal Khan Zamindar of Tibet, together with nine gold mohurs [coin] honored with his majesty's stamp, was brought into presence. Through the guidance of destiny and laudable exertions of Zafar Khan, governor of Kashmir…the said Abdal Khan had been induced to pay homage to the crown, and to have the Khutba read and coinage struck in the illustrious names and titles of the monarch of the age.'[484] The general use of the word in these texts should not be understood as the main land of Tibet but the generic name of *Tibet-e-Kalan* and *Tibet-e-Khurd* given to Ladakh and Baltistan region respectively.

The *Shahjahanama* gives an interesting account of the Mughal conquest of Ladakh and Baltistan and the political relations between the Ladakhis, Baltis and the Mughals. In fact, from the *Shahjahanama* we get the information about the varied subjects related to Ladakh and Baltistan—such as forts, the trade routes, Zamindars of the region, etc. The conquest of Tibet has also been described by Inayat Khan in a very intriguing manner. For him the subjugation of Tibet was a most consequential event of the Mughal

Empire. He not only gives an explicit description of the conquest of Tibet and Ladakh, but also discloses that Mughal Emperor Jahangir had earlier too made an attempt to subdue Ladakh, but failed to accomplish this task.

Consequently, Zafar Khan, who was the governor of Kashmir under Shahjahan, volunteered for the invasion of Ladakh and received Shahjahan's permission to conquer it, informs Inayat Khan, the son of Zafar Khan. Inayat Khan further informs that on the arrival of the royal army under Zafar Khan in that vicinity, they had to face a tough resistance from Abdal, a *Zamindar* (Chief) of Tibet. After defeating Abdal, Zafar Khan further proceeded to Skardu. Inayat Khan writes that forts of Tibet were the main obstructions in the way of the Mughal advancement. In fact, he was very much fascinated by the strength of the forts of Tibet especially those of Ali Rai, Shigar, Garewcha and Ganjak and mentions that there were 37 forts in Tibet and Ladakh and these forts provided considerable protection to the local rulers and the natives from the Mughal forces.

Inayat Khan acknowledges that one of the major factors that ensured Mughal victory in Tibet was that the soldiery and peasantry of Tibet were highly dissatisfied with Abdal's rule and this situation helped Zafar Khan and he exploited it to ensure his victory. The account of Inayat Khan ascertains the fact that Ladakh was strategically as well as commercially so important to the Mughals, that despite so many challenges and complications, they made every possible endeavor to retain their hold upon it. Very interesting information regarding the Mughal policy towards Baltistan and Ladakh comes from the French traveler Bernier too, who says that there was dissidence in the royal family of Baltistan (Little Tibet) and one of the princes of the royal family approached the Mughal governor of Kashmir for help. Accordingly, the Mughal Governor, under the orders of Shahjahan, went to help the prince.

This was a period of considerable turmoil in the Chinese history, with the Imperial Court having lost control over its peripheral territories, including Tibet, which in its own turn had lost suzerainty over Ladakh which had emerged as an independent empire. Neighboring Kashmir too had lost its autonomy, when the

Mughal emperor Akbar conquered it. In the emerging turmoil, the interference of Kashmir in the affairs Ladakh too had loosened. Bernier, has narrated about the conflict between Kashmir and Ladakh with the addition of interesting information that this conflict had serious repercussion for Ladakh. Soon thereafter, King Sinnge, in his annoyance, blocked the trade route to and from Kashmir and barred the movements of the caravans through Ladakh and also forbade any person to enter his territories from Kashmir. Bernier noticed this blockade even at the time of his visit to Kashmir in the year 1663. The result was that the traffic from India to Central Tibet drifted to the Patna-Nepal-Lhasa route, while the trade of Kashmir and Central Asia switched to another route via Peshawar, Skardu and Shigar to Kashgar. This act of Singge had serious repercussions on the economy and political influence of Ladakh, which had always been dependent upon transit trade. Thereafter began the weakening of the economy and strength of the kingdom of Ladakh, consequently, after the death of Singge Namgyal. This decision is generally attributed as the cause of Ladakh's decline.[485] Nevertheless, by loosening the general control of the big neighboring powers, Singge Namgyal, the 'lion king', had the opportunity to consolidate the western Himalayas into one political unit. By the time he died, 'his kingdom expanded to the border of Nepal in the east, Baltistan in the west, Karakoram in the north, and Spiti-Zanskar in the south.'[486] Domestically, he pursued a far-sighted policy for the expansion of trade with Tibet, Nepal, Spiti-Kangra Valley and Punjab. However, later when he pursued the self-defeating policy of closing the routes, things changed though prior to that he had paid great attention to developing trade with Kashmir as well as the fabled Silk Route towards west in Sinkiang (Xinjiang). Importantly, although born to a Muslim mother, he remained a devout Buddhist and offered legal rights over a series of monasteries near Mount Kailash to Bhutan's Shabdrung Ngawang Namgyal.

Unfortunately, his successors met a different fate since the conflict with Kashmir and the blocking of the trade routes had resulted in the diminishing strength of Ladakh and they ran into the aggressive policies of the Fifth Dalai Lama. China's Qing Dynasty too had regained some of its lost poise and was ready to take control of its peripheral regions. Thus, even as Tibet too lost its autonomy, Ladakh felt the full impact of the China sponsored Tibet aggression. As a result, Ladakh had to face the onslaught of the Chinese Mongol and Tibet Army and was forced to appeal for help to the Mughal Emperor Aurangzeb who deputed the Governor of Kashmir to provide military help. With the imminent threat averted, Ladakh was left floundering on the religious front since the Mughal emperor had stipulated that the new Namgyal not only build a mosque in Leh but also convert to Islam. The legend goes that though the Namgyal converted, none of his family members became Muslims and soon he too continued not only with his original name but also reverted to the Buddhist prayers and lifestyle.

Another version of this war was that, 'Tibet-Ladakh-Mughal War of 1679 was fought between Gelug Tibetan government and the Drukpa Kingdom of Ladakh. The Tibetan Ganden Phodrang government under Fifth Dalai Lama dispatched military mission in 1679 under the command of Zungar Mongol commander, Galdan Boshugtu Khan...who was a lama of the Tashilunpo monastery in Lhasa. The aim of the war was to subjugate Drukpa rule and impose the Gelug order in Ladakh.'[487] In the ensuing battle, Ladakhi forces were defeated and more than half of the kingdom built by Sinnge Namgyal was lost to Tibet but somehow, Ladakhi king Deldan held on to the forts of Basgo and Tingmosgang for at least three years before he sought the intervention of the Mughal emperor who sent help through the governor of Kashmir on the condition that a mosque will be built in Leh.[488] As a result of Mughal help, the Ladakh-Mughal Army defeated the Tibetan-Mongol Army near the plains of Nimoo, 25 kms west of Leh. A mosque was built in Leh but Ladakhi sources insist that neither their ruler nor the people embraced Islam. Whatever the truth, the consequence was that in 1684, the Fifth Dalai Lama again launched an attack to decimate Ladakh and this time, it is said, the Mughals were paid off[489] by him. The Ladakhis were defeated and Tibet wrested western Tibet or eastern Ladakh, including the regions of Rudok, Guge, Kailash, Burang up to Nepal border junction which were an integral part of Ladakh. Forced to sign the Treaty of Tingmosgang in 1684, Ladakh was compelled to part with the regions of Guge and Purang that constituted half of its territory. Ladakhis claim that partisan and selfish role was played by the Drukpa Lama, Sixth Drukchen Rinpoche Mipham Wangpo, who was brought in by Tibet to broker peace, and the brokered treaty not only stripped Ladakh of half of its territory but also authorized the Drukpa Lama to rule the entire Ngari-khor-sum region of eastern Ladakh comprising of Mount Kailash, Mansarover etc.

In fact, the provisions of the Tingmosgang Treaty of 1684[490] still reverberate in the Sino-Indian relationships since some of the provisions gave certain rights to Ladakh that have a bearing on contemporary times. Ladakhi sources claim that the Drukpa (red sect) Omniscient Lama, named Mee-pham-wangpo, who in his former incarnations had always been the patron Lama of the kings of Ladakh, from generation to generation, was sent from Lhasa to Tashis-gang (Tingmosgang), to arrange the conditions of a treaty of peace for the Ladakh king who could never refuse to abide by the decision of the Omniscient One. It also defined the borders though they were not demarcated in the modern sense. The Treaty reads as follows:

1. The boundaries fixed, in the beginning, when king Skyed-Ida-ngeema-gon gave a kingdom to each of his three sons, shall still be maintained.

2. Only Ladakis shall be permitted to enter into Ngarees-Khorsum wool trade.

3. No person from Ladak, except the royal trader of the Ladak Court, shall be permitted to enter Rudok.

4. A royal trader shall be sent by the Deywa Zhung (i.e. the grand Lama of Lhasa), from Lhasa to Ladak, once a year, with 200 horse-loads of tea.

5. A "Lo-chhak" shall be sent every third year from Leh to Lhasa with presents. As regards the quality and value of presents brought for all ordinary Lamas, the matter is of no consequences, but to the Labrang Chhakdzot shall be given the following articles, viz.: (a) Gold dust—the weight of 1 zho [about 3.7 g] 10 times. (b) Saffron—the weight of 1 srang (or thoorsrang) [about 185 g] 10 times. (c) Yarkhand cotton cloth—6 pieces. (d) Thin cotton cloth—1 piece.

> The members of the Lochak Mission shall be provided with provisions, free of cost, during their stay at Lhasa, and for the journey they shall be similarly provided with 200 baggage animals, 25 riding ponies, and 10 servants. For the uninhabited portion of the journey, tents will be supplied for the use of the Mission.
>
> 6. The country of Ngarees-khorsum shall be given to the Omniscient Drukpa Lama, Mee-pham-wang-po, and in lieu thereof the Deywa Zhung will give to the Ladak king three other districts (in Great Tibet).
>
> 7. The revenue of the Ngarees-khorsum shall be set aside for the purpose of defraying the cost of sacrificial lambs, and of religious ceremonies to be performed at Lhasa.
>
> 8. But the king of Ladak reserves to himself the village (or district?) of Monthser (i.e., Minsar) in Ngarees-khorsum, that he may be independent there; and he sets aside its revenue for the purpose of meeting the expense involved in keeping up the sacrificial lights at Kang-ree (i.e., Kailas), and the Holy Lakes of Manasarowar [Manasarovar] and Rakas Tal.
>
> With reference to the first clause of the treaty, it may be explained that, roughly speaking, King Skyed-Ida-ngeema-gon gave the following territories to his sons:
>
> a. To the eldest son—The countries now known as Ladak and Purig, extending from Hanley on the east to the Zojila Pass on the west, and including Rudok and the Gogpo gold district.
>
> b. To the second son—Googey, Poorang and certain other small districts.
>
> c. To the third son—Zangskar, Spiti, and certain other small districts.

This treaty, that should be the basis of border demarcation between India and Tibet—and, therefore China—, unequivocally gives the revenue districts of Mount Kailash, Manasarovar and a few other villages in that region to Ladakh. Thus, since Ladakh was a part of the Jammu and Kashmir State, it automatically became a part of India after the Accession to India in 1947. Though the treaty of 1684 stripped Ladakh of almost half its territory yet it had given right to the ruler of Ladakh revenue control over a few villages of Menser at the foot of Mount Kailash on the banks of Manasarovar

Lake.[491] It is also very interesting to notice that clause 5 of the treaty detailing the Lo-chhak or *Lo-phayag* mission that Ladakh was to pay triennial tribute to Dalai Lama in Lhasa, was religiously observed till the civil war in China between the communists and the Nationalist government disrupted it in the 1940. It finally came to an end with the takeover of Lhasa by the new Communist regime and the People's Liberation Army of China, and the flight of the Dalai Lama to India. It is also pertinent to mention that over a period of time this caravan meant to discharge an obligation under the Tingmosgang treaty evolved into a tribute-cum-trade mission since those carrying the tribute also carried with them goods to trade in Lhasa. This mission would, after a long and arduous journey, return the following year with Tibetan and Chinese goods in demand in Ladakh and Kashmir.

It is also very interesting to notice that the privilege to lead this mission was granted to a Muslim family—Radhu—based in Leh but originally from Srinagar. Abdul Wahid Radhu writes: 'It was a tribute-cum-trade mission, decreed by the 1684 Treaty of Tingmosgang. It was signed following a five-year war that was fought by monarchic (Buddhist) Ladakh in alliance with Mughal (Muslim) Kashmir against an army of ecclesiastic (Buddhist) Tibet in alliance with tribal (shamanist) Mongol.'[492]

The eclectic nature of the times can be judged by the fact that there were many families, particularly in trade, that had some members based in Lhasa or Kashgar because of the nature of their professions. Along with them, because of the significance of both the places on the Silk Road, there were numerous families from various nationalities living there. However, in the 1940s when the movement in China to right the wrongs of history that were inflicted upon them at a time when the Imperial Court was considerably weakened, led to a xenophobic trend, that made it difficult for the people from the Indian subcontinent to continue to live there. The 1684 Treaty of Tingmosgang had remained unaltered in the years after signing and not even the passing of Ladakh from the hands of local rulers to Dogras in 1834 had changed its status because this clause was retained in the 1842 treaty between Dogra Raja Gulab Singh and Tibet.

The negative fallout of the 1684 Treaty of Tingmosgang for Ladakh was that it had been rendered considerably weakened with the loss of territory and its economy and political independence became suspect. Not surprisingly, Ladakh's rehabilitation fell to the Dogra Raja Gulab Singh whose General Zorawar Singh dethroned the local ruler Tshepal Namgyal and subjugated Ladakh. It is intriguing to notice that not much attention has been paid by historians to the reasons of Zorawar Singh's campaign into western Tibet. Neither were his subsequent failure, death and annihilation of his army much written about. It is routinely described as a campaign of an intrepid and ambitious General who overstretched himself. But now, Phunchok Stobdan, a Ladakhi career diplomat and geostrategic thinker has suggested that 'It seems the Dogras wanted to recapture the lost territory of Ladakh from the Tibetans.'[493] This is not surprising since with the deprivation of the Guge region, Tibet had the option of trading with India from Almora or Bashahr routes at the cost of Ladakh. The conditions of the 1842 Treaty of Chushul and the Agreement between Tibet and Raja Gulab Singh made this very clear since it stipulated that all trade from Tibet will be routed through Leh.

It also needs recalling that the relationship between Ladakh and Tibet is the classic but rare case of 'two countries, one nation'.[494] Yet, history is replete with incidents involving border disputes between the two over grazing rights and trade issues. In fact, the Treaty of Chushul signed by the representatives of Raja Gulab Singh and Imperial China's representative from Lhasa had precisely tried to bury border disputes by mutual respect for the 'traditional' border between Tibet and Ladakh. Today, it has become as clear as daylight that India has not been aware to the geostrategic importance of the region and hence Kashmiri leaders were allowed for far too long to obstruct the growth and development of the region in India's interest. But as we can see, there is a long history of highs and lows in Ladakh's relationship with both India and Tibet. In congenial times, it has lived in happiness under the influence of India and has almost always had uneasy relationship with Tibet because of Tibet's cultural and sectarian hegemonic tendencies.

After 1947, Ladakh had become part of India but after 5 March

1948, when Sheikh Abdullah was appointed as the Prime Minister, it effectively came under Kashmir which in its arrogance, insensitivity and indifference, subjected it to neglect. This was a time when the world was changing around Ladakh. China was under the siege of the communists, who were winning and it was obvious that it was not long before the winds of change shook Tibet too. How this was going to affect Ladakh, was still a little way away in the future. But a note of caution was struck early by Karan Singh after his first visit to Ladakh in September 1952. On his return to Srinagar, he wrote to Prime Minister Nehru: 'As you know, the question of Ladakh has been troubling us for the last few years, and no satisfactory solution has yet been arrived at. The result is that the Ladakhis feel very distressed, insecure and unhappy, and the atmosphere makes the situation liable easily to be exploited by mischievous elements.'[495] Along with this note of caution was another note carrying detailed analysis of the region, the construct and contradictions and challenges, and the suggestions to deal with them. In the note he warned, 'With the recent political changes in Tibet, I feel there is a distinct possibility of attempts being made to win the sympathy of the Ladakhis away from India and towards Communism…My purpose in writing to you in this connection was to…urge that sympathetic consideration be given to requests of the Ladakhis. Ladakh is strategically very important, more so for India as a whole even than for the State, and it will be a tragedy if for lack of an accommodating spirit the people of Ladakh remain unhappy and discontented, and thus an easy prey to all kinds of exploitation, both communalist and communist.'[496]

This cautionary note had been written in the background of growing discontentment and frustration among the Ladakhis due to resource crunches and the step-motherly treatment it received from Kashmir. This had resulted in frequent agitations, demonstrations and violence. The Ladakhis had already started to drift away from the State of Jammu and Kashmir and the idea that it should be taken over by the center was gaining ground. In addition, like the Kashmiris, they too had begun to assert that they ought to have the freedom to choose their own course. Over the years, this resentment had only grown, for the leaders in the State failed to realize that the aspirations of the people were outstripping the meager resources that were being made available to Ladakh. It was only in 1957 that for the first time, the first Lama of Ladakh, Kushak Bakula, was appointed a minister of state for Ladakh affairs and trade agencies. He was also the President of the Ladakh unit of the National Conference. Yet the fact that he was given a minor status and responsibility only for Ladakh affairs demonstrated the reluctance to entrust a Ladakhi member of the Assembly with responsibility that is given to any other member from the rest of the State. However, even this tokenism was significant since it did recognize Ladakh as a responsible part of the State, in however small measures it may have been. But like any other palliative, this too was a temporary relief. Since the aspirations of Ladakhis only grew in a world where individual dignity and community identity was being increasingly recognized, it was a matter of time before the subterranean Buddhist sub nationalism came to the fore. Karan Singh's prophetic warning about the rise of communalism was about to come true in due time.

The rise of religious fundamentalism and terrorist acts of killings in the State in the late 1980s had also scalded the regions of Jammu and Ladakh. While the Kashmiri terrorists and their trainers and patrons from across the border considered Jammu a legitimate tool for activism, in Ladakh, because of the predominantly Muslim district of Kargil, these terrorist activities not only challenged the Buddhist hegemony of the region but aspired to take full control of the region, particularly Kargil, so that the national strategic interests of the country were harmed and the Indian Army's defence efforts were ham-strung. It is in this context that the creation of Ladakh as a Union Territory needs to be viewed.

Sadar-i-Riyasat Karan Singh had continued to press for justice for Ladakh and emphasize its geostrategic importance, all through his years as Head of the State. But he was only able to extract minor concessions from the myopic leadership from Kashmir. Its prejudice against Jammu can probably be explained by more than a century old perceived injury, but, that was no reason for Ladakh to be treated shabbily by them. However, finally, the inevitable had happened. After making Article 370 inoperative, the next political step was to dismantle the State of Jammu and Kashmir into two

Union Territories. The creation of Ladakh as a Union Territory was obviously welcomed by the predominantly Buddhist Leh region, who considered it as a liberation. However, gloom descended on Kargil, which was predominantly Muslim.

The Lok Sabha member for the Ladakh constituency, Jamyang Tsering Namgyal, praised the abrogation of Article 370 and welcomed the formation of a separate Ladakh Union Territory, hoping the move will encourage jobs and development. He did not fail to add, 'Under Kashmir, our development, our political aspiration, our identity, our language, all of this got lost, it is because of Article 370—and the Congress party is responsible for that.'[497] The move was also welcomed by the Ladakh Buddhist Association who then organized a thanksgiving celebration in Leh on 8 August 2019, which was attended by political and religious leaders. The Buddhist community in Leh and Ladakh stated that they had long been ignored and the revocation and reorganization will help them steer their own destiny. For the Ladakhis, this had been a long journey with a major breakthrough coming 'When the first Ladakh Hill Development Council (Leh) was sworn in on 3 September 1995, Leh District regained a measure of the autonomy that the Kingdom of Ladakh had lost in the 1830s to the Dogras. The Ladakh Autonomous Hill Development Councils Act 1995, decreed by the President a few months earlier, signified a major concession on the part of State and Central Government, especially considering the strategic and political importance of Ladakh in the overall Kashmir issue. The "Reasons for Enactment" accompanying the Act suggest a straightforward justification: a remote mountain region in need and desirous of decentralization of decision making is given its own administrative body. At first glance, then, this is the stuff that many indigenous peoples, many marginal groups in India and around the world, dream about: a responsive government recognizes the legitimate desires of a minority with a distinct identity.'[498]

It is significant to note that this change in favor of Ladakh's autonomy too had taken place when the State was under the Governor's Rule and the same provision of the Article 370 that was used in 2019 to neutralize it, was used. It is also important to notice that while addressing the grievance of people by constituting autonomous Council it had ignored then, as it did now, the aspirations of people of Jammu. It is also instructive to note that in the vanguard of the movement and agitation for autonomy of Ladakh since 1969 was the Young Buddhists Association. In 1989, this agitation had taken a violent turn and lives were lost. In the process a few paradigms were created: Ladakhis were supposed to be only Buddhists; Buddhists wanted to 'secede' from the State of Jammu and Kashmir and not India; and that Buddhists are nationalists while Muslims are not. It is contended by Martijen van Beek that Buddhists of Leh chose violence to silence the others, i.e. the Muslims. It is no wonder that soon a separate Kargil Hill Development Council had to be created because of the heavy communal divide in Ladakh. Not surprisingly, when Ladakh was carved out of Jammu and Kashmir State, Kargil expressed disappointment at the development. In Jammu, the people generally welcomed the move since they believed that the Article 370 had bred arrogance among the Kashmiri leadership making them immune to the needs and demands of others. However, it rued the fact that it had been downgraded from a State to Union Territory. Many also felt disappointment at the continued relationship with Kashmir because they were conscious that at the core of the Kashmir problem was the regional conflict, socio-economic, developmental and religious animosity, which had remained unaddressed.

Now Ladakhis hope that with the new Union Territory the wrongs of the past will be righted. However, change of status has the potential for China to create trouble since it contends that the Jammu and Kashmir dispute is not just between India and Pakistan but also involves China since the whole area of Aksai Chin in Ladakh is disputed by China as Chinese territory. With China claiming to be an all-weather friend of Pakistan, the possibility of it raking up the Jammu and Kashmir dispute as a tripartite matter cannot be ruled out. The coming years will be testing the military and diplomatic strength and acumen of India. In this, much will depend on the development and evolution of Ladakh as a truly integral and equal part of India. In fact, the political history of Ladakh as a respected part of India has only begun after it became a Union Territory.

17

Tense Present, Uncertain Future

'Every ending is a beginning. We just don't know it at the time.'

—Mitch Albom

The last Ruler of erstwhile State of Jammu and Kashmir was addressed as, 'Shriman Indra Mahindra Rajrajeshwar Maharajadhiraj Shri Hari Singhji, Jammu Kashmir Naresh Tatha Tibbet adi Deshadhipati Ruler of Jammu and Kashmir State'. These were not just pompous words; they announced the geographical expanse of his kingdom and asserted the fact that he was the Ruler of not only Jammu and Kashmir but also 'Tibbet adi' that is Ladakh, Baltistan and Gilgit etc. 'Adi' stood for the feudatory States like Punial, Ishkoman, Yasin, Kuh-Ghizer, Hunza, Nagar and Chilas. The reference to these regions as 'Tibbet adi' often creates confusion but all foreigners approaching this region on way to the land of Tibet realized that though the people shared a common culture, language and often religion too, they could only travel up to a certain point. Tibet as we know it, was a forbidden kingdom and hence they understood these vast lands of Ladakh and Baltistan etc. as Tibet. For a hundred years this is how the political geography of the State stood. Today, however, only a shadow of this huge and complex state remains, with the further possibility of reverting to the pre-1834 status before Ladakh was incorporated in Jammu kingdom and the annexation of Gilgit-Baltistan was still some years away.

No other State or region of India has undergone the kind of

changes in its construct, characteristics and fortune as the former State of Jammu and Kashmir. Diligent historians can dig a plethora of evidence tracing the continuity and connectivity of the region with the rest of the country and, indeed, there is a treasure of literature on the subject since antiquity. Kashmir, since ancient times, has been subject to the powerful forces descending upon it from central Asia. Sometimes, ambitious armies from the plains too have invaded it and occasionally, an intrepid ruler of Kashmir, like Lalitaditya, too has marched to the north and south to create an empire. It, however, remained the reservoir of the cultural and philosophical wealth, enriching many other states and societies with the wisdom of its learned men.

Jammu, on the other hand, not endowed with favorable geography or climate, often drew the ire of marauding armies because of the belligerent nature of its men even when they had little that could be looted. Consequently, the preferred career option was soldiering for the martial people and commerce and business for the traders. Ladakh, as we have seen, was different from these two regions but was important for its pursuit of spiritual journey and its significance as an important trading route to and from central Asia, Tibet and China. Ladakh, along with Baltistan and Gilgit held an important geostrategic location that drew ambitious conquerors to it. Close to the Silk Route and strategically placed for the ambitious, they offered riches as well as base for further expansion.

The Indian subcontinent has always been the crucible of new ideas and cultures but where the former State of Jammu and Kashmir differs from the rest of the country is that it was subjected to such cultural and religious changes that they made two of the three regions—Kashmir and Ladakh—distinct and exclusive. In its modern manifestation, by the exertions of Maharaja Gulab Singh and his son Maharaja Ranbir Singh, it fashioned itself as a strong State even when the fault-lines were clearly visible despite their suturing by their policies of tolerance and equitable justice. But even when stable, it was always unstable below the surface as cracks appeared when pressure was applied to it. Consequently, in the twenty-first century, the process of its unraveling began with the pressure coming, first from rising communalism, and then the awakening of regional ambitions that mutated into hegemonic tendencies. The latter arose mainly because of the violent secessionist movement in Kashmir and the equally ruthless response of the Indian State till on 5 August 2019 the Government of India finally decided in its wisdom to withdraw the special status given to it by the Constitution of India. In the process, only Ladakh has been made happy while Kashmir is understandably stunned, sullen and pummeled into submission for the time being. With the bifurcation of the State and downgrading to the status of a Union Territory, Jammu—the vigorous champion of abrogation of Article 370—does not now know if its aspirations have been met or if it has been asked to sacrifice its pride and swallow the humiliation of a downgraded status and silencing of its voice in public administration in order to 'teach' the Kashmiris a lesson. It is a bitter pill to swallow, particularly in the light of the fact that the State was given its modern shape and form by the exertions of the people and rulers of Jammu.

Looking back at history, there is little doubt that the making of the Jammu and Kashmir State, and its continuation after all other Indian states were reorganized on the basis of lingual solidarity, had bucked the historical trend. In fact, its creation in the nineteenth century itself was a throwback on an earlier era when the might of the sword could carve out kingdoms and states and redraw maps. It was era, when the fate and fortunes of the people hardly changed with the change of rulers or the boundaries; an era that was on the throes of death even though the new system and aspirations were a little way from taking shape. Even by 1846, the Dogras had considerably shrunk from the times when Dogri was spoken and written in areas spanning Lahore to the foothills of Pir Panjal, part of Punjab Doaba and the hill states of much of the lower Shiwaliks of north-west. However, with the arrival of waves of migrants from across the Himalayas and the rise of Hindi and Punjabi languages preferred by the new rulers, and the proselytizing Islamic saints respectively, not only did the Dogras suffer in status but also in the diminishing of their language. Though the Dogras loathe admitting, the gradual cultural submission to the Punjabis over the years, with the huge shift in the balance of political, economic and cultural power and influence towards Punjab and Punjabis has been a reality that is likely to come back to haunt them following the abrogation of Article 370.

The fate of Jammu and the Dogra region has once again driven home the lesson that those political parties that represent national interest, rarely understand, appreciate and defend the regional aspirations and are often prone to ignoring them. Earlier, the Congress used to ask the Dogras to accept the hegemony of the Kashmiris in governance because they were not only in majority but also because that was needed to further the national interests. Protests and voices of dissent were routinely dubbed as communalist rants and playing into the hands of Pakistan since it gave it the excuse to raise the bogey of the insecurity and vulnerability of the Muslims in India. This was taken to the extreme by Prime Minister Jawaharlal Nehru whose refusal to listen to the grievances of the Hindus of Jammu forced the people to devote themselves to, first the Praja Parishad, then the Bharatiya Jana Sangh, and later the BJP—the only political parties that were willing to carry their voice around the country. As Yuvraj and Sadar-i-Riyasat of the State, Karan Singh missed no opportunity to plead with Pandit Jawaharlal Nehru regarding the need to engage with the Praja Parishad,[499] but Nehru had developed a mental block which became an obstruction in the path of reducing the bitterness between Kashmir and Jammu.

There can be an endless debate about who has been more responsible for the unmitigated hostility between Kashmir and Jammu and which particular event triggered it. Kashmiris will say it is the Treaty of Amritsar, 1846 that yoked the Valley to Jammu as its fiefdom. This treaty, between the British and Raja Gulab Singh of Jammu and Ladakh, transferred to him and his successors, all the hilly and mountainous country between the Ravi and the Indus in perpetual possession, on his paying rupees 75 lakhs to the British. This was the amount of war indemnity that the Lahore Durbar was supposed to pay the British after they had lost the First Sikh War and was unable to pay. But ironically, the East India Company was not in a position to take control of this far-flung region, and this explains why they asked Raja Gulab Singh to pay the remaining indemnity and take control of Kashmir. The extensive territories thus transferred to Raja Gulab Singh included the whole of the outer hills between Ravi and Indus, the Valley of Kashmir and also Ladakh with Gilgit, Baltistan and the Indus Valley down to Chilas which had already been conquered by Raja Gulab Singh and incorporated in his territory. This Treaty also recognized him as the Maharaja of these lands.

Over a period of time, post signing the Treaty of Amritsar, 1846, the British had begun to have a second thought about the Treaty. They regretted, committing non-interference in the region, which was to be solely managed by Maharaja Gulab Singh to whom they had handed this region. But soon, as they realized the strategic and commercial importance of this region and discovered that the frontier of the Russian imperialism in Central Asia was getting alarmingly close to the Indian northern Frontiers, they began plans to contain it. The British anticipated it as a serious threat to their empire in India, which they regarded as 'The Brightest Jewel in the British Crown'. Therefore, they were very anxious about its security. They feared a Russian invasion of India from Caucasus or Central Asia—the regions where Russia was gradually but constantly creeping in. Consequently, Governor General Lord Hardinge had to face severe criticism for transferring Jammu and Kashmir to Maharaja Gulab Singh. The criticism came from his countrymen, both in India and abroad. It was now realized by the British how Kashmir and subsequently the regions of Ladakh and Gilgit, could have been utilized as a British colony. Ignoring the logistical inability of the British to defend the frontier region in 1846, the critics, in an effort to denigrate the Treaty, charged the East India Company for having 'sold' Kashmir to Gulab Singh for a paltry sum just to fill its coffers. Thus, the word 'sold' came to define Kashmir's relationship with Jammu. This has also become the central argument for all those inimical to the Dogras. In view of this criticism, Lord Hardinge in his correspondence (dated: 7 June 1846) to Lord Ellenborough, was constrained to justify his actions by giving details of the considerations that led him to conclude the Treaty of Amritsar, 1846. The letter clearly pinpoints some of the main considerations taken by British while signing the treaty. He argued that Maharaja Gulab Singh had not joined the Sikhs in their war against the British and that their main objective was to reduce the area and resources of the Sikh Empire, which then extended from Multan to Gilgit. But importantly, he pointed out that it was pragmatic at that point in time not to stretch the defence capabilities of East India Company when it had a strong and reliable kingdom to its north to ward off any threat. Furthermore, to understand the various dimensions associated with the transfer of Kashmir to Maharaja Gulab Singh one needs to also read the Treaty of Lahore (9 March 1846) signed between the British and Maharaja Duleep Singh of Punjab.

On reading the Lahore Treaty of 9 March 1846, the following points will emerge: number one, at the time of the Treaty of Amritsar (11 March 1846), which gave Kashmir in independent possession to Maharaja Gulab Singh, he was already undisputed hereditary ruler of Jammu, Baltistan and Ladakh. Number two, there was no sale of Kashmir. The myth of 'sale' was created by British elements opposed to Lord Hardinge but historically it was not true. Clause 12 of the Treaty of Lahore (1846) unequivocally declares that even before the Treaty of Lahore was signed, it was agreed that the area surrendered by the Lahore Durbar between the Ravi and the Indus were to be transferred to Raja Gulab Singh. Robert Thorpe, a young British army officer testifies the same, when he writes:

> By the conditions made with the Lahore durbar, after the first Punjab war, a certain sum of money was demanded by the British Government to defray the expenses of the campaign but the *Durbar* being unable to refund the full amount, it was resolved to take Cashmere and certain neighboring hill states in lieu of the deficiency, and to "transfer" these to Gulab Singh for an equivalent sum, which arrangement presented the further advantages of reducing the power of the Sikhs, and of gaining Gulab Singh as our ally.

For the record, Captain Thorpe was no sympathizer of the Dogras. On the contrary, historians suspect that he was sent to Kashmir as a part of the plot to annex it to the British India. His memoir is scathing in its condemnation of the Treaty of Amritsar, and has criticized the East India Company for putting the Kashmiris in a miserable life. His memoir, published in 1870 after his death, did not yield the desired result but they ultimately led to the appointment of a Political Resident in Kashmir. He has rued the fact that the British let go the chance to take direct control of Kashmir but nowhere finds any fault with the Treaty.

The English were aware of the strategic and commercial importance of the region and were also not unaware of the threat that loomed from Central Asia if Russia so desired. William Moorcroft[500], who wore a number of hats in his lifetime, had already published his adventures in Ladakh, Tibet and beyond and warned the British of various possibilities. He had also studied the sources of *pashm*, the wool from Western Tibet, which was the raw-material of the valuable shawl industry of Kashmir, and appreciated the significance of this region from the commercial and strategic point of view. Consequently, he had tried to persuade the British in India to extend their control over this region. What is, however, not discussed is the fact that in the British Parliament and political circles there was a constant and bitter conflict between the forces that advocated the 'forward policy' of imperialistic forces and those who believed that having friendly rulers in the frontier areas was much better and economical than directly controlling the regions and ruling them with many of the frontier tribes being fierce and hard to rule. The success of the Treaty of Amritsar (1809) between the Company and Maharaja Ranjit Singh stood testimony to it. But ever since a counter-narrative began to build, those politicians who were unable to make any headway, began a campaign among the Kashmiris to encourage their separate identity and build discontent. In this the 'sale' of Kashmir propaganda became a handy tool.

However, what remains unsaid about the Kashmiri resentment is that for the first time since the ascendancy of Islam in the Valley, it came to be ruled by the Hindus, and this was deeply resented by the Muslims of Kashmir and, surprisingly, Punjab. This narrative was no doubt countered by Jammu with the argument that the Kashmiris and Prime Minister Jawaharlal Nehru were responsible for unfairly and unjustifiably hoisting Sheikh Abdullah, a leader of the Valley, over Jammu and his mean and vindictive approach towards the Dogras that set the stage for confrontation between the two regions. Nehru, instead of being the honest broker, chose to be an unapologetic partisan of the Kashmiris. As for the charge of the Dogras being communal, it can be said with considerable justification that it was Sheikh Abdullah who was responsible for injecting communalism in the political discourse in the State. It must also be conceded that communalism always exists in a multi-cultural and multi-religious society but responsible and responsive governance can keep the temperatures low. It is public knowledge that all the Dogra rulers were devout Hindus and yet they strove to not be discriminatory towards the Muslims even though there were many in the courts of successive Maharajas who would have loved to keep the Muslims down. The only grouse can be about not enlisting of the Kashmiris in the State Forces. This too is unfair criticism since they were not categorized as martial, either by tradition within the State for close to seven centuries, or even the British, who debarred them from enlisting in the British Indian Army too.

It is also true that the founding ruler Maharaja Gulab Singh had created a Dharmarth Trust for the upkeep and day to day running of the Hindu temples and holy places and this clearly demonstrated his commitment to his religion. But it is significant that the Trust had been created by his personal donations and not State money. His successors too had added to the funds from their own purses. However, this commitment to Hindu religion in no way limited their duty towards their Muslim subjects and not surprisingly there is not even a single instance of any communal violence initiated by the Hindus before 1947. Muslims (mostly those from Jammu), under the Dogras, not only occupied high positions in the army and led campaigns in Ladakh and Baltistan, but also in the administrative set up. The last ruler Maharaja Hari Singh gave a prominent place to a number of Muslim courtiers who came to the State from as far as Hyderabad Deccan and Afghanistan. If the Dogra rule appeared economically oppressive at times, then, in defence it must be said that it was no more oppressive than what many other Princely states were or, for that matter, even the British Indian States. The fact that rural India had to launch a number of agitations against the British to secure justice is ample proof. The Kheda[501], Bardoli[502] and Champaran[503] farmers' agitation is a case in point. But it is a matter of pride for the Dogras that not only land reforms and freedom from the compound interest of the money lenders were legally given, justice too was delivered even-handedly. There is not even a single instance where a common citizen was condemned and punished without following the due process of law. In the administration of justice, they were second to none and that is the hallmark of a civilized state.

On the other hand, the Muslims of the Valley stand condemned for unleashing terror upon Hindus of the Valley in 1931, and that template has continued to be followed in the later years till terror and targeted killings almost wiped out the presence of Kashmiri Pandits from the Valley in the decade of 1990s. Muslims of the Valley cannot turn away from this crime nor can they be absolved of any culpability. This is an albatross they will continue to wear around their necks. In unleashing this violence, the Muslims of the Valley committed a historical and cultural crime that has not only deprived Kashmir of a legacy that was its crowning glory but also injected the element of Jihad that has turned the entire country against not just the Kashmiris, but Muslims in general. It is unfortunate that ever since 1931, communalism has been the bedrock on which has stood the edifice of politics in the Valley. The mosques became regular platforms for political activity and no political speech begins without invoking the authority of Allah and the Quran. Thus, what began as innocent and sincere invocation of God soon deteriorated to competitive claim towards Islam by rival political leaders and groups. In later years, if Jammu too fell to the lure of resorting to religious solidarity, then it can hardly be blamed. It is not that it was not tainted by the presence of communal elements even during the Dogra rule, but they were always kept under strict control and were never encouraged to display their preferences in state affairs since the Maharajas were aware (with the British breathing down their necks) of the responsibility of ruling a state that was predominantly Muslim.

As far as Ladakh is concerned, its isolation may have been a virtue during the earlier times, but in the modern era, it was a contributory cause for its backwardness and an invitation to resentment. Like many other Himalayan Buddhist states, Ladakh too was a forbidden region for outsiders and tourists. But what was an honest attempt to let the people live in pristine glory assumed miserable form when the winds of change had begun to reach Ladakh. Its neglect became manifest in several ways in comparison to Kashmir or even Jammu. This dereliction of duty on the part of the State has had its consequences in the form of the rise of the Young Buddhists Movement in Ladakh. It also created bad blood and became counter-productive as it threatened the security environment on the borders with two hostile neighbors waiting to pounce. The fact that no attempt had been made during the 1947-1948 Indo-Pak war to regain control over Gilgit-Baltistan, clearly exposed the ignorance of the leaders of free India and its military commanders regarding the geo-strategic importance of the regions. This had cost India dearly, as was demonstrated by the developments that followed.

It was only after the debacle of the 1962 Indo-China war that the project of linking Manali with Leh was undertaken in real earnest. It is hard to say if the general development of Ladakh was deliberately ignored by the State government so as to offer an advantage to a hostile neighbor or if it was a product of their myopic vision. But with changing times, as the Ladakhis were frequently exposed to the outside world thereby opening up their minds and ambitions, they grew more conscious of their unjust treatment and realized how far behind they had been left. In this not a mean part was played by the history of the region, which has lived with the competing ambitions of Tibet and Kashmir. The fact that for little favors they had to travel to either Srinagar or Jammu too was a cause of resentment and this was aggravated by the fact that they were also subjected to mockery and ridicule for being different from both the places. This added insult to their injury.

Now Ladakhis hope that with the new Union Territory this wrong will be righted. However, change of status has the potential for China to create trouble since it contends that the Jammu and Kashmir dispute is not just between India and Pakistan but also involves China since the entire area of Aksai Chin in Ladakh is disputed by it as Chinese territory. With China claiming to be an all-weather friend of Pakistan, the possibility of it raking up the Jammu and Kashmir dispute as a tripartite matter cannot be ruled out. The confrontation and deadly fracas of 2020, beginning with the Galwan Valley, is a case in point. The coming years will be testing the military and diplomatic strength and acumen of India. In this, much will depend on the development and evolution of Ladakh as a truly integral and equal part of India. In fact, the political history of Ladakh as a respected part of modern India has only begun after it became a Union Territory and there are already worrying signs.

There are disturbing trends that show the determination of the Ladakhis to distance Ladakh away from Kashmir. This has been facilitated by the very opportune opening of the Atal Tunnel under the Rohtang Pass connecting Kulu-Manali to Keylong and considerably shortening the distance to Leh. Ever since its opening, this has been the preferred route of Ladakhis from Leh to Chandigarh and Delhi. In the coming years this process of distancing from Kashmir will increase and only the Kargil region of Ladakh, dominated by Muslims, will retain the traditional route. The cause of concern is that this will only stoke flames of communalism in Ladakh, opening new challenges for India.

The further distancing of Ladakh from Kashmir as well as Jammu is today an inescapable outcome of the policies of the past. Ladakh, as its long history tells us, is more apprehensive about the moves of Tibet (read China) than any other country. It has found security with India in the past too, though there have been occasions when India has demanded its pound of flesh, as when Aurangzeb demanded building of a mosque in Leh and conversion to Islam by the Buddhist ruler. But these tactics have not had any lasting impact. What is different now is that the unfair treatment to Buddhist Ladakh has not only resulted in its distancing itself from Srinagar but also Kargil. Even when isolated cases of a Buddhist girl converting to Islam to marry a Ladakhi-speaking Muslim from Kargil happen, they become a destabilizing event that threatens the demography of an already diminished population. As a consequence, the Buddhists of Ladakh become xenophobic, and the Muslim Kargil lives in apprehension of being left out by Buddhists in alliance with the rightist India.

While this tug of war goes on in Kashmir and Ladakh, Jammu will most likely be the biggest loser if the Ladakhis continue to shun the Srinagar route to the plains, and thereby avoid Jammu too, and develop the Leh-Manali route even for their trade. As it is, Leh had lost its status of an entrepôt after the takeover of Tibet by the Chinese People's Liberation Army in 1951. But even then, the integrated economy of Jammu, Kashmir and Ladakh survived those events. One of the earliest casualties was the trade of high quality *pashm* from Tibet that had been protected by the 1684 Treaty of Tismosgang between Tibet and Ladakh and 1842 Treaty of Chushul between Tibet and Maharaja Gulab Singh. Today, the fabled *pashmina* shawls woven from those wools by the craftsmen of Kashmir have become a rarity. In addition, the trade with Central Asian countries has to take a longer route of Wagah in Punjab to Afghanistan when Pakistan allows it. Now, this integrated economy is being threatened by the new changes where avenging the past has become the driving force.

So, how did we reach here? The irony is that a State that was created in the midst of competing ambitions, intrigues and hostile forces and was so coveted, by the British to serve their geo-political interests after it had been created, met its end, not at the hands of forces that were hostile, but those that had a friendly face, assuring the people that the good of the people was their driving force. Much of the country is euphoric in the aftermath of the 'abrogation' of Article 370, not recognizing the fact that behind this constitutional change is the force of the military, and that, history has taught us again and again that there are no military solutions for political problems. History has also taught us that those leaders, nations and empires that have their image of powerful men, nations and empires have always failed to recognize the moment when offering concession, calling for peace and pressing the pause button is advisable. It is more than four years since the fateful decision of 'abrogation' was given effect and the outcome would be known only when military and para-military boots retire to their barracks and political 'normalcy' returns to the Valley. It is possible, though unlikely, that the mainstream politicians of Kashmir might have learnt the lessons that Delhi of today desires them to learn and, that, they go out to the people to exhort them to accept whatever Delhi is offering, just like they had accepted various conquerors of the past. The BJP, and the right-wing supporters certainly hope so, but no group of people have remained the same in history. For centuries, the Christian Hapsburg dynasty of the Holy Roman Empire of Austria-Hungary had ruled those regions of the Ottoman Empire that had converted to Islam but in modern times of liberalism, when the first opportunity arose, all the small ethnic groups of Islamic faith rose in rebellion and fought for their freedoms. History cannot be taken for granted and it rarely repeats itself and when it does, as the cliché goes, then it is in the form of a parody.

It is very clear that there is a long and arduous road ahead. None of the three regions of the former State are prepared to be ruled by outsiders, and that is what administrations of the two Union Territories are. The murmur of dissent and frustration is already audible in Jammu, and as said earlier, Kashmir is in a sullen mood. Its leadership has failed it and the new leadership is still in the cradle. Ladakh too has begun to show signs of unease with the local representatives finding themselves sidelined by officials from outside. The army cannot keep this level of presence indefinitely without producing a backlash in the world unless the America-led coalition concludes that it has to militarily engage with China in this part of the world and that a Sino-Russo military alliance will not become a reality. The state needs to do more than hunt and kill militants and arrest suspects and political workers to put them behind the bars for an indefinite period. That has been happening for a number of years but still home-grown militants keep replacing the eliminated. The bottom line is that perhaps, 'the tournament of shadows' has been revived, making the future tense and uncertain.

Notes

1. The Year After

1 Minar-e-Pakistan is a national monument located in Lahore, Pakistan. The tower was built between 1960 and 1968 on the site where the All-India Muslim League passed the Lahore Resolution on 23 March 1940—the first official call for a separate and independent homeland for the Muslims of British India, as espoused by the two-nation theory. The resolution eventually helped lead to the emergence of an independent Pakistani state in 1947.

2 Tashkent is the capital city of Uzbekistan. In 1966 it was part of the Soviet Union and as such host of the talks between Prime Minister Lal Bahadur Shastri and President Ayub Khan after the end of the 17- day Indo-Pak war in 1965. It was mediated by Alecksey Kosygin, Prime Minister of USSR. According the Tashkent Agreement both sides withdrew from the pre-war positions and gave up all territorial gains of war.

3 The RSS or the Rashtriya Swayemsewak Sangh is the mother organization that professedly works as a social organization. It is an umbrella over various other socio-cultural and political organizations. Bharatiya Jana Sangh was the first political outfit that was created by it. This merged with the short lived Janata Party in 1977 and after the split, it reinvented itself as the Bharatiya Janata Party or BJP.

4 Nasim Zehra, *From Kargil To The Coup: Events That Shook Pakistan*, (Lahore: Sang-e-Meel Publishers, 2018), p.61.

5 A.S. Dulat, *Kashmir: The Vajpayee Years*, (New Delhi: HarperCollins Publishers India, 2017), p. 15.

6 Michael Krepon, 'Looking Back: The 1998 Indian Pakistani Nuclear Tests' (Washington DC: Arms Control Association) https://www.armscontrol.org/act/2008-06/looking-back-1998-indian-pakistani-nuclear-tests

7 A.S. Dulat, Op cit, p. 17.
8 On the Srinagar-Leh road, after crossing Zoji La, Kargil was an important point since the caravans from Srinagar, Skardu and Leh met at the crossroads here. It is an important town linking Ladakh with the rest of India. Kargil heights, in control of Pakistan, could dominate the Srinagar-Leh highway thereby threatening the security of India.
9 The Siachen glacier is located in the north-eastern end of the Karakoram ranges where the Line of Control between India and Pakistan ends. It is part of the Union Territory of Ladakh. India took control of the whole Siachen Glacier and the Passes in 1984.
10 Christine Fair, *Fighting to the End: The Pakistan Army's Way of War* (New York: Oxford University Press, 2014), p. 151.
11 A.S. Dulat, Op cit, p. 24.
12 Khaled Ahmed, *Pakistan's Terror Conundrum* (New Delhi: Penguin Books India, 2021), p. 19.
13 Nasim Zehra, Op cit, p. 73.
14 Sartaj Aziz, Pakistan's Foreign Minister, 1997-1999; as quoted by Nasim Zehra in *From Kargil To The Coup*, p. 102.
15 Nasim Zehra, Op cit, p. 160-161.
16 Ibid, p. 17-18.
17 K.P.S. Gill and Ajay Sahni (ed.), *Faultlines: Writings on Conflict Resolution* (New Delhi: The Institute of Conflict Management)
18 The first hijacking of a plane took place in 1971 and it was followed by another in 1976, this time from Delhi. In the next decade—in 1984—two consecutive hijackings took place in the same year first the Srinagar-Delhi flight in July, followed by the the Chandigarh-Srinagar flight in August.
19 A.S. Dulat, Op cit, p. 36-37.
20 Azhar Masood is a radical Islamist and is the founder and leader of Jaish-e-Mohammad. His main area of operations is South Asia but he is also credited with bringing Jihad to Britain. He was declared an international terrorist by the United Nations Security Council on 1 May 2019.
21 Omar Shaikh is a British terrorist of Pakistani origin. He was arrested and jailed in India in 1994 on charges of kidnapping western tourists. He was released in 1999 after flight IC 814 was hijacked to Kandahar in exchange for the safe return of the passengers. He was provided a safe passage to the Talibans in Afghanistan.
22 Mushtaq Ahmed Zargar is a Kashmiri terrorist who was also released

in exchange for the release of passengers of IC 814. He is the founder of a terrorist organization, Al Umar Mujahideen, and has remained in Indian prison for many years.

23 'Ahrars' were those pre-partition Muslims who had come together as part of the Khilafat Movement. Later they opposed Jinnah's demand for a separate homeland though never fully merging with the Congress. After 1947, Ahrars were gradually marginalized.

24 Binori is a town in the neighborhood of Karachi with the religious complex of Jamia Uloom-ul-Islamia. This seminary was funded by a Deobandi cleric, Maulana Muhammad Yusuf Binori, who participated in the anti-Ahmadi movement.

25 Christophe Jaffrelot, *The Pakistan Paradox: Instability and Resilience* (New Delhi: Vintage/Penguin, 2016), p. 512.

26 Quoted by Christophe Jaffrelot from Ahmed Rashid's *Pakistan on the Brink: The Future of Pakistan, Afghanistan and the West.* Ibid, p.56.

27 Quoted by Christophe Jaffrelot from Mariam Abou Zahab and Oliver Roy's, *Islamic Networks: The Afghan Pakistani Connection.* Ibid, p. 33.

28 Myra MacDonald: *Defeat is an Orphan: How Pakistan Lost the Great South Asian War* (London: C. Hurst & Co., 2016), p. 28.

29 Zulfikar Ali Bhutto, 'Speech delivered at the UN Security Council on 22 September 1965 on Kashmir Issue' (https://bhutto.org/index.php/speeches/speeches-from-1948-1965/speech-delivered-at-the-un-security-council-on-september-22-1965-on-kashmir-issue/, Accessed December 2023).

2. Understanding Pakistan

30 Sir Muhammad Iqbal, widely known as Allama Iqbal, was a poet, philosopher and politician, as well as an academic, barrister and scholar in British India. He is widely regarded as having inspired the Pakistan Movement. He is called the "Spiritual Father of Pakistan."

31 He was a westernized Muslim and a lawyer par excellence who at one point in his life was a leading figure of the Indian National Congress. He parted with the Congress over his differences with Mahatma Gandhi in view of his launching the Khilafat Movement. Jinnah believed it was a regressive step for the Muslims. His drift away from the Congress gradually made him the leader of only the Muslim community.

32 Christophe Jafferlot is a French political scientist specialising in South Asia, particularly India and Pakistan. He is a professor of South

Asian politics and history at the Centre d'études et de recherches internationales (CERI) in Sciences Po (Paris), a professor of Indian Politics and Sociology at the King's India Institute (London), and a Research Director at the Centre national de la recherche scientifique (CNRS).

33 Ayesha Siddiqa is a Pakistani military scientist, a political commentator and author, who serves as a research associate at the SOAS South Asia Institute. She previously served as the inaugural Pakistan Fellow at the Woodrow Wilson Center between 2004 and 2005.

34 Sir Muhammad Iqbal's 1930 Presidential Address to the 25th Session of the All-India Muslim League Allahabad, 29 December 1930 (http://www.columbia.edu/itc/mealac/pritchett/00islamlinks/txt_iqbal_1930.html, Accessed December 2023)

35 'Ummah' is an Arabic word meaning 'community'. It is distinguished from 'Sha'b', which means a nation with common ancestry or geography. Thus, it can be said to be a supra-national community with a common history. It is a synonym for 'ummat al-Islām'—'the Islamic community'), and it is commonly used to mean the collective community of the Islamic people. In the Quran the ummah typically refers to a single group that shares common religious beliefs, specifically those that are the objects of a divine plan of salvation. In the context of pan-Islamism and politics, the word ummah can be used to mean the concept of a Commonwealth of the Believers (ummat al-mu'minīn).

36 Khaled Ahmed, *Pakistan's Terror Conundrum* (New Delhi: Penguin Books India, 2021), p. x

37 All India Muslim League, Mohammad Ali Jinnah's speech, 23 March 1940.

38 All India Muslim League Resolution, 23 March 1940.

39 However, within a few weeks after this speech, Karachi in particular and Sind Province in general was engulfed in communal violence. His speech failed to instill security among the Hindus and large scale bloodshed and migration followed.

40 Husain Haqqani, *Pakistan Between Mosque and Military*, (London: Penguin Books, 2016) p. 14.

41 Nicholas Mansergh and Penderel Moon, *Transfer of Power 1942-47: The Mountbatten Viceroyalty Formulation of a Plan*, 22 March-30 May 1947; quoted in Rajiv Dogra, *Where Borders Bleed: An Insider's Account of Indo-Pak Relations* (New Delhi: Rupa Publications India, 2015), p. 3.

42 Stanley Wolpert, *India and Pakistan: Continued Conflict or Cooperation?* (London: University of California Press, 2010)

43 Alex von Tunzelmann, *Indian Summer: The Secret History of the End of an Empire* (London: Simon and Schuster, 2012).

44 Mahir Ali, 'A Case of mistaken paternity?', *The Hindu*, September 2009. (https://www.thehindu.com/opinion/op-ed/A-case-of-mistaken-paternity/article16880558.ece, Accessed December 2023)

45 Sri Prakasa, *Pakistan: Birth and Early Days* (Meerut: Meenaksi Prakashan, 1965).

46 Alice Albania: *Empires of the Indus: The Story of a River* (London: John Murray, 2008)

47 Khaled Ahmed, *Pakistan's Terror Conundrum* (New Delhi: Penguin Books India, 2021),p. xi

48 The Federal Shariat Court was established in 1980 by General Zia-ul-Haq to examine and determine whether laws enacted by the State were in compliance with the principles and ideals of Sharia laws.

49 A body of Muslim scholars who are recognized as having specialist knowledge of Islamic sacred law and theology.

50 Laws in Pakistan that were enacted in 1979 as part of the then military ruler Zia-ul-Haq's 'Sharisation or Islamisation' process. It replaced parts of the British-era Pakistan Penal Code, adding new criminal offences of adultery and fornication, and new punishments of whipping, amputation, and stoning to death. After much controversy and criticism parts of the law were extensively revised in 2006 by the Women's Protection Bill. The Hudood Law was intended to implement Sharia law or bring Pakistani law into 'conformity with the injunctions of Islam', by enforcing punishments mentioned in the Quran and Sunnah for 'zina' (extramarital sex), 'qazf' (false accusation of zina), theft, and consumption of alcohol.

51 Zakat is an Islamic finance term referring to the obligation that an individual has, to donate a certain proportion of wealth each year to charitable causes. Zakat is a mandatory process for Muslims and is regarded as a form of worship.

52 As quoted Christine Fair, *Fighting to the End: The Pakistan Army's Way of War* (New York: Oxford University Press, 2014)

53 Mohammed Ayub Khan, 'Pakistan Perspective', *Foreign Affairs*, July 1960. (https://www.foreignaffairs.com/articles/india/1960-07-01/pakistan-perspective, Accessed December 2023)

54 Mohammed Ayub Khan, *Friends Not Masters: A Political Autobiography* (London: Oxford University Press, 1967), p. 194-195.

55 Pakistan's Commission on National Education, 1959. Constituted by President Ayub Khan, among its other purposes were ''preservation of the ideas which led to the creation of Pakistan and strengthening of the concept of it with the united nation and to create a sense of unity and of nationhood among the people of Pakistan.'

56 Sarmila Bose, 'Three Turbulent Years: A Re-appraisal of the Yahya Regime 1969-71' in Roger D. Long, *A History of Pakistan* (Karachi: Oxford University Press, 2015), p. 518.

57 Rizvi p. 256.

58 It is also known as Pakistan's 1984 Islamization Programme Referendum.

59 'Partial transcript of Pakistan President Musharraf's televised speech asking the people of Pakistan to support his course of action', The *Washington Post*, Spetember 2001 (https://www.washingtonpost.com/wp-srv/nation/specials/attacked/transcripts/pakistantext_091901.html, Accessed December 2023)

60 'Judgment in Referendum Case-Pakistan Supreme Court- 27/4/2002', *Advocatetanmoy Law Library: Legal Database and Encyclopedia* (https://advocatetanmoy.com/2020/12/07/judgment-in-referendum-case-pakistan-supreme-court-27-4-2002/, Accessed December 2023)

61 Martyrs' Day (Pakistan) or Youm-e-Shuda is a Pakistani holiday held on 30 April to pay tribute to Pakistani military who died in service of their country.

62 Quoted from Daily Times in Christine Fair, *Fighting to the End: The Pakistan Army's Way of War* (New York: Oxford University Press, 2014), p 79.

63 Husain Haqqani, *Pakistan Between Mosque and Military*, (London: Penguin Books, 2016), p. 2-3.

64 Christine Fair, Op cit, p. 86.

65 Ayesha Siddiqa, 'Why Imran Khan bats for Narendra Modi', *The Indian Express*, April 2019 (https://indianexpress.com/article/opinion/columns/narendra-modi-lok-sabha-elections-bjp-imran-khan-pakistan-5687359/, Accessed December 2023)

3. The Sentinels

66 Narendra Singh Sarila, *The Shadow of the Great Game: The Untold Story of India's Partition*, HarperCollins Publishers India with India Today Group, pp. 340-341.

67 The phrase 'Great Game' was accidentally coined by a young and

enthusiastic British captain, Capt. Arthur Connolly, who wrote in a letter to a friend: 'We are on the eve of stirring times; but if we play the great game that is before us, the results will be incalculably beneficial to us [the British] and to the tribes whose destinies may change from turmoil, violence, ignorance and poverty to peace, enlightenment and varied happiness.' Thus the phrase 'the Great Game' came to be used more than 60 years before Rudyard Kipling's 1901 novel *Kim*, about the Great Game made it popular. The Great Game was actually a big triangle consisting of Great Britain, Russia and China where often the British India would become a proxy for the Great Britain. The struggle was primarily for the control over the vast Afghanistan Empire that had spread into the central Asian countries and had also made inroads into the eastern end of the Chinese Empire. While Russia was fearful of British commercial and military inroads into Central Asia, Britain was fearful of Russia appropriating 'the jewel in the crown', India, to the vast empire that Russia was building in Asia. This resulted in an atmosphere of distrust and the constant threat of war between the two empires.

68 British diplomat, Sir Mortimer Durand, and Afghan Amir, Abdur Rehman Khan, reached an agreement to fix the areas of influence of the British and the Afghans in the Frontier region. It virtually took Tsarist Russia out of the Great Game since it allayed the fears of Russia.

69 Christine Fair, *Fighting to the End: The Pakistan Army's Way of War* (New York: Oxford University Press, 2014), p. 4

70 *Daily Times* 2006; quoted in Christine Fair, Ibid, p.1

71 *Ibid*, p. 3

72 Quoted by Stephen Cohen.

73 Ayesha Siddiqa, *Military Inc.: Inside Pakistan's Military Economy* (New Delhi: Penguin Random House India, 2017), p. 58.

74 Ibid, p. 69

75 C. Christine Fair, Op cit, p. 13

76 Anatol Leiven, *Pakistan: A Hard Country* (London: Allen Lane/ Penguin, 2011) pp. 185-86.

77 B.N. Mullik, *My Years with Nehru: Kashmir* (New Delhi: Allied Publishers, 1971)

78 Husain Haqqani, *Pakistan Between Mosque and Military* (London: Penguin Books, 2016), p. 33.

79 Margaret Bourke-White, *Halfway to Freedom: A Report on the New India in the Words and Photographs* (New York: Simon and Schuster, 1949), p.92.

80 Ibid.
81 Craig Baxter,'Mohammad Ayub Khan' in Roger D. Long, *A History of Pakistan* (Karachi: Oxford University Press, 2015), p. 498.
82 From the text of President Ayub Khan's Address to the Nation on 6 September 1965; quoted in Husain Haqqani, Op cit, p. 52
83 A.R. Siddiqui, *The Military in Pakistan*; quoted in Husain Haqqani, Op cit
84 Khaled Ahmed, *Pakistan's Terror Conundrum* (New Delhi: Penguin Books India, 2021), p. 8.
85 The US Embassy's telegram to the State Department, dated 8 September 1965; quoted in Husain Haqqani, Op cit, pp. 43-44.
86 Ibid, p. 55.
87 S. Mahmud Ali, *Understanding Bangladesh* (London: Oxford University Press, 2010), p. 31; quoted in Christophe Jaffrelot, *The Pakistan Paradox: Instability and Resilience* (New Delhi: Vintage/ Penguin, 2016), p. 119
88 Sarmila Bose, 'Three Turbulent Years: A Re-appraisal of the Yahya Regime 1969-71' in Roger D. Long, *A History of Pakistan* (Karachi: Oxford University Press, 2015), p. 524.
89 Christophe Jaffrelot Op cit, p. 216.
90 'Three Turbulent Years', Op cit, p. 534.
91 The Red Mosque, or Lal Masjid, as it is locally known, had developed as a stronghold of the Taliban and forces aligned to them. By 2006 they had become so powerful that the two brothers running the mosque, and the *madarsa* in the sprawling complex, had begun to call for the overthrow of the Pervez Musharraf government and the implementation of the sharia law in Pakistan. These forces had become so dominant that they clashed with the army and also took Chinese nurses as hostage from a health centre in the vicinity of the under-construction China-Pakistan Economic Corridor (CPEC). Finally, in July, the Pakistani Army's special forces stormed the complex leaving hundreds dead and thousands injured. The man and fire power in the complex pointed to the massive resources by these religious organizations to run a near parallel government.
92 Christophe Jaffrelot, Op cit, p. 586-87.
93 Anatol Leiven, Op cit, p. 162-163.
94 Ibid, p. 189.
95 Hein G. Kiessling, *Faith, Unity, Discipline: The Inter-Service-Intelligence (ISI) of Pakistan* (London: Hurst & Co., 2016), p. 116.
96 Ibid, p. 117.

97 Ibid, p.

98 Hamid Gul was a three star General of the Pakistani Army who headed the ISI during the crucial years of 1987-1989 when the Islamist Jihadist war against Soviet Union was at a critical juncture and seeds of militancy were being sown in Jammu and Kashmir. He carried this design even after retirement and during his last years was even closely aligned to Islamist Jihad, even against forces in Pakistan.

99 Sheikh Rasheed is currently the Interior Minister of Pakistan.

100 Christophe Jaffrelot, Op cit, p. 588

101 Former senior official of the Federal Investigation Agency and a politician of Pakistan aligned with Benazir Bhutto's Pakistan Peoples' Party.

102 Imtiaz Gul, *The Most Dangerous Place: Pakistan's Lawless Frontier* (London: Viking/Penguin, 2010), p. 213

103 'Global watchdog FATF puts Pakistan back on terrorist financing watchlist: Reports', *Firstpost*, February 2018. (https://www.firstpost.com/world/global-watchdog-fatf-puts-pakistan-back-on-terrorist-financing-watchlist-reports-4364147.html, Accessed December 2023)

104 Suhasini Haider, 'Pakistan retained on grey list of FATF', *The Hindu*, February 2020. (https://www.thehindu.com/news/international/pakistan-retained-on-grey-list-of-fatf/article30880521.ece, Accessed December 2023)

105 See Chapter 1 for more details

106 Bharatiya Janata Party is a party that owes its ideological philosophy to the Rashtriya Swayamsewak Sangh, a professed Hindu nationalist organization which also supported the Bharatiya Jana Sangh, the earlier incarnation of Bharatiya Janata Party. It professes Hindu superiority and also believes in the theory of irredentist India—Akhand Bharat.

107 Myra MacDonald: *Defeat is an Orphan: How Pakistan Lost the Great South Asian War* (London: C. Hurst & Co., 2016).

108 Christine Fair, Op cit, p. 16.

109 Ibid p.16.

4. The Threat of Jihad

110 The Salafi movement, also called the Salafist movement, Salafiya and Salafism, is a reform branch movement within Sunni Islam that developed in Al-Azhar Mosque in Egypt in the late 19th century as a response to Western European imperialism. It had roots in the 18th-century Wahhabi movement that originated in the Najd region

of modern-day Saudi Arabia. The name derives from advocating a return to the traditions of the *salaf*, the first three generations of Muslims, which they said was the unadulterated, pure form of Islam. Theoretically, those generations include the Islamic prophet Muhammad and his companions (the Sahabah), their successors (the Tabi'un) and the successors of the successors (the Taba Tabi'in). Practically, Salafis maintain that Muslims ought to rely on the Quran, the Sunnah and the consensus of the salafs alone, ignoring the rest of Islamic hermeneutic teachings. The contemporary questions too need to be answered by those ancient traditions associated with the life and times of the Prophet.

111 Juhayman ibn Muhammad ibn Sayf al-Otaybi was a Saudi militant and soldier who in 1979 led the Grand Mosque seizure of the Great Mosque of Mecca, Saudi Arabia's holiest mosque, to protest against the Saudi monarchy and the House of Saud. Juhayman said that his justification for the siege was that the House of Saud had lost its legitimacy through corruption and imitation of the West, an echo of his father's charge in 1921 against former Saudi king Ibn Saud. Unlike earlier anti-monarchist dissidents in the kingdom, Juhayman attacked the Saudi ulema for failing to protest against policies that betrayed Islam, and accused them of accepting the rule of an infidel state and offering loyalty to corrupt rulers in 'exchange for honors and riches.' He and his brotherhood propagated that moral and ethical answers to life are to be sought in the sunnah and not in the interpretation of the ulema.

112 The House of Saudis the ruling royal family of Saudi Arabia. It is composed of the descendants of Muhammad bin Saud, founder of the Emirate of Diriyah, known as the First Saudi state (1744–1818), and his brothers, though the ruling faction of the family is primarily led by the descendants of Ibn Saud, the modern founder of Saudi Arabia.

113 Imam Mahdi, al-mahdīy, meaning 'the Rightly Guided One' is an eschatological Messianic figure who, according to Islamic belief, will appear at the end of times to rid the world of evil and injustice.

114 Wahhabism is the Saudi kind of Salafist movement. Both are rooted in Islam as practiced during the Prophet's time.

115 Arif Jamal, *Call for Transnational Jihad: Lashkar-e-Taiba, 1985-2014* (Georgia: Avant-Garde Books, 2014), p. 29.

116 Yaroslav Trofimov, *The Seige of Mecca: The Forgotten Uprising in Islam's Holiest Shrine* (London: Allen Lane/Penguin, 2007), p. 6-8.

117 Arif Jamal, Op cit, p. 20.

118 Husain Haqqani, *Pakistan Between Mosque and Military*, (London: Penguin Books, 2016), p. 33.

119 Margaret Bourke-White, *Halfway to Freedom: A Report on the New India in the Words and Photographs* (New York: Simon and Schuster, 1949), p. 92.

120 Hein G. Kiessling, *Faith, Unity, Discipline: The Inter-Service-Intelligence (ISI) of Pakistan* (London: Hurst & Co., 2016), p. 29.

121 Ayesha Siddiqa, *Military Inc.: Inside Pakistan's Military Economy* (New Delhi: Penguin Random House India, 2017), p. 102.

122 Arif Jamal, Op cit, p. 77.

123 Ibid. p.77.

124 Ibid. p. 79.

125 Praveen Swami, '"Pro-Active" After Pokhran: A Perspective on Terrorism in J&K,' *Faultlines*, vol 1, (A South Asia Terrorism Portal, May 1999). (https://www.satp.org/faultline-chapter-details/volume-1/pro-active-after-pokhran-a-perspective-on-terrorism-in-jandk, Accessed December 2023)

126 Praveen Swami, 'A massacre and a message' *Frontline, The Hindu*, August 2002 (https://frontline.thehindu.com/cover-story/article30245638.ece, Accessed December 2023)

127 Praveen Swami, '"Pro-Active" After Pokhran', Op cit.

128 Praveen Swami, 'A massacre and a message', Op cit

129 'Militants massacre 23 kin of Army men, 7 HRTC passengers among 32 killed in Jammu area; all five terrorists shot', *The Tribune*, May 2002 (https://www.tribuneindia.com/2002/20020515/main1.htm, Accessed December 2023)

130 It is an Arabic term used to refer to various military groups willing to sacrifice themselves for a larger campaign.

131 The Ziarat of Baba Reshi is a popular shrine of Baramula, situated near the Alpather Lake, 13 km from Gulmarg and belongs to saint Baba payam-Din. Baba payam-Din was a well-known Muslim saint as well as a courtier of the king of Kashmir, Zain-ul-Abidin. This shrine is at the very site where Baba payam-Din died in 1480 after spending his days in prayer and meditation.

132 Praveen Swami, 'A war with three fronts', *Frontline, The Hindu*, July 2006 (https://frontline.thehindu.com/the-nation/article30210179.ece, Accessed December 2023)

133 Loosely translated as 'The System of the Prophet Muhammad', Nizam-e-Mustafa was a nine-party popular movement in Pakistan which was started by the Jamaat-e-Islami in 1977 to overthrow the secular

government of Zulfikar Ali Bhutto and establish an Islamic system of government in Pakistan.

134 Arif Jamal, Op cit, p. 97.

135 Ibid, p. 98.

136 'Six terror attacks that shook India,' *The Economic Times*, February 2020. (https://economictimes.indiatimes.com/news/defence/six-terror-attacks-that-shook-india/2001-parliament-attack/slideshow/74146279.cms, Accessed December 2023)

137 Gauri Gill, 'It's War, Put Diplomatically,' *Outlook*, February 2022. (https://magazine.outlookindia.com/story/its-war-put-diplomatically/214151, Accessed December 2023)

138 Bruce Riedel, *Deadly Embrace: Pakistan, America, and the Future of the Global Jihad*; quoted in by Rajiv Dogra, *Where Borders Bleed: An Insider's Account of Indo-Pak Relations* (New Delhi: Rupa Publications India, 2015), p. 191

139 Arif Jamal, Op cit, p. 102.

5. Disillusioned Followers

140 Henry Kissinger, *World Order: Reflections on the Character of Nations and the Course of History* (London: Penguin Books, 2015), p. 202-203.

141 Margaret Bourke-White, *Halfway to Freedom: A Report on the New India in the Words and Photographs* (New York: Simon and Schuster, 1949), p. 92.

142 He was also put in prison in June 1953 when he openly came out in favor of Pakistan and held a public meeting in Srinagar announcing the establishment of the Kashmir Political Conference. Slogans of *Pakistan Zindabad* were raised during the meeting.

143 In 1955, Mirza Afzal Beg established the Jammu and Kashmir Plebiscite Front with the objective of forcing the Government of India and the international community to hold a popular plebiscite to determine if the State wished to accede to India, Pakistan or state independent.

144 B.N. Mullik, *My Years with Nehru: Kashmir*, (New Delhi: Allied Publishers, 1971), p. 51.

145 Government agencies at that time had credible evidence that Begum Abdullah was an integral part of the Kashmir Conspiracy case but, according to B.N. Mullik in *My Years with Nehru: Kashmir*, 'Bakshi at this stage decided that whatever might be the strength of the evidence against Begum Abdullah, he would not agree to her prosecution. Muslim opinion in Kashmir valley would not excuse him for dragging this lady, who was known as 'Madr-e-Mehrban', to the courts.'

146 B.N. Mullik, Op cit, p. 67. Mullik writes, 'Rules regarding visitors were not observed strictly in respect of Sheikh Abdullah and Afzal Beg, and it was possible for visitors to go and meet them without being subjected to a search and Begum Abdullah was even allowed to stay with her husband...'

147 The intelligence had been gathering evidence of suspicious and anti-India activities among Sheikh Abdullah and his followers since 1953. The tipping point came in 1958 when Sheikh Abdullah was released when his utterances and acts left nothing to doubts. The agencies were convinced that they had a strong case against Sheikh Abdullah, Begum Abdullah, Mirza Afzal Beg and several others. To quote Mullik, 'His inflammatory speeches, his call to raise Razakars, the Hazratbal rioting and murder, the Plebiscite Front Manifesto and the receipt of large sums of money from Pakistan by the Begum during his presence in the house all went to further strengthen the case.' Prime Minister Nehru still hesitated from including name of Sheikh Abdullah in the case on the grounds that at international forums India had built its case around the support extended by Sheikh Abdullah to the State's accession to India and now if he was charged of India's secession in favor of Pakistan then not only that case would fall flat but also make India a laughing stock. However, by the end of the year he agreed to include the Sheikh's name in the face of irrefutable evidence. One of the letters that had been seized from the conspirators acknowledged that 'while weapons had been received from Pakistan, it was important to import saboteurs also, as it was not possible to raise them locally. A reliable man of Hyder Khan (Pakistan) came here last week. Long discussions were held with him and our position was explained to him in detail. They are preparing to come forward openly. I pointed out to him the harm that was occurring due to the indefinite postponement of the matter and it is possible, if it is delayed any further irreparable damage may be done. Secondly, I pointed to him the necessity of pruning the branches in the garden. They had sent the scissors and other material but a gardener is not available. So he was asked to send a good gardener from his village itself. The rot that has set in can be remedied by immediate pruning of branches. However, the case was withdrawn later on.' Chapter 6 of *My Years With Nehru: Kashmir* by B.N. Mullik

148 Ibid.

149 B.N. Mullik, Op cit, p. 78-83; The first confrontation took place on 17 January 1958 at Pathar Masjid, located opposite Mujahid Manzil,

the headquarters of the National Conference. In the Valley it was a popular belief that whoever controlled this headquarters controlled the Valley. On Abdullah's call people had begun to gather since morning and more than 20,000 had reached the venue. The plan appeared to be to storm the Mujahid Manzil, take control of it and then make a run for the Civil Secretariat. However, at the last moment, in a dramatic development, courage failed Abdullah and he never turned up. Instead he went to Hazratbal Mosque and delivered a vitriolic attack against Government of India and Bakshi. But soon he gathered courage and gave a call for complete boycott of the Republic Day function which was to follow the first confrontation. Again, Bakshi proved that he could muster popular nationalistic support in the valley and again got the better of Abdullah.

150 Though there is little evidence to suggest that Bakshi Ghulam Mohammad was personally involved in corruption, the people of the Valley were convinced of that his family members, particularly his brothers were corrupted. The people would sarcastically refer to them as BBC, i.e. Bakshi Brothers Corporation. One of the brothers made little effort to mitigate the effect of this virulent perception when he was accused of trying to outrage the modesty of the wife of an army officer, which resulted in a backlash from the army personnel.

151 Against the better judgment of Sardar Patel, Nehru had gone out of duty to concede to the unreasonable demands of more autonomy, thereby whetting his appetite for more and Indira Gandhi had heeded to the red flag raised by Dr Karan Singh regarding handing over power to Sheikh Abdullah without providing any safeguards for the integrity that had been achieved after 1953.

152 Wajahat Habibullah, *My Kashmir: The Dying of the Light* (New Delhi: Penguin India, 2014), p. 37.

153 Jawaid Alam (ed.), *Kashmir & Beyond, 1966-84: Select Correspondence between Indira Gandhi & Karan Singh* (New Delhi: Penguin India, 2020), pp. 262-266.

154 Colonel Muammar Qaddafi was a Libyan revolutionary, political leader and theorist. He ruled Libya after a coup in 1969 and continued to rule till his death in 2011 when a counter revolution overthrew him with US support. For as long as he remained in power, he defied the US and was therefore a long time ideal for many in the developing countries.

155 https://www.kashmirnewz.com/f000108.html and https://www.outlookindia.com/blog/story/india-news-dismantling-sheikh-abdullahs-legacy-one-historical-step-at-a-time/4148

156 Naya Kashmir is the name of the memorandum that was presented by the National Conference leaders to Maharaja Hari Singh in 1944 after his return from England. It outlined the change from absolute monarchy to constitutional monarchy in Jammu and Kashmir and also visualized radical socio-economic changes. Later it became the manifesto of the National Conference.

157 Syed Mohammad Yusuf Shah was a resident of Budgam district of the Valley. His early life was no different from that of ordinary citizens of the country but while pursuing his studies in the Kashmir University, Srinagar he became a follower of radical Islam. He was the joint candidate of Muslim United Front during the 1987 Assembly elections when the National Conference under Farooq Abdullah and the Congress under Rajiv Gandhi entered into an alliance. All opposition parties were decimated and it was widely believed that the elections had been rigged. It is considered to be a watershed moment since it drove away the Kashmiri youth from the democratic process. Yusuf Shah was the earliest to cross over to Pakistan-occupied-Kashmir and pick up arms. Before that he was imprisoned for his violent protests and was one of the six prisoners released after Mufti Mohammad Sayeed's (then Home Minister of India) daughter had been kidnapped. After crossing over, he joined the Hizb-ul-Mujahideen, an Islamist militant organization operating in the Kashmir region, and adopted the name of Salahuddin after the celebrated Islamic military leader of the Crusades of the twelfth century.

158 Walter R. Lawrence, *The Valley of Kashmir* (London: Henry Frowde/ Oxford University Press, 1895).

159 Bhagwan Singh, *Political Conspiracies of Kashmir* (Jammu: Light and Life Publishers, 1973)

160 In 1939, a group in the Muslim Conference, led by Sheikh Mohammad Abdullah, broke away from the parent body to rechristen as the National Conference.

161 Nehru's Note of 3 July 1952, recording his plans for Kashmir's integration; from *Selected Works of Jawaharlal Nehru, Second Series, Volume 18 (1 April-15 July 1952)* (New Delhi: Jawaharlal Nehru Memorial Fund, 1996), pp.423-425.

162 Alastair Lamb, *Kashmir: A Disputed Legacy, 1846-1990* (Hertford: Roxford Books, 1991), p. 304-305.

163 Ibid, p. 310.

164 Ibid, p. 304.

165 The agreement was reached well past midnight though it remains

dated as 2 July 1972, in Simla, now Shimla, the capital of Himachal Pradesh. For the first time, by this Agreement, Pakistan acknowledged that the Jammu and Kashmir dispute between India and Pakistan was a bilateral issue and excluded all outside interference including that of the United Nations.

166 Killed in 1990 by the terrorists, Moulvi Mohammad Shah Farooq was the Mirwaiz of Kashmir and the chairman of the All-Jammu and Kashmir Awami Party. He sought resolution to the Kashmir conflict and accepted the accession of the State to India.

167 Alastair Lamb, Op cit, p. 308.

168 Victoria Schofield, *Kashmir in the Crossfire* (London: I.B. Tauris, 1996), p.217

169 Alastair Lamb, Op cit, p. 308.

170 Balraj Puri, *Kashmir: Insurgency and After* (New Delhi, Orient Longman, 2010) p. 35.

171 Alastair Lamb, Op cit, p. 309.

172 Atal Behari Vajpayee, as leader of the Bharatiya Jana Sangh, became the Prime Minister of India for 13 days in 1996, 13 months in 1998 to 1999 and then for a full term from 1999 to 2004. He was also the first non-Congress Foreign Minister during the Janata Party government from 1977 to 1979.

173 She is the demon-killing Goddess worshiped all over India.

174 Prem Nath Bazaz, *Democracy Through Intimidation and Terror: The Untold Story of Kashmir Politics* (New Delhi: Heritage, 1978), p.24.

175 Gul Mohammad Wani, *Kashmir Politics: Problems and Prospects* (New Delhi: Ashish Publishing House, 1993), p.85.

6. The Flawed Federalism

176 Apart from India, Bangladesh and Pakistan are examples of this.

177 When the Constitution was adopted on 26 January 1950, Hindi was made the official language of India with English as the associate official language for 15 years, i.e. till 26 January 1965. As the day arrived, anti-Hindi agitation broke out and Tamil Nadu, then Madras, threatened secession over the issue. Officially 70 lives were lost during the violence and police firing, till the then Prime Minister Lal Bahadur Shastri assured them that English will remain the official language as long as the non-Hindi speaking States wanted it.

178 On 12 November 1969, Indira Gandhi was expelled from the Congress Party for violating party discipline. This came after a long-drawn

battle for supremacy between her and the Party bosses led by Morarji Desai, whose ambition to become the Prime Minister had already been thwarted twice, first by Lal Bahadur Shastri and then by Indira Gandhi. The Congress had put up Neelam Sanjeeva Reddy as the official candidate for the election of the President of India. Indira Gandhi supported V.V. Giri, leading to the charge of indiscipline. Giri won and the Congress split with Indira Gandhi's Congress coming to be known as Congress (R).

179 V.V. Giri is the only independent candidate to be elected the President of India. A trade unionist and a former minister, as member of the Congress party, he resigned from the party to contest the 1969 Presidential election that led to the defeat of the official Congress candidate.

180 In a concerted bid to oust Indira Gandhi from power, a Grand Alliance was formed for the 1971 Lok Sabha elections by the Samyukta Socialist Party (SSP), the Praja Socialist Party (PSP), the Swatantra Party and the Bharatiya Jana Sangh. This Alliance was badly trounced and it lost more than half of the seats held by its constituents.

181 Serious anti-Hindu riots with the intention of cleansing East Pakistan first took place in 1964 during the Moe-e-Muqaddas (The Holy Relic of Prophet Mohammad) crisis of Kashmir. When the Relic had been recovered, Pakistan declared it to be a fake and accused India of trying to hurt Muslim sentiments. It also declared 3 January 1964 as Kashmir Day. As a result, large scale killings of Pakistani Hindus took place, notably in Dhaka, Khulna, Narayanganj, Rajshahi, Mymensingh and Sylhet. However, the exodus of Hindus became a serious problem when East Pakistan erupted after the first general elections of Pakistan and the refusal of West Pakistan to hand over power to the Bangla-dominated Awami Party.

182 In response to Dhirendranath Datta's (a member of the National Constituent Assembly), call to have Bangla along with Urdu to be the lingua franca of East Pakistan, Liaquat Ali Khan, the Prime Minister, and Khwaja Nazimuddin, from the family of Nawabs of Dhaka, opposed the proposal on the grounds of Urdu being a unifying force; quoted in Anam Zakaria, *1971: A People's History from Bangladesh, Pakistan and India* (New Delhi: Penguin Random House India, 2019), p. 66-67.

183 Nawab Nazimuddin of the Nawab family of Dhaka was also Urdu speaking and barely appreciated the significance of Bengali. He later succeeded Jinnah as the Governor General of Pakistan and also

Liaquat Ali Khan as the Prime Minister upon his assassination. The family had been richly rewarded by the British for their loyalty and services during the Independence War of 1857.

184 Philip Oldenburg, '"A Place Insufficiently Imagined": Language, Belief, and the Pakistan Crisis of 1971.' *The Journal of Asian Studies* (44, no. 4, 1985), p. 716.

185 Anam Zakaria, Op cit, p. 64.

186 Ibid, p.66-67

187 Ibid, 74.

188 Quoted in Anam Zakaria, Op cit, p. 57.

189 Even though Pakistan was created on the basis of the Two Nation theory, the common factor of religion failed to keep West and East Pakistan together. The debate over language broke the two asunder and exposed the hollowness of the Two Nations theory in the subcontinent. The theme of linguist sub-nationalism had proved stronger, with the Pakistani Bengalis refusing to accept Urdu as the national language.

190 The Awami League of East Pakistan won a land slide victory by winning 160 of the 300 the National Assembly seats, all of them from East Pakistan. Zulfikar Ali Bhutto's Pakistan People's Party (PPP) could only win 81. This meant that the domination of the Punjabi and Pathan would have ended. The military and the western Pakistani establishment refused to see through the transfer of power leading to the agitation in the East and ultimate break up.

191 P.N. Dhar, *Indira Gandhi, the 'Emergency', and Indian Democracy* (New Delhi: Oxford University Press, 2000), p. 152-154

192 The tragedy was remembered by Sydney Schanberg, the *The New York Times* correspondent in the following words: 'The bodies have adjusted to those germs in their water, but suddenly they were drinking different water with different germs. Suddenly they've got cholera. People were dying all around us. You'd see that someone had left a body on the side of the road, wrapped in pieces of bamboo, and there'd be a vulture trying to get inside to eat the body. You would come into a school yard, and a mother was losing a child. He was in her lap. He coughed and coughed and then died. They went through holy hell and back.'

193 Gary J. Bass, *The Blood Telegram: India's Secret War in East Pakistan* (Noida: Random House India, 2013), p. 121.

194 The American President Richard Nixon and his National Security Advisor Henry Kissinger were convinced that India was capable of fighting a two front war and therefore tried to convince China to open the north front to teach Indira Gandhi a lesson. But India had

entered into a Treaty of Friendship with the USSR when the East Pakistan crisis had begun to unfold. China, on the other hand, though sympathetic to the cause of Pakistan was afraid that in case it entered into the fray it might lead to a direct confrontation with the USSR. In the end, all that China did was to ask both the parties for a ceasefire. India had played its diplomatic cards well.

195 *Garibi hatao and Roti kapada aur makan*, i.e 'remove poverty' and 'food, clothing and home', were the two slogans of Indira Gandhi during the 1971 Lok Sabha elections in response to her opponents slogan of *Indira hatao*, i.e. 'remove Indira'.

196 A coterie had come to control all the levers of power with Sanjay Gandhi being the leader of the pack. Other prominent members of this group were Information and Broadcasting Minister, V.C. Shukla, Haryana Chief Minister, Bansi Lal, S.S. Ray, Chief Minister of West Bengal, State Minister of Home, Om Mehta, and others. The bureaucrats too looked towards these for a lead as a result of which the parliamentary system of governance literally collapsed.

197 *Sampooran Kranti* or 'Total Revolution' was a call that originated from Bihar. What began as students protest regarding the quality of food available in university hostels, soon snowballed into a bigger protest that embraced the multiple ills that plagued society and governance. It moved forward from the 'revolution' of Gandhi to become an umbrella for all demands ranging from casteism, dowry etc. to corruption in public life. However, it fizzled out after the leadership of Jayprakash Narayan had guided to victory in 1977.

198 No one really knew what total revolution was except that it denoted changed. An aura of romance and idealism attracted the slogan for it was believed that it will usher a just system to pull India out of morass of corruption.

199 After being routed in the 1972 Punjab election, the Akali Dal put forward the Anandpur Sahib Resolution in 1973 to demand more autonomy to Punjab. The resolution included both religious and political issues. It asked for recognizing Sikhism as a religion separate from Hinduism. It also demanded that power be generally devolved from the Central to state governments. The demand for autonomy was phrased such a way that would have given more authority to Punjabis rather than the Central Government.

200 Indira Gandhi's election had been challenged by the losing candidate Raj Narain in the Allahabad High Court. The court unseated her on comparatively frivolous charges, while she was acquitted on more

serious charges. *The Times* described it as 'firing the Prime Minister for a traffic ticket'. Her supporters organized a mass pro-Indira demonstrations in the streets of Delhi close to the Prime Minister's residence. The persistent efforts of Narain were praised worldwide as it took over four years for Justice Sinha to pass judgement against the prime minister. Indira Gandhi challenged the High Court's decision in the Supreme Court. Justice V.R. Krishna Iyer, on 24 June 1975, upheld the High Court judgment and ordered that all privileges that Gandhi received as an MP be stopped, and that she be debarred from voting. However, she was allowed to continue as Prime Minister pending the resolution of her appeal. J.P. Narayan and Morarji Desai called for daily anti-government protests. The next day, J.P. Narayan organized a large rally in Delhi, where he said that a police officer must reject the orders of government if the order is immoral and unethical as this was Mahatma Gandhi's motto during the freedom struggle. Such a statement was taken as a sign of inciting rebellion in the country. Later that day, Indira Gandhi requested a compliant President Fakhruddin Ali Ahmed to issue a proclamation of a state of emergency. Within three hours, the electricity to all major newspapers was cut and the political opposition arrested. The proposal was sent without discussion with the Union Cabinet, who only learnt of it and ratified it the next morning.

201 Five Sikh separatists belonging to the Dal Khalsa carried out the hijacking of IC-423 Srinagar-Delhi flight to Lahore. However, Pakistani commandos freed the passengers and neutralized them. They were tried in a Lahore court where they were sentenced to life term in jail. On return to India they were arrested and tried in a Delhi court which released them saying that they had already served a jail sentence for that crime.

202 Seymour M. Hersh, *Price of Power: Kissinger in the Nixon White House* (New York: Simon and Schuster, 2013). The disclosure caused a storm in India and Morarji Desai, later Prime Minister of India, filed a suit of defamation in USA.

203 Katherine Frank, *Indira: The Life of Indira Nehru Gandhi* (London: HarperCollins Publishers, 2001), p. 443.

204 Henry Kissinger, *World Order: Reflections on the Character of Nations and the Course of History* (London: Penguin Books, 2015), p. 192.

205 Anshu Singh, 'Development of Cooperative Federalism in India', *Legal Services India* (https://www.legalserviceindia.com/article/l441-Cooperative-Federalsim-In-India.html, Accessed December 2023)

206 Robert L. Hardgrave, 'India in 1983: New Challenges Lost Opportunities', *Asian Survey* (24, no. 2), p. 209-218
207 Ashutosh Varshney, *India Today*, 30 November 1999
208 Ibid
209 The Shah Bano case was a controversial maintenance lawsuit in India, in which the Supreme Court delivered a judgment favoring maintenance given to an aggrieved divorced Muslim woman. Then the Congress government enacted a law—its most controversial aspect being the right to maintenance for the period of *iddat* after the divorce, and shifting the onus of maintaining the divorced wife to her relatives or the Waqf Board. It was seen as discriminatory as it denied right to basic maintenance available to Muslim women under secular law.
210 Ibid.
211 Sten Widmalm, *Kashmir in Comparative Perspective: Democracy and Violent Separatism in India* (London: RoutledgeCurzon/Taylor and Francis, 2002), p.61
212 Ibid, p. 61
213 Ibid, p. 62
214 The Jammu & Kashmir Grant of Permit for Resettlement in (or Permanent Return to) the State Act, 1982, was passed by the Assembly to 'provide for regulation of procedure for grant of permit for resettlement in or permanent return to the State of the permanent residents' and their descendants who had migrated to Pakistan between 1 March 1947 and 14 May 1954

7. Dangerous Moves

215 Alastair Lamb, *Kashmir: A Disputed Legacy, 1846-1990* (Hertford: Roxford Books, 1991), p. 328.
216 Apart from the report that Sir Owen Dixon presented to the UNCIP, he also advanced what came to be known as 'regional plebiscites'. It was either 'a plan for taking the plebiscite by sections or areas and the allocation of each section or area according to the result of the vote therein, without taking a vote therein.' The 1983 voting pattern reflected something like that.
217 Alastair Lamb, Op cit, p. 329; *Sten Widmalm, Kashmir in Comparative Perspective: Democracy and Violent Separatism in India* (London: RoutledgeCurzon/Taylor and Francis, 2002), p. 67.
218 Farooq Abdullah, *My Dismissal* (New Delhi: Vikas Publishing House, 1985)

219 'Concern over Srinagar Violence', *The Hindustan Times*, 16 October 1983

220 The National Conference used its clout to bully and intimidate opponents who either failed to file their nomination papers or whose papers were arbitrarily rejected. In Jammu the National Conference tactics had forced the leading opposition party, the Praja Parishad, to boycott the elections. Thus this Assembly was packed with National Conference representatives. It was this body that had drawn up the Constitution of the State.

221 Quoted in Sten Widmalm, Op cit, p. 63

222 'I never took oath as JKLF member: Farooq', *The Rising Kashmir*, 13 August 2017

223 Ibid

224 Jagmohan, *My Frozen Turbulence in Kashmir* (New Delhi: Allied Publishers, 1991), p. 2-3.

225 Ibid, p. 3.

226 Sten Widmalm, Op cit, p. 64.

227 Sheikh Abdullah, along with Chaudhary Ghulam Abbas co-founded the All-Jammu and Kashmir Muslim Conference in 1932. But soon a group, led by Sheikh Abdullah, realized that the name of the party was limiting its reach and therefore, in 1939 during the party convention it was renamed as the All-Jammu and Kashmir National Conference, to include all the segments of the State. This was deeply resented by a powerful group led by Ghulam Abbas, one of the founding fathers. This group broke away in 1941 to revive All-Jammu and Kashmir Muslim Conference.

228 There is no doubt that the reach of Sheikh Abdullah's leadership was confined to the Valley, but Prime Minister Nehru was convinced that the accession of the State to India will not be accepted by the Kashmiris without the support of Sheikh Abdullah and hence he made accession of the State and the sending of the troops to the Valley a precondition for it. Hence, Maharaja Hari Singh was forced into appointing the Sheikh, first as the Head of the Emergency Administration and then as Prime Minister by the Proclamation of 5 March 1948.

229 B.K. Nehru, ICS was not only the nephew of Pandit Jawaharlal Nehru but also a diplomat of note and of considerable clout. He was the Indian Ambassador to USA during the crucial years of 1961-1968. Later, he was appointed Governor of various States including the troubled States of Jammu and Kashmir and Assam.

230 N.T. Rama Rao was a Telugu actor, director and producer who turned

to politics and formed the Telugu Desam Party. He won a landslide victory in 1983 to be sworn in as Andhra Pradesh Chief Minister, but was controversially removed by Governor Ram Lal Thakur in 1984. He, however, had to be reinstated after he had mobilized all political parties at a national level. Thus he became one of the pioneers of opposition unity against Congress.

231 Between 1983 and 1988, Ramkrishna Hegde became the Chief Minister of Karnataka thrice. A product of opposition to the Congress hegemony, he was one of the architects of the Opposition parties.

232 The Telugu Desam Party, abbreviated as TDP, was founded by N.T. Rama Rao in 1983 as the regional answer to centralized Congress. Since 1995, the party is being led by his son-in-law Chandra Babu Naidu.

233 Between 1990 and 1991, Chandra Shekhar was the Prime Minister of India for seven months with the outside support of Congress. He had begun his career with the Praja Socialist Party (PSP) but later became a Congressman after the parent party merged with it. Known as one of the 'Young Turks' he was a staunch opponent of dictatorial tendencies and therefore became one of the most articulate voices of anti-Congressism and the proponent of Opposition unity.

234 Sten Widmalm, Op cit, p. 71.

235 Ibid, p. 72.

236 Jagmohan, Op cit, p. 267.

237 Ibid.

238 Katherine Frank, *Indira: The Life of Indira Nehru Gandhi* (London: HarperCollins Publishers, 2001), p. 440.

239 Ibid.

240 Ibid, p. 277.

241 Prabhu Chawala, *India Today*, 31 July 1984.

242 Jagmohan, Op cit, p. 288-89.

243 Ibid, p. 289.

244 Ibid, p. 291.

245 Sir John Marriot was an educationist, historian and a Conservative member of the British Parliament who also taught at the Oxford University from 1884 to 1920.

246 Dr Eugene Alfred Forsey was a constitutional expert who wrote on the reserved powers of the Crown. He served the Senate of Canada from 1970-1979.

247 Quoted in Jagmohan, Op cit, p.293.

248 This article, written in October 2019, was published in *The Guardian Weekly*.

249 Jagmohan, Op cit, p. 293.
250 Ibid, p.298.
251 The Sarkaria Commission was set up in June 1983 by the Central Government of India. Its charter was to examine the relationship and balance of power between state and central governments in the country and suggest changes within the framework of Constitution of India. The Commission was so named as it was headed by Rajinder Singh Sarkaria, a retired judge of the Supreme Court of India.

8. Erosion of Democracy

252 The year 1967 was landmark in the political history of India. The Congress had returned to power with 284 seats, the lowest till then. It was defeated in a number of states which formed non-Congress governments, but there were also states where the Congress returned to power with thin margins. In these states, defections from the Congress took place where the defectors—the Bharatiya Kranti Dal, the Samyukta Socialist Party, the Praja Socialist Party and the Jana Sangh—formed an alliance under the name of Samyukta Vidhhayak Dal and formed government. The first such government was formed in Madhya Pradesh and Govid Narain Singh became the first chief minister of such an alliance.
253 Haryana, created in 1966 from Punjab, also formed an opposition government with a breakaway group of the Congress—the Haryana Vishal Party of Rao Birender Singh.
254 In the Indian Constitution it was envisaged that English would be the lingua franca for only 15 years i.e. till 1965. After that the national language will Hindi. Thus on the passing of 15 years, Lal Bahadur Shastri declared Hindi as the national language. All the non-Hindi speaking states, including Tamil Nadu, then Madras, erupted in protests and violence. Consequently 70 people died over a period of two months. The agitation continued till the government withdrew its order. The result of the agitation was that it wiped out the Congress and the first Dravida Munnetra Kazhagam government, that championed the Dravid nationalism, was formed.
255 The seeds of separate Sikh identity from India were sown by the British on the eve of Partition in 1947. But, Nehru and the Congress had prevailed upon the Sikh leadership. However, the narrative took a turn after the 1973 Anandpur Sahib resolution of the Akali Dal, and gradually the political ineptitude led to the growth of separatism in Punjab till terror and deaths took a heavy toll.

256 Revolutionary fervor was always integral to Bengal but the rising socio-economic disparities and frustration of the youth and peasantry led to a peasant rebellion in a village called Naxalbari. From hence, the armed struggle of the peasants and the downtrodden came to be known as the Naxal movement that also aimed at secession.

257 Sten Widmalm, *Kashmir in Comparative Perspective: Democracy and Violent Separatism in India* (London: RoutledgeCurzon/Taylor and Francis, 2002), p. 60.

258 Ibid, p. 61

259 Balraj Puri, *Kashmir: Insurgency and After* (New Delhi, Orient Longman, 2010), p. 43.

260 Jawaid Alam (ed.), *Kashmir & Beyond, 1966-84: Select Correspondence between Indira Gandhi & Karan Singh* (New Delhi: Penguin India, 2020), p. 262.

261 Ibid, p. 263.

262 Ibid, p. 263-64.

263 Named after Justice Pralhad Balacharya Gajendragadkar, the seventh Chief Justice of India, it was the Sixth Law Commission of India that operated during the Emergency.

264 Ibid, p. 264.

265 Article 355 of the Indian Constitution gives reservation to the Scheduled Castes and Scheduled Tribes in government appointments. According to it, 'The claims of the members of the Scheduled Castes and the Scheduled Tribes shall be taken into consideration, consistently with the maintenance of efficiency of administration, in the making of appointments to services and posts in connection with the affairs of the Union or of a State.'

266 Ibid, p. 264.

267 Raghav Verma (ed.) *An Examined Life: Essays and Reflections by Karan Singh* (New Delhi: HarperCollins Publishers India, 2019), p. 270.

268 Ibid, p. 272.

269 Ibid, p. 280.

270 'Fundamentalists "Recruit Youths",' *The Tribune* Chandigarh, 18 September 1985; 'Shiv Sena Gaining Strength in Jammu', *The Times of India*, 17 January 1986.

271 'Every Kashmiri is a Pakistani: G.M. Shah', *The Hindustan Times*, 3 September 1987.

272 Arend Lijphart is a political scientist specializing in comparative politics, elections and voting systems, democratic institutions, and ethnicity and politics.

273 It is a form of power sharing in a democracy. Political scientists define a consociational state as one which has major internal divisions along with ethnic, religious, or linguistic lines, with none of the divisions large enough to form a majority group, but which remains stable due to consultation between the elites of these groups. Consociational states are often contrasted with states with majoritarian electoral systems. The goals of consociationalism are governmental stability, the survival of the power-sharing arrangements, the survival of democracy, and the avoidance of violence.

274 Syed Ali Shah Geelani (born 29 September 1929) is a Kashmiri separatist Hurriyat leader. He was previously a member of the Jamaat-e-Islami Kashmir but later on founded his own party by the name of Tehreek-e-Hurriyat. He has served as the chairman of All Parties Hurriyat Conference, a conglomerate of separatist parties in Jammu and Kashmir. He was an MLA from the Sopore constituency of Jammu and Kashmir three times (1972, 1977 and 1987).

275 Abdul Ghani Lone (born 6 May 1932–21 May 2002) was a Kashmiri lawyer, politician and Kashmiri separatist leader. He made his entry into politics serving in the State Assembly as a Congress candidate in 1967. In 1978, he formed a Kashmiri separatist organization called People's Conference, dedicated to what he called the restoration of 'internal autonomy' in Kashmir.

276 Qazi Nisar was the Mirwaiz of South Kashmir. He was a founding member of the Muslim United Front (MUF) that contested the 1987 Legislative Assembly elections in Jammu and Kashmir, and the Ummat-e-Islami. He was a vocal advocate of freedom for Kashmiris. Qazi Nisar founded the socio-religious organization, Ummat-e-Islami in 1985 as a collective resistance movement against the suspension of Muslim employees in the Kashmir Valley.

277 Mirwaiz-e-Kashmir Moulana Moulvi Muhammad Farooq Shah was the Mirwaiz of his time in Kashmir and the chairman of the All-Jammu and Kashmir Awami Action Committee, a coalition of disparate political parties in Jammu and Kashmir that sought the resolution of the Kashmir dispute in accordance to the wishes and aspirations of the people of Jammu and Kashmir. Moulvi Farooq was assassinated on 21 May 1990 by gunmen at his Nigeen residence. He is called Shaheed-e-Millat (Martyr of Nation).

278 Sten Widmalm, Op cit, p. 76-77.

279 Balraj Puri, Op cit, p. 35.

280 *The Indian Express* as well as *The Hindustan Times* reports corroborated

this news as the detentions and arrests continued even after the elections.

281 Sten Widmalm, Op cit, p. 80.

282 Jagmohan, *My Frozen Turbulence in Kashmir* (New Delhi: Allied Publishers, 1991), p. 529.

283 Ibid, p. 318.

284 Ibid, p. 322.

285 Ibid, p. 324.

286 Alastair Lamb, *Kashmir: A Disputed Legacy, 1846-1990* (Hertford: Roxford Books, 1991), p. 166.

287 On 24 December 1999, IC-814 with 178 passengers and 11 crew members left Kathmandu for Delhi. It entered Indian airspace at 5.30 p.m. and was hijacked shortly after. According to interviews with the crew later, first a masked man stood up and threatened to blow up the plane.

9. The Winter Chill

288 In the Kashmir Valley, the 40-day period of intense cold and winter is called *Chillai Kalan*. It begins on 21 December and ends on 29 January each year. It is followed by a shorter period of 20 days of slightly less cold, which is called *Chillai Khurd*. Kalan meaning big and *Khurd* meaning small.

289 Sikandar Shah was known as Sikandar *Butshikan*, that is, Sikandar the Iconoclast. Belonging to the Shah Miri dynasty, he reigned from 1389 to 1413. Large scale conversion of Brahmins and destruction of temples and manuscripts took place during that period.

290 Jagmohan, *My Frozen Turbulence in Kashmir* (New Delhi: Allied Publishers, 1991), p. 556-557.

291 Rahul Pandita, *Our Moon has Blood Clots: A Memoir of a Lost Home in Kashmir* (New Delhi: Penguin Random House India, 2014), p. 65-66.

292 Kashinath Pandit, *Ten Studies in Kashmir: History and Politics* (New Delhi: Academic Foundation, 2019), p. 148.

293 Ibid, p. 148.

294 Walter R. Lawrence, *The Valley of Kashmir* (London: Henry Frowde/ Oxford University Press, 1895), p. 197.

295 Ibid, p. 198.

296 Kashinath Pandit, Op cit, p. 284-285.

297 Rahul Pandita, Op cit, p. 116.

298 Ibid, p. 19.
299 B.L. Kaul, *My Kashmir in Peace and Turbulence: Story of a Native in Exile* (New Delhi: Peacock Books, 2019), p. 192.
300 Grants of public revenues of a district given to a person.
301 Ashok Dhar, *Kashmir As I See It: From Within and Afar* (New Delhi: Rupa Publications India, 2019), p. 142
302 Rahul Pandita, Op cit, p. 19.
303 Ibid, p. 77.
304 Jagmohan, Op cit, pp. 1-2.
305 Rahul Pandita, Op cit, p. 79.
306 Jagmohan, Op cit, p. 10.
307 Kashinath Pandit, Op cit, p. 150.
308 Ibid, p. 10.
309 As narrated by an eye witness friend of the author; Ashok Dhar, Op cit, p. 131.
310 Jagmohan, Op cit, p. 485-486; Rahul Pandita, Op cit, p. 115-116.
311 Rahul Pandita, Op cit, p. 117-118.
312 Jagmohan, Op cit, p. 486-487.
313 The definition of genocide has been debated by experts with divided results. One set of experts believes it is too narrow and allows many genocides to go unpunished. The other, believes that the term has been overused. The contentious part is concerning 'intent'. To constitute genocide, there must be a proven intent on the part of perpetrators to physically destroy a national, ethnical, racial or religious group. Cultural destruction does not suffice, nor does an intention to simply disperse a group. It is this special intent, or dolus specialis, that makes the crime of genocide so unique. In addition, case law has associated intent with the existence of a State or organizational plan or policy, even if the definition of genocide in international law does not include that element. Importantly, the victims of genocide are deliberately targeted—not randomly—because of their real or perceived membership of one of the four groups protected under the Convention (which excludes political groups, for example). This means that the target of destruction must be the group, as such, and not its members as individuals. Genocide can also be committed against only a part of the group, as long as that part is identifiable (including within a geographically limited area) and 'substantial.' The dictionary meaning of 'ethnic cleansing' is the mass expulsion or killing of members of one ethnic or religious group in an area by those of another.

314 Kashinath Pandit, Op cit, p. 154.

315 Ibid, 489.

316 Ibid, p. 155.

10. The Churning

317 Srinagar born, Gowhar Geelani is an established and renowned Kashmiri political commentator, analyst and journalist who is regularly sought by *BBC World*, *CNN News 18*, *NDTV*, *India Today* etc.

318 'Khoon e Shahidan rang laya' was a song that was most played out during that fateful period. It is credited to S.A.S. Geelani, the hardcore separatist leader and chairman of the All Parties Hurriyat Conference (APHC), which has openly advocated accession of Jammu and Kashmir State with Pakistan.

319 Ahmed Ali Fayyaz, 'A Kashmiri Journo Explains the History of Militancy in the Valley', *The Quint*, February 2020 (https://www.thequint.com/voices/opinion/kashmiri-pandit-exodus-militancy-congress-national-conference-party-hindus-muslims-polarisation#read-more, Accessed December 2023)

320 Jagmohan, *My Frozen Turbulence in Kashmir* (New Delhi: Allied Publishers, 1991), p. 15.

321 Ibid, p. 10.

322 Ibid, 13.

323 Ibid, pp. 10-11.

324 Basharat Peer, *Curfewed Night* (New Delhi: Penguin Random House India, 2009), p. 14.

325 Ibid, p. 10.

326 Ibid, p. 11.

327 Ibid, p. 22.

328 Jagmohan, Op cit, p. 16.

329 'ILF-2017: Kashmir: Two Sides to a Question (16.4.2017)' Karachi Lit Festival, YouTube, 19 June 2017 (https://www.youtube.com/watch?v=B-JiAbb-lXQ, Accessed December 2023)

330 Jagmohan, Op cit, p. 12.

331 Hein G. Kiessling, *Faith, Unity, Discipline: The Inter-Service-Intelligence (ISI) of Pakistan* (London: Hurst & Co., 2016), p. 191.

332 Ibid, p. 191.

333 Zafar Meeraj and Pankaj Pachauri, 'J&K: Secessionists hold sway as Farooq Abdullah's Government is paralysed', *India Today*, October 2013 (https://www.indiatoday.in/magazine/special-report/

story/19900115-j-k-secessionists-hold-sway-as-farooq-abdullah-government-is-paralysed-812247-1990-01-15, Accessed December 2023)

334 The Jammu Kashmir Liberation Front (JKLF) is a political organization active in both Pakistan-administered and Indian-administered Kashmir. It was founded by Amanullah Khan, with Maqbool Bhat also credited as a co-founder. Originally a militant wing of the Plebiscite Front, it changed its name to JKLF in Birmingham, England on 29 May 1977. From then until 1994 it was an active militant organization. It first established branches in several cities and towns of the UK, and other countries of Europe, United States and Middle East. In 1982, it established a branch in Pakistan-administered Azad Kashmir; in 1987, a branch in Indian-administered Kashmir Valley.

335 Kashinath Pandit, *Ten Studies in Kashmir: History and Politics* (New Delhi: Academic Foundation, 2019), p.145.

336 The first quarter of 1952 had seen the widening of differences between Sheikh Abdullah and Nehru and by extension, the Government of India. On 11 April 1952, while addressing a public rally at Ranbirsighpura (Jammu), Sheikh Abdullah made a speech that dogged him and the National Conference endlessly. In that oft quoted speech, he said: 'We are prepared to welcome application of India's constitution to Kashmir in its entirety once we are satisfied that the grave of communalism has been finally dug in India. Of that we are not clear yet…Many Kashmiris are apprehensive as to what will happen to them and their position if, for instance, something happens to Pandit Nehru.'

337 Indus Water Treaty was signed in Karachi on 19 September 1960 between Pakistan's President Ayub Khan and India's Prime Minister Jawaharlal Nehru. The Treaty gives control over the waters of the three 'eastern rivers'—the Beas, Ravi and Sutlej with a mean annual flow of 33 million acre-feet (MAF)—to India, while control over the waters of the three 'western rivers'—the Indus, Chenab and Jhelum with a mean annual flow of 80 MAF—to Pakistan. The treaty allows India to use the western river waters for limited irrigation use and unlimited non-consumptive use for such applications as power generation, navigation, floating of property, fish culture, etc.

338 'Who took me hostage?' *The Independent*, 4 February 1997 (https://www.independent.co.uk/life-style/who-took-me-hostage-1276790.html, Accessed December 2023)

339 Murali Manohar Joshi, a senior member of Atal Behari Vajpayee's NDA government between 1999 and 2004, and was also the president

of the BJP from 1991 to 1993 at the time of demolition of the Babri Masjid on 6 December, 1992, and was named in the case for making inflammatory speeches.

340 Under the aegis of Murali Manohar Joshi, President of BJP, an Ekta Yatra (the journey for unity) from Kanyakumari to Srinagar was taken out to unfurl the national flag on Republic Day in 1992. It was organized to send a message to secessionist forces.

341 One of the founders of BJP and also Deputy Prime Minister of India, Lal Krishna Advani, led a Rath Yatro (chariot journey) to the site of the Babri Masjid in Ayodhya, Uttar Pradesh to reclaim the site as the place where many Hindus believed Lord Rama was born. This marked the aggressive rallying of the forces of Hindutva as against the Islamic influence and symbols. The Babri Masjid was claimed to have been built after demolition of the Rama temple there.

342 Zahoor Malik, *Kashmir Times*, 20 January 2020.

343 Frantz Fanon, was a French-West Indian psychiatrist and political philosopher from the French colony of Martinique (today a French department). His works have become influential in the fields of post-colonial studies, critical theory and Marxism,. Along with being an intellectual, Fanon was a political radical, Pan-Africanist, and Marxist humanist concerned with the psychopathology of colonization and the human, social, and cultural consequences of decolonization.

344 Badri Raina, *Kashmir: A Noble Tryst in Tatters* (Paranjoy, 2017)

345 Ibid, p.6

346 Nasim Zehra, *From Kargil To The Coup: Events That Shook Pakistan*, (Lahore: Sang-e-Meel Publishers, 2018), p 89.

347 Nund Rishi, also known as Nooruddin, is the founder of the Rishi school of Sufism which presented the benign and tolerant face of Islam. It used syncretism to spread Islam. There are many legends about Nund Rishi including the most popular that linked him to Lalleshwari (Lal Ded, a Kashmiri mystic of the Kashmir Shaivism school of Hindu philosophy) who is said to have breastfed him since the newborn had refused to suckle the mother's milk.

348 Nasim Zehra, Op cit, p. 89.

11. Reclaiming Democracy

349 'Remembering PV Narasimha Rao: When India stood together for Kashmir', *HW News*, 18 June 2018 (https://hwnews.in/news/opinion/pv-narasimha-rao-india-kashmir/47630, Accessed December 2023)

350 Satinder Kumar Lambah, *In Pursuit of Peace: India-Pakistan Relations under Six Prime Ministers* (Gurugram: Penguin Random House India, 2023), p. 93.
351 Ibid.
352 Ibid, p. 94.
353 Ibid.
354 Ibid, p. 126.
355 Ramesh Vinayak, 'Abduction of five foreign tourists by militants and blast in Jammu keep Valley on boil', *India Today*, 15 August 1995 (https://www.indiatoday.in/magazine/special-report/story/19950815-abduction-of-five-foreign-tourists-by-militants-and-blast-in-jammu-keep-valley-on-boil-807642-1995-08-15, Accessed December 2023)
356 'Sky is the limit: Continuity in Congress' Kashmir policy', *Early Times*, 23 December 2015 (http://www.earlytimes.in/newsdet.aspx?q=166352, Accessed December 2023)
357 https://www.indiatoday.in/magazine/cover-story/story/19951130-spurning-of-p-v-narasimha-rao-pre-election-package-turns-into-another-example-of-his-sham-808040-1995-11-30
358 Inderjit Badhwar,'Spurning of P.V. Narasimha Rao's pre-election package turns into another example of his sham', *India Today*, 27 June 2013 (https://www.indiatoday.in/magazine/cover-story/story/19951130-spurning-of-p-v-narasimha-rao-pre-election-package-turns-into-another-example-of-his-sham-808040-1995-11-30, Accessed December 2023)
359 A.S. Dulat, *Kashmir: The Vajpayee Years*, (New Delhi: HarperCollins Publishers India, 2017), p. 104.
360 Ibid
361 Ibid, p. 72-76
362 Ibid, p.76.
363 Ibid, p. 76.
364 Radha Kumar, *Paradise at War: A Political History of Kashmir* (New Delhi: Aleph Book Company, 2018), p. 216.
365 'Lok Sabha Debates: Discussion Regarding Resolution Passed By Jammu And Kashmir…on 26 July, 2000', *Indian Kanoon* (https://indiankanoon.org/doc/638146/, Accessed December 2023)
366 Radha Kumar, Op cit, p. 217.
367 A news report in *The Pioneer* by A.K. Dhar and G. Sudhakar Nair, 'JK Groups warn Pakistani mercenaries.'
368 http://www.defencejournal.com/2000/sept/kashmir-talks.htm
369 Ibid, p.218.

370 Parveen Swami, 'A chance for peace', *Frontline, The Hindu*, 8 December 2001 (https://frontline.thehindu.com/other/article30252816.ece, Accessed December 2023)

371 *The Tribune*, 9 August 2000.

372 'Shock And Outrage', *Outlook*, 3 February 2022 (https://www.outlookindia.com/website/story/shock-and-outrage/219532, Accessed December 2023)

373 Ibid, pp. 220-221.

374 As reported in the Outlook, 8 August 2003.

375 Ibid.

376 https://mea.gov.in/in-focus-article.htm?18987/Fact+Sheet+on+Jammu+amp+Kashmir

12. Peace Efforts—2003-2008

377 A.S. Dulat, *Kashmir: The Vajpayee Years*, (New Delhi: HarperCollins Publishers India, 2017), p. 77.

378 A.G. Noorani, 'Vajpayee and Mehbooba: Myths and Falsehoods', *Greater Kashmir*, 18 May 2017.

379 Radha Kumar, *Paradise at War: A Political History of Kashmir* (New Delhi: Aleph Book Company, 2018), p. 230.

380 Ibid, p. 236.

381 On 22 October 1947, raiders from Pakistan connived with the Muslim forces of the 4th Jammu and Kashmir Battalion to capture the bridge on river Jhelum at Kohala. Thus the road from Srinagar to Muzaffarabad went into Pakistan control and remained closed for traffic till the Srinagar-Muzaffarabad bus service was started.

382 London's *The Guardian*, 22 January 2004.

383 'Musharraf To Visit India On April 17 To Watch Match', *Arab News*, 17 March 2005 (https://www.arabnews.com/node/263844, Accessed December 2023)

384 Radha Kumar, Op cit, p. 239.

385 Sumita Kumar, 'The Earthquake In Kashmir', *Strategic Analysis* (29, no. 3, Manohar Parrikar Institute for Defence Studies and Analysis, July 2005) (https://www.idsa.in/strategicanalysis/TheEarthquakeinKashmir_skumar_0705, Accessed December 2023)

386 Radha Kumar, Op cit, p. 239.

387 Ibid, p. 241.

388 'Hurriyat leaders call on Musharraf', *The Hindu*, 7 January 2006

389 Radha Kumar, Op cit, p. 242-243.

390 Sandeep Dikshit, 'Hurriyat has reneged on promise: Manmohan', *The Indian Express*, 19 October 2007

391 Raj Chengappa, 'Why the 2005-08 Back-Channel talks could be a better option for Modi and Sharif', *India Today*, 21 September 2015 (https://www.indiatoday.in/magazine/ground-zero/story/20150921-the-secret-indo-pak-talks-820425-1999-11-30, Accessed December 2023)

392 European Parliament Committee on Foreign Affairs, *Report on Kashmir: Present Situation and Future Prospects.*

13. Hope and Despair

393 'Jammu agitation more than Amarnath land issue', *The Economic Times*, 4 August 2008 (https://economictimes.indiatimes.com/news/politics-and-nation/jammu-agitation-more-than-amarnath-land-issue/articleshow/3322590.cms, Accessed December 2023)

394 'Indian Fatalities: 1994-2018', South Asia Terrorism Portal

395 Harinder Baweja, 'Exclusive: Shopian truth', *India Today*, 14 February 2014 (nailedhttps://www.indiatoday.in/latest-headlines/story/exclusive-shopian-truth-nailed-67271-2010-02-13, Accessed December 2023)

396 Radha Kumar, *Paradise at War: A Political History of Kashmir* (New Delhi: Aleph Book Company, 2018), p. 256.

397 'Hurriyat holds secret meeting with Chidambaram', *The Hindu*, 17, November 2009.

398 Muzamil Jaleel, 'Fake encounter at LoC: 3 arrested, probe ordered', *The Indian Express*, 29 May 2010 (https://indianexpress.com/article/news-archive/web/fake-encounter-at-loc-3-arrested-probe-ordered/, Accessed December 2023)

399 Mudasir Ahmad, 'As Institutions Fail Kashmiris, Machil Fake Encounter Victims' Families Vow to Keep Fighting', *The Wire*, 29 July 2017 (https://thewire.in/government/machil-fake-encounter-armed-forces-tribunal-verdict-kashmir, Accessed December 2023)

400 'Manmohan announces over Rs 1000 crore sops for J&K' *The Hindu*, 8 June, 2010.

401 Samir Yaseer, '2010 Kashmir unrest: Scathing report on Omar Abdullah's govt asks Mehbooba not to deploy CRPF', *Firstpost*, 9 January 2017 (https://www.firstpost.com/india/2010-kashmir-unrest-scathing-report-on-omar-abdullahs-govt-asks-mehbooba-not-to-deploy-crpf-3194886.html, Accessed December 2023)

402 Shabir Choudhry, 'Another Round Of Jihad Is To Start Soon In Kashmir', *CounterCurrents.org*, 10 February 2010 (https://www.countercurrents.org/choudhry100210.htm, Accessed December 2023); Quoted in Radha Kumar, Paradise at War: A Political History of Kashmir (New Delhi: Aleph Book Company, 2018)

403 'Kashmir's bizarre new normal', *The Hindu*, 23 July 2010.

404 Sameer Arshad, 'J&K stone throwers an illiterate, frustrated lot', *The Times of India*, 19 January 2011

405 Quoted from a *Times of India* report 27 February 2010.

406 Sanjeev Pargal, 'Masrat Alam admits to taking Rs 40 lakhs to fuel protests' *Daily Excelsior*, 14 December 2010

407 Zulfiqar Ali, 'Pakistani militants "hijacking" Kashmir cause' *BBC News*, 28 September 2010 (https://www.bbc.com/news/world-south-asia-11425831, Accessed December 2023)

408 *The Hindustan Times*, August 8, 2010.

409 *The Hindustan Times*, August 20, 2010.

410 'Police being trained to play greater role than army: Omar', *The Indian Express*, 24 November 2009

411 'Entrusting law & order to J&K police ultimate aim.', *Daily Excelsior*, 31 January 2010

412 Quoted in Radha Kumar, Op cit, p. 265.

413 Sameer Yasir, Op cit.

414 Ibid.

415 Rajesh Venugopal and Sameer Yasir, *Natural Disasters Amidst Political Crisis: The 2014 Floods in Kashmir*, 2015 (https://personal.lse.ac.uk/venugopr/kashmir%20flood%20venugopal%20yasir%202015.pdf, Accessed December 2023)

416 Soutik Biswas, 'Did Kashmir "abandon" its flood-hit people?', *BBC News*, 12 September 2014 (https://www.bbc.com/news/world-asia-india-29170087, Accessed December 2023)

417 Ibid.

418 Ibid

14. The Unraveling

419 Muralidhar Reddy, 'It's official: Modi is BJP's choice', *The Hindu*, 13 September 2013 (https://www.thehindu.com/news/national/its-official-modi-is-bjps-choice/article5124375.ece, Accessed December 2023)

420 The Radia tapes controversy relates to the telephonic conversations of

Niira Radia, a political lobbyist in India. The (then) Indian telecom minister A. Raja, and senior journalists, politicians, and corporate houses, were taped by the Indian Income Tax Department in 2008-09. The tapes were leaked to the press, and were eventually published by some media outlets and shown by television channels.

421 'Jitendra Singh says Article 370 to be repealed, then backtracks', *Firstpost*, 28 May 2014 (https://www.firstpost.com/india/jitendra-singh-says-article-370-to-be-repealed-then-backtracks-1545923.html, Accessed December 2023)

422 Press release, 11 December 2015

423 'BJP, PDP formally announce alliance, to form govt in Jammu and Kashmir', *The Economic Times*, 24 February 2015 (https://economictimes.indiatimes.com/news/politics-and-nation/bjp-pdp-formally-announce-alliance-to-form-govt-in-jammu-and-kashmir/articleshow/46358760.cms?from=mdr, Accessed December 2023)

424 Shubhajit Roy, 'India objects to Pakistan NSA Sartaj Aziz meeting Kashmiri separatists ahead of NSA-level talks', *The Indian Express*, 21 August 2015 (https://indianexpress.com/article/india/india-others/india-advised-pakistan-against-meeting-hurriyat-leaders-before-nsa-talks-foreign-ministry/, Accessed December 2023)

425 Shujaat Bukhari, 'Matter of choice', *Frontline*, *The Hindu*, 14 October 2015 (https://frontline.thehindu.com/cover-story/matter-of-choice/article7756964.ece, Accessed December 2023)

426 Asiya Andrabi remains one of the most important women separatists in the Valley. She was married to Qasim Faktoo (a founding member of the Hizbul Mujahideen) in 1990. Her husband is in jail since 1992. Andrabi also played a leading role during the 2010 agitation, notorious for stone-pelting, and was the main supporter of the agitation's front man, Masarat Alam.

427 Asiya was already the head of Kashmir's biggest network of 'women jihadis' (as she describes her 'lieutenants of Dukhtaran-e-Millat').

428 'J-K high court order enforcing beef ban on hold for 2 months: SC', *The Hindustan Times*, 5 October 2015 (https://www.hindustantimes.com/india/j-k-high-court-order-enforcing-beef-ban-on-hold-for-2-months-sc/story-CDNVdAtgijRLqsKsFf8LCN.html#:~:text=india%20news-,J%2DK%20high%20court%20order%20enforcing%20beef%20ban%20on%20hold%20for,bench%20to%20decide%20the%20issue, Accessed December 2023)

429 Javid Iqbal, 'Modi needs no advice', *Greater Kashmir*, 14 November 2015

430 Gowhar Geelani, *Kashmir: Rage and Reason* (New Delhi: Rupa Publications India, 2019), p. 8.

431 Ghulam Mohiuddin Karra was the organizational backbone of the National Conference till he parted with Sheikh Abdullah. Both had started their political careers simultaneously but political ambitions and claim to leadership proved too difficult a hurdle for them. He passed away in 1996.

432 B.N. Mullik, *My Years with Nehru: Kashmir*, (New Delhi: Allied Publishers, 1971), p. 66.

433 The name comes from Tupac Amaru II, the Peruvian leader who led a rebellion against the Spanish in the eighteenth century. This operation was sanctioned by President Zia-ul-Haq and was run by the ISI of Pakistan with the objective of disintegrating India.

434 Radha Kumar, *Paradise at War: A Political History of Kashmir* (New Delhi: Aleph Book Company, 2018), p.322.

435 Ibid.

436 Gowhar Geelani, Op cit, p. 3.

437 Ibid, p. 3.

438 Radha Kumar, Op cit, p. 323.

439 Ashfaq Majeed Wani was the first commander-in-chief of the Jammu and Kashmir Liberation Front (JKLF). He was killed in March 1990 at the age of 24.

440 Muzaffar Raina, 'Militancy 1st target rewinds', *The Telegraph*, 21 December 2017 (https://www.telegraphindia.com/india/militancy-1st-target-rewinds/cid/1329799, Accessed December 2023)

441 Karan Singh, *Autobiography*, (New Delhi: Oxford University Press India, 1994), p. 324.

442 Sten Widmalm, *Kashmir in Comparative Perspective: Democracy and Violent Separatism in India* (London: RoutledgeCurzon/Taylor and Francis, 2002), p. 102-103.

15. Redeeming a Pledge

443 Asad Durrani, *Pakistan Adrift: Navigating Troubled Waters* (London: Hurst & Co, 2018), p. 157.

444 Huỳnh Công Út, known professionally as Nick Ut is a Vietnamese-American photographer for the Associated Press (AP). He won both the 1973 Pulitzer Prize for Spot News Photography and the 1973 World Press Photo of the Year for 'The Terror of War', depicting children in flight from a napalm bombing during the Vietnam War.

His best-known photo features a naked nine-year-old girl, Phan Thị Kim Phúc, running toward the camera from a South Vietnamese napalm strike that mistakenly hit Trảng Bàng village instead of nearby North Vietnamese troops. This photograph shook the world and greatly contributed to the withdrawal of the US Forces from Vietnam.

445 *The Economic Times*, 15 December 2015

446 *The Tribune*, 20 March 2020.

447 Ellen Berry, *The New York Times*, 28 August 2016.

448 Billy Perrigo, 'Faces in the Darkness: The Victims of 'Non-Lethal' Weapons in Kashmir', *Time*, 6 September 2018 (https://time.com/longform/pellet-gun-victims-kashmir/, Accessed December 2023)

449 Saiba Varma, 'Inequality of suffering: Why images of Kashmir's pellet victims have failed to evoke India's empathy', *Scroll.in*, 19 December 2018 (https://scroll.in/article/905247/inequality-of-suffering-why-images-of-kashmirs-pellet-victims-have-failed-to-evoke-indias-empathy, Accessed December 2023)

450 'Has there been no major terror attack in India since 2014?', *BBC News*, 23 January 2019 (https://www.bbc.com/news/world-asia-india-46902935, Accessed December 2023)

451 Prabhash K. Dutta, *India Today*, June 19, 2018.

452 Col (Dr) P K Vasudeva, 'Success Story: Surgical Strike-2 Retaliation of the Pulwama Attack', *Indian Defence Review*, 05 March, 2019 (http://www.indiandefencereview.com/news/success-story-surgical-strike-2-retaliation-of-the-pulwama-attack/, Accessed December 2023)

453 'Shooting down of Mi-17 was a big mistake, admits IAF chief', *The Hindu*, 4 October 2019 (https://www.thehindu.com/news/national/shooting-down-our-own-chopper-big mistake-says-iaf-chief/article29593737.ece#:~:text=The%20Indian%20Air%20Force%20(IAF,Bhadauria%20said%20on%20Friday.&text=The%20CoI%20had%20confirmed%20that,air%20missile%20of%20the%20IAF, Accessed December 2023)

454 Lok Sabha Debates, 4 December 1964, Volume XXXIII, columns 3449-65.

455 Jammu and Kashmir: A timeline of recent events, *The Hindu*, 5 August 2019 (https://www.thehindu.com/news/national/jammu-and-kashmir-a-timeline-of-events-leading-to-imposition-of-144-crpc-and-house-arrest-of-leaders/article61587382.ece, Accessed December 2023)

456 Zeba Siddiqui, and Mayank Bhardwaj, 'Kashmir communications blackout angers some in the Indian media,' *Reuters*, 8 August 2019 (https://www.reuters.com/article/us-india-kashmir-media/kashmir-communications-blackout-angers-some-in-the-indian-media-idUSKCN1UY1YH, Accessed December 2023)

457 Ibid

458 Ibid.

459 'Necessary to stop talks between terrorists: Jaishankar justifies curb on phone services in Kashmir', *The Statesman*, 3 September 2019 (https://www.thestatesman.com/india/necessary-stop-talks-terrorists-jaishankar-justifies-curb-phone-services-kashmir-1502795404.html, Accessed December 2023)

460 Ibid.

461 Jawaid Alam (ed.), *Jammu and Kashmir 1949-64: Select Correspondence Between Jawaharlal Nehru and Karan Singh*, (New York: Penguin/ Viking, 2006), p. 60-61.

462 Ramchandra Guha, *The Telegraph*, 9 November 2019.

463 Karan Thapar's interview with Faizan Mustafa, Vice Chancellor, NALSAR University of Law, *The Wire*.

464 Ibid.

465 *The Tribune*, 24 June 2020.

466 Ibid.

16. Ladakh

467 August Hermann Francke, *A History of Western Tibet: One of the Unknown Empires*, (New Delhi: Asian Educational Services, 1907), p. 20.

468 The Licchavis were a clan amongst the Vajji Mahajanapada of ancient India. Licchavi, also spelled Lichchhavi, were people of northern India. They settled (sixth–fifth century BCE) on the north bank of the Ganges (Ganga) River in what is now Bihar; their capital city was at Vaishali. They were known for their republican form of government. Vaishali, the capital and homeland of the Licchavis, was also the capital of the Vajji Mahajanapada. It was later occupied by Ajatashatru, who annexed the Vajji territory into his kingdom during the Magadha-Vajji war. Kautilya in his Arthaśāstra (Ch. XI), describes the Licchavis as a republic (gana sangha), whose leader uses the title of rājā (rājaśabdopajīvinah). A Buddhist text, the Mahāparinibbāna Suttanta refers them as Kshatriyas and one of the claimants of the relics of Shakyamuni Buddha.

469 In the seventeenth year of Emperor Ashoka's reign the Third Council of Buddhism was called to rid the Sangha and Dhamma of the corruption and impurities that had infiltrated through opportunistic monks. Thera Moggaliputta Tissa headed the proceedings and chose

one thousand monks from the sixty thousand participants for the traditional recitation of the Dhamma and the Vinaya, which went on for nine months. The Emperor himself questioned monks from a number of monasteries about the teachings of the Buddha. Those who held wrong views were exposed and expelled from the Sangha immediately. In this way the Bhikkhu Sangha was purged of heretics and bogus bhikkhus.

470 Prem Singh Jina, *Ladakh: Past & Present* (New Delhi: Gyan Publishing House, 2001), p.43

471 Janet Rizvi, *Ladakh: Crossroads of High Asia* (New Delhi: Oxford University Press, 1983), p.56

472 Ibid, p. 56-57.

473 Kalhana was a Kashmiri who wrote the history of Kashmir written between 1148 and 1149 CE. Not much is known about him and whatever has been gathered is from deductions from his writings. His work is the first written historical record of any part of ancient India.

474 *Rajtarangini*, meaning the river of kings, has also been written by Jonaraj. While Kalhana wrote about the Hindu Kashmir, Jonaraj wrote about Kashmir after it had passed into the hands of Muslims and had Sultans for rulers.

475 Jogesh Chandra Dutt, *The Rajatarangini of Jonaraja*, (New Delhi: Gyan Publishing House, 2012), p.28-30

476 Mohibbul Hasan, *Kashmir Under the Sultans*, (Delhi: Aakar Books, 1959), p. 77.

477 Jogesh Chandra Dutt, *Medieval Kashmir* (New Delhi: Atlantic Publishers & Distributors, 1993), p. 68.

478 Luciano Petech, *The Kingdom of Ladakh, C. 950-1842 A.D.* (Rome: Istituto italiano per il Medio ed Estremo Oriente, 1977), p.23.

479 Ibid, p. 26.

480 Jahangir, *Tuzuk-i-Jahangiri*, p.148

481 Francois Bernier, *Travels in the Mogul Empire, A.D. 1656-1668.* (London: Oxford University Press, 1916), p.403

482 *The Ain-i-Akbari*, Vol. II, p. 38-39; *Tarikh-i-Rashidi*, Vol. II, p. 411-412; *The Shah Jahan Nama of Inayat Khan*, p. 218

483 Abul Fazl, *The Akbarnama*, Vol. III, p. 838.

484 *The Shah Jahan Nama*, Op cit, p. 122.

485 Janet Rizvi, Op cit, p. 68-69.

486 *The Great Game in the Buddhist Himalayas* by Phunchok Stobdan p. 21.

487 Ibid. p. 25.

488 *Kingdom of Ladakh* by Luciano Petech, Opp. Cit. pp. 171-172.

489 Phunchok Stobdan, *The Great Game in Buddhist Himalayas: India and China's Quest for Stategic Dominance* (New Delhi: Penguin Random House India, 2019), p. 26.

490 *The Sino-Indian Boundary: Texts of Treaties, Agreements and Certain Exchange of Notes Relating to the Sino-Indian Boundary*, (New Delhi: The Indian Society of International Law, 1962), p. 1-2.

491 Phunchok Stobdan, Op cit, p. 27.

492 Abdul Wahid Radhu, *Tibetan Caravans: Journeys from Leh to Lhasa* (New Delhi: Speaking Tiger Books, 2017), p. xi.

493 Phunchok Stobdan, Op cit, p. 27.

494 Abdul Wahid Radhu, Op cit, p. 2.

495 Jawaid Alam (ed.), *Jammu and Kashmir 1949-64: Select Correspondence Between Jawaharlal Nehru and Karan Singh*, (New York: Penguin/ Viking, 2006), p. 58.

496 Ibid, p.60-61.

497 Pretika Khanna, 'With Article 370 gone, future of Ladakh now is very bright', *Mint*, 9 August 2019

498 Martijn van Beek, 'True Patriots: Justifying Autonomy for Ladakh', *Himalaya, the Journal of the Association for Nepal and Himalayan Studies* (18, no 1, article 9, 1998) (https://core.ac.uk/reader/46723084, Accessed December 2023)

17. Present Tense, Future Uncertain

499 Jawaid Alam (ed.), *Jammu and Kashmir 1949-64: Select Correspondence Between Jawaharlal Nehru and Karan Singh*, (New York: Penguin/ Viking, 2006), p. 63, 74-75, 86-87, 113.

500 William Moorcroft was a Veterinarian with the East India Company and had ostensibly visited Ladakh and beyond the Karakoram on the pretext of scouting horses for the army of the Company. Another purpose for this journey was to search for goats that yielded *pashm* wool. It is believed that Moorcroft had procured a small herd of the animals which were duly ferried to Scotland for rearing. However, the experiment had failed. He also pretended to be an emissary of the British and was the first to goad the British to play a more pro-active role in the Himalayan States.

501 In 1918, the British increased taxes on the farmers of the Kheda (Gujrat) region by 23 percent. However, the peasants were unable to pay the taxes because of continuing famine conditions and epidemic.

Finally, the Government had to agree to the suspension of tax collection for the year and next, and released all confiscated lands and also reduced the taxes.

502 The Bardoli farmers' agitation began in 1925 when the government decided to raise taxes on farming by 22 percent. It was resolved in 1928 when the government conceded to the farmers' demands. The agitation firmly established Sardar Patel among the top nationalist leaders.

503 The Champaran agitation was the first organized act of civil disobedience during the British rule. It was against the forced cultivation of indigo for Britain's textile industry. But indigo cultivation led to the degradation of the land making in fallow. It established Mahatma Gandhi as the undisputed leader of freedom movement.

Bibliography

Abdullah, Farooq. *My Dismissal.* New Delhi: Vikas Publishing House, 1985

Ahmed, Khaled. *Pakistan's Terror Conundrum.* New Delhi: Penguin Books India, 2021

Alam, Jawaid (ed.). *Kashmir & Beyond, 1966-84: Select Correspondence between Indira Gandhi & Karan Singh.* New Delhi: Penguin India, 2020

———. *Jammu and Kashmir 1949-64: Select Correspondence Between Jawaharlal Nehru and Karan Singh.* New York: Penguin/Viking, 2006

Bazaz, Prem Nath. *Democracy Through Intimidation and Terror: The Untold Story of Kashmir Politics.* New Delhi, Heritage, 1978

Bernier, Francois. *Travels in the Mogul Empire, A.D. 1656-1668.* London: Oxford University Press, 1916

Bourke-White, Margaret. *Halfway to Freedom: A Report on the New India in the Words and Photographs.* New York: Simon and Schuster, 1949

Dhar, Ashok. *Kashmir As I See It: From Within and Afar.* New Delhi: Rupa Publications India, 2019

Dhar, P.N. *Indira Gandhi, the 'Emergency', and Indian Democracy.* New Delhi: Oxford University Press, 2000

Dogra, Rajiv. *Where Borders Bleed: An Insider's Account of INDO-PAK Relations.* New Delhi: Rupa Publications India, 2015

Dutt, Jogesh Chunder. *The Rajatarangini* of *Jonaraja.* New Delhi: Gyan Publishing House, 2012

———. *Medieval Kashmir.* New Delhi: Atlantic Publishers & Distributors, 1993

Dulat, A.S. *Kashmir: The Vajpayee Years.* New Delhi: HarperCollins Publishers India, 2017

Durrani, Asad. *Pakistan Adrift: Navigating Troubled Waters.* London: Hurst & Co, 2018

Fair, Christine. *Fighting to the End: The Pakistan Army's Way of War.* New York: Oxford University Press, 2014

Frank, Katherine. *Indira: The Life of Indira Nehru Gandhi.* London: HarperCollins Publishers, 2001

Geelani, Gowhar. *Kashmir: Rage and Reason.* New Delhi: Rupa Publications India, 2019

Habibullah, Wajahat. *My Kashmir: The Dying of the Light.* New Delhi: Penguin India, 2014

Haqqani, Husain. *Pakistan Between Mosque and Military.* London: Penguin Books, 2016

Hardgrave, Robert L. 'India in 1983: New Challenges, Lost Opportunities.' *Asian Survey* 24, no. 2 (1984): 209–18. https://doi.org/10.2307/2644440.

Hasan, Mohibbul. *Kashmir Under the Sultans.* Delhi: Aakar Books, 1959

Hersh, Seymour M. *Price of Power: Kissinger in the Nixon White House.* New York: Simon and Schuster, 2013

Jaffrelot, Christophe. *The Pakistan Paradox: Instability and Resilience.* New Delhi: Vintage/Penguin, 2016

Jagmohan, *My Frozen Turbulence in Kashmir.* New Delhi: Allied Publishers, 1991

Jamal, Arif. *Call for Transnational Jihad: Lashkar-e-Taiba, 1985-2014.* Georgia: Avant-Garde Books, 2014

Jina, Prem Singh. *Ladakh: Past & Present.* New Delhi: Gyan Publishing House, 2001

Kaul, B.L. *My Kashmir in Peace and Turbulence: Story of a Native in Exile.* New Delhi: Peacock Books, 2019

Kiessling, Hein G. *Faith, Unity, Discipline: The Inter-Service-Intelligence (ISI) of Pakistan.* London: Hurst & Co., 2016

Kissinger, Henry. *World Order: Reflections on the Character of Nations and the Course of History.* London: Penguin Books, 2015

Kumar, Radha. *Paradise at War: A Political History of Kashmir.* New Delhi: Aleph Book Company, 2018

Lamb, Alastair. *Kashmir: A Disputed Legacy, 1846-1990.* Hertford: Roxford Books, 1991

Lawrence, Walter R. *The Valley of Kashmir.* London: Henry Frowde/ Oxford University Press, 1895

Leiven, Anatol. *Pakistan: A Hard Country.* London: Allen Lane/Penguin, 2011

Long, Roger D. *A History of Pakistan.* Karachi: Oxford University Press, 2015

MacDonald, Myra. *Defeat is an Orphan: How Pakistan Lost the Great South Asian War*. London: Hurst & Co., 2016

Mahmud Ali, S. *Understanding Bangladesh*. London: Oxford University Press, 2010

Mullik, B.N. *My Years with Nehru: Kashmir*. New Delhi: Allied Publishers, 1971

Oldenburg, Philip. '"A Place Insufficiently Imagined": Language, Belief, and the Pakistan Crisis of 1971', *The Journal of Asian Studies* 44, no. 4 (1985): 711–33. https://doi.org/10.2307/2056443

Pandit, Kashinath. *Ten Studies in Kashmir: History and Politics*. New Delhi: Academic Foundation, 2019

Pandita, Rahul. *Our Moon has Blood Clots: A Memoir of a Lost Home in Kashmir*. New Delhi: Penguin Random House India, 2014

Peer, Basharat. *Curfewed Night*. New Delhi: Penguin Random House India, 2009

Petech, Luciano. *The Kingdom of Ladakh, C. 950-1842 A.D.* Rome: Istituto italiano per il Medio ed Estremo Oriente, 1977

Puri, Balraj. *Kashmir: Insurgency and After*. New Delhi, Orient Longman, 2010

Radhu, Abdul Wahid. *Tibetan Caravans: Journeys from Leh to Lhasa*. New Delhi: Speaking Tiger Books, 2017

Raina, Badri. *Kashmir: A Noble Tryst in Tatters*. Paranjoy, 2017

Rizvi, Janet. *Ladakh: Crossroads of High Asia*. New Delhi: Oxford University Press, 1983

Sarila, Narendra Singh. *The Shadow of the Great Game: The Untold Story of India's Partition*. New Delhi: HarperCollins Publishers India with India Today Group, 2005

Schofield, Victoria. *Kashmir in the Crossfire*. London: I.B. Tauris, 1996

Selected Works of Jawaharlal Nehru, Second Series, Volume 18 (1 April-15 July 1952). New Delhi: Jawaharlal Nehru Memorial Fund, 1996

Siddiqa, Ayesha. *Military Inc.: Inside Pakistan's Military Economy*. New Delhi: Penguin Random House India, 2017

Singh, Bhagwan. *Political Conspiracies of Kashmir*. Jammu: Light and Life Publishers, 1973

Singh, Karan. *Autobiography*. New Delhi: Oxford University Press India, 1994

Stobdan, Phunchok. *The Great Game in Buddhist Himalayas: India and China's Quest for Strategic Dominance*. New Delhi: Penguin Random House India, 2019

The Sino-Indian Boundary: Texts of Treaties, Agreements and Certain

Exchange of Notes Relating to the Sino-Indian Boundary. New Delhi: The Indian Society of International Law, 1962

Trofimov, Yaroslav. *The Seige of Mecca: The Forgotten Uprising in Islam's Holiest Shrine*. London: Allen Lane/Penguin, 2007

Tunzelmann, Alex von. *Indian Summer: The Secret History of the End of an Empire*. London: Simon and Schuster, 2012

Wani, Gul Mohammad. *Kashmir Politics: Problems and Prospects*. New Delhi: Ashish Publishing House, 1993

Widmalm, Sten. *Kashmir in Comparative Perspective: Democracy and Violent Separatism in India*. London: RoutledgeCurzon/Taylor and Francis, 2002

Wolpert, Stanley. *India and Pakistan: Continued Conflict or Cooperation?* London: University of California Press, 2010

Zakaria, Anam. *1971: A People's History from Bangladesh, Pakistan and India*. New Delhi: Penguin Random House India, 2019

Zehra, Nasim. *From Kargil To The Coup: Events That Shook Pakistan*. Lahore: Sang-e-Meel Publishers, 2018

Index

A MODERN HISTORY OF JAMMU AND KASHMIR, VOLUME ONE

THE TROUBLED YEARS OF MAHARAJA HARI SINGH (1925-1949)

Harbans Singh

The modern history of Jammu and Kashmir is often focused mainly on the Kashmir valley, leaving out the other regions that make up the bulk of the erstwhile Princely State. A similar limitation marks most discussions of the rule of the fourth-generation Dogra ruler of Jammu and Kashmir, Maharaja Hari Singh. After his inheritance of the throne in 1925, Hari Singh introduced a number of progressive reforms—among them, programmes for girl education, opening temple doors for Dalits and abolishing the exploitative *begar* system of labour. However, contemporary historians look past these reforms and focus only on the issue of the accession of the State to India.

At a time when the entire subcontinent was reeling from the shock and violence of Partition, the Maharaja had to decide which dominion—India or Pakistan—the State would join. How was he to choose where to put his trust, especially after Pakistan-backed Pashtun tribals invaded the State and India refused to offer military help? Was any decision possible that would appease all—the Muslim majority of Kashmir, the Hindu majority of Jammu and the Buddhist majority of Ladakh?

Those tumultuous times took a toll on Hari Singh during the final years of his reign. Accession to India was not as easy as he had hoped, and pressurised by Nehru and Sardar Patel, the Maharaja was forced to choose exile in 1949 and spent the rest of his days in Bombay. Harbans Singh's *A Modern History of Jammu and Kashmir, Volume One: The Troubled Years of Maharaja Hari Singh (1925-1949)* offers a more rounded history of the State than most available scholarship. The first volume in a trilogy, this book offers a strong and nuanced defence of the last ruler of Jammu and Kashmir and is a valuable document in understanding its evolving history.

A MODERN HISTORY OF JAMMU AND KASHMIR, VOLUME TWO

THE KARAN SINGH YEARS (1949-1967)

Harbans Singh

The Modern History of Jammu and Kashmir, Volume Two: The Karan Singh Years (1949-1967) examines the politics of the period that followed Maharaja Hari Singh's exile from the State in 1949. Focusing on Hari Singh's son, the book examines the history of Jammu and Kashmir through Yuvraj Karan Singh's journey from becoming the Regent at the young age of eighteen, then the Sadar-i-Riyasat and finally the Governor.

During the challenging time when the Sheikh Abdullah-led National Conference and the Dogra-backed Praja Parishad were locked in a fierce tug-of-war for control of the State, it was the Yuvraj who prevailed as the voice of reason. He strove to maintain equitable power sharing between the three major provinces—Jammu, Kashmir and Ladakh—throughout the eighteen years of his career in Jammu and Kashmir.

The major political changes during Karan Singh's time—the judicious use of the provisions of Article 370 and the further integration of Jammu and Kashmir with India, among others—also had a crucial effect of consolidating the future of the State with that of the country. A sense of mutual respect and cooperation was forged between Delhi and the Jammu and Kashmir leaders.

Relying on both historical sources and the vast correspondence Karan Singh had with Jawaharlal Nehru and later Indira Gandhi, this second volume of Harbans Singh's magisterial trilogy is both a biography of a remarkable man as well as a fresh look at the history and politics behind the making of modern-day Jammu and Kashmir.